The Thought of C. S. Peirce

THE THOUGHT
OF C. S. PEIRCE

THOMAS A. GOUDGE

*Professor of Philosophy in
the University of Toronto*

DOVER PUBLICATIONS, INC.
NEW YORK

Published in Canada by General Publishing Company, Ltd., 30 Lesmill Road, Don Mills, Toronto, Ontario.
Published in the United Kingdom by Constable and Company, Ltd., 10 Orange Street, London WC 2.

This Dover edition, first published in 1969, is an unabridged and unaltered republication of the work originally published by the University of Toronto Press in 1950.

Standard Book Number: 486-22216-0
Library of Congress Catalog Card Number: 72-94324

Manufactured in the United States of America
Dover Publications, Inc.
180 Varick Street
New York, N.Y. 10014

TO
HELEN AND STEPHEN

PREFACE

A NUMBER of years ago I became interested in C. S. Peirce through the account of him given in Muirhead's *The Platonic Tradition in Anglo-Saxon Philosophy*. Shortly afterwards, my interest in him was heightened by the writings and lectures of Professor C. I. Lewis. I thus began a study of Peirce's ideas which has continued, with some major interruptions, down to the present. This book is one of the fruits of that study.

My first intention was to deal with Peirce's thought as a systematic whole. But I soon became convinced that no such whole exists, and that an adequate appraisal of his work must try to account for the obvious inconsistencies which occur in it. Accordingly, I came to adopt the hypothesis stated in the opening chapter, and have undertaken to interpret Peirce's thought in terms of a basic conflict which I believe it exhibits. By proceeding thus I have been able to survey his main ideas without brushing any of them aside as "unrepresentative" because they do not fit into a coherent system. I have also been able to take his *ipsissima verba* at their face value without feeling called on to construe them in such a way as to render them consistent. Every interpretation of Peirce must be to some degree controversial, and I am far from believing that what follows is the final word on the subject. It is probable that I have made mistakes in regard to specific points. But on the whole, I think that my interpretation is illuminating and in accord with the facts.

All students of Peirce are under obligation to the editors of the *Collected Papers*, Charles Hartshorne and Paul Weiss. To them, and to other commentators such as Justus Buchler, James K. Feibleman, and Philip Wiener, I must acknowledge indebtedness. Where I have differed from their estimate of Peirce, it has only been after due consideration.

The Department of Philosophy, Harvard University, has graciously given me permission on two separate occasions to examine Peirce's original manuscripts. The Harvard University Press has kindly consented to the publication of the passages from the *Collected Papers* which are here quoted. By granting me leave of absence during the Michaelmas Term of the session 1948-49, the University of Toronto made it possible for me to complete the writing of the book. For all these favors I express my gratitude.

I must thank Miss F. G. Halpenny, Assistant Editor, University of Toronto Press, for her careful scrutiny of my manuscript, and for numerous improvements in style and expression which she suggested. To my colleagues in the Department of Philosophy I owe the stimulus of many informal discussions over the Thursday luncheon-table. I wish also to express appreciation of the assistance towards publication provided by the Humanities Research Council of Canada and the University of Toronto Press Publication Fund.

Finally, I should like to record my indebtedness to Peirce himself. "The best thing for a fledgling philosopher," he once remarked, "is close companionship with a stalwart practical reasoner." To one fledgling philosopher the benefits of such companionship, though perhaps not obvious, have been incalculable.

T. A. G.

December 1, 1949

CONTENTS

Contents

Part Two

PEIRCE'S TRANSCENDENTALISM

‑≫≫≫≪≪‑≪≪

The Thought of C. S. Peirce

If philosophic eminence were measured not by the number of finished treatises of dignified length, but by the extent to which a man brought forth new and fruitful ideas of radical importance, C. S. Peirce would easily be the greatest figure in American philosophy.

—Morris Cohen

The condemnation which a great man lays upon the world is to force it to explain him.

—G. W. F. Hegel

I

THE INTERPRETATION
OF PEIRCE'S THOUGHT

1. THE PROBLEM OF INTERPRETING PEIRCE

AMONG philosophers of the recent past who are making an impact on contemporary thought, a foremost place must be given to Charles Sanders Peirce. During his own lifetime (1839-1914) he was neglected and unknown. Today he is almost a vogue. The reason for this change of status is that between 1931 and 1935 six large volumes of his *Collected Papers* were published.[1] These quickly revealed to students what his own age failed to appreciate, that Peirce was a thinker of the first magnitude. The result has been a steadily mounting interest in his ideas, and numerous publications have appeared which bear witness to his influence. Recently, there has been formed "The Charles S. Peirce Society," whose object is to promote the study and development of his philosophy in its manifold aspects.

From one point of view, this sudden popularity is easy to understand. It springs from the remarkable anticipation in Peirce of themes that are in the foreground of current philosophical discussion. Such subjects as the foundations of logic and mathematics, semantics, induction and probability, phenomenology, chance and determinism in nature, evolutionary metaphysics—all are dealt with in the *Collected Papers*. Moreover, much of the exposition has a freshness, originality, and penetration which cannot fail to impress the reader. No matter

---

[1]*Collected Papers of Charles Sanders Peirce,* edited by Charles Hartshorne and Paul Weiss (Cambridge, Mass., Harvard University Press, 1931-35). All subsequent references to this work will be given in the body of the text by noting the number of the volume and of the paragraph concerned. Thus a reference to volume 5, paragraph 234 will be indicated as (5.234), and so on.

how widely he may differ from Peirce's conclusions, he is bound to be stimulated by the new avenues of reflection opened up, and by the unusual perspectives in which ancient problems are viewed. Even the language used has a surprisingly contemporary ring. Part of the tragedy of Peirce's career lay in the fact that his thinking was so far in advance of his own time. He had, indeed, a twentieth- not a nineteenth-century mind.

From another point of view, however, the present interest in Peirce is somewhat surprising. For his ideas have appeared in a form scarcely designed to attract a wide circle of readers. Despite expert editorship, the *Collected Papers* remain fragmentary, repetitious, and rambling. Peirce was by nature incapable of sustained, orderly reflection. In short articles he could focus his thought brilliantly. But when working on a larger scale, he frequently wandered off into profitless and irrelevant by-paths. This tendency was aggravated by his isolation from the intellectual community of his day. Not only was he obliged more and more to become his own audience, but he was deprived of the discipline of regular discussion with fellow-scholars. It should be added that his arguments are often interrupted by out-of-the-way bits of knowledge which his astonishing erudition led him to insert into the text.

Another characteristic which may baffle a reader of the *Collected Papers* is their alternate clarity and obscurity. When the spirit moved him, Peirce could be admirably lucid in discussing complex issues. At other times he seems to glory in dark sayings. Josiah Royce summed the matter up very well when he observed:

It is not always easy to understand Peirce. On occasion he could be brilliantly clear . . . although this clearness was a capricious fact in his life and in his writings, and was frequently interrupted by a mode of expression which often seemed to me to be due to the fear, after all, that in case mediocre minds found themselves understanding too many of his ideas, they would be led to form too high an impression of their own powers. One finds this tendency towards what might be called "impenetrability" in his manuscripts. Too often the reader meets with a thought of surpassing brilliancy, and follows it eagerly, only to have it disappear like the cuttlefish in the inky blackness of its own secretion.[2]

But the most puzzling feature of the *Collected Papers* has yet to be mentioned. Scattered throughout the six volumes are a large number of statements extremely difficult to reconcile with one another.

[2]*Journal of Philosophy, Psychology and Scientific Methods*, vol. XIII (1916), p. 707.

Many of these represent contradictory points of view on the same subject; others are at least incompatible propositions. Thus—to give one or two examples by way of anticipation—scientific method is declared to be the only reliable way of establishing belief (5.377 ff.); yet, feeling or sentiment is held to be the ultimate authority in ethics, religion, and the practical affairs of life (1.634 ff.). Again, philosophy is affirmed to be a positive observational science (1.126) whose concepts are meaningless unless defined in terms of their experimental consequences (5.412); but in his metaphysics Peirce reaches conclusions that have no observational basis, and are speculative in the extreme sense of the term (1.409; 6.33). In some places he insists that it is impossible to observe any distinctively psychical facts in the world (e.g., 1.253); but he also argues that what we call "matter" is really mind in an inchoate form (6.25). These and other discrepancies are a constant source of embarrassment to the student who is seeking in Peirce a consistent set of ideas.

The situation is not made any easier when one reads Peirce's report of his method of philosophical composition.

A student might infer that I have been given to expressing myself without due consideration; but in fact I have never, in any philosophical writing—barring anonymous contributions to newspapers—made any statement which was not based on at least half a dozen attempts, in writing, to subject the whole question to a very far more minute and critical examination than could be attempted in print, these attempts being made quite independently of one another, at intervals of many months, but subsequently compared together with the most careful criticism, and being themselves based upon at least two briefs of the state of the question, covering its whole literature, as far as known to me, and carrying the criticism in the strictest logical form to its extreme beginnings. . . . My waverings, therefore, have never been due to haste. (5.146)

Anyone who has seen Peirce's original manuscripts will probably agree that this account of his procedure is not exaggerated.

If so much be granted, it becomes an important task to examine the nature and possible causes of Peirce's "waverings." There are at least three ways of dealing with this problem.

First, we might seek to show that the discrepancies in Peirce's text are mainly verbal; that they are diverse, and perhaps occasionally careless, formulations of thought which is at bottom consistent; and that, with a little re-wording, they can be incorporated into a system. This I take to be the general position favored by Professor Weiss and

Mr. Feibleman.[3] In the very nature of the case, their view cannot be *proved* false. But I am convinced that its inadequacy is shown by the extensive reinterpretation of Peirce's pronouncements which they often have to make, and by the degree to which they charitably avert their eyes from statements that cannot be readily fitted into the "system."[4] This procedure seems to me quite unwarranted. At any rate, I propose to assume that Peirce meant exactly what he said, and that therefore *all* his statements must be taken seriously. I shall not, however, argue in detail against the "systematic interpretation," but shall seek to make my counter-view as convincing as possible.

A second way in which the problem might be tackled is this. By attaching dates to the various incompatible statements we might try to see whether Peirce's ideas exhibit a temporal development. On such an approach, earlier doctrines could conflict with later ones, yet the later doctrines might conceivably form a system, and thus be accepted as Peirce's official philosophy. But it is relatively easy to demonstrate that the discrepancies are not thus removable. They do not appreciably diminish in the writings which belong to the close of his career. Some development in Peirce's thought there undoubtedly was, but not the sort that issued in a system.

According to a third method of interpretation, the most illuminating procedure is to sort out the contradictory statements and see whether they can be arranged in a meaningful pattern. This is the method I have chosen. In consequence, I have been led to form the hypothesis (a) that Peirce's ideas fall naturally into two broad groups whose opposite character is a reflection of a deep conflict in his thinking; and (b) that the conflict can be best understood in terms of what I shall call his "naturalism" and his "transcendentalism." The precise content of each of these tendencies and the way they interact throughout the *Collected Papers*, form the subject of the present study. In other words, taking Peirce's text as my data, I shall attempt to validate the above hypothesis by an appeal to the evidence. Before turning to the latter, I must first indicate in what sense I am using the terms "naturalism" and "transcendentalism."

[3]Cf. Paul Weiss, "The Essence of Peirce's System," *Journal of Philosophy*, vol. XXXVII (1940), pp. 253-64; and James Feibleman, *An Introduction to Peirce's Philosophy, Interpreted as a System* (New York and London, 1946).

[4]Thus Mr. Feibleman makes the candid, but to my mind damaging admission that he has proceeded on the principle that "where statements conflict (and this situation is not uncommon), a choice has been made of the one which is most consistent with his [Peirce's] leading principles and the others abandoned" (*An Introduction to Peirce's Philosophy*, p. xix).

2. NATURALISM AND TRANSCENDENTALISM IN PEIRCE

When William James drew his famous distinction between "tough-minded" and "tender-minded" philosophers, he underlined the important truth that a thinker's temperament has a great deal to do with the sort of conclusions he affirms. The relationship implied here, I think, is this. A philosopher's temperament determines in large measure the *assumptions* he makes, consciously or unconsciously, in working out his ideas. Such assumptions are a necessary part of every philosophy, and constitute the basis on which it rests. They include various fundamental matters such as the philosopher's conception (*a*) of the method proper to his discipline (e.g., empiricism, rationalism, etc.); (*b*) of the locus of the real in contrast to the illusory or fictitious; (*c*) of the proper weight to be attached to the results of the empirical sciences in relation to the deliverances of feeling, emotion, instinct, etc.; and so on. Whatever conclusions he reaches will be conditioned by the premisses[5] from which he sets out. The consistency or inconsistency of the latter will inevitably be reflected in the former. It is not suggested that such assumptions are immune from scrutiny. The point is that *if* they are scrutinized, it can only be in terms of *other* assumptions that are made. Furthermore, since temperament is largely determined by inherited and environmental influences, there is a significant connection between a philosopher's assumptions and his personal history. Because of the peculiarly basic role of these ultimate premisses, they may be referred to as *metaphysical*. Every philosopher, then, can be said to have either a tacit or an explicit metaphysics in the light of which his reflection is conducted.

Now Peirce's temperament, I believe, harbored a conflict which exhibits itself philosophically in the espousal of two incompatible sets of premisses for his thought. One of these is his naturalism; the other is his transcendentalism. The consequences of the former are "tough-minded"; those of the latter "tender-minded." Each is a relatively, but not a rigorously, consistent doctrine. Yet between them there exists a fundamental antagonism.

By "naturalism" I mean a philosophical position whose major prin-

---

[5]Throughout this study I shall adopt Peirce's spelling of "premiss" and "premisses." He quite rightly points out that the more usual words, "premise" and "premises," are "of legal provenance," and hence inappropriate to philosophy, or at least to logic. "Premiss" is derived from the medieval Latin *praemissa;* whereas "premise" comes from the French *premise,* which is a noun derived from the phrase *les choses premises,* used in inventories. (Cf. 2.253; 2.582.)

ciples are somewhat as follows. (1) Scientific method—i.e., the process which starts with observation, goes on to formulate hypotheses, deduces their consequences, and terminates in inductive verification—is the only means of obtaining knowledge. (2) Theory and practice are interdependent and inseparable components of human life. (3) Conceptual precision achieved by logical analysis is a primary desideratum in philosophy. (4) There is no good reason for accepting a Platonic realism with regard to universals. (5) Man is a product of the natural world, with which he is continuous; and his philosophical account of that world requires the use of non-subjective or non-personal categories. (6) All *a priori* modes of thought about matters of fact are illegitimate. (7) The attempt to construct a "system" of philosophy in which the nature of the world is "explained," should be regarded with suspicion. (8) The conclusions of philosophy must be broadly compatible with the ideas of common sense.

By "transcendentalism," on the other hand, I mean a doctrine which includes the following propositions among its premisses. (1) The appeal to feeling, sentiment, or instinct is a more important source of knowledge than the appeal to reason or science. (2) Theory and practice have no intrinsic connection with one another. (3) Since the most important philosophical ideas are of necessity vague, no precise definition of them is possible. (4) Metaphysical construction is a more significant activity than logical analysis. (5) There are convincing reasons for espousing a Platonic realism of universals. (6) Since man's inner life provides him with the truest insights into the nature of the universe, he may properly interpret the latter in terms of highly personal or anthropomorphic categories. (7) *A priori* modes of reasoning are both necessary and legitimate in dealing with such matters as the origin and destiny of man and the universe. (8) The aim of philosophical thought is to produce a comprehensive system of knowledge which will be ultimate and final. Its conclusions must inevitably differ from the superficial opinions of common sense.

The above descriptions, it should be made clear, do not purport to be an account of two historical positions in philosophy. They are rather delineations of certain broad doctrines, some or all of which can function as the premisses of a philosopher's thought. Many of them have so functioned historically. But to argue for this generally is not my intention. Nor do I wish to imply that the views sketched constitute a *fundamentum divisionis,* so that every philosophy must be either naturalistic or transcendentalist. That would involve a gross over-simplification. Finally, I have not attempted to elaborate the details of each of the above points, since to do so would require a complete study in itself. The form which they take in Peirce's work, however, will emerge as we proceed.

My contention, then, is (*a*) that there are genuine discrepancies in the philosophy of Peirce; (*b*) that the *major* discrepancies are due to the presence of the two sets of premises just indicated; and (*c*) that at various places there is a conflict between the consequences which flow from these premises, so that no single, coherent doctrine results. It must be added that the assumptions in question do not play an equally important role in determining his conclusions. As we shall discover, the naturalistic "moment" of his thought was far stronger and more influential than his transcendentalism. It was the former that led him to pursue his researches in formal logic, semiotics, scientific method, phenomenology, and critical metaphysics, and to make such impressive contributions to those fields. His transcendentalism is most apparent in his views on cosmology, ethics, and theology, though traces of it are visible elsewhere. His speculative conclusions, while often highly original and suggestive, are on the whole the least cogent aspect of his work. As we pass from the logical studies through phenomenology to his metaphysics, the coexistence of the two tendencies becomes increasingly apparent. The upshot is diversity rather than unity of thought.

The marshalling of evidence in support of the above interpretation will now be undertaken. In Part One, I shall give a full account of Peirce's naturalism, noting at certain points where his transcendentalism impinges on the course of the argument. In Part Two, his transcendentalism will be considered separately in its various aspects. No claim will be made that *all* the inconsistencies in Peirce's text can thereby be explained, but only the major inconsistencies. A concluding chapter will seek to show how the circumstances of his life and intellectual development helped to produce the opposite tendencies in his thought.

PART ONE

Peirce's Naturalism

II

THE PATTERN OF HUMAN INQUIRY

1. PEIRCE'S INTEREST IN METHODS OF INQUIRY

PEIRCE's naturalism has its basis in his view of human inquiry. This was a subject of profound and perennial interest to him. Thus, in 1898 he declared: "From the moment when I could think at all, until now, about forty years, I have been diligently and incessantly occupied with the study of methods of inquiry, both those which have been and are pursued and those which ought to be pursued" (1.3). Four years later he wrote: "I only say that since my youth I have been associated with strong thinkers and have never ceased to make it a point to study their handling of their problems in all its details" (2.110). Accordingly, he devoted some of his best thought to analyzing human inquiry. In this chapter I shall present the general results of his analysis, and subsequently we shall grapple with the details.

Few men were as well equipped as Peirce to undertake such a study. His first-hand acquaintance with the procedures employed in mathematics and logic, his training in chemistry, his practical experience in astronomy, experimental psychology, geodesy, and optics, provided him with a wealth of material for examination. His great generalizing power enabled him to use this material for the formulation of principles exhibited in all types of inquiry. And his naturalistic orientation led him to insist that since inquiry does not take place in a void, it must be exhibited as a mode of human activity. The *raison d'être* of inquiry lies in the biological and social nature of man.

2. THE BIOLOGICAL BASIS OF INQUIRY

Peirce gives a clear explanation of this at the start of his paper of 1880 "On the Algebra of Logic." He there seeks to show that "thinking, as cerebration, is no doubt subject to the general laws of nervous action" (3.155), and that these laws in turn depend on the fundamental properties of protoplasm (cf. 5.563). The first point he makes is that when a nerve is stimulated, it displays an automatic tendency to react in such a way as to remove the stimulus. Now since all vital processes become easier on repetition, and since every type of nervous irritation sooner or later produces the action that removes it, "a strong habit of responding to the given irritation, in this particular way, must quickly be established" (3.157). Habits thus acquired can, Peirce thinks, be transmitted by inheritance (3.158). One of the most important habits is that "by virtue of which certain classes of stimuli throw us at first, at least, into a purely cerebral activity" (*ibid.*).

Since the category of habit is a central one in Peirce's thought, it should be noted that he employs it in two senses. The wider sense occurs in the context of his transcendentalism. Here he treats *habit* as a synonym for *natural law,* and applies it to the interpretation of inorganic, as well as organic phenomena. In the narrower sense, *habit* denotes any acquired form of behavior, produced by repeated responses of an *organism* to stimuli of a determinate kind. Thus conceived, habits are regarded not as passive modes of behavior, but as positive determinants of action.

Peirce considers that habits constitute the core of human personality. "Man is a bundle of habits" (6.228). But men also have the distinctive characteristic of becoming conscious of their habits, and what is called "belief" is identical with this consciousness. Peirce early came to the conclusion, following a suggestion of Bain's which he used to hear expounded at the Cambridge Metaphysical Club by Nicholas St. John Green (cf. 5.12), that belief is just "a habit of which we are conscious" (4.53), "a cerebral habit of the highest kind, which will determine what we do in fancy as well as what we do in action" (3.160). "A genuine belief, or opinion, is something on which a man is prepared to act, and is therefore, in a general sense, a habit" (2.148). It follows that a belief is not simply a matter of abstract, intellectual conviction, but is a dynamic force which finds its primary manifestation in behavior. "The feeling of believing is a more or less sure indication of there being established in our nature some habit which will determine our actions" (5.371).

Now every habit is exposed to the possibility of being blocked, or rendered ineffectual, by the appearance in the environment of factors with which it has not previously had to deal. In that case, a new habit must be formed to cope with the unfamiliar stimuli. Where the original habit is a belief, the blocking manifests itself as a state of doubt.

Doubt, then, is the privation of habit (5.417) arising from the surprise or shock which comes with a novel environment (5.512). Now whereas belief is a calm and satisfactory state which we do our utmost to preserve, doubt is the precise opposite. It is "an uneasy and dissatisfied state from which we struggle to free ourselves" (5.372). To this struggle Peirce gives the name of *Inquiry* (5.374). The aim of inquiry is to re-establish and "fix" beliefs, i.e., to render them secure against future surprise and disappointment (2.173). "With the doubt, therefore, the struggle begins, and with the cessation of doubt it ends. Hence, the sole object of inquiry is the settlement of opinion." (5.375) It is worth observing that although the last three statements quoted were made in 1877, Peirce refers with approval to them in 1906 (cf. 5.563). He must, therefore, have considered them to be a permanent and essential part of his doctrine.

3. ERRONEOUS CONCEPTIONS OF INQUIRY

Peirce next goes on to show how this conception of inquiry sweeps away certain influential but erroneous notions. The first is the view propounded by Descartes that the proper starting-point for inquiry is a state of complete absence of belief. For Descartes, such a state is achieved by the activity of doubting systematically all one's beliefs, and subsequently accepting just those which are certified by rational inquiry. Only thus can the individual make sure that his knowledge is solidly grounded. The Cartesian method of doubt, which inaugurated the period of modern thought, referred specifically to *philosophical* inquiry; so Peirce proceeds to attack the doctrine in that form.[1]

His objection to it is twofold. (*a*) It is in fact impossible to pursue the method of universal doubt. For "genuine doubt cannot be created by a mere effort of will, but must be compassed through experience" (5.498). Some surprising or novel feature of our environment which interferes with an existing belief-habit is the only source of "real and living doubt." *All* our beliefs can never be challenged in this way by any experience. If it be objected that the method of doubt which Descartes advocated does not involve any reference to habits, but only

[1]His attack forms part of a general criticism of "that strangely influential hodge-podge, the salad of Cartesianism," which he undertook in his important early papers: "Questions concerning Certain Faculties Claimed for Man," "Some Consequences of Four Incapacities," and "Grounds of Validity of the Laws of Logic," *Journal of Speculative Philosophy,* vol. II (1868). Other aspects of his rejection of Cartesianism will emerge below.

requires the adoption of a certain intellectual attitude, Peirce replies
that this reduces it to a mere "make-believe." "Some philosophers have
imagined that to start an inquiry it was only necessary to utter a question whether orally or by setting it down upon paper. . . . But the
mere putting of a proposition into the interrogative form does not
stimulate the mind to any struggle after belief. There must be a real
and living doubt, and without this all discussion is idle." (5.376)
"Do you call it *doubting* to write down on a piece of paper that you
doubt? If so, doubt has nothing to do with any serious business."
(5.416) (*b*) Thus, if we adopt the universal scepticism recommended
by Descartes as a necessary propaedeutic to philosophy, we expose
ourselves to an insidious form of self-deception. For we shall end by
recovering all those beliefs which we began by rejecting, because our
rejection was in reality only formal. The method of doubt is therefore
like going to the North Pole in order to get to Constantinople by coming down regularly upon a meridian. Accordingly, if we want to make
our thinking real and vital, we must recognize that there is much that
we do not in the least question. "Let us not pretend to doubt in philosophy what we do not doubt in our hearts" (5.265).

Another mistaken view of inquiry, which stems from Aristotle, is
that it must begin with certain first principles as its premises. These
first principles are commonly regarded as "self-evident truths," or propositions which the light of reason has declared to be cognitively certain. Sometimes, they are affirmed to be necessarily true because their
denial is inconceivable. Only on such a basis, it is held, can scientific
demonstration be established, for otherwise we should have an infinite
regress in thought. The ultimate premises of demonstration cannot
themselves be in need of proof. They must be in the nature of "first
cognitions."

As early as 1868, Peirce settled accounts with this "intellectualist"
conception of inquiry. First of all, he shows that even if we take it on
its own terms and equate inquiry with the process of logical thought,
there is no ground for asserting the presence of first cognitions. For if
such cognitions existed they would have to be known either immediately by a kind of intuition, or mediately by inference. Several considerations militate against the former possibility (cf. 5.213 ff.), the
chief of which is that since any cognition requires a finite span of time
in which to take place, no cognition can arise in the immediate present,
i.e. in intuition. Peirce's view that thought necessarily involves signs
and symbolic reference led him to reject all forms of the doctrine of

intuitive knowledge, as we shall see in more detail below. The other possibility, that we apprehend the existence of first cognitions "by hypothetical inference from observed facts," leads to a contradiction. For to *conclude* that X is a first cognition is to admit that X is not an ultimate premiss of thought, but rather the *result* of thought (cf. 5.260). "No cognition not determined by a previous cognition, then, can be known. It does not exist, then, first, because it is absolutely incognizable, and second, because a cognition only exists so far as it is known." (5.262)

Quite apart from this argument, however, there are other facts which Peirce thinks fatal to the notion of absolute first principles. Historical evidence shows that there never has been any general agreement either as to their number or as to their precise content. What has seemed "self-evidently true" to some individuals has proved wholly unacceptable to others. A similar difficulty faces those who want to establish the primacy of certain propositions by showing that their denial is "inconceivable."

By this denial being inconceivable is meant that it is quite impossible to definitely realize in imagination a state of things in which that would be false which the denial asserts to be false. Those who believe in the criterion innocently think that in order to ascertain whether the denial is thus inconceivable, all they have to do is to try an easy experiment and so find out, at once, whether they can imagine the state of things in question, or not. But as J. S. Mill puts it, "the history of science teems with inconceivabilities which have been conquered." What is required, therefore, is that "inconceivable" should mean not merely unrealizable in imagination today but unrealizable after indefinite training and education. (2.29)

In this sense, "inconceivability of the denial" would apply to the final results of inquiry, not to its premisses.[2]

4. THE PRESUPPOSITIONS OF INQUIRY

If neither a state of universal doubt nor a set of first principles can provide the starting-point for inquiry, where is it to begin? At what point, for instance, must the philosopher commence his activities? Peirce's answer is that he must commence at whatever point in his career he happens to be when he starts to think philosophically. There can be no other point of departure; certainly, there is no absolute

---

[2]Exactly the same objections apply to attaching the word "inconceivable" to the affirmation of a proposition, not merely to its denial. Peirce goes so far as to say that "nothing is 'inconceivable' to a man who sets seriously about the conceiving of it" (4.68).

starting-point from which a philosopher *has* to set out. As he put it in 1868: "We must begin with all the prejudices which we actually have when we enter upon the study of philosophy. These prejudices are not to be dispelled by a maxim, for they are things which it does not occur to us *can* be questioned." (5.265) By 1905, Peirce came to realize that what he had referred to as "prejudices," were more appropriately conceived as beliefs possessing an important cognitive status. Hence he writes that "in truth, there is but one state of mind from which you can 'set out,' namely, the very state of mind in which you actually find yourself at the time you do 'set out'—a state in which you are laden with an immense mass of cognition already formed, of which you cannot divest yourself if you would" (5.416). This "mass of cognition" turns out to be a number of fundamental beliefs adopted by the individual as the result of his experience. When formulated, they constitute a group of indubitable propositions, i.e. propositions *not in fact doubted,* which serve as the basis for his investigations. Not only philosophic inquiry, but *all* inquiry, rests on a foundation of such beliefs.

Towards the close of his life, Peirce devoted considerable attention to these unquestioned beliefs which underlie inquiry. The subject was one which interested him greatly, and formed an important part of what he liked to call his "Critical Common-sensism." But he was far from thinking that he had explored its implications fully. In a footnote appended to a brief discussion of it in 1905, he remarks: "I wish I might hope, after finishing some more difficult work, to be able to resume this study and to go to the bottom of the subject, which needs the qualities of age and does not call upon the powers of youth. A great range of reading is necessary; for it is the belief men *betray* and not that which they *parade* which has to be studied." (5.444) Such a study was, he felt, essential to the full understanding of human inquiry.

In the broadest sense, indubitable beliefs represent for Peirce the accumulated wisdom of the race. "That is to say, they rest on . . . the total everyday experience of many generations of multitudinous populations" (5.522). They may also be called "instinctive beliefs" inasmuch as they are the result of biological and social adjustments made at an unreflective level of life (5.511). Hence they remain broadly invariant from group to group, and from age to age.[3] The only

---

[3] Peirce reports that he at first thought "that the indubitable propositions changed with a thinking man from year to year," but later came to realize that they remain relatively the same from generation to generation (cf. 5.444).

specific illustrations which Peirce gives of these "social indubitables"[4] are: the conviction that fire burns (5.498), that there is an element of order in the universe (6.496), and that incest is a crime (5.445). But he undoubtedly had in mind the whole corpus of common-sense opinions about physical nature, human society, and man—in particular, the belief that the world of things, persons, and events exists independently of the experience of any individual or individuals.

A man may say "I will content myself with common sense." I, for one, am with him there, in the main. I shall show why I do not think there can be any *direct* profit in going behind common sense—meaning by common sense those ideas and beliefs that man's situation absolutely forces upon him. . . . I agree, for example, that it is better to recognize that some things are red and some others blue, in the teeth of what optical philosophers say, that it is merely that some things are resonant to shorter ether waves and some to longer ones. (1.129)

It is in this connection that Peirce signifies his agreement "under inevitable modification," with the Scottish philosophy of common sense, and with "the opinion of that subtle but well-balanced intellect, Thomas Reid" (5.444). Yet he differs from thinkers like Reid and Stewart in several important respects. (*a*) He insists that indubitable beliefs are always essentially vague, and stand in need of criticism and clarification before they can be placed in the same class with the results of inquiry (5.505 ff.). (*b*) Indubitable beliefs must have grown up in the course of the evolutionary process; and during the process cannot have been indubitable (5.512). This recognition of evolution is one of the main features which distinguishes a Critical Commonsensist from the old Scottish philosophers who lived in the days when "Adam was an undoubted historical personage" (5.444). Hence, although changes in indubitable beliefs are slight from one generation to the next, such changes are by no means imperceptible (5.512). (*c*) In general, beliefs remain indubitable only in relation to affairs that resemble a primitive mode of life (5.511; 5.445). Consequently, when inquiry has proceeded for some time, such beliefs may become dubious. In that case they will be replaced by scientific hypotheses. Indubitable beliefs therefore cannot be said, strictly speaking, to belong to the systematic part of any inquiry. At most, they serve as its vague, ultimate premises (5.515) which need to be constantly subjected to scrutiny (5.517). For "the whole history of thought shows

---

[4]I borrow this useful expression from Justus Buchler, *Charles Peirce's Empiricism* (New York and London, 1939), p. 59.

that our instinctive beliefs, in their original condition, are so mixed up with error that they can never be trusted till they have been corrected by experiment" (1.404).[5]

5. THE FIXATION OF BELIEF

We have seen that for Peirce the limits of human inquiry are set by the states of doubt and belief. Belief is always prior to doubt, both for the individual and for the race. Now a belief has three properties.

First, it is something that we are aware of; second, it appeases the irritation of doubt; and, third, it involves the establishment in our nature of a rule of action, or, say for short, a *habit*. As it appeases the irritation of doubt, which is the motive for thinking, thought relaxes, and comes to rest for a moment when belief is reached. But, since belief is a rule for action, the application of which involves further doubt and further thought, at the same time that it is a stopping-place, it is also a new starting-place for thought. (5.397)

The general aim of thought, however, is always the fixation of belief, the production of habits which will be forever proof against surprise and disappointment.

The question now arises, What are the various possible ways of establishing beliefs, and which, if any, can be accepted as reliable? This is the subject to which Peirce addresses himself in his essay of 1877 on "The Fixation of Belief." The focal point of the essay consists of the four methods of fixing belief which he distinguishes and evaluates. They are: (1) the method of tenacity, (2) the method of authority, (3) the *a priori* or metaphysical method, and (4) scientific method. His discussion is of such importance for his theory of inquiry that we must examine it in detail.

1. The majority of men prefer to adopt the method of tenacity as a means of escaping the annoyance of doubt. That is to say, they cling tenaciously to doctrines taught them at their mother's knee, and turn with contempt and hatred from anything that might disturb them. Such doctrines tend to be of a congenial and consolatory character. The individual persists in their acceptance because to surrender them would make him uncomfortable or unhappy. This, according to Peirce, is like the alleged behavior of the ostrich which buries its head in the sand whenever danger approaches. It is a policy deliberately adopted by those who are unwilling to face the necessity for frequent suspense

---

[5] A different view of the reliability and importance of instinctive beliefs will be considered in connection with Peirce's transcendentalism.

of judgment. They go through life systematically keeping out of view all that might cause a change in their opinions.

Now it is beside the point to object that this attitude is irrational. For that only amounts to saying that we do not accept such a method of settling our own beliefs. The real weakness of the method is its inability to sustain itself *in practice.* "The social impulse is against it" (5.378). For whoever follows it is bound to discover that other persons think differently from him on many subjects. Hence it cannot but occur to him in some saner moment that their opinions are quite as good, if not better, than his own; and this will be a constant threat to his peace of mind. Unless we become hermits we cannot avoid influencing each other's opinions; so that the problem really is one of fixing belief not in the individual, but in the *community.* And here appeal may first be made to some source of authority.

2. The situation envisaged by Peirce as typical of the method of authority is all too familiar in the modern world, and sounds like the description of a contemporary totalitarian state.

Let an institution be created which shall have for its object to keep correct doctrines before the attention of the people, to reiterate them perpetually, and to teach them to the young; having at the same time power to prevent contrary doctrines from being taught, advocated, or expressed. Let all possible causes of a change of mind be removed from men's apprehensions. Let them be kept ignorant, lest they should learn of some reason to think otherwise than they do. Let their passions be enlisted, so that they may regard private and unusual opinions with hatred and horror. Then, let all men who reject the established belief be terrified into silence. . . . When complete agreement could not otherwise be reached, a general massacre of all who have not thought in a certain way has proved a very effective means of settling opinion in a country. . . . This method has, from the earliest times, been one of the chief means of upholding correct theological and political doctrines, and of preserving their universal or catholic character. (5.379)

Peirce goes on to remark ironically that judged in terms of its material efficiency, the method of authority is vastly superior to the method of tenacity. "The mere structures of stone which it has caused to be put together—in Siam, for example, in Egypt, and in Europe—have many of them a sublimity hardly more than rivaled by the greatest works of Nature" (5.380). True, the method outrages the sensibilities of any rational man, because of the premium it puts on cruelty, ruthlessness, and intellectual slavery.[6] But its chief defect is

[6]Yet Peirce adds: "For the mass of mankind, then, there is perhaps no better method than this. If it is their highest impulse to be intellectual slaves, then

that no institution, however efficient, can undertake to regulate opinions on *every* subject. Only the most important can be attended to, while in regard to the rest, "men's minds must be left to the action of natural causes." Moreover, there is an intrinsic spontaneity possessed by thought which renders it incapable of being completely regimented. Hence, even in the most tyrannical of states, individuals will arise who are to some degree emancipated from official dogma. They will come to perceive that it is just the accident of their having been surrounded by the manners and associations they have, that has caused them to believe as they do, and not far differently. Nor will they be able to escape the reflection that there is no good reason to rate their own views at a higher value than those of other nations and other centuries. All this will serve ultimately to undermine the established beliefs of the community. Therefore, the wilful adhering to an opinion, and the arbitrary forcing of it on others, must both be given up.

3. A more respectable and sophisticated method of fixing belief is that adopted by the metaphysicians. Its essence consists in the establishment of a set of propositions that are "agreeable to reason." No question of conformity to experience or to observed facts is raised. The sole issue is whether the beliefs fit into a scheme which reason can accept. Plato, for example, found it agreeable to reason to believe that the distances of the celestial spheres from one another should be proportional to the different lengths of string which produce harmonious sounds. Descartes found it agreeable to believe that God cannot be a deceiver. Hegel "simply launches his boat into the current of thought and allows himself to be carried wherever the current leads. He himself calls his method *dialectic*, meaning that a frank discussion of the difficulties to which any opinion spontaneously gives rise will lead to modification after modification until a tenable position is attained. This is a distinct profession of faith in the method of inclinations." (5.382 n.) The vast majority of metaphysicians have been led to their conclusions by such *a priori* routes.

The basic objections to this procedure are two in number. (i) It is unavoidably infected with subjectivity because of the fact that it involves no appeal to an external reality. "It makes of inquiry some-

---

slaves they ought to remain." (5.380)   This is the kind of judgment that can easily lead to the excesses of the method of authority. It is a good example of how Peirce was occasionally betrayed into making statements not only unsupported by evidence, but also at variance with his own position.

thing similar to the development of taste" (5.383). But taste is notoriously unstable and ephemeral. Consequently, metaphysicians have never been able to agree on even the most rudimentary principles of their discipline. From the earliest times to the latest, the pendulum has swung back and forth between the extremes of monism and pluralism, idealism and realism, depending on the predilections of particular thinkers. (ii) The method has also fostered an individualistic attitude to the search for knowledge. Instead of becoming a steadily progressive, co-operative enterprise, it has been from the outset a series of controversies among rival metaphysicians, each of whom defends his private system of thought against all the others. Thus the *a priori* method of establishing belief can provide no guarantee of reliability. "To satisfy our doubts, therefore, it is necessary that a method should be found by which our beliefs may be determined by nothing human, but by some external permanency—by something upon which our thinking has no effect. . . . But which, on the other hand, unceasingly tends to influence thought. . . . Such is the method of science." (5.384)

4. A distinguishing characteristic of science is its realistic foundation. It starts with the hypothesis that there exists prior to and apart from the investigating scientist, an objective order of nature. It assumes that: "There are Real things, whose characters are entirely independent of our opinions about them; those Reals affect our senses according to regular laws, and, though our sensations are as different as are our relations to the objects, yet, by taking advantage of the laws of perception, we can ascertain by reasoning how things really and truly are" (*ibid.*). Has this hypothesis any weight of evidence in its favor? Peirce contends that the following considerations make its acceptance reasonable. (i) None of the conclusions so far reached by scientific method have proved incompatible with it. On the contrary, the method and the assumption on which it rests remain ever in harmony. No doubts regarding the method, therefore, spring from its practical application, as is the case with all the other procedures. (ii) The feeling of dissatisfaction engendered in the minds of rational individuals when confronted with a pair of contradictory existential propositions, is a vague concession that there must be a single state of affairs which determines the truth or falsity of *one* of the propositions. "Nobody, therefore, can really doubt that there are Reals, for, if he did, doubt would not be a source of dissatisfaction. The hypothesis, therefore, is one which every mind admits." (*Ibid.*) (iii) As a matter of fact, we all employ the scientific method to some extent, and only

cease to employ it when we do not know precisely how it ought to be applied. (iv) Lastly, a long experience of the method has not led us to doubt it—quite the opposite. For scientific investigation has gone from triumph to triumph in the process of settling opinion, and it is highly probable that it will continue to do so in the future. Consequently, we are more than justified in adopting it as a means of fixing our beliefs.

When scientific method is contrasted with the other three, its strength becomes obvious. Thus, if we adopt the method of tenacity, and isolate ourselves from all disturbing influences, whatever we think necessary to doing this *is* necessary according to that method. Similarly with the method of authority. The state may try to put down heresy by means which are extremely ill adapted to their ends, if the matter be viewed scientifically. Nevertheless, the only test *on that method* is what the state thinks; so that it cannot pursue the method wrongly. The same is true of the *a priori* method. Since its very essence is to think as one is inclined to think, all metaphysicians will tend to do just that, however much they may be inclined to judge each other wrong. But with the scientific method the case is different. We may propose to start with known and observed facts and proceed to the unknown; yet the rules we follow in doing so may not be such as investigation would ultimately approve. The test of whether we are truly following the method is not an immediate appeal to feelings and purposes, but on the contrary, involves the *application* of the method itself. For, as we shall see, Peirce holds scientific method to be intrinsically self-corrective and capable of eliminating its own errors. Accordingly, it alone can bring about that coincidence between our ideas and the objective world which is the sole condition of stable beliefs.

6.   THE CHARACTERISTICS OF SCIENTIFIC INQUIRY

It seems clear from the above that in his essay of 1877 Peirce tended to identify scientific method with the procedures employed by the physical sciences. I think he continued to regard these procedures as exhibiting most clearly the virtues of soundly conducted inquiry. Thus, when he describes himself as "saturated, through and through, with the spirit of the physical sciences" (1.3), and as "having all his life associated mostly with experimentalists . . . with a confident sense of understanding them and of being understood by them" (5.411), he leaves us in little doubt about the pre-eminent place which the natural sciences occupied in his thinking. Yet, as he penetrated more deeply into the essence of scientific inquiry, he broadened his conception of what it should include, so as to make a place for pure mathematics and the various branches of philosophy. Indeed, by 1902 he was prepared to adopt the ancient division of sciences into theoretical and practical, including under the latter heading such pursuits as printing, book-binding, ink-making, pigeon-fancying, etc! While this represents a much wider use of the word "science" than he ordinarily made, it shows that he was not prepared to limit it to laboratory disciplines alone. These are subsumed under the title "Idioscopy" in his classification of the sciences, and, together with Mathematics and Philosophy, make up what Peirce calls "the sciences of discovery."⁷ The latter are what he generally means when he speaks about inquiry as scientific.

What are the distinctive characteristics of the sciences in this wider sense? A science is, of course, a method of fixing belief, as we have seen. But in addition to that, it has certain further traits to which Peirce calls attention. (1) A science is primarily a persistent, disinterested pursuit of truth; (2) it is a co-operative, social venture, not an individual affair; (3) its data must be obtained by some form of *observation;* (4) its method of dealing with these data is that of rational or logical thought; (5) its conclusions must be verifiable by observation, experiment, or both; and (6) its conclusions are intrinsically provisional and susceptible of further refinement or correction as inquiry is continued. Some remarks must now be made about each of these points.

1. Peirce's repeated declaration that we must conceive science as consisting neither in organized knowledge nor in the activity of knowing, but rather "in diligent inquiry into truth for truth's sake, without any sort of axe to grind" (1.44), is amenable to two interpretations. One of these belongs to the transcendental tendency in his thought. The other is part of his naturalism. The naturalistic interpretation, with which we are concerned at the moment, is based on the relation which he sees between truth and belief. The central point here is that for Peirce truth and falsity must be *defined* in terms of belief and doubt. "All you have any dealings with are your doubts and beliefs, with the course of life that forces new beliefs upon you and gives you power to doubt old beliefs. . . . But if by truth and falsity you mean

---

⁷See section 8 of the present chapter.

something not definable in terms of doubt and belief in any way, then you are talking of entities of whose existence you can know nothing." (5.416) In other words, that which you do not in the least doubt, you must and do hold to be completely true. But, it may be objected, surely I have to recognize that despite the fact that there are scores of things which I do not doubt, I may very well be mistaken about some of them? To deny this, would be to make truth wholly subjective, a mere matter of private satisfaction. Peirce's reply is that the beliefs in terms of which truth is defined are those stable beliefs reached by an indefinitely long application of scientific method. Thus, for example, we say that the proposition "Caesar crossed the Rubicon" is true because the further we push our historical investigations, the more strongly a belief in that proposition is established in our minds. Conversely, to say that the proposition is false means that we *must* ultimately be led to disbelieve it as our inquiry is carried on indefinitely. If, inspired by the artificial procedure of Cartesianism, you keep insisting that there is something more to truth than this, you will "only puzzle yourself by talking of this 'metaphysical truth' and 'metaphysical falsity,' that you know nothing about" (*ibid.*).

The same point is stated by Peirce in another way. Suppose two reasonable men engage in a dispute over some question. Underlying the dispute is an assumption made by both parties that they will in the end find themselves forced to a common belief which will be definitive and final. Otherwise, their argument is irrational and pointless. Hence, we may say that "to reach a final and compulsory belief is, therefore, what the reasonable disputant aims at. But what he aims at is the truth. Therefore, by the truth he means nothing more than a finally compulsory belief." (2.29) Precisely the same situation obtains in all human inquiry. Truth, then, may be described as "that concordance of an abstract statement with the ideal limit towards which endless investigation would tend to bring scientific belief" (5.565).[8]

One consequence of this view is that for Peirce truth consists in a state of satisfaction. When he affirmed this in his essay of 1877, he did not foresee the use which would be made of the doctrine by William James and F. C. S. Schiller, a quarter of a century later. These men interpreted "satisfaction" in purely individualistic terms in formulating

[8]Professor Dewey mentions this as one of the best definitions of truth from the logical point of view with which he is acquainted. Cf. *Logic: The Theory of Inquiry* (New York, 1938), p. 345.

their pragmatic version of truth. Hence in 1908, Peirce felt obliged to clarify his own position by emphasizing that when he declared that truth consists in satisfaction, he did not mean actual satisfaction for any individual, but rather "the satisfaction which *would* ultimately be found if the inquiry were pushed to its ultimate and indefeasible issue. This, I beg to point out, is a very different position from that of Mr. Schiller and the pragmatists of today." (6.485) Accordingly, a belief is satisfactory only when all possible doubt in regard to it has been removed by scientific method. To ask for more than this is to seek the unattainable. The true is that at which inquiry aims (5.557); and the search for truth is the search for the ideally complete set of stable, satisfactory beliefs arrived at by continuous scientific inquiry.

2. Peirce makes frequent references to the co-operative nature of inquiry. For "the progress of science cannot go far except by collaboration; or, to speak more accurately, no mind can take one step without the aid of other minds" (2.220). In the physical sciences, co-operation is an accomplished fact. Unlike "those intellectual nomads" the traditional metaphysicians, workers in the experimental disciplines are not individualists in their search for truth. They are highly sensitive to the opinions and results of their co-workers. A true scientist attaches positive value to the views of every man as competent as himself. He therefore regards wide divergence from the convictions of the great body of scientific men as tending of itself to argue incompetence. Nor will he attach much weight to the opinions of eminent "back-numbers" long since dead, who were necessarily ignorant of much that has since been discovered which bears on the question in hand. Thus, the physical sciences constitute a vast, co-operative enterprise in which an issue is not regarded as settled until all intelligent and informed doubt about it has ceased, and all competent persons have come to a catholic agreement. This is the main reason why they make such steady progress. Their proponents envisage the quest for truth as essentially the task of the scientific community—"not as the work of one man's life, but as that of generation after generation, indefinitely" (5.589).

Peirce is firmly of the opinion that *all* inquiry requires a co-operative community of minds. In his papers of 1868, he stressed the fact that the notion of such a community is involved in the philosophic definition of the real.

And what do we mean by the real? It is a conception which we must first have had when we discovered that there was an unreal, an illusion; that is, when we first corrected ourselves. Now the distinction for which alone this fact logically called, was between an *ens* relative to private inward determinations, to the negations belonging to idiosyncrasy, and an *ens* such as would stand in the long run. The real, then, is that which, sooner or later, information and reasoning would finally result in, and which is therefore independent of the vagaries of me and you. Thus, the very origin of the conception of reality shows that this conception essentially involves the notion of a COMMUNITY, without definite limits, and capable of a definite increase of knowledge. (5.311)

One of the implications of this is that philosophical inquiry must become scientific if it is to emerge from its present infantile condition—"for as long as earnest and industrious students of it are able to come to agreement upon scarce a single principle, I do not see how it can be considered as otherwise than in its infancy" (1.620). Peirce wants to remedy the situation by encouraging philosophers to espouse the scientific method, and to collaborate in their researches after the manner of the physical scientists.[9] "I wish philosophy," he says, "to be a strict science, passionless and severely fair" (5.537). In a letter to James in 1909 he repeats these sentiments, adding that he has a deep conviction "that philosophy is either a science or is balderdash."[10] At a later stage, the details of his view of philosophy as a science will be examined. Here we merely note that an important aspect of it is that philosophers should be more favorably disposed to team-work in their investigations. For "we individually cannot reasonably hope to attain the ultimate philosophy which we pursue; we can only seek it, therefore, for the *community* of philosophers" (5.265).

The intimate connection between inquiry and the community in Peirce's thought appears in several different forms. The one so far indicated fits quite naturally, I think, into the pattern of his naturalism. For since inquiry is a struggle to escape doubt, and since the only effective procedure for doing so is the scientific method of fixing belief, it follows that this is the method everyone will ultimately come to adopt. The whole community will eventually practice it in determining

[9]He praises the scholastics for their practice in this regard. Willingness to collaborate in research, together with a tendency to be minute and thorough in the treatment of every question they handled, "affiliates them with men of science and separates them, world-wide, from modern so-called philosophers" (1.33). Peirce would presumably have welcomed such recent attempts at philosophical co-operation as *The New Realism,* edited by E. B. Holt (New York, 1912); *Essays in Critical Realism,* edited by Durant Drake (New York, 1920); *Creative Intelligence* by J. Dewey, A. W. Moore *et al.* (New York, 1917); and *Naturalism and the Human Spirit,* edited by Y. H. Krikorian (New York, 1944).

[10]R. B. Perry, *The Thought and Character of William James* (Boston, 1935), vol. II, p. 438.

its beliefs. Hence the philosophical meaning of conceptions such as truth and reality refers to the ideal state of complete information which would be accepted by the community after inquiry of indefinite duration. The individual who refuses to espouse scientific method will find himself in a precarious position, because no other method will enable him to achieve a stable and satisfactory relationship to his world. In the majority of cases, the weight of circumstances will force the individual to turn to the right method. But if not, Peirce seems to feel that we are warranted in saying to such a person: "You *ought* to make your beliefs reliable." This is a categorical or unconditional obligation having its roots in a sentiment which makes the individual identify his interests with those of an unlimited community. Thus, certain ethical considerations, such as the recognition of the *summum bonum*, become an indispensable requirement of inquiry. How this turn of the argument affects Peirce's naturalism, we shall note in due course.

3. That scientific inquiry requires material provided by observation is a cardinal point with Peirce. For this material is the source of all our knowledge. Just as a machine cannot do work perpetually without being fed with power in some form, so "the machinery of the mind can only transform knowledge, but never originate it, unless it be fed with facts of observation" (5.392). So important is the observational element in inquiry that Peirce uses it as one of the criteria in classifying the sciences. Thus, each of the three sciences of discovery, Mathematics, Philosophy, and Idioscopy, obtains its data by a special mode of observation. Mathematics produces imaginary constructions, or diagrams, according to a set of abstract rules, and then observes these constructions with a view to finding in them relations of parts not specified in the rules. Hence, as the mathematician Gauss remarked, algebra is "the science of the eye." Philosophy's domain of observation is ordinary macroscopic experience such as occurs to every man in every moment of his waking life. Idioscopy (i.e., the special sciences) depends upon "special observation, which travel or other exploration, or some assistance to the senses, either instrumental or given by training, together with unusual diligence, has put within the power of its students" (1.242). The use of instruments is of particular importance, as the history of the sciences shows. The great landmarks are placed at the points where new observational devices have been invented. In the sciences of discovery, then, inquiry must have sensory data to work on before it can get under way.

Now it is one thing to affirm the importance of observation, and quite another to know in detail what that affirmation entails. For the epistemological problems connected with the process of observing are notoriously difficult, and require systematic and painstaking analysis. Peirce can hardly be said to have provided any such analysis. Moreover, this is one of the places where the consistency of a philosophy receives an acid test, which is likely to reveal any latent discrepancies it contains. Consequently, the conflict in Peirce's thought shows itself here in certain incompatible pronouncements which he is led to make. Since our interest at the moment is in his naturalism, we must try to select and piece together the particular pronouncements which belong to this position. Other aspects of the question will claim attention later on.

First, we must note that Peirce employs a number of closely allied expressions in discussing the observational phase of inquiry. In addition to "observation" itself, we encounter "observed facts," "perception," "perceptual facts," "perceptual judgments," "experience," "percepts," etc. Thus, for example, he speaks of all knowledge as coming from observation (1.238); as resting on observed facts (6.522); as depending on what we directly experience (6.492); as having its immediate object in the percept (4.539); and so on. By examining the context, however, it is possible to interpret these as alternative descriptions of a single situation, and to establish some measure of equivalence among the various terms used.

The situation in question seems to amount to this. Observation is a process of attentive experience involving some, often great, effort (2.605). As such it may be denominated *perception,* provided we mean by this an activity which includes analysis (1.34) or abstraction. To mark off this type of analysis or abstraction from other types, Peirce uses the scholastic term *prescission.* Hence, "the most ordinary fact of perception, such as 'it is light,' involves *precisive* abstraction, or *prescission*" (4.235). But from what is "*precisive* abstraction" made, and what epistemological resultant does it yield?

Peirce's view on this matter seems to have undergone a change which is reflected in the terminology he used to deal with it. In his important paper "On a New List of Categories" (1867), the exposition is conducted in terms of "impressions" and "conceptions," with a strongly Kantian emphasis. In observation, prescission is made from our direct impressions, and the result is "a definite conception or *supposition* of one part of an object, without any supposition of the other" (1.549). This conception reduces the impressions to unity.

Elementary conceptions only arise upon the occasion of experience; that is, they are produced for the first time according to a general law, the condition of which is the existence of certain impressions. Now if a conception does not reduce the impressions upon which it follows to unity, it is a mere arbitrary addition to these latter; and elementary conceptions do not arise thus arbitrarily. . . . Hence, the impressions . . . cannot be definitely conceived or attended to, to the neglect of an elementary conception which reduces them to unity. (1.549)

As his thought moved away from Kantianism, Peirce dropped the view that concepts reduce impressions to unity at the level of perception. His change of attitude is clearly reflected in a criticism of Kant's doctrine made about 1890. "Kant gives the erroneous view that ideas are presented separated and then thought together by the mind. This is his doctrine that a mental synthesis precedes every analysis. What really happens is that something is presented which in itself has no parts, but which nevertheless is analyzed by the mind, that is to say, its having parts consists in this, that the mind afterward recognizes those parts in it." (1.384) Thus, in his later discussions, Peirce substitutes the term "percept" for "impression," and the term "perceptual judgment" for "conception." Observation is then seen to have two epistemological components, (*a*) the direct sensory material or *percept*, and (*b*) the characterization of that material in a *perceptual judgment*.[11] The latter interprets the percept, i.e., asserts that it has such-and-such features. Thus, the sentence "This looks red" is the linguistic expression of a perceptual judgment in all cases where "this" denotes a certain kind of percept. The word "experience," in at least one of the senses in which Peirce uses it, is identified with percepts—"the percepts . . . constitute experience proper" (2.142). The final product of the act of observation or perception is referred to as the "observed facts" or the "perceptual facts." Bearing in mind these correlations, certain further aspects of the two components of observation must be noted.

[11]The substitution of "percept" for "impression" makes it clear that Peirce intended to designate the *total content* of immediately present awareness, not just that *part* of the content which is the referent of a perceptual judgment. In other words, a percept is not a sense-datum or a mosaic of sense-data, as might have been suggested by the word "impression." Peirce puts the matter thus in the *Nation* for July 7, 1892 (p. 15): "There is no such thing as an 'immediate' sense-impression; the only things immediately given are total states of feeling, of which sense-impressions are mere elements; and to say that they are elements is a metaphorical expression, meaning not that they are in the immediate feeling in its immediateness, but that the act of reflective judgment is irresistible which perceives them there."

Percepts. The occurrence of percepts is temporally prior to that of perceptual judgments, though the interval separating them is infinitesimally small. This priority arises from the transience which is a feature of all human awareness. "It is plain enough that all that is immediately present to a man is what is in his mind in the present instant. His whole life is in the present. But when he asks what is the content of the present instant, his question always comes too late. The present has gone by, and what remains of it is greatly metamorphosed." (1.310) What remains of it is, of course, that which has been recorded in a perceptual judgment.

A percept is not a mental occurrent, but a portion of the external world which impinges directly on us. It exerts a brute compulsion from which we cannot escape, and is therefore properly described as physical rather than psychical. "The percept brutally forces itself upon us; . . . it appears under a physical guise. . . . The psychical, then, is not contained in the percept." (1.253) Indeed, for Peirce, "no psychical fact, as such, can be observed" (*ibid.*). But how can we be absolutely sure that a given percept *is* part of the external world? We cannot be *absolutely* sure, Peirce replies. Yet we can be reasonably sure, provided the percept sustains itself in the face of three tests. If it cannot be dismissed by an act of will; if other people agree with us about its characteristics; and above all, if we can use it as a basis for prediction and experiment—then we have excellent grounds for believing that the percept belongs to the real world (2.142).

The bare occurrence of a percept in the immediate present is not a cognition. For the percept is just "a single event happening *hic et nunc* . . . an actual passage at arms between the non-ego and the ego" (2.146). As a direct experience, it "is neither certain nor uncertain, because it affirms nothing—it just *is*. . . . It involves no error, because it testifies to nothing but its own appearance. For the same reason, it affords no certainty. It is not *exact,* because it leaves much vague; though it is not *inexact* either; that is, it has no false exactitude." (1.145) Hence, while it serves as the occasion of knowledge, the direct presentation of a percept is not *per se* an instance of knowing. For this to occur, we require a perceptual judgment.

Perceptual judgments. From the frequent but scattered remarks which Peirce makes on this subject, the following picture seems to emerge.

A perceptual judgment is a cognitive act, "an act of formation of a mental proposition combined with an adoption of it or act of assent to it" (5.115). The proposition is to be sharply distinguished from the written or spoken perceptual statement, for the latter is wholly linguistic whereas the former is at most "quasi-linguistic."

A perceptual judgment interprets or describes a percept. The judgment is "directly expressive of and resulting from the quality of a present percept" (5.151), and hence affirms a proposition of existence. As we have seen, it follows immediately upon the occurrence of the percept.

A perceptual judgment is totally different from a percept. "It is as unlike it as the printed letters in a book, where a Madonna of Murillo is described, are unlike the picture itself" (5.54). "The percept is the reality. It is not in propositional form. But the most immediate judgment concerning it is abstract. It is therefore essentially unlike the reality, although it must be accepted as true to that reality." (5.568) The relation between the two, therefore, cannot be one of simple correspondence or resemblance. On the contrary, the perceptual judgment is "true to" the percept if on the basis of the judgment we can make successful predictions about the future course of events. Hence the only justification of a perceptual judgment "is that it subsequently turns out to be useful" (1.538).

Perceptual judgments are the vehicles by which generality and universality enter into our knowledge (5.150). For although the subject of such a judgment always refers to a "singular actually reacting upon the mind," the predicate involves generality or "thirdness" (5.152). The judgment itself is always particular, never universal; but since it contains general elements, the presumption is that a universal proposition can be derived from it (5.156).

Now the question arises whether a percept *causes* a perceptual judgment to be formed, so that the latter is essentially beyond our control, or whether the perceptual judgment is a wholly voluntary act. Peirce does not discuss the psychological aspect of this question, which he rightly holds to be of secondary importance. "You may adopt any theory that seems to you acceptable as to the psychological operations by which perceptual judgments are formed" (5.55). But he does have something to say about the epistemological character of perceptual judgments, particularly in regard to their cognitive certainty or uncertainty. His remarks suggest, however, that he never finally made up his mind on this issue, and hence advocates two different positions.

(i) On the one hand, Peirce appears to insist that perceptual judgments must be taken as completely certain because it is impossible to correct them. They are incorrigible for two reasons. First, the process of forming a perceptual judgment is so swift that it is incapable of being controlled. The judgment seems literally thrust on us *ab extra*. Because of its involuntary character, Peirce sometimes speaks of it as a "subconscious process" (5.181), or as belonging to the "instinctive" part of the mind (5.212). It is akin to the flash of insight which is the means of providing the scientist with his hypotheses (5.173). Hence, it represents a limiting case of the more general procedure of abduction, as will appear later. It differs from ordinary abductive inference, however, in transcending all criticism (5.55; 5.108; 5.116, etc.).

Moreover, the epistemological referents of perceptual judgments are percepts; and percepts by their very nature are transient and fleeting. One cannot recapture a percept and discover whether one's original judgment about it was accurate. For example, I may judge that a certain sheet of paper appears perfectly red. (The fact that I am making a perceptual judgment is indicated by the word "appears." I am not judging that the paper *is* red.) But a moment later I may question whether that judgment is a reliable report of what I saw, and may look again more sharply. If my second judgment is that I see a perfectly red surface, the theory of the *facts* will be simpler than if on my second look I were to judge that the surface appears orange in color. Nevertheless, my second judgment cannot refer to identically the same percept as my first, but must refer to a different percept (5.115). Therefore, the original judgment is beyond all possibility of criticism. As Peirce puts it:

If I judge a perceptual image to be red, I can conceive of another man's not having that same percept. I can also conceive of his having this percept but never having thought whether it was red or not. I can conceive that while colors are among his sensations, he shall never have had his attention directed to them. Or I can conceive that, instead of redness, a somewhat different conception should arise in his mind; that he should, for example, judge that this percept has a warmth of color. I can imagine that the redness of my percept is excessively faint and dim, so that one can hardly make sure whether it is red or not. But that any man should have a percept similar to mine and should ask himself the question whether this percept be *red*, which would imply that he had already judged *some* percept to be red, and that he should, upon careful attention to this percept, pronounce it to be decidedly and clearly *not* red, when I judge it to be prominently red, *that* I cannot comprehend at all. An abductive suggestion, however, is something whose truth *can* be questioned or even denied. (5.186)

In other words, given the linguistic usage of the word *red,* it is meaningless to say that I may be in error when I judge that a certain percept is red; for (*a*) there is no conceivable way in which my judgment could be disproved; and (*b*) I should not have made *that* particular judgment unless the percept *had been* red. Thus, perceptual judgments appear as the infallible first premisses of all scientific inquiry, because they present the raw material of knowledge in logical form. "All our other judgments are so many theories whose only justification is that they have been and will be borne out by perceptual judgments" (5.116).

(ii) A rather different picture from the above is implied by statements which appear in chapter 2 of the "Minute Logic." Peirce there varies his usage and talks not about perceptual judgments, but about "perceptual facts." The latter are "the intellect's description of the evidence of the senses [percepts], made by my endeavor. These perceptual facts are wholly unlike the percept, at best; and they may be downright untrue to the percept." (2.141) So far as their interpretative function is concerned, perceptual judgments and perceptual facts are simply the same thing under a different name (cf. 5.568). But they are markedly unlike in this, that perceptual facts are *not forced on our attention.* They arise from a *voluntary* effort to describe percepts, and are thus the result of purposive endeavor (2.141).

Since whatever is produced by conscious effort may easily be mistaken, it follows that perceptual facts are always exposed to error. Consequently, we do not accept them because we know them to be reliable; we accept them because we have nothing better, fully recognizing that they may be a crude and inaccurate registration of the percepts. Peirce sometimes denies that there is *any* cognitive relation at all between percepts and perceptual judgments.

You look at an object and say "That is red." I ask you how you prove that. You tell me you see it. Yes, you see *something;* but you do not see *that it is red;* because *that it is red* is a proposition; and you do not see a proposition. What you see is an image and has no resemblance to a proposition, and there is no logic in saying that your proposition is proved by the image. For a proposition can only be logically based on a premiss and a premiss is a proposition. (6.95)

Hence, we cannot *validate* a perceptual judgment by referring to the percept with which it is correlated. We can only validate the judgment in terms of other judgments; and since the series thus involved is infinite, no particular judgment can have more than a degree of cognitive certainty. Complete certainty is out of the question. Finally, the very temporal character of perception makes it impossible for perceptual judgments to be more than approximate. Consider again the judgment "This wafer looks red."

It takes some time to write this sentence, to utter it, or even to think it. It must refer to the state of the percept at the time that it, the judgment, began to be made. But the judgment does not exist until it is completely made. It thus only refers to a memory of the past; and all memory is possibly fallible and subject to criticism and control. The judgment, then, can only mean that so far as the character of the percept can ever be ascertained, it will be ascertained that the wafer looked red. (5.544)

But we cannot infer from this that the judgment itself, at the time it is made, is necessarily accurate. The upshot here seems to be that the perceptual facts on which science rests can never be known to be free from error. So far from being absolutely certain premises, they are unavoidably fallible, and may be modified or even rejected as investigation proceeds. To seek any other basis for science is to desire the impossible.

I think Peirce never committed himself unequivocally in regard to these two interpretations. That they are incompatible with one another is, of course, obvious. If perceptual judgments are taken to be completely veracious and incorrigible, they constitute an invariant foundation for scientific knowledge. If they are taken to be merely approximate and corrigible, then scientific knowledge has no invariant foundation, but must operate wholly within the realm of the approximate and the probable. It can hardly be denied that the second of these interpretations accords better with other aspects of Peirce's naturalism, such as his doctrine of fallibilism and his theory of signs. For these preclude the possibility of any synthetic proposition being cognitively certain. Nevertheless, the total evidence makes it clear that he did not succeed in working his way through to a definite conclusion on the matter.[12]

Summing up the discussion, then, we may say that observation for Peirce is construed in broadly Kantian terms as a combination of matter and form. The matter is produced by the external world im-

---

[12]Cf. Buchler, *Charles Peirce's Empiricism*, pp. 58 ff., for a different view on this question. Buchler contends that Peirce has a consistent position, and that he never really treats perceptual judgments as incorrigible.

pinging upon us in our percepts; the form is provided by our characterization of these percepts in perceptual judgments. The bare "having" of percepts does not constitute knowledge. They are known
mediately through the perceptual judgments which interpret them.
The kind of proposition yielded by a perceptual judgment is always a
singular whose predicate involves a modicum of generality. It is exclusively on the basis of these judgments that the inference found in
all inquiry takes place.

4. This brings us to the heart and center of inquiry, namely, its
inferential phase.[13] In exploring the methods and criteria of reasoning,
Peirce's great gifts as a logician reveal themselves. The details of his
analysis will be exhibited in their proper place, when we come to the
subject of logical inquiry. Here we shall simply note the broad outlines
of his doctrine.

Reasoning or thinking is not regarded by him as a psychical activity which goes on somewhere "in the mind." Nor is it treated as
radically different from everything else in nature. On the contrary,
"the possibility of science depends upon the fact that human thought
necessarily partakes of whatever character is diffused through the
whole universe, and that its natural modes have some tendency to be
the modes of action of the universe" (1.351). More specifically, reasoning is a complex form of behavior; so that when a formal logician
makes an inference in *Barbara*, "something . . . takes place within the
organism which is equivalent to the syllogistic process" (5.268). In
the course of his paper of 1883 on "A Theory of Probable Inference,"
Peirce even tries to show the precise physiological analogues of inference in the nervous system. And in 1902 he remarks that reasoning
exhibits "the singular phenomenon of a physiological function which
is open to approval and disapproval" (2.152). It must be admitted,
however, that these attempts to link logic with physiology are not very
illuminating.

Certain other general features of his view of reasoning may be
indicated here. (*a*) Reasoning is "essentially a voluntary act, over
which we exercise control" (2.144). For this reason it can be criticized

[13]The distinction between phases (3) and (4) is mainly one of degree rather
than of kind, since for Peirce inference itself involves a kind of observation.
Indeed, in the article "Observation," in Baldwin's *Dictionary of Philosophy and
Psychology*, it is stated that "whatever else there is in the act of reasoning is only
preparatory to observation, like the manipulation of a physical experiment"
(2.605). This article was written partly by Peirce and partly by J. M. Baldwin,
the editor.

or evaluated as good or bad, valid or invalid. Such criticism is the
proper task of logic. (*b*) The determination of logical goodness or badness is, at least initially, dependent on certain norms of reasoning.
Every valid argument conforms to a rule which governs the class of
inferences of which it is a member. This rule is the "leading principle"
of the argument. (*c*) Subjectively considered, "thinking always proceeds in the form of a dialogue" (4.6). The vernacular phrase "I say
to myself" correctly reports the situation which occurs when reflection
takes place. (*d*) All reasoning is conducted in signs or symbols. This
was a conclusion reached by Peirce about 1868, and held throughout
the remainder of his life as a doctrine of primary importance. Logic,
therefore, must bring the process of signification within its purview.
By so doing, it becomes "the science of the general necessary laws of
Signs and especially of Symbols" (2.93).

Peirce's analysis of reasoning leads to the recognition of "three
grand classes," Deduction, Induction, and Abduction. They are inter-
related in every process of inquiry, though each form of inference has
its own specific features. These are indicated compactly and lucidly
in a passage which occurs in the fifth of his "Lectures on Pragmatism"
(1903).

Deduction is the only necessary reasoning. It is the reasoning of mathematics. It starts from a hypothesis, the truth or falsity of which has nothing
to do with the reasoning; and of course its conclusions are equally ideal.
The ordinary use of the doctrine of chances is necessary reasoning, although it is reasoning concerning probabilities. Induction is the experimental
testing of a theory. The justification of it is that, although the conclusion
at any stage of the investigation may be more or less erroneous, yet the
further application of the same method must correct the error. The only
thing that induction accomplishes is to determine the value of a quantity.
It sets out with a theory and it measures the degree of concordance of that
theory with fact. It never can originate any idea whatever. No more can
deduction. All the ideas of science come to it by the way of Abduction.
Abduction consists in studying facts and devising a theory to explain them.
Its only justification is that if we are ever to understand things at all, it
must be in that way. (5.145)

Now I take it to be Peirce's view that any given piece of inquiry
embodies *all three* forms of reasoning. Even a relatively unsophisticated investigation carried on at the level of common sense—for
example, a person looking for a misplaced article—has its abductive,
deductive, and inductive phases. Peirce was emphatic in holding that
the refined procedures of science are continuous with the ordinary
practical activity out of which they grew. Indeed, as we shall see, he

believed that scientific method was rooted in certain instinctive modes
of response which humans have inherited from their animal ancestors.
"Side by side, then, with the well-established proposition that all
knowledge is based on experience, and that science is only advanced
by the experimental verifications of theories, we have to place this
other equally important truth, that all human knowledge, up to the
highest flights of science, is but the development of our inborn animal
instincts" (2.754).

But while every inquiry makes use of abduction, deduction, and
induction, Peirce was quite clear that these are not always present in
the same degree. Any one may predominate; or, perhaps, any two.
Thus, to take an obvious example, mathematics gives a far larger place
to deductive reasoning than to either of the others—so much so that
it is permissible to speak as though mathematical investigations were
wholly deductive. On the other hand, the special sciences of nature,
particularly in their early stages of development, are mainly abductive
and inductive. Furthermore, all three types of reasoning are susceptible of varying degrees of refinement. Hence, a particular inquiry may
combine elementary forms of abduction and deduction with a highly
complex form of induction, and so on. Peirce was very sensitive to the
manifoldness of the scientific enterprise, as one would expect from a
man equally at home in chemistry, astronomy, mathematics, and philosophy. His discussions of method may at times be open to the charge
of being unsystematic; they can never properly be described as over-
simplified.

5. Scientific inquiry must yield conclusions that are verifiable by
observation, experiment, or both. Theoretical elaborations must lead
to experiential tests. Strictly speaking, verification is part of the
process of induction; but for the sake of convenience we may examine
it briefly as detached therefrom. Such a procedure will not involve any
distortion of Peirce's meaning.

Two major aspects of verification need to be borne in mind. (i) It
marks the point in inquiry where doubt is removed and belief established (2.643). The belief is in the hypothesis which has survived the
process of testing. But belief being of the nature of habit, the result is
the production of a rule of action. And since verification is susceptible
of degrees, there will be considerable variation in the firmness with
which different beliefs are fixed. (ii) From the logical point of view,
verification determines the degree of probable truth of the initial hypothesis. The typical situation is where predictions made on the basis of
the hypothesis are fulfilled in a manner certified by observation and

experiment. While observation may occur without any accompanying experiment—as, for example, in the elementary verifications of astronomy—the more usual procedure is for experimentation to produce observed results. Hence Peirce thinks that the distinction between sciences of observation and sciences of experiment is "chiefly one of degree, and from a philosophical point of view is of quite secondary importance" (2.606). We have already seen what observation involves. But how does experiment function as a technique of verification?

Peirce holds that there are two forms of experimentation, "ideal" and "real." The former is the sort carried on in the deductive disciplines—mathematics and logic—where "operations upon diagrams, whether external or imaginary, take the place of the experiments upon real things that one performs in chemical and physical research" (4.530). Such ideal experiments lead the reasoner, through the observation of their result, "to discover unnoticed and hidden relations" among parts of the diagram (3.363). In "real" experimentation, on the other hand, the entities manipulated are not human constructions but the objects and processes of the perceptible world. The investigator sets up his experiment in such a way as to force nature to answer his question. Nature in turn reacts in a determinate way; so that ultimately, the force of the facts produces the verification. Both types of experimentation, however, are exposed to the possibility of error, and both are capable of correction through repeated trials. Such trials are not only a matter of individual performance, but are intrinsically social and public.

By generalizing the analysis, Peirce is able to give the following account of the essential ingredients of an experiment.

First, of course, an experimenter of flesh and blood. Second, a verifiable hypothesis. This is a proposition relating to the universe environing the experimenter, or to some well-known part of it and affirming or denying of this only some experimental possibility or impossibility. The third indispensable ingredient is a sincere doubt in the experimenter's mind as to the truth of that hypothesis. Passing over several ingredients on which we need not dwell . . . we come to the act of choice by which the experimenter singles out certain identifiable objects to be operated upon. The next is the external (or quasi-external) ACT by which he modifies those objects. Next comes the subsequent *reaction* of the world upon the experimenter in a perception; and finally, his recognition of the teaching of the experiment. (5.424)

Only when this stage of inquiry has been completed are we in a position to make warranted assertions about the "constitution of the universe."

6. The last general feature of scientific inquiry follows directly from what has just been said. Since verification requires an appeal to experience, the conclusions it warrants must always be approximate and provisional. Inquiry can never yield results that are completely certain, exact, necessary, or universal (1.55; 1.142). For, in the first place, observation is unable by its very nature to escape an element of vagueness. "No cognition and no Sign is absolutely precise, not even a Percept" (5.543). Further refinements in methods of empirical discrimination are always possible.[14] This consideration is, indeed, a commonplace in the special sciences of measurement which are the least subject to error, but it has been grossly overlooked elsewhere. Hence, "in those sciences . . . no man of self-respect ever. now states his result, without affixing to it its *probable error;* and if this practice is not followed in other sciences it is because in those the probable errors are too vast to be estimated" (1.9). In the second place, "observed facts relate exclusively to the particular circumstances that happened to exist when they were observed. They do not relate to any future occasions." (6.523) When we generalize on the basis of a limited number of observations, we inevitably enter the region of the uncertain and the probable. Our relation to the universe does not permit us to have any universal and necessary knowledge of positive facts (1.608). "On the whole, then, we cannot in any way reach perfect certitude nor exactitude. We can never be absolutely sure of anything, nor can we with any probability ascertain the exact value of any measure or general ratio. This is my conclusion, after many years study of the logic of science." (1.147) To designate his position, Peirce invented the name "Fallibilism."

In its widest formulation, fallibilism affirms that "every proposition which we can be entitled to make about the real world must be an approximate one" (1.404). Several objections to this doctrine may immediately be raised. It may be argued that we cannot consistently assert the proposition: "There is no absolutely certain knowledge," for the proposition itself makes a claim of absolute certainty. Peirce seems prepared to admit the objection, though he does not consider it particularly significant. "If I must make any exception, let it be that the assertion that every assertion but this is fallible, is the only one that is absolutely infallible" (2.75). The important point is that no assertions about existential facts are completely certain.

[14]Peirce made this the subject of one of his pieces of scientific investigation. Cf. "On the Theory of Errors of Observation," *Report of the Superintendent of the U.S. Coast Survey* (1870), pp. 220-24.

But what about the propositions of mathematics? Are they, too, only approximate? Is it only probable, not certain, for example, that $2 \times 2 = 4$? Although he discusses these questions in a number of places, Peirce is curiously ambiguous in his answers to them. Thus, he remarks: "It is often said that the truths of mathematics are infallible. So they are, if you mean practical infallibility. . . ." (1.248) Yet he also says just the opposite of this. "*Theoretically*, I grant you, there is no possibility of error in necessary reasoning. But to speak thus 'theoretically,' is to use language in a Pickwickian sense. In practice, and in fact, mathematics is not exempt from that liability to error that affects everything that man does. Strictly speaking, it is not certain that twice two is four." (5.577) But again: "It would be quite misunderstanding the doctrine of fallibilism to suppose that it means that twice two is probably not exactly four," since "numbers are merely a system of names devised by men for the purpose of counting," and fallibilism does not say that men cannot attain a sure knowledge of the creations of their own minds (1.149; 2.192). Nevertheless, because "the greatest mathematicians sometimes blunder . . . it is *possible*— barely possible—that all have blundered every time they added two and two." Hence, "mathematical certainty is not absolute certainty" (4.478).

With the best will in the world, I do not think that anyone can make these pronouncements *wholly* consistent. However, the contradictions can, perhaps, be softened if we imagine Peirce to have meant something like this. Mathematical *inquiry* is not the same thing as mathematical *reasoning*. The former, like all inquiry, needs a flesh-and-blood person to undertake it, and makes use of the operations of perception and ideal experimentation. Both these components make its results intrinsically fallible. Mathematical reasoning, on the other hand, is that *part* of inquiry which is purely explicative, and therefore necessary. It is merely an analysis of our premises with a view to eliciting their consequences, and it functions exclusively in terms of conditional propositions. Since these are "the creations of the mind, concerning which there is no obstacle to our learning whatever is true of them," we can "accept the reasonings of pure mathematics as beyond all doubt" (2.192). But pure mathematics, as the tracing out of formal implications, is just a part of mathematical inquiry, which itself can never claim infallibility. I do not pretend that this interpretation is without difficulties, or that it makes all Peirce's statements harmonious. The best it can do is to offer a suggestion as to what he may have had in mind.

The principle of fallibilism may give rise to a misconception unless it is taken in conjunction with the fact that as inquiry is repeated over a long period of time, the margin of error attaching to any existential proposition is inevitably reduced. The truth-value of the proposition approximates asymptotically to a given measure which represents its absolute truth. Hence, the longer it has been sustained by inquiry, the less fallible the proposition is, and the more adequately it expresses a stable belief. Peirce calls attention to this fact in a variety of ways. Thus, he speaks of the self-corrective feature of reasoning (5.575), of the "activity of thought by which we are carried, not where we wish, but to a fore-ordained goal" (5.407), of "the predestined result to which sufficient inquiry would lead" (5.494), and so on. At bottom, however, the tendency of inquiry to approximate more and more closely to the truth is due to the nature of induction. This point will call for more detailed examination at a later stage.

7. OBSTACLES TO SCIENTIFIC INQUIRY

Even after scientific inquiry, as delineated above, has been adopted as the only reliable method for fixing belief, certain obstacles to its successful employment have to be guarded against. In the main, these obstacles are due to philosophical dogmas explicitly or implicitly accepted by inquirers, without adequate scrutiny. The effect of such dogmas is to stop investigation at the points where they occur, and so to prevent the further discovery of truth. Consequently, the cardinal rule for a scientific philosophy is: "Do not block the way of inquiry" (1.135). Philosophy can usefully apply this rule in relation to the special sciences, by appraising critically the metaphysical and other assumptions on which they rest. "The philosopher alone is equipped with the facilities for examining such 'axioms' and for determining the degree to which confidence may safely be reposed in them. . . . In short, there is no escape from the need of a critical examination of 'first principles.'" (1.129) The purpose of the examination is to release inquiry from arbitrary hindrances to its progress.

Now the placing of barricades on the road to truth is the "one unpardonable offence . . . to which metaphysicians have in all ages shown themselves the most addicted" (1.136). Peirce therefore proceeds to expose several of the common forms in which "this venomous error assails our knowledge." The first is the error against which fallibilism warns us, viz., the temptation to declare that some propositions are absolutely certain. The second form of the error is that of "maintaining that this, that, and the other can never be known" (1.138). The history of science shows us countless cases where things affirmed to be forever beyond human comprehension have subsequently been accounted for. One of the most glaring examples was Comte's assertion that men would never be able to discover the chemical composition of the stars—an assertion almost immediately disproved by the invention of the spectroscope and the development of spectroscopic analysis. In philosophy, Kant's *Ding an sich* and the *Unknowable* of Spencer, Hamilton, *et al.*, represent a prevalent form of the error. Peirce rejected the notion of the absolutely incognizable as early as 1868, on the ground that it is meaningless. For "all our conceptions are obtained by abstractions and combinations of cognitions first occurring in judgments of experience. Accordingly, there can be no conception of the absolutely incognizable, since nothing of that sort occurs in experience. But the meaning of a term is the conception which it conveys. Hence, a term can have no such meaning." (5.255) We cannot properly talk about the unknowable, or about things that forever transcend human experience. "An absolutely incognizable existence is a nonsensical phrase" (6.419).

"The third philosophical stratagem for cutting off inquiry consists in maintaining that this, that, or the other element of science is basic, ultimate, independent of aught else, and utterly inexplicable—not so much from any defect in our knowing as because there is nothing beneath it to know" (1.139). The "atoms" of Democritus, the "simple natures" of Descartes, the "monads" of Leibniz are the sort of elements alluded to here. When he rejected the doctrine of "inexplicable ultimates" in the course of his early reaction against Cartesianism, Peirce did so quite categorically. His argument followed a pattern which he often used at the time. "That anything *is* thus inexplicable can only be known by reasoning from signs. But the only justification of an inference from signs is that the conclusion explains the fact. To suppose the fact absolutely inexplicable, is not to explain it, and hence this supposition is never allowable." (5.265) In other words, since from a cognitive standpoint the sole purpose of inquiry is to render things intelligible, to conclude that a given thing is unintelligible is a self-stultification. Reasoning can never justify such a conclusion.

Before long, however, Peirce saw that there were things in the universe which he had to admit to be philosophically ultimate. The two sets of characteristics designated by his categories of Firstness and Secondness were of this kind. Hence, he came to modify his objection to the doctrine of inexplicables. By 1890 he was saying that the only sort of facts which ought never to be assumed inexplicable are those of a *general* or *orderly* nature. Moreover, the principle that warns us against making this assumption is a purely regulative one, in Kant's sense of the term. "We must therefore be guided by the rule of hope, and consequently we must reject every philosophy or general conception of the universe, which could ever lead to the conclusion that any given general fact is an ultimate one" (1.405). Such a principle alone will keep the road of inquiry open. At a subsequent stage, we shall note the connection which this doctrine has with Peirce's theory of continuity (Synechism) and his logic of Abduction.

A fourth sort of obstacle to the advance of knowledge is the idea that a given generalization or law has received its final and perfect formulation. In view of what Peirce has already told us, this issue requires little comment. Clearly, if a margin of error, however slight, always attaches to the results of inquiry, every statement of a law must be capable of indefinite refinement in the interests of precision. The history of the experimental sciences again provides relevant illustrations, e.g., in the increasingly exact determination of the velocity of light. It seems likely that by calling attention to this obstacle Peirce wished to suggest that inquiry should be prepared to admit the occurrence of genuinely new phenomena in any field, no matter how well established the laws there may happen to be. For "there is no kind of inference which can lend the slightest probability to any such absolute denial of an unusual phenomenon" (1.140).

One final obstacle to inquiry which Peirce touches on may appropriately be mentioned here. It arises from interference with the scientific enterprise by some non-scientific body. For the practitioners of inquiry, both individually and collectively, must fail in their task if they are subject to direction or control from any outside source. "The health of the scientific communion requires the most absolute mental freedom. . . . It thus becomes one of the first duties of one who sees what the situation is, energetically to resist everything like arbitrary dictation in scientific affairs." (2.220) Freedom of inquiry is thus a *sine qua non* of every community which values truth. This does not mean that an atmosphere of intellectual *laissez-faire* should be encouraged; quite the contrary. Scientific method has its own strict canons of procedure which must be observed by all who engage in it. These canons are necessary to the attainment of its objective, and are therefore imposed by the scientific community on itself. Any other form of control will prove fatal. Progress on the road to truth can only be made "provided the march of scientific intelligence be unchecked" (2.769).

8. THE CLASSIFICATION OF THE SCIENCES

Reference has been made to the very wide sense in which Peirce came to employ the term "science." This is most strikingly evident in his proposed scheme for classifying the sciences—a project of the highest importance for the understanding of his thought. Apart from its intrinsic interest, the classificatory scheme brings into sharp relief the conflict of naturalism and transcendentalism on certain crucial issues. This matter will only become fully apparent at the conclusion of our study. For the present we may simply note that while his classification is carried out in a broadly naturalistic spirit, its results tend to negate his naturalism in the interests of an architectonic pattern. Our immediate concern will be to sketch the outlines of his project, and thereby pave the way for much that is to follow.

Peirce began to devote special attention to the classification of the sciences around 1900. Yet his interest in the matter probably dates back to the brief period when he was a student of Louis Agassiz, author of the famous *Essay on Classification* (1857). Peirce was well aware that "this business of classifying sciences is not one to be undertaken precipitately or offhand" (1.203). It presupposes philosophical maturity, as well as a wide acquaintance with the special sciences, and a grasp of the principles of classification. It also involves a recognition of the provisional and incomplete character of all classificatory schemes. For one cannot presume to catalogue all possible sciences, but only the *existing* ones. Hence, "classifications in all cases perfectly satisfactory hardly exist" (2.636). One's catalogue is bound to be unfinished and exposed to modification with the passage of time.

As a prolegomenon to the subject, Peirce raises the question whether, and in what sense, there are natural classes of elements in the world. Many scientists and logicians dismiss this question in negative terms. For them, classes are artifacts, arbitrary divisions of the matrix of nature, which depend wholly on human purposes and interests. They hold such an opinion mainly because they attach a metaphysical signification to the term *natural* or *real* class; and also because they have embraced a system of metaphysics which makes natural classes impossible. Peirce sympathizes with this position so far as to agree that it is unnecessary in positive science to decide whether there are or are not "metaphysically real" classes. "To my apprehension the business of classification has no concern with them, but only with true and natural classes, in another and a purely experiential sense" (1.204). That is to say, classes can be treated empirically without bothering about their ontological status. When we adopt this attitude we see that their reality is an indubitable fact. For we mean by a class simply "the total of whatever objects there may be in the universe which are of a certain description" (*ibid.*). Empirical investigation reveals that the vast majority of objects—tables, chairs, lamps, quadrupeds, trees, clouds, and so on—fall naturally into distinct groups; and that is all which interests, or should interest, the experimentalist.

So far everything is tolerably clear. It soon becomes apparent, however, that Peirce does in fact attach metaphysical import to the notion of natural classes. For he enters on an obscure, rambling argument designed to show that they involve a necessary reference to final causation, since the individual members of any class "owe their existence" to a common final cause. The full meaning of this sort of doctrine will emerge only in connection with his transcendentalism. But a partial interpretation, consistent with his naturalism, may be attempted along the following lines. If we take any collection of human productions, say the class of lamps, we may plausibly contend that the members of that class "owe their existence" to a final cause. For the sole reason lamps were constructed was that man felt the need of artificial illumination, and the objects in question satisfied the need. They serve a definite purpose, and are, in that sense, the products of final causation. But when we turn to "natural" groups, like birds or fishes, the same situation does not seem to obtain. It is hard to see what could be meant by attributing their existence to final causes. Our difficulty here is due, Peirce argues, to a gratuitous identification of a final cause with a purpose in some mind. Actually, "a purpose is merely that form of final cause which is most familiar to our experience" (1.211). The two things are by no means identical. Hence, a final cause may be conceived to operate without being a purpose in anybody's mind, as, for example, in the process of biological evolution. It is true that in regard to most natural objects we do not know what their final causes are. "But need that prevent us from ascertaining whether or not there is a common cause by virtue of which those things that have the essential characters of the class are enabled to exist?" (1.204)

The upshot is that a natural class is defined as "a family whose members are the sole offspring and vehicles of one idea, from which they derive their peculiar faculty" (1.222). Peirce goes on to relate this to his doctrine of "the reality and potency of ideas," which we shall examine later. He also tries to show the intimate connection between final and efficient causation. The relevance of all this to the project of classifying the sciences is not very obvious. It is a striking illustration

of the double tendency in his thought that Peirce should introduce
such issues into the discussion after having insisted that they are
irrelevant to the classificatory enterprise.

The actual categories of classification which Peirce employs were
taken from his teacher, Agassiz. The latter, in his *Essay on Classification,* divides the animal kingdom into *branches, classes, orders,
families, genera,* and *species.* Although, as Peirce admits, this scheme
long ago ceased to attract the majority of biologists, it has the merit,
he believes, of being the outcome of deep study, and it does not
involve unwarranted accuracy of statement. He therefore proposes to
adopt it with certain minor amendments. As a consequence, the first
division of science (made in terms of the basic purpose being served)
yields its *branches.* A modification of a basic purpose will produce
sub-branches. Since all the sciences rest on observation, groups based
on this consideration are called *classes,* and modifications of the same
nature, *subclasses.* Two departments of science, *A* and *B,* belonging
to one class, may be such that *A* derives from *B* certain special facts
for further generalization, while supplying *B* with principles which the
latter adopts ready-made. *A* will then rank higher than *B,* by virtue
of its greater generality; but *B* will be richer and more varied than *A.*
Groups based on these considerations are *orders;* or, if based on
modifications of the same sort of idea, *sub-orders.* A given science
with a special name, a special journal, a special society, studying one
group of facts, forms a *family.* A subdivision of it on the same principle but taken more minutely is a *subfamily.* Peirce admits that this
is as far as he is prepared to carry his classification, since definitions
in terms of *genera* and *species* require almost microscopic distinctions.
With regard to the scheme as a whole, he is careful to add: "I have not
first fixed my definitions of *branch, class, order,* and *family,* and then
adapted the classification to those definitions, but, on the contrary, the
classification was first entirely formed . . . before any idea of employing the terms *branch, class, order,* and *family* entered my head, and
it was not until this was done that first the appropriateness of these
terms struck me" (1.238).

Turning now to the specific divisions of Peirce's scheme, we find
him distinguishing two main branches of science: "Theoretical, whose
purpose is simply and solely knowledge of God's truth; and Practical,
for the uses of life" (1.239). The theoretical sciences form two sub-
branches: (*a*) the sciences of discovery, whose concern it is to ac-
cumulate, organize, describe, and explain all possible facts in the
universe; and (*b*) the sciences of review, which are occupied with

arranging the results of discovery, beginning with digests, and going on to form a philosophy of science (1.182). Their aim is to sum up the conclusions of the special sciences, and study them as forming one system. Such works as Humboldt's *Cosmos,* Comte's *Philosophie positive,* and Spencer's *Synthetic Philosophy* belong to this department, as does the classification of the sciences itself.

Among the sciences of discovery, Peirce finds three classes. The first is Mathematics, which does not undertake to ascertain any material truths whatever, but merely posits hypotheses and then traces out their necessary consequences. It seeks to discover all the possible "facts" of implication. It is observational in the sense that it makes imaginary constructs according to sets of abstract rules, and then observes these constructs with a view to finding in them relations of parts not specified in the rules of construction. The second science of discovery is Philosophy, which deals with such positive truth as can be derived from those observations that "come within the range of every man's normal experience, and for the most part in every waking hour of his life" (1.241). No special techniques are required for this pursuit, only the ability to discern what is being directly experienced in ordinary thought, perception, or feeling. Yet it does require considerable training, for the most pervasive aspects of experience are the hardest to discriminate accurately. The third and last science of discovery Peirce calls, after Bentham, Idioscopy. Under it come all the special sciences devoted to the accumulation of the more obscure facts. Here, special types of observation involving instrumental aids to the senses are employed. This class divides into two subclasses, the physical and the psychical sciences, or "physiognosy" and "psychognosy." The former studies the working of efficient causation; the latter studies the working of final causation, and continually borrows principles from the physical sciences. The above classes of science have certain general inter-connections, inasmuch as mathematics and philosophy both have their application in all the other sciences. But mathematics itself is not dependent on philosophy; whereas certain parts of philosophy, notably logic, presuppose the existence of mathematical reasoning.

Proceeding next to the orders of science, Peirce specifies the three divisions of mathematics as (*a*) the Mathematics of Logic; (*b*) the Mathematics of Discrete Series; and (*c*) the Mathematics of Continua and Pseudo-continua. Philosophy also has three orders: (*a*) Phenomenology; (*b*) Normative Science; (*c*) Metaphysics. Phenomenology ascertains and studies the kinds of elements universally present in phenomena, i.e., in whatever is present at any time to the mind in any way. Normative science distinguishes what ought to be from what ought not to be in the realms of conduct, feeling, and thought. It requires the assistance of both phenomenology and mathematics. Metaphysics seeks to give an account of the universe of mind and matter. Its basis is provided largely by phenomenology and normative science.

The physical and psychical sciences have three orders each. Under the former Peirce notes: (*a*) Nomological or General Physics, which "discovers the ubiquitous phenomena of the physical universe, formulates their laws, and measures their constants. It draws upon metaphysics and upon mathematics for principles" (1.188); (*b*) Classificatory Physics, whose concern it is to catalogue the various kinds of physical forms, and explain them by means of the laws which are discovered in (*a*); (*c*) Descriptive Physics, concerned with describing individual objects—the earth and the heavens—and showing how they can be accounted for in terms of the principles enunciated by the other two orders. The psychical sciences are: (*a*) Nomological Psychics or Psychology; (*b*) Classificatory Psychics or Ethnology; and (*c*) Descriptive Psychics or History. The first of these discovers the general elements and laws of mental phenomena. It is greatly influenced by phenomenology, logic, metaphysics, and biology (a suborder of classificatory physics). The task of classificatory psychics or ethnology is to catalogue the products of mind, and explain them according to psychological principles; it is at present "far too much in its infancy." Descriptive psychics endeavors to describe individual manifestations of mind, whether they be permanent works or actions; and to that task it adds the one of endeavoring to explain them on the principles of psychology and ethnology. It borrows from many other sciences in pursuit of its goal.

This brings us to the sub-orders of the sciences. The first set which Peirce distinguishes belongs to normative science, and consists of Esthetics, Ethics, and Logic. "Esthetics is the science of ideals, or of that which is objectively admirable without any ulterior reason. I am not well acquainted with this science; but it ought to repose on phenomenology. Ethics, or the science of right and wrong, must appeal to esthetics for aid in determining the *summum bonum*. It is the theory of self-controlled, or deliberate, conduct. Logic is the theory of self-controlled, or deliberate thought; and as such, must appeal to ethics for its principles. It also depends upon phenomenology and upon mathematics." (1.191) Since all thought involves the operation of signs, logic may be regarded as the science of the general laws of signs.

PEIRCE'S CLASSIFICATION OF THE SCIENCES

BRANCHES	SUB-BRANCHES	CLASSES	SUBCLASSES	ORDERS
		Mathematics		Mathematics of Logic Mathematics of Discrete Series Mathematics of Continua & Pseudo-Continua
		Philosophy	Phenomenology	
			Normative Science	
			Metaphysics	
A. THEORETICAL SCIENCE	Sciences of Discovery			
		Idioscopy	Physical Sciences	Nomological or General Physics
				Classificatory Physics
				Descriptive Physics
			Psychical Sciences	Nomological Psychics or Psycholo
				Classificatory Psychics or Ethnolo
				Descriptive Psychics or History
	Sciences of Review, e.g. Humboldt's *Cosmos*, Comte's *Philosophie positive*, Spencer's *Synthetic Philosophy*; also, Classification of the Sciences			

B. PRACTICAL SCIENCE, e.g. pedagogics, gold-beating, book-binding, ink-making, pigeon-fancying, &c.

hetics

ics

gic ———————————————— { Speculative Grammar
Critic
Methodeutic }

ology
igious Metaphysics
sical Metaphysics

lar Physics, Dynamics & Gravitation
lecular Physics, Elaterics & Thermodynamics
erial Physics, Optics & Electrics

stallography

mistry ———————————————— { Physical Chemistry
Organic Chemistry
Inorganic Chemistry }

ogy ———————————————— { Physiology
Anatomy }

gnosy
onomy

ospective Psychology
erimental Psychology
iological Psychology
d Psychology

ial Psychology ———————————— { Individual Psychology
Psychical Heredity
Abnormal Psychology
Mob Psychology
Race Psychology
Animal Psychology }

uistics ———————————————— { Word Linguistics
Grammar }

ology ———————————————— { Ethnology of Social Development
Ethnology of Technology }

ry proper ———————————————— { Monumental History
Ancient History
Modern History
Political History
History of Sciences
History of Social Developments }

raphy

cism ———————————————— { Literary

Art ———————————— { Criticism of Military Operations
Criticism of Architecture
&c. } }

It subdivides into three families: (a) Speculative Grammar, or the general theory of the nature and meaning of signs; (b) Critic, which classifies arguments and determines the validity of each kind; (c) Methodeutic, which studies the methods that ought to be pursued in the investigation, exposition, and application of truth. Each family depends on that which precedes it.

The sub-orders of metaphysics are: (a) Ontology, (b) Religious Metaphysics, concerned chiefly with the questions of God, freedom, and immortality, and (c) Physical Metaphysics, which discusses the real nature of space, time, matter, causation, etc. The second and third branches, Peirce comments, "appear at present to look upon one another with supreme contempt" (1.192).

It is hardly necessary to enumerate the long list of sub-orders of the physical and psychical sciences. The accompanying table indicates their general arrangement, and Peirce himself does little more than designate them by name. However, attention may be called to one or two points. (i) It is interesting to note that biology is represented as a division of classificatory physics. Apparently, Peirce was not altogether satisfied with this placing of the subject, for he elsewhere suggests that "biology might be regarded . . . as the chemistry of the albumoids and of the forms they assume" (1.195). (ii) Crystallography also presents a problem. In one context it appears as coordinate with chemistry and biology; in another, it is treated as a division of chemistry (1.260). (iii) Peirce makes a curious distinction between introspective psychology and individual psychology, the former being the first family of nomological psychics, and the latter being a subfamily of special psychology. He does not explain the basis of this division in any way. It is also queer to read that "both experimental and physiological psychology are dependent upon introspective psychology" (1.199). (iv) Descriptive psychics appears as a class of very heterogeneous elements. It embraces the various kinds of history, biography, literary appreciation, and even the criticism of military operations, which is represented as a sub-family of Art Criticism! One suspects that the sole factor common to most of these subjects consists in their refusal to be subsumed under any other category.

A word must be said in conclusion about the Practical Sciences. Although this is the second of the two main branches of science, Peirce does not attempt to deal with it systematically. Indeed, he confesses that he is "utterly bewildered" by the motley crowd of pursuits which it embraces. He accordingly contents himself with giving a very long list (which his editors have wisely and humanely abbreviated) of them. Among the typical "sciences" noted are: pedagogics, gold-beating, etiquette, pigeon-fancying, vulgar arithmetic, horology, surveying, navigation, librarian's work, ink-making, book-binding, engraving, etc. No wonder Peirce remarks that "fortunately the natural classification of this branch will not concern us in logic—at least, will not do so as far as I can perceive" (1.243).

9. SUMMARY AND CONCLUSION

This brings to a close our survey of the most general features of inquiry according to Peirce. We have seen that inquiry is an elaborate struggle to escape from the condition of blocked activity which we call "doubt," and to reach the state of smooth-running, habitual behavior which we call "belief." Proceeding always in terms of those beliefs which are not in fact doubted, and making use of observational data, hypotheses, deductive elaboration, and inductive verification, it arrives at conclusions that are reliable, but not infallible. The ideally complete set of such conclusions which inquiry of indefinite duration would lead the scientific community to accept is what we mean by "Truth," and that to which the set of conclusions refers is "Reality." At any given time, therefore, the results of scientific inquiry fall short of complete truth; that is to say, they are probable. Yet inquiry fully carried out has the capacity to purge itself of its errors. It therefore gradually but inevitably approximates to the ideal of absolute truth. At no point, however, does any trans-experiential reference enter. Inquiry functions exclusively within the confines of the human and the natural.

Our next task is to investigate the details of inquiry in certain classes and orders of the sciences of discovery. Mathematics, being the first of these, will be dealt with in chapter iii. Then we shall proceed to philosophy, and devote chapter iv to phenomenology, chapters v and vi to one part of normative science, viz., logic, and chapter vii to metaphysics. Central interest in each case will attach to the elements which illustrate his naturalism. Since the other parts of normative science—esthetics and ethics—yield nothing that is relevant here, they will be omitted from the discussion. What material there is on these subjects falls entirely within the orbit of his transcendentalism. As for idioscopy—the last of the three classes of sciences of discovery—I shall consider it sufficiently dealt with for our purposes in chapter vi, where the salient features of its method are reviewed.

III

MATHEMATICAL INQUIRY

1. PEIRCE'S ORIENTATION IN MATHEMATICS

In approaching Peirce's discussion of mathematical inquiry, we need to remind ourselves that he was no amateur in this field. As a son of the eminent Harvard mathematician, Benjamin Peirce (1809-80), he was introduced to the science at an early age, and quickly showed that he had the family gift for it. Even while an undergraduate at Harvard, he discussed advanced mathematical problems with his father.[1] Mainly out of deference to the latter's wishes, he took an A.M. in mathematics at Harvard in 1862. When Benjamin Peirce's "Linear Associative Algebras" appeared posthumously in 1881, Charles not only contributed the notes, but also added an appendix in which he proved an important theorem (cf. 3.289 ff.).[2] Thus, he did not need to give ground to anyone in the matter of technical competence in mathematics. His paramount interest, however, was in its philosophical significance—particularly in its aim and method. This is the topic, with its various ramifications, that will concern us in the present chapter.

Before coming to grips with details, it will be in order to say a word or two about the influences which his doctrine reflects. There was, first of all, his father's well-known characterization of mathe-

---

[1]Their association continued until at least 1870, when, Peirce reports, "we were . . . working simultaneously upon closely related subjects, and continually discussing them together" (4.301 n.). So intimate was the collaboration that each occasionally attributed some discovery to the other (cf. 4.322 n.). Charles greatly admired and respected his father. He "boasts" about being Benjamin Peirce's son (4.229), and freely declares, "in mathematics, he was my master, and vastly my superior in genius" (4.301 n.).

[2]E. T. Bell, in his *The Development of Mathematics* (New York and London, 1940), p. 234, states the theorem thus: "The only linear associative algebras in which the co-ordinates are real numbers, and in which a product vanishes only if one factor is zero, are the field of real numbers, the field of ordinary complex numbers, and the algebra of quaternions with real coefficients."

matics as "the science which draws necessary conclusions."[3] As a
description of the *method* of mathematics, Peirce thought this struck
for the first time "the true note" (3.558). He himself, however, preferred to define the science "by its aim and subject-matter" (4.238).
In this connection, his study of the *Critique of Pure Reason* was an
important influence. Kant's rejection of the prevailing view that mathematics is the science of quantity, and his psychological description of
it as the study of constructions or diagrams,[4] Peirce holds to be "un-
questionably correct" (3.556). The description expresses the fact that
mathematics is concerned wholly with hypothetical states of things,
and emphasizes that these are dealt with by means of special schemata.
In Kant's logical doctrine that mathematical propositions are synthetic
a priori judgments, Peirce finds only "this much truth, that they are
not, for the most part, what he called analytical judgments; that is,
the predicate is not, in the sense he intended, contained in the definition of the subject" (4.232). Another work which he says influenced
him considerably (2.76), was F. A. Lange's *Logische Studien* (1877).
This again was mainly on the psychological side. Lange's neo-Kantian
contention that mathematical truth is derived from observation of
objects created by our visual imagination is substantially the one
Peirce adopts. Yet other aspects of Lange's doctrine, relating to the
validity of deductive reasoning, he finds "rather ridiculous" (4.354).
His own conception of validity in mathematics will have to be investigated below.

2. HOW MATHEMATICAL INQUIRY PROCEEDS

A simple way of finding out what mathematical inquiry involves
is to consider how the mathematician goes to work in a specific situation. A paradigmatic case, according to Peirce, is this. Some investigator—an engineer, physicist, insurance company, etc.—wishes to ascertain what the consequences of certain possible facts would be; but the
facts are so complicated that they cannot be handled readily. The
problem is then presented to the mathematician for solution. Now the
mathematician does not regard it as any part of his responsibility to
verify the facts given to him. He accepts them without question. In
the great majority of instances, he cannot determine their consequences
with any exactitude by tackling them directly. So what he does is to
construct a simpler but quite fictitious problem, sufficiently like the

[3]Benjamin Peirce, "Linear Associative Algebras," with notes and addenda by
C. S. Peirce, *American Journal of Mathematics*, vol. IV (1881), p. 97.
[4]*Critique of Pure Reason*, A713-17 = B741-45.

original one to serve as a substitute for it. The constructed problem is thus highly abstract, i.e. it leaves out all features that have no bearing on the relation of the premisses to the conclusion. Being abstract, it can be manipulated in various ways without difficulty. The mathematician now examines the "skeletonization" of the problem with a view to "seeing" what relations it exemplifies and what necessary results may be derived from it by permissible transformations. In other words, "the mathematician does two very different things: namely, he first frames a pure hypothesis stripped of all features which do not concern the drawing of consequences from it, and this he does without inquiring or caring whether it agrees with the actual facts or not; and, secondly, he proceeds to draw necessary consequences from that hypothesis" (3.559).

Like all inquiry, then, mathematics sets out from some kind of problem. This may be presented by one of the positive sciences; or the problem may arise within the body of pure mathematics in the course of its development. Either way, the problem is essentially one of deduction, of discovering what follows from something given. The inquiry is always pursued in terms of certain clear and definite assumptions (1.417). Thus, as Peirce repeatedly insists, mathematics is the study of what is true of hypothetical states of things (4.238). In other types of inquiry, the problem is a factual one, and the investigation proceeds on the basis of a number of vague, instinctive beliefs. Not deduction, but explanation is sought. The special scientist and the philosopher deal with problems set by the real world. The pure mathematician, restricting himself to hypotheses, deals with "creatures of his own imagination; but he discovers in them relations which surprise him sometimes" (5.567).

Mathematical discovery for Peirce hinges on two things, (*a*) the production of an appropriate diagram, and (*b*) the observation of it. The initial hypothesis cannot be examined in merely general terms. "It is necessary to set down, or to imagine, some individual and definite schema, or diagram—in geometry, a figure composed of lines with letters attached; in algebra an array of letters of which some are repeated" (4.233). The diagram is constructed so as to reproduce in exact form the characteristics of the hypothesis. This is followed by the performing of certain operations or experiments on the diagram— such as the drawing of subsidiary lines in geometry or the making of permissible transformations in algebraic formulae; "thereupon, the faculty of observation is called into play" (*ibid.*).

Peirce recognizes that the observation employed by the mathematician is of a special kind. For it does not need to be, and perhaps is usually not, directed towards diagrams inscribed on some external surface, such as a sheet of paper or a blackboard. It may be observation of "constructions in the imagination" (1.240), a "seeing with the mind's eye" of figures or formulae, and the discovery in them of relations not specified in the precept of their construction. Yet this is still properly called observation, he thinks, since although it is "directed to the creations of our own minds," it implies "some degree of fixity and quasi-reality in the object to which it endeavors to conform" (2.305). In other words, it involves the interpretation of data directly presented to the mind. To distinguish the sort of interpretation used in mathematics from other forms, Peirce speaks of it as *subjectal abstraction* (in contrast to the *prescisive abstraction* of philosophy and the special sciences). Subjectal abstraction "consists of seizing upon something which has been conceived as a ἔπος πτερόεν , a meaning not dwelt upon but through which something else is discerned, and converting it into an ἔπος ἀπτερόεν, a meaning upon which we rest as the principal subject of discourse" (1.83). Thus, for the mathematician an operation is something which itself can be operated on. The collection of places of a moving particle is itself a place which can at a single instant be occupied by a filament. If this in turn be imagined to move, the aggregate of all its places, considered as possibly occupied in one instant, is a surface; and so forth. Subjectal abstraction is, therefore, "one of the most constantly employed tools of the mathematician" (4.332).

The final step in the inquiry, closely allied to abstraction, is generalization. For mathematical thought "can have no success where it cannot generalize" (4.236). As Plato pointed out long ago, the mathematician is not interested in proving something to be true of the particular figure before him. He seeks to prove what is universally true. Hence, while he "supposes an individual case, his hypothesis is yet perfectly general, because he considers no characters of the individual case but those which must belong to every such case" (3.92). As a result of generalization, the mathematician obtains universal propositions; and with these, as demonstrated conclusions, his inquiry terminates.

3. MATHEMATICAL DEMONSTRATION

But what does mathematical demonstration mean for Peirce? We have already caught a glimpse of the difficulty of answering this question satisfactorily, in our discussion of fallibilism. Now, we must look at it in a different light. The fundamental issue is whether mathematical demonstration is simply an explication of what is assumed in the premises from which it starts; or whether it entails more than this. The former view seems to have been accepted by Peirce prior to the eighteen-eighties. Thus the opening paragraph of his paper of 1867, "Upon the Logic of Mathematics," states that its aim "is to show that there are certain general propositions from which the truths of mathematics follow syllogistically, and that these propositions may be taken as definitions of the objects under the consideration of the mathematician without involving any assumption in reference to experience or intuition" (3.20). That is to say, mathematics derives its conclusions by explicative or analytic reasoning from definitions. But by 1905, Peirce could say of his early paper: "It is now utterly unintelligible to me, and is, I trust, by far the worst I ever published" (4.333). Even making allowance for the rhetorical flourish of this statement, it strongly suggests a shift in doctrine.

Although the textual evidence is inconclusive, I believe the shift can be plausibly reconstructed as follows. The view that mathematics is exclusively a matter of analytical inference accounts for one of its salient traits, viz., that it draws conclusions apodictically. For on such an approach, the conclusion merely restates in different form what the premises of the reasoning have already asserted. That is why the conclusion is necessary. Demonstration is a disguised process of affirming tautologies where nothing genuinely "new" is introduced. This last consequence was one Peirce could not bring himself to accept. He felt that it did not give a satisfactory explanation of the element of "discovery" in mathematics. For the history of the science reveals innumerable cases where unforeseen and novel results have been reached—results unforeseen and novel in much more than just a psychological sense. Should it be concluded, then, that mathematical novelty has its source in some experiential element, so that the propositions involved are, as J. S. Mill contended, empirical generalizations? If we say this, it becomes impossible to defend the strictly apodictic character of the mathematician's demonstrations. The upshot is that both the necessity and the novelty in the science must be accounted for, if we are to do full justice to the facts. As Peirce put it in 1885:

It has long been a puzzle how it could be that, on the one hand, mathematics is purely deductive in its nature, and draws its conclusions apodictically, while on the other hand, it presents as rich and apparently unending

a series of surprising discoveries as any observational science. Various have
been the attempts to solve the paradox by breaking down one or other of
these assertions, but without success. (3.363)

It seems to have been his study of the logic of relatives that provided Peirce with a "solution" to this paradox. A relevant passage
occurs in his discussion of 1893, where he examines Kant's view that
analytic judgments are those in which the predicate is involved in the
conception of the subject. Peirce takes Kant to mean by this that the
predicate is "confusedly thought" in the subject whenever we think
the latter; and such a psychological doctrine he rejects as "monstrous."

To be *involved*, is phrase to which nobody before Kant ever gave such a
psychological meaning. Everything is involved which can be evolved. But
how does this evolution of necessary consequences take place? We can
answer for ourselves after having worked awhile in the logic of relatives.
It is not by a simple mental stare, or strain of mental vision. It is by manipulating on paper, or in the fancy, formulae or other diagrams—experiment-
ing on them, *experiencing* the thing. Such experience alone *evolves* the
reason hidden within us. (4.86)

Mathematical inquiry, then, *does* involve experience; but inner not
outer experience. It is an observational and experimental science which
deals with diagrams, or signs, created by the human mind. These
signs, which Peirce calls *icons* and *indices* (cf. 3.429; 2.305), are constructed in accordance with rules we ourselves have made. The experiential component is the source of novelty in mathematical reasoning. The necessity which belongs to mathematical reasoning has its
source in the fact that the diagrams are our own creations (3.560).
Nevertheless, if we press Peirce to be more explicit about how the
validity of a given mathematical demonstration is guaranteed, we find
that ultimately he has to fall back on an intuitive criterion. The demonstration is "seen" to be necessary; it is immediately "evident." In
algebra, for example, the mathematician constructs his schemata in
accordance with certain rules of formation. Then he experiments with
the array of characters, in the light of his rules of permissible transformation. "By virtue of these rules, become habits of association,
when one array has been written or assumed to be permissibly scriptible, the mathematician just as directly perceives that another array is
permissibly scriptible, as he perceives that a person talking in a certain tone is angry, or is using certain words in such and such a sense"
(4.246). Presumably, however, he must also directly perceive that
what holds for the particular case confronting him will hold for *all*

cases of that kind, since that is what *qua* mathematician he wishes to prove. But this jump "from the particular to the universal" would seem to require a special mathematical "intuition," rather like Mr. W. E. Johnson's "formal intuitive induction."[5] Such a doctrine can scarcely be said to have been espoused by Peirce, and, indeed, is explicitly attacked by him in several places. Yet it is not easy to see how on his own premises he can escape something very like it.

4. MATHEMATICS AND LOGIC

Further light may be shed on this matter if we turn to what he has to say on the relation between mathematics and logic. Here again, his ideas underwent a change. In the passage already quoted from the opening part of his paper "Upon the Logic of Mathematics," it is clear that he thought of the science as resting on a foundation of logical definitions. Indeed, in the last section of the paper there is a definite foreshadowing of the theme later elaborated by Frege in his *Grundlagen der Arithmetik* (1884) and by Whitehead and Russell in *Principia Mathematica* (1910-13), that arithmetic is derivable from logic. Peirce, of course, merely hints how this might be done; but his suggestion shows that at this stage in his career, he regarded logic as having a significant priority over mathematics.

It was probably as a consequence of accepting his father's definition of mathematics that Peirce came to reverse his position on this question. For he tells us that at the time the definition was being formulated, he and his father were holding "daily discussions upon a large subject which interested us both" (4.239). And he rejects Dedekind's view that mathematics is a branch of logic,[6] on the ground that "this would not result from my father's definition, which runs, not that mathematics is the science of *drawing* necessary conclusions—which would be deductive logic—but that it is the science which *draws* necessary conclusions. It is evident, and I know as a fact, that he had this distinction in view." (*Ibid.*) The more philosophically conscious son followed out the implications of the distinction, and was led to the conclusion that mathematics must be prior to logic. At least three things were implied by this conclusion: (1) logic is existentially dependent on mathematics; (2) mathematics cannot be derived from logic; and (3) mathematics cannot be, and does not need to be, evaluated by logic. A few comments on each of these points will now be made.

[5]*Logic* (Cambridge, England, 1922), vol. II, pp. 192 ff.
[6]Cf. *Was sind und was sollen die Zahlen?* (1888), "Vorwort."

1. Logic for Peirce is the science which studies and criticizes human reasoning. But in order that such a science may come into being, the object of its study must already exist. Reasoning necessarily precedes the theory of reasoning; and while the latter presupposes the former, the reverse is not the case. "Just as it is not necessary, in order to talk, to understand the theory of the formation of vowel sounds, so it is not necessary, in order to reason, to be in possession of the theory of reasoning. Otherwise, plainly, the science of logic could never be developed." (4.242) Moreover, the objects which logic studies need to exist in their purest and most genuine form. This is precisely what mathematics contributes, for it exemplifies the highest type of human reasoning. By contrast with what the special scientists and philosophers do, "mathematicians alone reason with great subtlety and great precision" (4.425). Hence, without their activity to examine, logic would not amount to anything, that is to say, would not really exist as a science.

2. But, it may be objected, while all this is perhaps true historically, is it not quite possible that mathematics may be derivable from meta-mathematical premisses, and that these are of an exclusively logical character? Not, Peirce would reply, if we remain true to the facts, and consider mathematics as a living inquiry rather than as a collection of static "propositions." For if it is the science which *draws* necessary conclusions, this can only be owing to "our natural power of reason" (4.242) or "a natural instinct for right reasoning" (2.3). How, otherwise, can it happen that a man may be a gifted mathematician without having any knowledge of, or any interest in logic? Peirce frequently employs the scholastic distinction between *logica utens* and *logica docens* to express his meaning here. "Mathematics performs its reasonings by a *logica utens* which it develops for itself" (1.417). From this a *logica docens* may be obtained by the secondary inquiry of the logician. That is why it may be truly said that "mathematics lays the foundation on which logic builds" (2.197). In short, our native capacity for thinking rigorously (susceptible, of course, to development through training and practice) is the only thing from which mathematics can be "derived."

3. Yet if logic criticizes reasoning, and formulates the norms which distinguish valid from invalid thought, surely it must be concerned to evaluate mathematical reasoning? Again Peirce answers in the negative. "Mathematical reasoning derives no warrant from logic. It needs no warrant. It is evident in itself. . . . The recognition of mathe-

matical necessity is performed in a perfectly satisfactory manner antecedent to any study of logic." (2.191) Several reasons are given by
Peirce for this view. In the first place, since mathematical inference is
far more exact than any doctrine of logic proper, "an appeal in mathematics to logic could only embroil a situation" (4.243). What advantage could the highest type of reasoning gain from any appeal to an
inferior type? In the second place, mathematics reposes on clear and
definite suppositions; and its only problem is to determine what other
suppositions follow from them. "Since we ourselves create these suppositions, we are competent to answer them," purely as mathematicians. "But it is when we pass out of the realm of pure hypothesis
into that of hard fact that logic is called for" (2.191). When a dispute
arises in mathematics, and one of its practitioners says that a certain
consequence follows from a hypothesis, while his opponent says that
it evidently does not, it might seem that a logician could properly be
called in to adjudicate the dispute. "However, because this dispute
relates merely to the consequences of a hypothesis, the mere careful
study of the hypothesis, which is pure mathematics, resolves it; and
after all, it turns out that there was no occasion for the intervention of
a science of reasoning" (1.247). Finally, have there ever been any
actual cases where logicians have put mathematicians right? Certainly
not, Peirce replies.

No case is adducible in which the science of logic has availed to set mathematicians right or to save them from tripping. On the contrary, attention
once having been called to a supposed inferential blunder in mathematics,
short time has ever elapsed before the whole mathematical world has been
in accord, either that the step was correct, or else that it was fallacious;
and this without appeal to logic. . . . Thus, historically mathematics does
not, as *a priori* it cannot, stand in need of any separate science of reasoning. (1.248)

Once committed to the priority of mathematics over logic in the
above senses, Peirce clearly had to have recourse to an intuitive criterion of demonstration. There was no alternative but to declare that
"we simply recognize a mathematical necessity" (2.191), and that
"mathematics has no occasion to inquire into the theory of the validity
of its own argumentations; for these are more evident than any such
theory could be" (2.120). This appeal to a special "mathematical intuition" is not unconnected, as I shall try to show later, with that
divorce of theory from practice which is one aspect of his transcendentalism.

Occasionally, however, even in his later writings, Peirce admits that logic might have a beneficial effect upon mathematics. Thus, in 1903 he says:

> There is reason to believe that a thorough understanding of the nature of mathematical reasoning would lead to great improvements in mathematics. For when a new discovery is made in mathematics, the demonstration first found is almost always replaced later by another much simpler. Now it may be expected that, if the reasoning were thoroughly understood, the unnecessary complications of the first proof would be eliminable at once. Indeed, one might expect that the shortest route would be taken at the outset. (4.428)

This improvement would presumably be brought about by the discipline which attempts to "understand mathematical reasoning"—that is to say, by logic. Again, at the end of his article "The Regenerated Logic" (1896), in which he discusses volume III of Schröder's *Vorlesungen über die Algebra der Logik,* he remarks that the new symbolic logic "will certainly be applied to settle certain logical questions of extreme difficulty relating to the foundations of mathematics. Whether or not it can lead to any method of discovering methods in mathematics it is difficult to say. Such a thing is conceivable." (3.454) Ten years earlier he had referred to this problem of discovering a method for the discovery of methods in mathematics as "one of the main problems of logic" (3.364). Such statements show that his position of 1867 continued to exert some influence on his thinking even after 1880.[7]

One very important relation between mathematics and logic remains to be mentioned, viz., the application of mathematics to logic. By virtue of the fact that in the classification of the sciences mathematics stands first, it not only requires no support from any other science, but it contributes an essential element to each of them. It "meddles with every other science without exception. There is no science whatever to which is not attached an application of mathematics." (1.245) Consequently, in addition to a mathematical physics and a mathematical economics, we have a mathematical logic, which is simply formal logic properly studied. This is perhaps the basic sense in which "logic depends upon mathematics" (4.240). For as the history of logic amply illustrates, it was only with the importation of mathematical techniques into the subject that its true nature began

[7]Other illustrations of this occur in chapter 17 of the "Grand Logic" (1893). For example, he asserts there that "arithmetical propositions may be syllogistic conclusions from ordinary particular propositions" (4.88).

to be disclosed. The techniques used, however, are "so excessively simple as neither to have much mathematical interest, nor to display the peculiarities of mathematical reasoning" (4.244).

The primary purpose of mathematical logic does not reside for Peirce in the developing of a symbolic calculus. The purpose "is simply and solely the investigation of the theory of logic, and not at all the construction of a calculus to aid the drawing of inferences" (4.373). Indeed, these two projects are incompatible. The investigation of logical theory has to be minutely analytical, breaking up inference into the maximum number of steps and arranging them under the most general categories possible. A calculus of reasoning, on the other hand, would seek to reduce the number of individual steps to a minimum, and to specialize the symbols so as to adapt them to the various kinds of inference. Furthermore, the use of algebraic devices in the treatment of logic "is open to the danger of degenerating into idle trifling of too rudimentary a character to be of mathematical interest, and too superficial to be of logical interest" (3.619). It is exposed to the additional danger that the rules for the manipulation of the symbols may be mistaken for first principles of logic. Peirce remained sceptical about the feasibility of the Leibnizian project of constructing a universal calculus of reasoning. He believed little profit would accrue from any "semi-mechanical method for performing all reasoning" (3.618), though the subject of "logical machines" did have a certain fascination for him. The primary value of mathematical methods in logic is that they force us to formulate "with precision, definiteness, and simplicity, the general facts of experience which logic has to take into account" (*ibid.*).

Peirce did not mean to imply by the above that a logical calculus is of no use in the exploration of necessary inference. His own contributions to the subject make this quite clear. Thus, the paper "On the Algebra of Logic" aims "to develop an algebra adequate to the treatment of all problems of deductive logic," and thereby attain three objectives. "The first is the extension of the power of logical algebra over the whole of its proper realm. The second is the illustration of principles which underlie all algebraic notation. The third is the enumeration of the essentially different kinds of necessary inference." (3.364) The great advantage of conducting the analysis by means of algebra is that the subject can be explored more thoroughly and more systematically than is otherwise possible. Such a calculus is not without interest to the pure mathematician. But he looks at it from a very different point of view, asking such questions as, "Can it be applied to unravelling a complicated question? Will it, at one stroke, produce a remote consequence?" (4.239); and so on. His concern, in short, is with the calculus in so far as it may provide him with an efficient method of reasoning which he can extend to new problems. Hence, that which is a merit in a logical algebra for a mathematician will be a demerit for a logician, and *vice versa*. Yet it is of decided interest to both.

As he followed during his own lifetime the development of mathematical logic, Peirce grew increasingly aware that the border-line between it and pure mathematics is difficult to draw. The two disciplines are so intimately related that "no small acumen is required to find the joint between them" (1.245). In the work of a man like Dedekind, the boundary becomes "almost evanescent" (2.215). The same thing is true of some of Peirce's own investigations. Thus, in a paper of 1902 headed "The Simplest Branch of Mathematics," he attacks the question of the constitution of the most rudimentary form of the science and quickly arrives at what would today be called the propositional calculus. His discussion seems worth following in a little detail, both for its intrinsic interest and for its relevance to his philosophy of mathematics.

The simplest hypothesis from which a mathematical system can be generated is that there are two objects. For clearly, if nothing at all be supposed, nothing can be derived; and if only one unit be assumed, no question is possible because there would be but a single possible answer. Given the initial pair of objects, designated by v and f, we can produce a dichotomic algebra which is applicable to every case where we have two possible alternatives. "Then the first kind of problem of this algebra will be, given certain data concerning an unknown object, x, required to know whether it is v or f. Or similar problems may arise concerning several unknowns, x, y, etc." (4.250) Once the original dichotomy is made, others can be generated by means of the binary operations of the calculus. Using his own symbolism, Peirce examines a number of these operations, as well as certain other features of the system. It would scarcely be profitable, however, to enter into the minutiae of his deductions here.

Now v and f are called by Peirce the two possible *values* of the algebra, one of which must be attached to any unknown. "This idea of a system of values is one of the most fundamental abstractions of the algebraic method of mathematics. An object of the universe, whose

value is generally unknown, though it may in special cases be known
. . . is called, when we speak of it as *'having'* a value, a *quantity.*"
(4.251) I am not sure what this last statement means; but if Peirce
is saying that the values of dichotomic algebra are always quantitative,
the matter is highly doubtful. For he himself recognizes that "we might
call the *v* the truth, and *f* falsity" (*ibid.*). In that case, dichotomic
algebra becomes the familiar two-valued propositional calculus, since
"true" and "false" attach exclusively to propositions. Moreover, since
the affirmations of the algebra, treated abstractly, must be propositions
which are themselves either true or false but not both, the two-valued
propositional calculus would seem to be peculiarly basic. But Peirce
is adamant in maintaining that abstract dichotomic algebra is mathematics, not logic. As mathematics, it must involve quantitative elements. Hence, *v* and *f* are quantities, even when interpreted as "true"
and "false." Since the latter terms apply only to propositions, these
terms must be "admitted to the universe of quantities" (4.263). Jevons
was wrong when he presented a form of Boolean algebra as "a science
of quality."[8] For "the algebra of Boole is nothing but the algebra of
that system of quantities which has but two values—the simplest conceivable system of quantity" (3.561).

Considered thus, dichotomic algebra is too trivial an enterprise to
be of interest to the mathematician. But the logician finds it important
as an organon for the study of his subject, particularly of those
branches which Peirce calls "speculative grammar" and "critical logic."
Quite apart from this utilitarian function, however, there is the note-
worthy fact that "*for logical reasons* [italics mine], every mathematical
doctrine involves dichotomic mathematics. Where, for example, would
be the algebra without a sign of equality? Yet that sign is a dichotomic
sign." (4.275) It is a little hard to understand how, if mathematics is
independent of logical theory, there can be "logical reasons" for the
involvement of dichotomic algebra in every other algebraic system.
Here again one cannot help feeling that Peirce is glossing over certain
difficulties in his thesis that mathematics is prior to logic. The reverse
relationship seems much easier to defend. At any rate, one can readily
see why he concluded that it is "almost impossible to separate" the
two sciences (1.283).

In the paper on "The Simplest Branch of Mathematics," Peirce
offers a sketch of the type of mathematics which follows dichotomic

[8]W. S. Jevons, *Pure Logic: The Science of Quality* (London and New York, 1864).

algebra in order of complexity. This is the calculus of three elements, or trichotomic mathematics. It "is not quite so fundamentally important as the dichotomic branch; but the need of a study of it is much greater, its applications being most vital and its difficulties greater than the dichotomic. Nevertheless; it has hardly received any direct attention." (4.308) Such a calculus will not be without its dichotomic elements. "For how is a mathematician to take a step without recognizing the duality of truth and falsehood? Hegel and others have dreamed of such a thing; but it cannot be." (*Ibid.*) Peirce therefore concludes that trichotomic algebra must be a sixfold affair, since the true-false dichotomy is necessarily superimposed on the three primary elements. This, of course, complicates his assignment enormously. Yet he would scarcely have accepted the current device of transforming the dichotomy into a trichotomy by means of a third truth-value (e.g., "doubtful"), and then identifying the elements of his calculus with the three truth-values. Although he anticipated many later trends, there is little prevision in his thought, so far as I can see, of the contemporary doctrine of "multi-valued logics."[9] For him, the two-valued logic was the only true one.

5.   THE DIVISIONS OF MATHEMATICS

This analysis gave Peirce a basis for suggesting a new division of mathematics into its various branches. Traditionally, two such branches have been recognized, viz., geometry and algebra. They are differentiated on the ground that they use totally dissimilar schemata. Geometry employs linear figures with letters attached; algebra, arrays of characters, sometimes in series, sometimes in blocks, with associated rules of transformation. Peirce disagrees with this way of dividing mathematics, because it suggests that geometry and algebra deal with wholly separate subjects. But in fact, "any mathematical subject, from the theory of numbers to topical geometry, may be treated

[9]However, in a letter to F. C. Russell, quoted by Paul Carus (*Monist*, vol. XX (1910), p. 45), Peirce remarks: "Before I took up the general study of relatives, I made some investigations into supposing the laws of logic to be different from what they are. It was a sort of non-Aristotelian logic, in the sense in which we speak of non-Euclidean geometry. Some of the developments were somewhat interesting, but not sufficiently so to induce me to publish them. The general idea was, of course, obvious to anybody of sufficient grasp of logical analysis to see that logic reposes upon certain positive facts, and is not mere formalism. Another writer afterward suggested such a false logic, as if it were the wildest lunacy, instead of being a plain and natural hypothesis worth looking into (notwithstanding its falsity)."

either algebraically or geometrically" (4.247). Hence a more appropriate way of proceeding is to consider the nature of the general hypotheses used in the various parts of the science, "taking for the ground of primary division the multitude of units, or elements, that are supposed; and for the ground of sub-division that mode of relationship between the elements upon which the hypotheses focus the attention" (4.248).

Applying this principle, Peirce concludes that there are three major departments of mathematics: (*a*) that in which the hypotheses relate to systems as finite collections, (*b*) that in which the hypotheses relate to systems as infinite collections, and (*c*) that in which the hypotheses relate to systems that are true continua. The study of finite collections has two sub-orders: (i) the simplest mathematics, i.e., the dichotomic and trichotomic algebra already mentioned; and (ii) the general theory of finite groups. The study of infinite collections likewise splits into two sub-orders: (i) arithmetic, or the study of the least multitudinous of infinite collections, and (ii) the calculus, or the study of collections of higher multitude. The third major division of mathematics consists of topical geometry or topology. This is defined by Peirce as "the study of the continuous connections and defects of continuity of loci which are free to be distorted in any way so long as the integrity of the connections and separations of all their parts is maintained" (4.219). Despite the little progress it had made in his day, Peirce was much impressed by the potentialities of this discipline. He speaks of it as the "highest kind of mathematics" (1.283), and regards the analysis of its procedure as "one of the first tasks of exact logicians" (3.526). No doubt part of his interest in topology was dictated by the central place which it gives to the notion of continuity—an idea of great philosophical significance in Peirce's eyes. He even suggests that the advance of topical geometry has been retarded because of "the lack of a developed logic of continua" (3.642). The limits of mathematics, then, are defined by simple dichotomic algebra at the bottom and topology at the top.

6. THE NATURE OF NUMBER

In view of the fact that "number is *the* mathematical conception *par excellence*" (4.659), we must turn next to a brief survey of Peirce's views on this subject. As already noted, Peirce repudiated his youthful attempt to derive mathematical notions from logic; and this carried with it a repudiation of the attempt to give "a definition of cardinal numbers considered as multitudinal" (4.333). The word *multitude* is used by Peirce to denote an attribute of a collection of discrete units, by virtue of which the collection is greater than some collections and less than others—the attribute being determined by means of one-to-one correlation of the units of the respective collections (cf. 3.546; 4.175). Hence, his paper of 1867, "Upon the Logic of Mathematics," belongs to the general tradition of Cantor and Frege. Cantor used the term cardinal number to mean any multitude (*Menge*) whatsoever (4.657). Frege, in like vein, defined cardinal number as the class of all those classes similar to the given class. Such definitions became quite unacceptable to Peirce. Not only do they represent a logical treatment of mathematical concepts, but they consider numbers in illegitimate abstraction from the process of mathematical inquiry.

It is quite in character for Peirce to seek light on the subject by asking what end or purpose numbers serve in relation to human thought. Once this question is raised, the answer becomes obvious. "A cardinal number, though confounded with multitude by Cantor, is in fact one of a series of vocables the prime purpose of which, quite unlike any other words, is to serve as an instrument in the performance of the experiment of counting." (3.628) Men are constantly being faced with the problem of dealing with collections of items, and one of the most effective methods is to count the items involved. This is done by discriminating each of them in a determinate order, the numbers being pronounced in their order from the beginning, one as each member of the collection is disposed of. If the counting terminates because the collection is exhausted, the last cardinal number pronounced is applied adjectivally to the collection and expresses its multitude. Thus, in contradistinction to those who identify cardinal numbers with classes, Peirce holds that cardinal numbers are *signs* of classes, or "indices, of abnumerable multitudes" (4.657). Now the function of indexical signs, like the words "this" and "that," is to direct the person addressed to perform an act of observation. In themselves, they have no "connotation," and to that extent are meaningless. Such is the case with the cardinal numbers. Like the children's vocables, "Eeny, meeny, miney, mo" (which Peirce thinks may originally have been gipsy numerals), the cardinals "are without meaning" (4.157). But within the class of meaningless expressions, "the cardinal numerals possess the unique distinction of being mere instruments of experimentation." The sole uses to which they can be put are, "first, to count with them, and second, to state the results of such counts" (4.158).

Once the numerals have been developed in the concrete activity of counting, they are amenable to abstract treatment. This is undertaken by the mathematician, "who, generalizing upon them, creates for himself an ideal system" (4.159). The system conforms to certain precepts which Peirce formulates as follows:

First, There is a relation, G, such that to every *number, i.e.,* to every object of the system, a different number is G and is G to that number alone; and we may say that a number to which another is G is "G'd" by that other;

Second, There is a number, called zero, 0, which is G to no cardinal number;

Third, The system contains no object that it is not necessitated to contain by the first two precepts. That is to say, a given description of number only exists provided the first two precepts require the existence of a number which may be of that description. (4.160)

Peirce shows how these precepts are applied to the theory of arithmetic. He deduces from them a variety of corollaries, including such propositions as: (*a*) No number is G of more than one number; (*b*) No number is G'd by two numbers; (*c*) No number is G to itself; (*d*) Every number except zero is G of a number; and (*e*) There is no class of numbers every one of which is G of a number of that class. He then goes on to prove the Fermatian principle, which follows from the above three precepts. The demonstration is worth quoting in full.

Theorem I. The Fermatian Principle: *Whatever character belongs to zero and also belongs to every number that is G of a number to which it belongs, belongs to all numbers.*

Proof. For were there any numbers which did not possess that character, their destruction could not conflict with the first precept, since by hypothesis no number without that character is G to a number with it. Nor would their destruction conflict with the second precept directly, since by hypothesis zero is not one of the numbers which would be destroyed. Hence, by the third precept, there are no numbers without the character. (4.165)

Peirce regards this as "the truly fundamental theorem of pure arithmetic" (*ibid.*). The principle that customarily goes by that name (roughly, that an enumerable collection always has the same cardinal number), he holds to be of subsidiary importance.

The question arises whether cardinals or ordinals "are the pure and primitive mathematical numbers" (4.658). Peirce discusses the matter "after the fashion of a scholastic disputation," reviewing the arguments *pro* and *con.*

In favor of the primacy of the cardinals, there are five main considerations. (*a*) The vast majority of writers of arithmetic text-books,

68 *The Thought of C. S. Peirce*

from Leonardo of Pisa[10] to Pliny Earl Chase[11] and Horace Mann,[12] make cardinals fundamental. (*b*) The forms of the words in all languages suggest that the cardinals are older than the ordinals. Since they appear to have been conceived first, they must constitute the simpler conception. (*c*) The primacy of the cardinals accords with the convictions of common sense. (*d*) No clear account of multiplication is possible without the cardinals. For 3×5 is a collection of 3 members, each a collection of 5 units. But no sense can be attached to the expression "third fifth," unless we mean by it that we produce three collections of five each. (*e*) With ordinals alone, we can have no fractions, "except perhaps in Washington, where there is a '4½ th' street!" (*ibid.*).

To each of these arguments serious objections can be offered. With regard to (*a*), appeals to authority are illegitimate as a means of settling any question; and, in this case, the authorities cited are worthless. "The only opinions worth consideration are those of the modern mathematicologicians, Georg Cantor, Richard Dedekind, Ernest Schröder, and their fellows" (4.660). So far as the testimony of these men is concerned, Peirce thinks it is mainly on the side of the ordinals, though Cantor's position is rather equivocal. To (*b*) the obvious retort is that the earliest forms of numbers are not necessarily the neatest and purest. Indeed, the history of mathematical ideas supports just the opposite view. Moreover, "there can hardly be a doubt that the original numbers were meaningless vocables used for counting, such as children invent; and there is no reason to suppose that these were at first less purely ordinal than the children's are" (4.661). Argument (*c*) merits no reply, since the gist of it is that the less thought a man has bestowed upon a question, the more valuable his opinion about it is likely to be. Such a contention is "beneath contempt" (4.662).

The fourth argument for the primacy of cardinals is "the most respectable of the list" (4.663). Its strength depends on the alleged difficulty of providing an adequate conception of multiplication in ordinal terms. Peirce, however, not only undertakes to remove this difficulty, but also to demonstrate that an ordinal definition of multiplication is the only one that really does justice to the facts. Unfortun-

[10]*Liber Abaci* (1202). Leonardo was "the effective introducer into Europe of what we call the Arabic system of numerical notation" (4.658).
[11]*Elements of Arithmetic* (1844). "The best introduction to the art I ever saw; from which I learned to cipher as a boy" (4.658).
[12]*Elements of Arithmetic* (1851).

ately, whether because of its subtlety or its obscurity, I find his argument very hard to follow. The best I can make of it is this. A thorough analysis of multiplication shows that it presupposes the linear arrangement, or *order*, of the units with which it deals. Therefore, ordinal considerations alone make multiplication possible.

The final argument, (*e*), has the defect of failing to prove that we *can* define fractions in terms of cardinals. Peirce holds that such a proof cannot be given. For the cardinal numbers being indices of multitudes, refer to characters of collections. But it seems obvious "that there is no such thing as a fractional collection" (4.667). If not, how can fractions be derived from cardinal numbers? An even more serious objection is that the cardinal method is utterly helpless "when it attempts to represent the multiplication of fractions" (*ibid.*). Hence, the only alternative is to admit that fractions can be generated in terms of an ordinally defined series.

The above criticisms reflect Peirce's own conviction that the ordinals must be prior to the cardinals. Three positive arguments are formulated by him in support of the doctrine. (*a*) When we state precisely what it is that the cardinals indicate, we must say that "they signify the *grades* of multitude. Now a grade is a rank; it is an ordinal idea. . . . Thus, cardinal numbers are nothing but a special case of ordinals." (4.659) To say, for instance, that a plural is five means that it is of the fifth grade of multitude. It would be the sixth, if *none* were taken as the first number—or, as we might say, if we were to begin with the "*none-th*" number. However, the important thing is that "all that is essential to the mathematics of numbers is *succession* and definite relations of succession, and that is just the idea that ordinal number develops" (*ibid.*). (*b*) The essence of any object lies in what it is designed to do. Now numbers are designed for counting, and they are able to accomplish their purpose precisely because they are vocables arranged in a determinate sequence. Hence, their most distinctive feature is ordinal. (*c*) But the aim of counting is to assist reasoning. "In order to do that, it must carry a *form* akin to that of reasoning. Now the inseparable form of reasoning is that of proceeding *from* a starting-point *through* something else, *to* a result. This is an ordinal, not a collective idea." (*ibid.*)

All the evidence, then, according to Peirce, points to the conclusion that the ordinals are "the pure and primitive numbers." While it can hardly be said that his arguments are coercive, or even wholly clear, they have an impressiveness about them which springs from the consistent appeal they make to mathematics as a mode of human inquiry. In this respect, they have a certain affinity with the arguments used by the contemporary school of mathematical "Intuitionism."

7. GEOMETRY AND SPACE

The last topic about which a word must be said is the relation between geometry and the properties of space. I shall confine my remarks to the two main questions Peirce deals with here: (1) Does geometry entail one kind or many kinds of space? and (2) What is the connection, if any, between geometrical space and the space of ordinary perception and of physics?

1. Peirce accepts unconditionally the revolutionary developments in non-Euclidean geometry that began in the decade before his birth with the work of Lobachewsky and Bolyai. "The question of non-Euclidean geometry may be said to be closed," he wrote in 1902 (1.249). Five years earlier, he had declared that Euclid himself really ought to be "classed among the non-Euclideans," for "he puts his famous postulate about parallels into the form in which it most obtrusively displays its hypothetic character. He ranks it, too, as a postulate, that is as a dubitable proposition not demonstrated." (4.186 n.) The fact that Euclidean geometry was set up as a deductive system also left open the possibility that there might be other systems. It was Euclid's successors, not Euclid, who converted his geometry into the complete and final truth.

The recognition that non-Euclidean systems are co-valid with the Euclidean enables one to see that geometrical space must be multidimensional, not just tri-dimensional. Peirce expresses the matter clearly in his review of Sylvester's *Collected Mathematical Papers:*

Universal geometry can testify concerning no other space than its own, which is a space not of three, but of an infinite number of dimensions; and nothing is more striking in this more generalized geometry than that it is decidedly easier for the human mind to comprehend a space of four dimensions than one of three. Give a higher geometer sixty days to accustom himself to a four dimensional space, and he would be ever so much more at home there than he can ever be in this perverse world.[13]

This agrees with Peirce's conception of mathematics as the science which deals with hypothetical states of things. The n-dimensional spaces of pure geometry are suppositions of the human mind which have their being only in the mathematician's imagination.

[13]*Nation*, vol. LXXIX (1904), p. 203.

2. It follows from this that pure mathematics cannot be expected to throw any light on the nature of the "real space" of ordinary experience and of physics. The most geometry can do is to elaborate possible systems of spatial relations which might be existentially (and approximately) exemplified. Whether they are in fact exemplified is a matter to be determined by those sciences which are positive and experiential—namely, philosophy and certain branches of physics (3.557). The space of unaided observation is certainly three-dimensional. "But are we quite sure that the corpuscles into which atoms are now minced have not room enough to wiggle a little in a fourth? Is physical space hyperbolic, that is, infinite and limited, or is it elliptic, that is, finite and unlimited? Only the exactest measurements upon the stars can decide. Yet even with them the question cannot be answered without recourse to philosophy." (1.249)

Just as pure mathematics cannot settle anything about the properties of actual space, so, Peirce affirms, it has nothing to say about whether space is or is not *a priori*. This is a philosophical question, i.e., a question of logic. Some people have held that the researches of Lobachewsky have undermined the Kantian doctrine that space is *a priori*. For if Lobachewsky is correct, we cannot hope to know in advance of empirical evidence what the nature of space is. The conception of space involves an arbitrary constant to which values can only be given *a posteriori*. Even so, Peirce replies, it may still be the case "that the general properties of space, with the general fact that there is such a constant, are *a priori*, while the value of the constant is only empirically determined" (3.134 n.). Moreover, the discussion of this whole matter takes us out of the realm of hypotheses into that of fact. Hence, physical as well as mathematical considerations must be introduced. It might, therefore, turn out that we could accept Lobachewsky's denial of Euclid's postulate of parallels as true of actual space, and still, by means of appropriate *physical* assumptions, retain the view that space is Euclidean. For all Lobachewsky has shown is that it is conceivable that actual space should be such as to permit two straight lines in a plane and inclined to one another to exist without ever meeting, no matter how far produced. But he has not shown that the facts implied in that supposition are inconsistent with the view that space has a Euclidean structure while the properties of *things in it* change in certain ways. Peirce gives the following illustration of his meaning:

In Lobachewsky's geometry a star at an infinite distance has a finite parallax. But suppose space to have its present [i.e. Euclidean] properties, and suppose that there were one point in the universe towards which anything being moved should expand, and away from which being moved should contract. Then this expansion and contraction might obey such a law that a star, the parallax of which was finite, should be at an infinite distance measured by the number of times a yardstick must be laid down to measure off that distance. (*Ibid.*)

Accordingly, no matter what suppositions akin to Lobachewsky's are made, they can always be theoretically squared with the supposition that actual space is Euclidean. In short, Peirce concludes, "it appears to me plain that no geometrical speculations will settle the philosophy of space, which is a logical question" (*ibid.*).

Although he is generally quite clear about it, Peirce sometimes confuses pure with applied geometry. This is particularly so when he wants to find support for his doctrine of fallibilism. He affirms, for example, that mathematicians are now "fully agreed that the axioms of geometry (as they are wrongly called) are not by any means evidently true" (1.130); and he quotes Gauss to the effect that "there is no reason to think that the sum of the three angles of a triangle is exactly equal to two right angles" (1.401). As evidence, however, he takes the case of a stellar triangle having for its base the diameter of the earth's orbit and for its apex the furthest star, and contends that the sum of the internal angles will be found by observation to deviate from 180 degrees, by perhaps as much as 0.1 seconds. Indeed, there are an infinite number of possible values for the result of such observation, only one of which is precisely 180 degrees; "so that the probability is as 1 to ∞ or 0 to 1, that the value is just 180 degrees" (1.130). The obvious retort to this argument is that it confounds mathematics with mathematical physics. Peirce himself has sufficiently stressed the fact that mathematics makes no "external observations." Hence the appeal to stellar triangles has absolutely no bearing on the question of the validity of the above axiom as a proposition of pure geometry. Of course, it is not true that the internal angles of a triangle *must* equal 180 degrees; it is only true in Euclidean geometry. Given a Euclidean triangle, does it make sense to say that this proposition is only approximately true? Surely it must be true by definition; and hence not approximate, but necessary.

8. BRIEF EVALUATION OF PEIRCE'S DOCTRINE

Reviewing Peirce's account of mathematical inquiry in the light of his naturalism, we can see both strong and weak points. Among the former, I should place first his keen awareness of mathematics as a living process of inquiry—something human beings do to solve certain problems, not a vast, incomprehensible collection of desiccated formulae. Secondly, there is his perception of the hypothetical character of the entities with which the mathematician is concerned. These in no way depend on existential or empirical considerations, but are creations of the human mind. That is to say, mathematics is a postulational science whose aim is to trace the necessary consequences of its assumptions. In the third place, there is the contention that the tracing of consequences is performed by means of the purest variety of deductive reasoning. The high degree of abstraction achieved in mathematics empties it of material content, leaving the formal structure sharply delineated. This permits the reasoning to be complex, subtle, and yet rigorous. Finally, there is the explanation Peirce gives of the *modus operandi* of mathematics in terms of the manipulation of diagrams or signs. It seems to me that he is on solid ground when he insists that the practice of the mathematician involves a kind of experimentation with such diagrams or signs, together with the observation of the results of the experimentation. In these four respects, at least, Peirce's interpretation appears consistently naturalistic and in accord with the facts.

The weakest point in his doctrine is the treatment of the nature of mathematical demonstration. Had he continued to work out the position he held until about 1885 (cf. 3.252), that the basic propositions of mathematics are strictly syllogistic consequences from a small number of logical definitions, he would probably have reached a conception consonant with his naturalism. For he could then have concluded (*a*) that mathematical reasoning is explicative or analytical of certain postulated meanings, (*b*) that it conforms to the rules which govern all deductive inference, and (*c*) that the necessity of its demonstrations is at bottom a matter of the formal equivalence or identity of statements. Instead, he sought in the latter part of his career to make mathematical reasoning something *sui generis,* wholly independent of logic, and possessing a quality of "evidence" in the light of which its conclusions are "seen" to hold apodictically. The source of this non-naturalistic view (together with his occasional tendency to "Platonize" the entities with which mathematics deals) will be discussed in connection with his transcendentalism.

It seems a pity that Peirce did not "prescind" more carefully the logical from the psychological features of mathematical inquiry. His failure to do so had unfortunate consequences, particularly in regard to the observational element which he came to consider so important. That the observing of signs or diagrams is, psychologically, an essential part of the procedure of thinking mathematically seems to be true. But should it be counted a part of the logical structure of the thinking? If we say it should, as Peirce apparently does, then we shall be forced to accept the doctrine of "fallibilism" in mathematics. For since the reasoning of a mathematician depends on observations, it must be a sort of induction (cf. 2.782; 4.478), and so "every mathematical inference is merely a matter of probability" (1.248). But then we must give up once for all the notion that its conclusions are "necessary." True, we may endeavor to wriggle out of the difficulty by asserting that "when we talk of deductive reasoning being necessary, we do not mean, of course, that it is infallible" (4.531); or that in mathematics "we can be certain of our conclusions, *provided no blunders have been committed*" (2.778). But such equivocations contribute nothing in the way of a solution. A more promising approach seems to be the one implied, though never developed, by Peirce, namely, to recognize the concrete process of mathematical inquiry as a matrix within which "precise, necessary reasoning" is embedded as one (albeit the most important) of several components.[14]

[14]Peirce's philosophy of mathematics was unfavorably influenced by his study of the *Critique of Pure Reason*. For Kant, the content of mathematics is provided by "pure intuitions" having the convenient property of being particular, sensible representations which are also *a priori*. But Peirce's "diagrams," unlike their Kantian counterpart, are exclusively *a posteriori*, and hence cannot yield universal and necessary conclusions. Both men hold that mathematics possesses a unique content which is secure independently of all logic. Mathematics can therefore never be based on logic alone. This is also the view of Hilbert. Cf. H. Weyl, *Philosophy of Mathematics and Natural Science* (Princeton, 1949), p. 64.

IV

INQUIRY IN PHENOMENOLOGY

1. MATHEMATICS, PHILOSOPHY, AND PHENOMENOLOGY

WE have seen that in Peirce's classification of the sciences the place next to mathematics is occupied by philosophy. That the latter yields a kind of knowledge incapable of being provided by any other science, he never doubted for a moment. Now philosophy differs from mathematics in several important respects. (*a*) "Mathematics studies nothing but pure hypotheses, and is the only science which never inquires what the actual facts are; while philosophy, although it uses no microscopes or other apparatus of special observation, is really an experimental science, resting on that experience which is common to us all" (3.560). The one discipline is abstract and concerned with possibilities; the other is concrete and concerned with actualities. (*b*) Specially constructed schemata are essential to the reasoning of the mathematician. The philosopher reasons with words (4.233). Yet Peirce was convinced that a philosopher's words should not be limited to expressions taken over from popular speech, but should include a technical vocabulary peculiar to his subject (cf. 5.413). "If philosophy is ever to stand in the ranks of the sciences, literary elegance must be sacrificed—like the soldier's old brilliant uniforms—to the stern requirements of efficiency, and the philosophist must be encouraged—yea, and required—to coin new terms to express such new scientific concepts as he may discover, just as his chemical and biological brethren are expected to do" (5.13). Certain thinkers in the past, of course, such as Aristotle, the scholastics, and Kant, have followed this policy. But Peirce believes that it should become a universal requirement for philosophers; and he tries to practice what he preaches. (*c*) Both mathematics and philosophy employ "necessary" reasoning, though in somewhat different senses. For philosophical thought is "only necessary in the sense that all the world knows beyond all doubt those truths of experience upon which [it] is founded" (3.560). In other words, mathematical reasoning "is frightfully intricate, while the elementary conceptions are of the last degree of familiarity; in contrast to philosophy, where the reasonings are as simple as they can be, while the elementary conceptions are abstruse and hard to get clearly apprehended" (*ibid.*).

Philosophy, then, is an observational science whose subject-matter is whatever can be present to the waking consciousness of all men. Now the most fundamental question that can be asked about this subject-matter is whether it possesses any pervasive or universal features, and if so, how these are to be described. The branch of philosophy which tackles that question is phenomenology.

2. GENERAL FEATURES OF PHENOMENOLOGY

The enterprise of phenomenology was one Peirce came to recognize explicitly only towards the close of his life. No instances of the word occur in his writings before 1900, though anticipations of the idea can be found in papers completed during the eighteen-nineties, and even as early as 1867. It was apparently Hegel's *Phänomenologie des Geistes* which suggested the title to him (5.37). But he is always careful to emphasize that his phenomenology, while it "has a general similarity to Hegel's" (1.544), is also significantly different. "I will not restrict it," he says, "to the observation and analysis of *experience*, but extend it to describing all the features that are common to whatever is *experienced* or might conceivably be experienced or become an object of study in any way direct or indirect" (5.37). To facilitate analysis, Peirce invents the technical term *phaneron* to stand for "the collective total of all that is in any way or in any sense present to the mind, quite regardless of whether it corresponds to any real thing or not" (1.284). The advantage of the term is that, unlike "phenomenon" or "appearance," it does not suggest any contrast with an opposite (e.g., "noumenon" or "reality"). It is also free from irrelevant psychological connotations such as attach to the word "idea." *Phaneron* is a neutral expression, and thus conforms to one of the prime purposes of the science. Increasingly, after 1904, "phenomenology" was replaced by "phaneroscopy"; but I shall mainly use the former title.

Like all inquiry, phenomenology seeks an answer to the question which initiated it. This question is, briefly, whether the phaneron possesses any ubiquitous or universal characteristics, and, if so, what these characteristics are. Such a problem is not likely to stimulate the majority of mankind to inquiry. It affects only the philosophically minded. Yet the finding of an answer to it is a most difficult task, demanding very peculiar powers of thought (1.280). In particular, three faculties are essential. "The first and foremost is that rare faculty . . . of seeing what stares one in the face, just as it presents itself, unreplaced by any interpretation, unsophisticated by any allowance for this or for that supposed modifying circumstance" (5.42). The perceptual sensitivity of the artist who is able to see the colors of nature as they appear in their pristine purity is a basic requirement. The second faculty needed is the power of resolute discrimination of the particular feature being investigated, so that it can be detected in all its various manifestations. The third faculty "is the generalizing power of the mathematician who produces the abstract formula that comprehends the very essence of the feature under examination" (*ibid.*). Throughout the inquiry no question is raised as to the "reality" or "unreality" of what is studied. The intention is simply to scrutinize the direct appearances, and "to combine minute accuracy with the broadest possible generalization" (1.287).

A grave misconception will arise here if we do not keep two points constantly in mind. The first is that Peirce has no intention of identifying phenomenology with introspective psychology. The latter science seeks to provide as complete a description as possible of man's "inner world" of thoughts, feelings, and volitions, taking due account of individual differences found there. But phenomenology embraces both the "inner" and the "outer" worlds, though it draws no such distinction between them. The items it studies are not predesignated "mental" or "material"; and it is interested not in their individual but in their universal traits. The second point is that these traits, when isolated by phenomenology, must never be thought of as *existing separately* from one another in the phaneron. Each is rather a genuine *aspect* of the phaneron, separated from it by prescision, i.e., by the act of attending to one element and neglecting others. Such prescisive abstraction "is not an analysis into existing elements" (1.294). The phaneron exhibits an essential unity—not a homogeneous or structureless unity, but a unity of distinguishable parts which it is the business of phenomenology to investigate.

Since it does not draw on any other inquiry except mathematics, Peirce regards phenomenology as "the most primal of all the positive sciences" (5.39). It is a "science," however, in a rather special sense. Ordinarily a positive science is taken to be one that obtains knowledge capable of being expressed in categorical propositions. These represent publicly verifiable conclusions arrived at by reasoning from observations and experiments. But phenomenology "can hardly be said to involve reasoning; for reasoning reaches a conclusion, and asserts it to be true however matters may seem; while in Phenomenology, there is no assertion except that there are certain seemings; and even these are not, and cannot be asserted, because they cannot be described. Phenomenology can only tell the reader which way to look and to see what he shall see." (2.197)   In other words, the science does not consist of a body of established propositions, but rather of a set of prescriptions or instructions which each student must follow for himself, if his inquiry is to be meaningful. "Indeed, he must actually repeat my observations and experiments for himself," Peirce insists, "or else I shall more utterly fail to convey my meaning than if I were to discourse of effects of chromatic decoration to a man congenitally blind" (1.286). The indubitable beliefs underlying the whole investigation are (*a*) that *phanera* are fundamentally the same for everyone, and (*b*) that they are completely open to the observation of anyone who takes the trouble to examine them. Thus phenomenology is an exclusively descriptive science, making no inferences and drawing no conclusions! We can scarcely be surprised when in actual practice Peirce has to deviate from this conception.

The description which phenomenology undertakes cannot hope to encompass *every* aspect of the phaneron. This would be an impossible assignment. Attention is therefore confined to the phaneron's general or pervasive traits. These can be detected because of the fact that they are "indecomposable"—either "logically indecomposable, or indecomposable to direct inspection" (1.288). All attempts to analyze them into simpler constituents fail. Now phenomenology is concerned to sort out these indecomposable elements and classify them under a few distinct headings. Peirce notes two different bases of classification that can be used. The first takes account of the form or structure of the elements; the second takes account of their matter. He reports that he spent "two most passionately laborious years" trying to work out a classification on the second basis, but finally abandoned the attempt as beyond his powers. He then turned to differences of structure as a basis for attacking the problem. If it be asked how an indecomposable element can possibly have any differences of structure, the answer is that what is meant is not internal logical structure, but external structure, "that is to say, structure of its possible compounds" (1.289). To elucidate his point Peirce refers to the phenomenon of chemical valency. Just as the elements of the periodic table exhibit certain systematic modes of combination, so the elements of the phaneron "may have structure through valency." This is the sole respect in which they vary. But whereas chemical valency is exceedingly complex, extending from monadic relations through dyads, triads, tetrads, etc., to octads and so on, in the case of the phaneron, "it can be proved . . . that no element can have a higher valency than three" (1.292).

This last contention is a most important principle of phenomenology. For the proof of it recourse must be had to the prior science of mathematics, or more specifically, to that application of mathematics called the "logic of relatives." Peirce believes that this discipline proves that every relation must be monadic, dyadic, or triadic; that each of these three types is irreducible; and that relations which appear to be of greater complexity are logically analyzable into two or more triads (cf. 3.456 ff.). That a monadic relation, or predicate (e.g., "is virtuous") is totally different from a dyadic relation (e.g., "loves") is sufficiently obvious not to require elaboration. A triadic relation, likewise, is indecomposable, since, for example, "we cannot build up the fact that A presents C to B by any aggregate of dual relations between A and B, B and C, and C and A. A may enrich B, B may receive C, and A may part with C, and yet A need not necessarily give C to B. . . . Thus we see that a triad cannot be analyzed into dyads." (1.363) But every relation of higher *rank* (or *adinity*, as Peirce calls it; cf. 3.465) than a triad is compounded of triads. For if we take the quadruple fact that A sells C to B for price D, it is really a complex of two other facts, viz., that A makes a certain transaction, called E, with B, and that E is the sale of C for price D. "Each of these two facts is a triple fact, and their combination makes up as genuine a quadruple fact as can be found" (1.363).

The reason for this interesting situation lies in the logical form of the relations concerned. A dyadic relation, such as "loves," has a form involving two blank places; a triadic relation, such as "gives," has a form involving three blanks. In each case, when the blanks are suitably filled in, the result is a relational proposition. Now we can take a pair of triadic relations and join them by filling in one blank of each with the same letter or symbol, say *x*, which has the force of a pronoun or identifying index. Then the pair will constitute a whole having *four* blank places. If we combine three triads in the same way we obtain *five* blanks, and so on. But if we try to imitate the procedure with dyads, we find that conjoining a pair by means of *x* leaves us with only two blanks, i.e., we still have only a dyadic relation. Graphically, the matter can be represented thus. Let —*— stand for any dyadic relation. Then the conjunction of dyads will give —*— —*—, or —*— —*— —*—, both of which are dyads, since each has only two termini. Let —*— stand for any triadic relation. Then the conjunction of triads will give —*— —*— or —*— —*— —*—, the first of which is a tetrad (with four termini) and the second a pentad (with five termini). In this way all relations of greater complexity than the triadic can be constructed.

Phenomenology thus begins its investigations with a principle taken over from mathematical logic, namely, that there can be only three logically irreducible types of structure, represented by monads, dyads, and triads. This principle seems to play two very different roles in Peirce's thought, one of which is compatible with his naturalism, and the other not. In the first role, the principle appears as a hypothesis by which phenomenological inquiry is guided, but which stands in need of "inductive examination" before its validity can be determined. In the second role, the principle functions deductively by enabling us to infer *a priori* that empirical observation can reveal three and only three ultimate elements in the phaneron. The conflict between these two interpretations has various implications which will emerge as we proceed.

3. PHENOMENOLOGY AND THE CATEGORIES

Peirce not only follows Hegel in adopting the title of phenomenology; he also believes that "Hegel was quite right in holding that it was the business of this science to bring out and make clear the *Categories* or fundamental modes" (5.38). With such a declaration the full import of phenomenology stands revealed. The "indecomposable elements" of the phaneron are to be nothing less than exemplifications of the most basic categories of phenomena. Peirce feels that he is following a well-established precedent here. "The word *Category* bears substantially the same meaning with all philosophers. For Aristotle, for Kant, and for Hegel, a category is an element of phenomena of the first rank of generality." (5.43) This is precisely the sense in which

Peirce uses the term. Many philosophers, however, distinguish between
two orders of categories. Kant, for instance, subsumes his list of twelve
under four more inclusive headings, Quantity, Quality, Relation, and
Modality. Hegel presents the long array of categories in his *Encyclopedia,* but they are really subordinate to the three stages of thought,
Thesis, Antithesis, and Synthesis. In the case of each of these men,
the second set of categories is what Peirce calls the "universal" as distinct from the "particular" categories. He admits the correctness of
differentiating two types, but states that his own investigations have
been limited to those categories which are universal in scope. At any
rate, phenomenology deals only with the universal categories; and in
connection with them, its business "is to draw up a catalogue of categories and prove its sufficiency and freedom from redundancies, to
make out the characteristics of each category, and to show the relations of each to the others" (*ibid.*).

Peirce's interest in "the problem of the categories" was of long
standing, and had its roots in his youthful study of Kant. He tells us
that about 1860 he "was much struck with a certain indication that
Kant's list of categories might be a part of a larger system of conceptions" (1.563). Various attempts to arrive at some independent
conclusions on the matter by tackling it "in a direct speculative, a
physical, a historical, and psychological manner" proved fruitless. "I
finally concluded," he says, that "the only way was to attack it as Kant
had done from the side of formal logic" (*ibid.*). One of the first fruits
of this was his paper "On a New List of Categories" (1867). We must
examine it in outline because of the light it throws on the sources of
his mature doctrine.

The central argument of the paper is this. The universal conception
closest to sense, prior to any judgment and expressing the "pure denotative power of the mind," is that of something being present, or of
the present in general. "This conception of the present in general, of IT
in general, is rendered in philosophical language by the word 'substance' in one of its meanings" (1.547). Now the function of the understanding is to reduce the manifold of sensuous impressions to unity
in the proposition. Hence the proposition which characterizes the content of the present has a subject term representing the substance, and
a copula expressing the universal conception of *being,* i.e., the joining
of predicate to subject. "If we say 'The stove is black,' the stove is the
substance, from which its blackness has not been differentiated, and
the *is,* while it leaves the substance just as it was seen, explains its con-

fusedness, by the application to it of *blackness* as a predicate" (1.548). Substance and being are accordingly the beginning and the end of all conception. They are two absolutely basic categories.

They are not, however, the *only* basic ones. Three others are required to complete the analysis. The first is that which the predicate of the proposition expresses, viz., the notion of *quality*. It is the joining of quality to substance that is performed by the conception of being. "Quality, therefore, in its very widest sense, is the first conception in order in passing from being to substance" (1.551). We might be tempted to argue that quality must precede both being and substance since it is given in the direct impression. But Peirce thinks any such conclusion based on "the results of introspection" is untrustworthy. His attitude shows how far logical considerations take precedence over observational data at this stage in his thinking about the categories. "A proposition asserts the applicability of a mediate conception to a more immediate one. . . . Take, for example, the proposition 'This stove is black.' Here the conception of *this stove* is the more immediate, that of *black* the more mediate, which latter, to be predicated of the former, must be discriminated from it and considered *in itself*, not as applied to an object, but simply as embodying a quality, *blackness*." (*Ibid.*)   That is to say, blackness is apprehended by a process of abstraction (or prescision) which takes a mediate conception and makes it immediate, i.e., represents it as a *quale* or "pure species." "But, taken immediately, it transcends what is given (the more immediate conception), and its applicability to the latter is hypothetical" (*ibid.*). Quality, then, although a fundamental notion, is logically derivative, not primary.

Now empirical psychology has offered convincing evidence that we can only know a quality by means of its contrast with or similarity to another. Because of this, abstraction must involve reference to a correlate. Such reference is most appropriately indicated by the logical notion of *relation*. It is a factor embedded in every conception. Relation is consequently the category which comes after quality.

The third category in this group arises from the necessary reference to an interpretant which every proposition implies. For in bringing the manifold of impressions to unity, we not only have to differentiate this impression from that, but the impressions cannot become a unity "until we conceive them together as being *ours,* that is, until we refer them to a conception as their interpretant" (1.554). The logical notion of *representation* may be used to express this mediating activity which the interpretant performs. Representation is, therefore, the final conception in passing from being to substance.

Summing up, we find that the "new list of categories" which Peirce proposes has the following arrangement:

> *Being*
>> Quality (reference to a ground)
>> Relation (reference to a correlate)
>> Representation (reference to an interpretant)
> *Substance*

To indicate their slightly subordinate position, Peirce calls the three intermediate categories "accidents" (1.555).

As his thought develops, this Kantian method of "deducing the categories" is modified by two significant factors: (*a*) his study of the logic of relatives, and (*b*) his growing emphasis on the place of observation and experiment in human knowledge. As a result of (*a*) he became convinced that since there were ultimately only three modes of logical combination, the number of categories could not exceed three. As a result of (*b*), he was led to the view that phenomenology is a science which deals exclusively with what appears. Hence it cannot properly have any traffic with such ontological notions as "being" and "substance." This pair was accordingly dropped from the list of categories, and the remaining three became the basis for his mature doctrine. He tried out several alternative designations for them, searching always for titles that would express his meaning most suitably. In the end he settled on *Firstness, Secondness,* and *Thirdness,* as being scientific terms, "entirely new" and "without any false associations whatever" (4.3).

Before turning to Peirce's discussion of the individual categories, I must state in a little more detail what I take to be involved in a phenomenology which is naturalistic. It seems to me that this discipline can be regarded as the part of philosophy which tries to discover what conceptions, if any, are applicable to every phenomenon or item of experience. It seeks notions which have maximum generality. It is primarily an observational science, using logical analysis at those points where conceptual formulation and definition are involved. All conclusions reached are tentative in the sense that they cannot claim completeness or finality. The inquirer simply affirms that as far as he is able to see, taking into account not merely his own observations but those of others, such-and-such notions are universally exemplified, and hence fit to rank as categories. At some future time, however, others may well be discovered, or his own list extensively modified. Moreover, the content of the categories must be designated in terms as neutral and non-subjective as possible. Words with strongly human or personal connotations should be eschewed. The reason for this is that the investigation is proceeding on naturalistic premises, and these do not entitle man to read his own traits into everything that comes within his purview. Since the basic naturalism involves certain "metaphysical assumptions," phenomenology cannot pretend to be *completely* neutral on this score. But it can avoid all assumptions which might prejudice its inquiry from the start, such as that whatever is open to observation is "mental" or "material," "real" or "unreal," etc. In regard to these matters it not only can, but must, be non-committal. It stands for a procedure that is broadly empirical in spirit.

Now it seems to me that much of what Peirce has to say about phenomenology conforms to the above pattern. That it is *par excellence* an observational science has perhaps been sufficiently shown already. In any case, the matter will be illustrated further as we proceed. That the conclusions of the discipline are asserted not dogmatically but provisionally, is also implied by Peirce. "Each category has to justify itself by an inductive examination which will result in assigning to it only a limited or approximate validity" (1.301). In focusing attention on Firstness, Secondness, and Thirdness, he says: "I by no means deny that there are other categories. On the contrary, at every step of every analysis, conceptions are met with which presumably do not belong to this series of ideas." (1.525) In the strictest sense, the three notions can hardly be called conceptions at all; "they are so intangible that they are rather tones or tints upon conceptions" (1.353). The temper implicit in all this is certainly empirical and tentative. In specifying the content of the individual categories, Peirce employs many naturalistic terms, as we shall see. He is likewise very interested in finding empirical corroboration for his doctrine in the findings of the special sciences—notably psychology, physiology, biology, and physics (cf. 1.374-416).

I do not deny—on the contrary, I shall insist—that there is a side of Peirce's phenomenology which is very far from being naturalistic. In it, the categories are deduced *a priori*, given a highly anthropomorphic content, and linked to a speculative cosmology. All that will concern us at a later stage. Now, we must go on to examine the individual categories as they appear in their naturalistic setting.

4. FIRSTNESS

Every phaneron exhibits a certain unique and irreducible feature which Peirce calls Firstness. By its very nature, this feature is incapable of being described; but it can be denoted or identified through the performance of the appropriate act of abstraction. To suggest to the reader "which way to look," Peirce deliberately employs a number of alternative expressions. Some of these are individual terms which name exemplifications of Firstness; others are phrases descriptive of imaginary operations which partially detach the category from the matrix in which it is embedded. Both methods are indirect approaches to Firstness; but they are the only ones that can be taken in view of the inability of language to describe everything.

The most familiar individual terms which point in the direction of the category are the names of the secondary qualities (1.303). Specific instances of these, such as "the color of magenta, the odor of attar, the sound of a railway whistle, the taste of quinine" (1.304), considered in the immediacy of their occurrence, help to convey what is intended. If we expand the catalogue to include characteristics such as "heart-rending," "noble," "the emotion upon contemplating a fine mathematical demonstration," and so on, we quickly come to realize that "everything has its quality." Even the tragedy of *King Lear* can be said to have its Firstness, "its flavor *sui generis*." Hence, "that wherein all such qualities agree is universal Firstness" (1.531).

The category is also predominant in that to which a number of other words refer. Freedom and spontaneity, freshness and originality, measureless variety and multiplicity, self-containedness, and feeling, are all saturated with Firstness (1.302). It is, of course, only one aspect of them; and, as Peirce agrees, a peculiarly elusive aspect.

It cannot be articulately thought: assert it, and it has already lost its characteristic innocence; for assertion always implies a denial of something else. Stop to think of it, and it has flown! What the world was to Adam on the day he opened his eyes to it, before he had drawn any distinctions, or had become conscious of his own existence—that is first, present, immediate, fresh, new, initiative, original, spontaneous, free, vivid, conscious, and evanescent. Only, remember that every description of it must be false to it. (1.357)

The connection of Firstness with the present leads Peirce to suggest certain imaginary experiments as a means of isolating it further. "Let us now consider what could appear as being in the present instant were it utterly cut off from past and future. We can only guess; for nothing is more occult than the absolute present." (2.85) It is a fair surmise, however, that we would find simply sheer quality, undifferentiated and unspecified, "something *which is what it is without reference to anything else* within it or without it, regardless of all force and of all reason" (*ibid.*). This is the monadic aspect of the phaneron. Hegel was therefore right when he spoke of presentness, or immediacy, as the first and simplest character to be noted when anything is before the mind. He was wrong in holding presentness to be abstract, to be pure Being. This, Peirce insists, is "a falsity so glaring, that one can only say that Hegel's theory that the abstract is more primitive than the concrete blinded his eyes to what stood before them" (5.44). The true state of affairs is the precise opposite of what Hegel thought. The present is the locus of maximum concreteness. "Go out under the blue dome of heaven and look at what is present as it appears to the artist's eye" (*ibid.*). Contemplate the quality of the *tout ensemble,* not as having any relation to an underlying substance or substratum but simply in and for itself. The result will be a good approximation to Firstness.

Occasionally, Peirce applies the terms "possibility" or "potentiality" to the category (cf. 1.422 ff.). What he has in mind is not wholly clear; but the context suggests that these words are used in two quite different senses. (*a*) After various exemplifications of Firstness have been abstracted and suitably symbolized, they can be described as "possibilities" or "potentialities" in a purely logical sense. They are not so describable as they occur concretely in the phaneron. Thus, for instance, the word *red* names a particular manifestation of Firstness which can be directly observed. By reflective abstraction the *concept* of redness can be formed, and this, of course, is not observable but thinkable. Now it is to redness alone that the terms "possibility" or "potentiality" can be properly applied, by virtue of the fact that there are many possible red things, or many things potentially red. Indeed, redness as a mere concept, apart from particular red things, is a universal or general (1.447). Hence, "when we say that qualities are general, are potential determinations, are mere potentialities, etc., all that is true of qualities reflected upon; but these things do not belong to the quality-element of experience" (1.425). (*b*) The other sense in which Peirce employs the terms links them not with logical possibility but with material potentiality or "power." Firstness seems to refer to the power of bodies to determine future manifestations of inefficacious qualities. A quality *per se* and its actualization are related as potential to kinetic energy.[1] It is therefore perfectly intelligible to talk of things being colored in the dark, or being hard when no one is touching them, for what we mean is that they possess the "material potentiality" of determining such qualities under certain conditions.

A quality is a mere abstract potentiality; and the error of those [nominalistic] schools lies in holding that the potential, or possible, is nothing but what the actual makes it to be. . . . That the quality of red depends on anybody actually seeing it, so that red things are no longer red in the dark, is a denial of common sense. I ask the conceptualist, do you really mean to say that in the dark it is no longer true that red bodies are capable of transmitting the light at the lower end of the spectrum? Do you mean to say that a piece of iron not actually under pressure has lost its power of resisting pressure? If so, you must either hold that those bodies under the circumstances supposed assume the opposite properties, or you must hold that they become indeterminate in those respects. If you hold that the red body in the dark acquires a power of absorbing the long waves of the spectrum, and that the iron acquires a power of condensation under small pressure, then, while you adopt an opinion without any facts to support it, you still admit that qualities exist while they are not actually perceived. . . . Consistency, therefore, obliges you to say that the red body is red (or has some color) in the dark, and that the hard body has some degree of hardness when nothing is pressing upon it. If you attempt to escape the refutation by a distinction between qualities that are real, namely the mechanical qualities, and qualities that are not real, sensible qualities, you may be left there, because you have granted the essential point. . . . You forget perhaps that a realist fully admits that a sense-quality is only a possibility of sensation; but he thinks a possibility remains possible when it is not actual. . . . It is impossible to hold consistently that a quality only exists when it actually inheres in a body. (1.422)

While the meaning of this passage is not unequivocal, it seems to contain a clear identification of perceptible qualities with material potentialities.

Neither of the above interpretations seems to me compatible with what Peirce has previously said about Firstness. For on his own admission, once we have begun to think discursively about the category, we distort its true nature. Firstness "is so tender that you cannot touch it without spoiling it" (1.358). It can be directly experienced, and by abstraction denoted or named. But when we describe it in terms of possibility, potentiality, generality, etc., we are dealing not with Firstness but with a conceptual entity or Thirdness. Another way of putting this is to say that a perceived quality is a particular, whereas its con-

[1] Cf. John Dewey, "Peirce's Theory of Quality," *Journal of Philosophy,* vol. XXXII (1935), pp. 701-7.

ceptual description is a universal. The point will be elaborated when
we come to Peirce's discussion of his "scholastic realism." Meanwhile,
we must note that there is a tendency in his phenomenology to treat
qualities as quasi-Platonic essences. More than a hint of this is evident
in the passage just quoted, and additional examples of it will be forth-
coming as we proceed.

5. SECONDNESS

In addition to quality, phenomenological inquiry locates another
indecomposable element in the phaneron—its Secondness. Like Firstness, this can only be denoted, not defined. But we do not require so
careful an act of abstraction to grasp it in its purity. For the category
is one "which the rough and tumble of life renders most familiarly
prominent. We are continually bumping up against hard fact." (1.324)
That is to say, the phaneron is not merely qualitatively such-and-such;
it is also ineluctably before us, an actuality, *hic et nunc*. The here-ness
and now-ness are not reducible in any way to a matter of spatio-
temporal location. Nor can they be reconstrued in terms of quality.
Together they constitute an ultimate feature of phenomena, best designated by the word *fact*.

Because of its greater familiarity, the content of Secondness can be
isolated effectively by means of various descriptive phrases. Peirce
offers a number of these in a lengthy, but unsystematic, discussion of
the main features of fact. His "promiscuous list" includes the following
descriptions.

1. A fact is a particular. No element of generality belongs to it.
Hence, "Secondness, strictly speaking, is just when and where it takes
place, and has no other being; and therefore, different Secondnesses,
strictly speaking, have in themselves no quality in common" (1.532).
Both quality and generality are thus excluded from the sheer particularity of fact.

2. A fact is a contingent, or accidentally actual, particular. It
"involves an unconditional necessity, that is, force without law or
reason, *brute* force" (1.427). Peirce thinks there should be no difficulty
in understanding this, so long as we remember that we are concentrating not on the total phaneron but only on one phase of it. Thus,
for example, a flash of lightning considered as a total event is certainly
governed by law. Yet there is an aspect of it, namely, its bare *happening*, or *haecceitas*, that is irrational and accidental. The same is true
of human action. "After I have determined how and when I will exert

my strength, the mere action itself is in itself brute and unreasoning" (1.432). This is the case with fact everywhere.

3. The phrase *hic et nunc,* which Peirce associates with Duns Scotus, points to another important characteristic of fact. "It is a forcible phrase if understood as Duns did understand it, not as describing individual existence, but as suggesting it by an example of the attributes found in this world to accompany it" (1.458). Every fact has a here and now.

4. Just as quality is the monadic element in the phaneron, so fact is the dyadic element. The phenomenon in which this appears most obtrusively is that of exerting muscular effort. If we try to push open a door which stubbornly refuses to move, the sense of effort and resistance overwhelms everything else in our perception. "We can make no effort where we experience no resistance, no reaction. The sense of effort is a two-sided sense, revealing at once a something within and another something without. There is binarity in the idea of brute force; it is its principal ingredient." (2.84) The phaneron, then, has a polarity which is its dyadic aspect.

5. The particularity of fact makes it perfectly determinate in regard to the possession or lack of possession of any quality. Accordingly, the principle of excluded middle applies only to what is individual, and does not hold of the general; for the latter is partially indeterminate (1.434).

6. "Every fact has a subject, which is the grammatical subject of the sentence that asserts the existence of the fact" (1.436). In the strict logical sense there are two subjects, for the fact, as we have seen, is a dyad. But it is possible to limit our attention to one of them sufficiently to make it the referent of a subject-predicate proposition. What is thus attended to is a *thing* in the widest meaning of the word.

These are the main characteristics which phenomenological inquiry establishes about the factual aspect of the phaneron. I have omitted several other characteristics which Peirce mentions in his discussion, because they seem to be components not of *every* phaneron, but only of those which we regard as belonging to the physical world. In other words, Peirce occasionally forgets that he has committed himself to a *phenomenological* investigation, and talks about fact as though it were exclusively restricted to what forces itself upon us "from without." The natural associations of the word probably encouraged this way of thinking. Thus, in pointing out that every fact has a subject which is a thing, Peirce remarks that "this subject, whose actions all have single objects, is material, or physical substance, or *body*" (*ibid.*). Here he has momentarily slipped into regarding a thing as necessarily a material or physical object. But this is erroneous if we are in earnest about examining "whatever appears to normal waking consciousness" with no ontological preconceptions. That is to say, if the traits which phenomenology discriminates are to be general, and exhibited by all phenomena without exception, they must be present in what we should ordinarily call "memory-images," "products of the imagination," "thoughts," etc., as well as in objects of external perception. And while we may be willing to admit that from a phenomenological standpoint a memory-image, for instance, has an element of brute, irrational particularity which forces itself upon our attention *hic et nunc*, that it is a dyad, that it either possesses or does not possess every quality, and that it is a subject or thing, we should hardly be prepared to admit that it is also a material substance or body. On the other hand, the six features specified do seem to have the sort of generality which phenomenology demands.

A somewhat puzzling note is sounded by Peirce's assertion that Secondness has two varieties, a "genuine" and a "degenerate" form. This is apparently a distinction which arises at the level of reflection upon the *concept* of Secondness, and is not exhibited by the category as directly present in the phaneron. The distinction is required, Peirce thinks, because of the "prior" category of Firstness. By combining Firstness with Secondness, two "mixed concepts" are generated. "One is the second whose very Firstness is Secondness. The other is a second whose Secondness is second to a Firstness." (1.528)   In other words, when we endeavor to get the purest possible notion of Secondness, what we are seeking is the Firstness of Secondness (1.530). That is the genuine form of the category. But we may also consider Secondness as amounting to "nothing but this, that a subject, in its being a second, has a Firstness, or quality" (1.528). Here we obtain the degenerate form of the category. Since the relation between Firstness and Secondness is asymmetrical, there can be no Secondness of Firstness.

My difficulties with this distinction are as follows. (*a*) What it refers to is not "pure" Secondness, i.e. the concrete element in the phaneron, but rather a conceptual elaboration, or Thirdness. This is exactly analogous to the objection raised in connection with the applying of the term "possibility" to Firstness. If phenomenology is to remain a genuinely observational science, I do not see how it can resort to distinctions which do not have their basis in what can be directly

discovered in the phaneron. (*b*) To say that the Firstness of Secondness is the genuine form of the category is surely to imply that Secondness is a *quality*. But this is just what Peirce has previously denied.
(*c*) If the categories are *ultimate* distinctions within what is presented,
I do not see how we can be entitled to apply one category to another.
Certainly, if Secondness is really an indecomposable element in the
phaneron, we cannot consistently "decompose" it into genuine and
degenerate varieties! That Peirce himself was not without certain
qualms about the distinction may be inferred from his statement that
"it appears to be a conception of an entirely different series of categories" (*ibid.*).

6. THIRDNESS

This brings us to Thirdness. In certain respects it is the hardest of
the categories to elucidate. For one thing, it is the most complex, and
requires unusually close examination to be discriminated (1.338).
Unlike Firstness and Secondness it cannot be denoted, but only
described or defined. This does not mean that it is incapable of being
observed, as we shall see. Thirdness is, moreover, a category of the
highest importance in Peirce's thought. Perhaps just because of this,
it seems to me to focus with peculiar sharpness the conflict of tendencies in his philosophy. At the same time, the naturalistic and transcendentalist elements are often so intertwined that the disentangling
of them is no simple task.

The content of Thirdness will begin to grow clear if we notice that
the phaneron permits us to make reliable forecasts of the future. "Five
minutes of our waking life will hardly pass without our making some
kind of prediction; and in the majority of cases these predictions are
fulfilled in the event" (1.26). Now this would be an utterly inexplicable occurrence were the phaneron merely particular. It must,
therefore, contain something which links it with what is to happen,
and also with what has happened. This something can only be an element of generality. The very process of prediction is of a general
nature, for it refers, in the vast majority of cases, not to a uniquely
specific outcome, but to some *kind* of outcome. The cook who follows
the rules in her recipe-book for making an apple pie, can predict that
an apple pie will result, but she cannot predict, nor indeed is she interested in, *the* specific apple pie which will be produced. What she
desires is a certain kind of object. Moreover, she feels confident but
not absolutely certain that the recipe will produce the desired result;

that is, she feels that her prediction has a decided tendency to be fulfilled. But this "is to say that future events are in a measure really
governed by a law" (*ibid.*). Generality and law are the heart of Thirdness.

Human discourse contains an important exemplification of the
category in the phenomenon of meaning. Thus, every general term has
a meaning which is specifiable only in the conditional prediction of an
inexhaustible series of consequences. Take the case of any simple
predicate.

> I say of a stone that it is *hard*. That means that so long as the stone remains
> hard, every essay to scratch it by the moderate pressure of a knife will fail.
> To call the stone *hard* is to predict that no matter how often you try the ex-
> periment, it will fail every time. That innumerable series of conditional pre-
> dictions is involved in the meaning of this lowly adjective. Whatever may
> have been done will not begin to exhaust its meaning. (1.615)

This situation clearly involves the presence of a law in the form of an
established rule of usage for the term *hard*. The law expresses a regularity which holds of an indefinite future. In similar manner, the vast
majority of terms in a language are saturated with Thirdness.

Now the vehicle whereby meaning is conveyed is always a sign or
symbol. For a symbol to function as such, there must always be three
factors present, the symbol itself, its object (i.e., what it denotes or
signifies), and an interpretant. Where these obtain, the symbol possesses a meaning. It appears, then, that this form of Thirdness is
irreducibly triadic; and the presumption is that all forms of the category have a like structure. Just as Firstness and Secondness are monadic and dyadic notions respectively, so Thirdness is triadic. To express
this character, Peirce sometimes speaks of Representation or Mediation
as synonyms for the category (5.105; 2.86).

The intimate connection between generality and mediation serves
to elucidate another side of Thirdness. The scholastics defined a
general as *quod natum aptum est dici de multis*. This is sufficiently
accurate, Peirce thinks, provided we remember that the "many" of
which the general is apt to be predicated cannot be a denumerable
collection of items. Since he uses the word *multitude* only in connection with enumerable and denumerable collections, it can be
said that those objects of which the general "is fit to be predicated,
form an aggregate that exceeds all multitude" (5.103). The point may
be illustrated by considering any two objects that might be called
suns. The generality attaching to this word consists in the fact that

however alike the objects are to which it applies, any multitude of intermediate suns are alternatively possible "between" them. And similarly with any pair taken from these intermediate possible suns; and so on. "In short, the idea of a general involves the idea of possible variations which no multitude of existent things could exhaust but would leave between any two not merely *many* possibilities, but possibilities absolutely beyond all multitude" (*ibid.*). This state of affairs is usually described by the term *continuity.* So the upshot of the argument is that generality is simply another name for continuity (4.172). Discreteness is an essential component of Secondness; continuity is an essential component of Thirdness.

In the light of the above, it is to be expected that Peirce would find thought to consist predominantly of Thirdness. A thought is general in at least two respects. "I had it. I imparted it to you. It is general on that side. It is also general in referring to all possible things, not merely to those which happen to exist." (1.420) Furthermore, every thought is of the nature of a sign (5.594), and hence possesses the triadic character which belongs to every process of representation. Thinking or inference is carried on in signs that are mainly of the same general structure as words (6.338). Finally, the particular form of law which we call *habit* dominates the domain of reflective activity— so much so that intellectual power can be defined as "facility in taking habits and in following them in cases essentially analogous to, but in non-essentials widely remote from, the normal cases . . . under which those habits were formed" (6.20). So adequately does thought exemplify the major aspects of Thirdness that Peirce is tempted to regard it as the purest (and indeed, the only) form of the category. In his transcendentalist metaphysics he succumbs to this temptation, as will appear.

Phenomenological inquiry, then, finds the most prominent illustrations of Thirdness to be generality, law, meaning, representation, mediation, continuity, triplicity, and thought or inference. These arise from the examination of the phaneron, and are observable features of it. This point will only be clear if we remember that for Peirce observation is a process which includes a judgmental as well as a non-judgmental factor. The process characterizes a percept in a direct perceptual judgment, itself quite spontaneous and uncontrollable. Translating this view into phenomenological terms, it would seem to imply that the phaneron embraces both the percept (Firstness and Secondness) and the perceptual judgment (Thirdness). That is why

Peirce can say that Firstness and Secondness are "given in perception" (5.194), and why he holds that in themselves they are non-conceptual, being denotable but not describable. By "perception" Peirce means that aspect of consciousness which is predominantly receptive; in which, as he puts it, the "effect of things on us is overwhelmingly greater than our effect on them" (1.324). It is thus properly thought of as a component of the more inclusive activity of observation, which is not only receptive but contributory and out-going. Thirdness, however, is not something capable of being directly perceived.[2] Peirce refers to Aristotle's doctrine that the general is directly perceived in the particular as "an extraordinarily crude opinion" (2.26). For as the great medieval realists have shown, "the general is not capable of full actualization in the world of action and reaction but is of the nature of what is thought" (1.27). Thirdness, then, can emerge only with the occurrence of the perceptual judgment. It is, however, part of the phaneron, and so can be detected by phenomenological observation.

As with Secondness, Peirce argues that Thirdness has both pure and degenerate forms. But where Secondness has only a single degree of degeneracy, Thirdness has two degrees. These are the Firstness of Thirdness, i.e., the sheer qualitative character of generality, "the peculiar flavor or color of mediation" for which we really have no word (1.533); and the Secondness of Thirdness, i.e., the factuality or ineluctable presence of generality in the phaneron, best illustrated in such a phenomenon as the "compulsion" of a valid argument, or the "logical necessitation of a *meaning*" (1.530). In genuine Thirdness, on the other hand, "the first, the second, and the third are all three of the nature of thirds, or thought" (1.537). That is to say, our conceptual description of Thirdness, as contrasted with our "perception" of the degenerate aspects of it, can discriminate, for example, "thought in its capacity as mere possibility; that is, mere *mind* capable of thinking, or a mere vague idea" (*ibid.*). Or our description can relate to a thought as an occurrence or specific event. Or, finally, our description can consider a thought as governing Secondness.

This doctrine of the degenerate forms of Thirdness seems no more

[2] In the last of the 1903 "Lectures on Pragmatism" (especially 5.209 ff.), Peirce seems to say that Thirdness *is* directly perceived. Yet the context strongly suggests that he is using "perception" here rather as a synonym for "observation," since the whole tenor of his argument in the lecture is that generality cannot be "given otherwise than in the perceptual judgment" (5.186). Hence, the "perception" required is, as he himself admits, of the world of ideas (5.194), and must therefore contain an element of thought.

satisfactory than the parallel doctrine in connection with Secondness. There is again an insufficient treatment of crucial issues and some downright inconsistency. Thus we are informed that the "purest conception" we can have of Thirdness is the Firstness of Thirdness (1.530). Yet in the section previously quoted (1.537), this appears as a degenerate form of the category. In Peirce's defense it may be urged that he does not profess to be giving more than a "slight glimpse" of these matters (1.535), his aim being to point the way to the sort of analyses that might busy a student of phenomenology. Even so, the slight glimpse seems to raise as many problems as it solves.

7. NOMINALISM AND REALISM

The category of Thirdness has a consequence to which Peirce makes repeated reference in the *Collected Papers*. It marks off his philosophy as "realistic," in contradistinction to the nominalism which is so prominent a feature of modern thought. Although this question falls a little outside the scope of phenomenology, I propose to discuss it here, because of its connection with the matters just reviewed.

Peirce takes nominalism to be the belief that "*laws* and general *types* are figments of the mind" (1.16), so that particular facts or events are the only realities. Since we need to understand these events, it is useful to record our findings by means of abstract expressions. Some of the latter, for example the laws of motion, simply summarize the way in which certain events have followed one another. Other expressions, such as "hardness" and "intelligence," summarize what we have found to obtain in numerous individual instances. All such abstractions are convenient devices which have absolutely no status apart from the function they serve in knowing. They designate nothing in the natural world. It is clear that Peirce intends to include under the one heading both the extreme nominalists who argue that abstract terms or generals are nothing but *words,* and the conceptualists who admit that abstract terms are words which designate purely mental *concepts* or thoughts. Conceptualism has often tried to represent itself as an independent position. But Peirce considers it to be a muddle-headed form of nominalism (1.27).

The rise of this doctrine in the medieval period with Roscellinus, Ockham, and their followers, culminated in the "tidal wave of nominalism" which has swept over modern philosophy. Peirce holds that most philosophers since the Renaissance have subscribed to the creed. Descartes, Leibniz, the British Empiricists, Kant, and even Hegel, have all been in agreement here. No small part of the prestige of nominalism has sprung from the assumption that it is implied by science. Peirce reports that he once accepted this view himself, and gave expression to it in his review of Fraser's edition of Berkeley in 1871. But he abandoned the idea on reading "the very remarkable introduction" to Francis Ellingwood Abbot's *Scientific Theism* (1885), which "showed on the contrary, quite conclusively, that science has always been at heart realistic, and must always be so" (1.20). Those features of it which suggest the opposite conclusion are superficial and transient. Hence the nominalism of modern philosophy, so far from being "allied to the conceptions of modern science . . . is anti-scientific in essence" (2.166).

From the vantage-point of his own realism Peirce kept up a running-fire attack on nominalism for many years. His attitude toward it alternated between contempt and a grudging admission that it had some merits. Modern nominalists "are mostly superficial men" (5.312), addicted to a "loose and slapdash style of thinking" (1.27). Indeed, "they do not reason logically about anything" (1.165). The average representative of the class reminds Peirce of the blind spot of the retina, "so wonderfully does he unconsciously smooth over his field of vision and omit facts that stare him in the face" (4.1). Yet the nominalistic doctrine has the great virtue of being simple; and the methodological principle of Ockham's razor, which "is the very roadbed of science," instructs us to always select the simplest hypothesis. Now realism cannot successfully establish itself if it ignores this principle (4.35). Hence, the burden of proof rests on the realists to show that full justice can only be done to the facts on their hypothesis. Because of this, "everybody ought to be a nominalist at first, and to continue in that opinion until he is driven out of it by the *force majeure* of irreconcilable facts" (4.1). Apparently, then, while the doctrine can never be a defensible terminus for thought, it is a proper starting-point.

In his later years, Peirce became hypersensitive to nominalistic tendencies. He sees them cropping out in many quarters, even in some of his own early writing, and attributes to them various undesirable consequences, both philosophical and social. Thus, the "realist" Paul Carus is said to vitiate his argument by nominalistic lapses from time to time (6.593). The pragmatism of James and Schiller is inadequate because it does not rest on a thorough-going realism.[3] Even Duns

[3] See letter to James, in R. B. Perry, *The Thought and Character of William James* (Boston, 1935), vol. II, p. 430.

Scotus, to whose realism Peirce proclaims his allegiance so often, is lightly rapped over the knuckles because he inclines too much towards nominalism (1.560). In a published paper of 1892, Peirce indicates that a certain doctrine which he held in 1868 was "too nominalistic" to be satisfactory (6.270). Near the close of his article entitled "Postulate," in J. M. Baldwin's *Dictionary of Philosophy and Psychology* (1902), he remarks that those who seek to found geometry on definitions alone represent "an extreme nominalistic position" (3.633). Inasmuch as his own aim about 1867 was to prove that the truths of mathematics follow syllogistically from a few propositions taken as definitions (cf. 3.20), he is probably right in thinking that there were elements of "nominalism" in his thinking at that time. They may, perhaps, be traceable to his early Kantianism. But even then, his realism was quite explicit, though not as extreme as it subsequently became. Among the social consequences of nominalism, Peirce mentions the view that since *genus homo* has no reality apart from particular men, they must be the repository of ultimate values. For on this approach the community is a fiction. Accordingly, nominalism logically implies that there is nothing higher in worth than "individual happiness, individual aspiration and individual life."[4] Such conclusions were as repugnant to Peirce as the root from which they grew.

To all shapes and varieties of nominalism, the one effective alternative lies in Thirdness. The core of Peirce's "scholastic realism" is contained in this category, affirmed in a metaphysical as well as a phenomenological sense. Generality is not only an ultimate feature of whatever is capable of being observed; it is also "an indispensable ingredient of reality" (5.431). Universals are therefore *real*, not just figments or creations of the human mind. Exactly what is involved in this doctrine will be considered in a moment. But first we may note two things that it does not entail.

1. It is an ancient and important insight that the acceptance of realism does not commit one to any form of Platonism. Peirce, at least in his naturalistic moments, is entirely clear on this point. "Every realist must, as such, admit that a general is a term and therefore a sign. If, in addition, he holds that it is an absolute exemplar, this Platonism passes quite beyond the question of nominalism and realism; and indeed the doctrine of Platonic ideas has been held by the extremest nominalists." (5.470) Berkeley is a case in point here, as

[4] *North American Review*, vol. CXIII (1871), p. 472.

Peirce remarked in his review of Fraser's edition of Berkeley's *Works*. The trouble with all such Platonizing is that it falls into the absurdity of treating the general as a particular, subsisting eternally in some mysterious realm of being. Quite apart from other difficulties, this view simply fails to recognize Thirdness. It is disguised conceptualism, with subjective concepts treated as hypostasized entities.

2. The affirmation of realism does not necessarily imply that generals exist in the same way individual facts do. Realists are sometimes thought to believe that, for example, the law of gravity is "in nature" precisely as particular falling bodies are. Since no such thing is empirically perceivable, it is easy to conclude that a *universalia in re* must be a metaphysical fiction. This path to nominalism is blocked by Peirce's distinction between Secondness and Thirdness. According to it, existence is limited to individual facts, and cannot properly be talked of in connection with generals. A realist does not need to assert the *existence* of universals; he only needs to assert their *reality*.

Now what precisely does "the reality of generals" mean for Peirce? We have caught some glimpse of his meaning in the phenomenological account of Thirdness. But when we look for enlightenment on specific details, it remains unfortunately true, as Dr. Buchler has remarked, that "a clear or concise statement of his realism is not to be found in his writings."[5] One is consequently obliged to reconstruct his doctrine as best one can from scattered sources, taking due account of any changes in emphasis which may appear. My own efforts in this direction have led me to conclude that Peirce "declared for realism" in several different senses, but that only one of these falls properly within the orbit of his naturalism. I shall deal with it first, and then go on to make some remarks about the other versions.

The controversy between nominalists and realists is stated by Peirce in 1871 as though it were concerned exclusively with what is involved in judgments about classes of things. "The question, therefore, is whether *man, horse,* and other names of natural classes, correspond with anything which all men or all horses have in common, independent of our thought, or whether these classes are constituted simply by a likeness in the way in which our minds are affected by individual objects which have in themselves no relationship whatsoever."[6] The realist obviously takes the former of these alternatives.

[5] Justus Buchler, *Charles Peirce's Empiricism* (New York and London, 1939), p. 123.
[6] *North American Review*, vol. CXIII (1871), p. 454.

The question then immediately arises as to the precise character of
the "something" which all members of a class have in common, and
how it is related to the concrete individual on the one hand and to the
abstract universal concept on the other. The answer which Peirce finds
most satisfactory here was given by Duns Scotus, whose position he
proceeds to sketch.

The gist of that "subtle and difficult" doctrine is taken by Peirce
to be as follows. Apart from thought, only singular things exist. But
there are in singulars certain "natures," themselves neither universal
nor particular, which constitute the ground of intelligibility. In things,
these natures are particular; when brought into relation to an act of
the intellect, they are universal. "It is the very same nature which in
the mind is universal and *in re* is singular."[7] Elsewhere, Peirce quotes
directly from Scotus to emphasize the point. "*Eadem natura est, quae
in existentia per gradum singularitatis est determinata, et in intellectu,
hoc est ut habet relationem ad intellectum ut cognitum ad cognoscens,
est indeterminata.*"[8] Thus, for example, the directly experienced hard
surface of a particular stone is determinate, whereas the universal
hardness which the intellect grasps is indeterminate or general. A consequence of this view is that the individual *per se* is not a proper object
of knowledge. What we know are genera and species, themselves the
product of mental action. Yet because complete being embraces both
universality and particularity, because man *perceives* the singular with
his senses while *cognizing* the universal with his intellect, it is possible
for him to attain to the singular by relating universals to something
which is *this*.

The objection may be raised that such a view destroys the reality
of the universal by making it depend on a relation to thought. Peirce
replies that this objection springs from the belief that the real must be
wholly independent of reflective activity, i.e. must be a thing in itself.
But the notion of a thing in itself is self-contradictory, for it requires
us to think about what is *per definitionem* out of relation to thought.
We can have no conception of any incognizable reality (cf. 5.254 ff.).
Indeed, "a realist is simply one who knows no more recondite reality
than that which is represented in a true representation" (5.312). It is
the nominalist who wants to introduce something more than this, and
so gets into insurmountable difficulties. Let it be noted that the realist
does not hold that reality is dependent on the thinking of any *indi-*

[7]*Ibid.*, p. 459.
[8]*Quaestiones in metaphysicam Aristotelis* VII. 18. 8.

vidual. On the contrary, the real is precisely that which is independent
of what you, or I, or anyone else happens to think about it. But it does
not follow that the real is independent of thought in general, i.e. of
"the ultimate decision of the community" (5.316). A parallel case will
serve to show that this is not an unfamiliar manner of thinking. We all
recognize the relativity of the sensory quality *red* to the human visual
apparatus. "But the fact that this or that is in that relation to vision
that we call being red is not *itself* relative to sight; it is a real fact"
(5.430). Similarly, although the real natures which exist in things are,
apart from all action of the intellect, singular, they are nevertheless
real universals in relation to human thought. Our judgments about
types or classes, then, do not refer to metaphysical fictions, but to
divisions that have a basis in the actual world.

It was a simple matter for Peirce to make this doctrine include
laws as well as general types. The realist, he felt, is bound to account
for the frequency with which our predictions about the future are
verified by the course of events. That this frequency of verification
depends on wholly contingent regularities of events, or that it is an
ultimate fact incapable of being explained, as the nominalists admit
(when pushed into a corner), Peirce found unacceptable. He could
see only one satisfactory conclusion, viz., that there is a tendency in
individual things to manifest *ways* of behaving. This tendency, when
elicited by reflective thought upon what is observed, is a law. Its mode
of being is *esse in futuro* (2.148). As a general, it not only transcends
what can be perceived in the present; it also "goes beyond any accomplished facts and determines how facts that *may be,* but *all* of which
never can have happened, shall be characterized" (1.420). On Scotistic
grounds it follows that the tendency of things to behave in a certain
determinate way is a law only in relation to thought. Nevertheless,
in that relation the law is a real component of the world, to which
individual things conform.

So far, Peirce would seem to be in broad agreement with Scotus.
We must now specify one important respect, perhaps already obvious
from what has been said, in which their doctrines diverge. For Scotus,
as for all the scholastics, the thought required for the apprehension of
the universal is that of the individual intellect. Moreover, the result of
this apprehension is *necessary* knowledge of being. Hence, the one
criterion which governs the pursuit of knowledge is absence of contradiction. The pursuit is exclusively an adventure of reason. For
Peirce, however, the thought which grasps the reality of the universal

is that of the community of minds employing the method of scientific inquiry throughout an unlimited period of time. Intellectual activity is construed as a social and historical enterprise. Because scientific inquiry has an inherent tendency to correct itself as it proceeds, it is slowly leading humanity towards a state of absolute knowledge. But at any given time, our apprehension of universals is *probable* only; and this is the case not only for the individual but also for the scientific community. While Peirce agrees with Scotus, then, that a universal resulting from the activity of thought is the proper object of knowledge, he disagrees with the view that the individual or finite intellect can grasp that object in its totality. In this respect the Scotistic position is a "halting realism" which helped to pave the way for nominalism.

Peirce's doctrine of universals appears to be consistent with what he has said about the categories. Particular existents as directly presented or perceived are characterized by Firstness and Secondness. These same existents, when observed and thought about, are characterized by Thirdness. On every occasion of their appearance, Firstness and Secondness are completely determinate; but Thirdness is indeterminate because it refers to an indefinite future as well as to what is present. Although it does not exist in the realm of fact, Thirdness may be said to "govern" that realm, since future manifestations of Firstness and Secondness will conform to it. Furthermore, thought, when directed upon the concrete particularity of a quality, finds therein a basis for the construction of a universal concept (e.g., whiteness, redness, etc.) and is thus able to make judgments about genera and species. Like the "natures" of Scotus, sensory qualities are singular as perceived and universal as thought. We have already noticed how Peirce blurs this distinction when he slips into talking about Firstness as "possibility" or "potentiality." From the perspective of phenomenology, whatever can be observed is a complex of the three categories. From the perspective of realism, everything observable is a complex of particular and universal.

It seems to me that the version of realism presented here is of the "moderate" variety, which is not incompatible with naturalism. For it involves no reification of universals, no attributing to them of an efficacy superior to that of individual existents, no suggestion that they have some status in the universe independent of human thought. On the contrary, laws and general types are genuine features of the world as investigated by the scientific community. They are features with a quite different mode of being from that of singular existents, but they have an ineluctable reality none the less. The question may arise whether on this view universals would disappear if all minds in the universe were destroyed. Peirce would say, I imagine, that we cannot hope to know the answer to such a question. Indeed, the question itself has little, if any, meaning. Lurking behind it is the inadmissible notion of incognizable being. However, if we wish to attribute a modicum of meaning to the question, and make a *guess* at the answer, we should probably have to give an affirmative reply. Apart from all minds, only particulars with their various singular characteristics would occupy a place in nature. Yet these same characteristics, if they were subsequently to be observed and thought about, would become genuine universals.

In the last few paragraphs I have gone beyond anything that Peirce actually says in the *Collected Papers*. But I have tried to reconstruct what he might have said had he worked out some of the implications of his "Scotistic realism" in more detail.[9] That he failed to do so may be explained by the fact that his thinking moved on towards a more extreme form of the doctrine (cf. 5.470). Even in 1871 he recognized that the views of Scotus "were only separated from nominalism by a hair."[10] By 1900 he was convinced that Duns inclined too much towards nominalism, and hence described his own position as that of "an Aristotelian of the scholastic wing, approaching Scotism, but going much further in the direction of scholastic realism" (5.77 n.). Since the development suggested here is one which takes him away from naturalism, we may refer to it briefly.

A comment which Peirce makes in his paper "What Pragmatism is" (1905) contains a clue to the shift in his opinions. "Not only may generals be real," he says, "but they may also be *physically efficient*" (5.431). He goes on to add that he does not mean this to be taken "in every metaphysical sense, but in the common-sense acception in which human purposes are physically efficient" (*ibid.*). Nevertheless, he does elsewhere talk as though a natural law, for instance, had a power of *compelling* events to happen as they do. The compulsion exerted by a law is not, of course, the brute compulsion of an efficient cause. It is the kind of compulsion which a final cause exerts (1.211 ff.). Because of this we cannot escape the conclusion "*that general principles are*

[9]I hardly need to say that my interest here has been limited to expanding the doctrine which Peirce attributes to Scotus, rather than the doctrine of Scotus himself.
[10]*North American Review*, vol. CXIII (1871), p. 452.

really operative in nature" (5.101). He expresses the same idea in another way when he affirms that the laws of nature are "habits," which are akin to human habits, and exercise a similar determining capacity. Just as a habit *makes* a person behave in a certain way, so a law makes the individual events behave the way they do (cf. 5.99 ff.). It would be inappropriate at the moment to explore these themes more closely, for they would take us into the center of Peirce's transcendentalism. For this tendency in his thinking drew him towards a realism "of a somewhat extreme stripe," not far removed from Platonism.

8. THE CATEGORIES IN THE SPECIAL SCIENCES

Returning to phenomenology proper, we may wind up our discussion by considering what Peirce has to say about the categories in relation to the special sciences. If the categories are pervasive features of whatever can be observed, we should be able to find them exemplified in every special science. Moreover, the detection of their presence would constitute an important confirmation of phenomenology's findings. Peirce, however, does not tell us in precisely what sense he thinks the categories can be thus exemplified. Presumably, they do not belong to the explicit theory of a science, for if they did, it must have performed a kind of phenomenological analysis of its own in order to obtain them. Such a consequence would contradict what has been said about the procedure of phenomenology as an independent discipline. Similarly, the categories can hardly be among the characteristics which it is the proper task of a science to study. The most that can be allowed, it would seem, is that when the total subject-matter (including both theory and observational elements) of a science *is surveyed by phenomenology*, the three categories are found to be involved. So much is mere conjecture, for Peirce does not make his position clear. His whole discussion is fragmentary and impressionistic. The only justification for introducing it is that it reflects his concern to find empirical support for his doctrine of the categories. The four sciences whose subject-matter he touches on are psychology, physiology, biology, and physics. I shall follow that order in summarizing his remarks.

Psychology, for Peirce, is "the systematic study of the mind" (2.210), whose aim is to find "the general elements and laws of mental phenomena" (1.189). Its condition is that of a science which has made an admirable beginning, but only a beginning, and whose advance is being retarded by the lack of a well-defined method. Hence, "matters of brain-physiology and matters of consciousness elbow one another in unsympathetic juxtaposition, in a way which can only be transitional, and is a sign for us . . . that psychologists do not yet understand what mind is, nor what it does" (2.42). Peirce does not pretend to have found the remedy for this situation. He is convinced, however, that the data of psychology must be "self-observations," since the science "has no dealings with objects out of the mind" (2.64). It does not follow that the observation required will be identical with what has been traditionally called "introspection." For the latter has been held to be concerned exclusively with what is "psychical" or "mental," whereas Peirce belongs to "the party which thinks that no psychical fact, as such, can be observed" (1.253). Moreover, introspection in the older sense was a kind of immediate knowledge, whereas Peirce considers it to be "wholly a matter of inference" (5.462). In the light of these uncertainties regarding its method, and the rudimentary character of its conclusions, psychology can hardly be expected to provide the best illustrations of the categories. Here, more than elsewhere, phenomenology is faced with the necessity of re-interpreting the data.

Most psychologists since the time of Kant have accepted, Peirce contends, the division of the mind's operations into feelings of pleasure and pain, acts of willing, and acts of knowing. As it stands, this division can hardly be said to embody the categories. But it can be shown to do so if we make some slight modifications which seem to be warranted by the facts. Thus, close examination shows that pleasure and pain "can only be recognized as such in a judgment; they are general predicates which are attached to feelings rather than true feelings" (1.376). The latter are rather the passive "having" of all sorts of qualities, without recognition, analysis, or comparison. This element of immediate experience is an aspect of all consciousness, and deserves a special title, viz. feeling. Similarly, in willing, which is mere activity, the feature which dominates consciousness is the·sense of resistance, of something reacting upon us which we seek to overcome. "We are conscious of hitting or getting hit, of meeting with a *fact*" (*ibid.*). Another way of describing the phenomenon would be to say that we have a consciousness of polarity. "For will, then, as one of the great types of consciousness, we ought to substitute polar sense" (1.380). Finally, the act of knowing is one phase of a more extensive process which includes learning, inference, synthesis—in short, *thought* in the widest sense of the term.

It seems, then, that the true categories of consciousness are: first, feeling, the consciousness which can be included with an instant of time, passive consciousness of quality, without recognition or analysis; second, consciousness of an interruption into the field of consciousness, sense of resistance, of an external fact, of another something; third, synthetic consciousness, binding time together, sense of learning, thought. (1.377)

Not only does Peirce hold that these "three radically different elements of consciousness" illustrate Firstness, Secondness, and Thirdness respectively, but he even affirms that the degenerate forms of the categories appear as well. For example, "the polar sense splits into two, and that in two ways, for first, there is an active and a passive kind, or will and sense; and second, there are external will and sense, in opposition to internal will (self-control, inhibitory will) and internal sense (introspection)" (1.383). I take Peirce to mean here that "degenerate Secondness" is exemplified in the passive polar sense and in internal will and sense. Synthetic consciousness also conforms to the phenomenological analysis of Thirdness. The first degenerate variety is manifested in cases where we have an external compulsion to think things together, e.g. association by contiguity. The second degenerate variety is manifested in cases where we have a natural proclivity to think things together, i.e. where we are "internally compelled" to synthesize them or sunder them, as in association by similarity. The genuine form of synthetic consciousness is manifested in cases where the mind produces a synthesis made in the interests of intelligibility alone, by means of an idea "not contained in the data, which gives connections which they would not otherwise have had" (*ibid.*). This is thought in its genuinely creative function—a matter insufficiently explored by psychology.

If it be granted that there are three different modes of consciousness, "it follows as a matter of course that there must be something threefold in the physiology of the nervous system to account for them" (1.385). The implication here has its source in that intimate dependence of mind on body which everybody now recognizes. Peirce has no intention of dogmatizing in his search for physiological illustrations of the categories. All he proposes is to employ the results of phenomenological inquiry as hypotheses, and to trace out the consequences which they should have for physiology if the analysis of the categories has been adequately performed. Judgment on the empirical validity of the consequences must be the prerogative of the physiologists alone.

The first two modes of consciousness, feeling and the polar sense, can, Peirce believes, be correlated readily with physiological facts. The former is connected with the active condition of the protoplasmic content of the nerve-cells, following excitation by some stimulus. While we cannot be sure that every nerve-cell in an active state has feeling, there is little room for doubt that the activity of such cells is the major physiological requisite for immediate consciousness. "On the other hand, the sense of action and reaction, or the polar sense . . . is plainly connected with the discharge of nervous energy through the nerve-fibres" (1.386). For example, in external volition a discharge of nervous energy takes place along efferent nerves to a muscle; in external sense a similar discharge occurs from the terminal nerve-cell along afferent paths to cells in the brain. Now, bearing in mind that the polar sense "is the sense of the difference between what was before and what is after a dividing instant . . . we see clearly that the physiological concomitant of it must be some event which happens very quickly and leaves a more abiding effect, and this description suits the passage of a nervous discharge over a nerve-fibre so perfectly, that I do not think we need hesitate to set this phenomenon down as the condition of dual consciousness" (*ibid.*).

The physiological basis of synthetic consciousness in its genuine form is "the most characteristic property of the nervous system, the power of taking habits" (1.390). Several principles determine this capacity, the most important of which is the tendency for a nerve-impulse to flow more easily along a path which it has travelled on previous occasions. Peirce does not connect that fact, as he might easily have done, with the hypothesis of decreasing resistance of the synapses as a nerve-path is repeatedly used. But he does insist that the tendency to form habits is not a rigid, unvarying affair like the operation of a mechanical law. The response of a nerve to stimulation, which leads to the instituting of habit through repetition, is directed, as we have seen (chapter II, section 1), towards the removal of the stimulus. Those responses which are successful in achieving this objective become stable habits. We may appropriately say, therefore, that our actions always have the general aim of removing a stimulus. "Every man is busily working to bring to an end that state of things which now excites him to work" (1.392).

The cardinal functions of the nervous system, then, are "first, the excitation of cells; second, the transfer of excitation over fibres; third, the fixing of definite tendencies under the influence of habit" (1.393). Here again we see the imprint of the categories. But Peirce is not content to stop at this point. His enthusiasm leads him to delve "yet deeper into physiology" in search of illustrative material. Consequently, he speculates on the possible neurological basis of the degenerate forms of Thirdness, and then tries to show that even the properties of proto- plasm "can all be summed up under the heads of sensibility, motion, and growth" (*ibid.*), in conformity to his categorial scheme. A good deal of his argument in this connection is impenetrable to me. Where I do catch a glimmer of meaning, I get the impression that he is not only forcing the issue unjustifiably, but is also going beyond the limits of his competence in dealing with what is, after all, a very technical field of science. I shall therefore pass over the rest of his discussion in silence.

Coming now to biology, we find Peirce focusing his attention on the central concept of Darwinian evolution, i.e., the theory of natural selection. "A very remarkable feature of it is that it shows how merely fortuitous variations of individuals together with merely fortuitous mishaps to them would, under the action of heredity, result, not in mere irregularity, nor even in statistical constancy, but in continual and indefinite progress toward a better adaptation of means to ends" (1.395). The process of selection requires that certain physical charac- teristics should appear fortuitously in some members of a species, and should enable them to adapt themselves to their environment more successfully than those who lack these characteristics. The latter group is gradually eliminated; while the former, transmitting its favorable qualities from generation to generation, survives. Such a "survival of the fittest" does not mean the survival of the fittest individuals but rather of the fittest types, "for the theory does not at all require that individuals ill-adapted to their environment should die at an earlier age than others, so long only as they do not reproduce so many off- spring as others" (1.397). Now this process surveyed in its entirety contains, Peirce argues, three major factors which correspond in a rough way to the categories. They are: (*a*) the chance variations, in- determinate and irregular (Firstness); (*b*) the hereditary transmission of characteristics, involving the determination of something by what went before (Secondness); and (*c*) the elimination of unfavorable characteristics, "which is the principle of generalization by casting out of sporadic cases" (Thirdness). If such correlations seem imperfect, this may be attributed, Peirce suggests, to "the imperfection of the theory of development" (1.399). Apparently, the results of phenomen- ology must remain above suspicion!

The final science to be mentioned in connection with the categories is physics. Unfortunately, what purports to be a discussion of this in the *Collected Papers* (1.400-416), seems to me far more concerned with metaphysics. Peirce shows comparatively little interest in examining the special science to locate illustrations of his categories. Rather, what he does is to draw certain speculative consequences from his phenomenology, and offer them as hypotheses which physics in the future might put to empirical test. That such a procedure is not without value is shown by the fact that it led him to anticipate two prominent doctrines of twentieth-century physical theory. But the procedure obviously does not provide the sort of scientific corroboration of the categories which was originally sought.

It is not difficult to see why Peirce followed such a pattern. The physics of his day was still dominated in the main by the ideas of classical mechanics. Two of these ideas, that of dynamic action or force, and that of universal laws governing events, may be taken as rough examples of Secondness and Thirdness respectively. But it is difficult to find in the subject-matter of classical physics any example of Firstness. Peirce therefore proceeds to argue that the physicist needs to revise his conception of law so as to bring it into line with the empirical evidence. For the belief that the laws of nature are inviolable and permit no exceptions is not one which the actual practice of science establishes. "We know that when we try to verify any law of nature by experiment, we always find discrepancies between the observations and the theory. These we rightly refer to errors of observation; but why may there not be similar aberrations due to the imperfect obedience of the facts to law?" (1.402) If this hypothesis is correct (and there can be nothing in experience to negative it), two things immediately follow. (*a*) The physicist will find that the laws of nature are more adequately construed as approximate rather than as absolute regularities. In other words, experimental evidence will increasingly suggest that a law is a statistical generalization having a high degree of probability only. (*b*) It will no longer be thought absurd to admit that an element of indeterminacy or chance exists in nature. "To the ancients, there was nothing strange in such notions; they were matters of course; the strange thing would have been to have said that there was no chance" (1.403). The reason modern physics has scoffed at the idea is that scientists have assumed the validity of a certain view of the physical world, namely, mechanistic determinism. It is this "unconscious metaphysics" rather than experimental considerations that has dictated their notion of law. In urging that the hypothesis of chance be admitted into physics, Peirce probably believed he was helping the science to maintain a closer accord with empirical fact.

His metaphysical position, of course, was that all the arguments were hostile to "necessitarianism" and favorable to "tychism"—the doctrine that chance is objectively real. We shall have to examine these arguments in the appropriate place. Here we may simply observe that Peirce's adumbration, on purely speculative grounds, of the statistical conception of law and of the notion of indeterminacy in nature fore-shadowed two of the ideas that have challenged the supremacy of classical physics since the turn of the century.[11] Were he alive today, he would doubtless enjoy pointing to quantum theory as an area where Firstness makes its presence felt. At any rate, indeterminacy or chance, dynamical action or force, and statistical regularity or law, are the three elements which he took to illustrate the categories as they occur in physics.

We may sum up this project of seeking scientific verification of his phenomenological conclusions in the following table:

		Firstness	*Secondness*	*Thirdness*
Phenomenology		Quality	Fact	Law
Psychology	*or*	Feeling	Action and reaction	Thought
		Sensation	Perception	Belief
Physiology		Cell excitation	Passage of nerve impulse	Habit
Biology		Fortuitous variations	Hereditary transmission of traits	Elimination of unfavorable traits
Physics		Indeterminacy	Force	Statistical regularity

This by no means completes the list of illustrations of the categories. We shall find others cropping up in his logic, theory of signs, and metaphysics.

[11]That Peirce did not break completely with the classical doctrine is shown by such statements as: "The laws of physics know nothing of tendencies or probabilities; whatever they require at all they require absolutely and without fail, and they are never disobeyed" (1.390). Cf. Philip P. Wiener, "The Peirce-Langley Correspondence and Peirce's Manuscript on Hume and the Laws of Nature," *Proceedings of the American Philosophical Society,* vol. XCI, no. 2 (1947), pp. 201-28.

Peirce was well aware that the frequent occurrence of triadic divisions in his thought might lead to the charge that he attached "a superstitious or fanciful importance to the number three," and forced everything upon a Procrustean bed of trichotomy. At the very close of his life, he began a paper entitled "Triadomany" (1910), designed to show that he was not the victim of an *idée fixe,* but that his analyses were determined by the character of the world and our manner of investigating it. Only a few paragraphs of the paper got written. Perhaps that is just as well, for it is doubtful whether anything he could have said would have produced more conviction than his other discussions. No one, surely, can come away from the study of his phenomenology without recognizing Peirce's sincerity when he says: "I find myself obliged, for truth's sake, to make . . . a large number of trichotomies" (1.568). Whether the reader feels a similar obligation is another matter. Personally, I find it hard to believe that Peirce's categories are mere arbitrary inventions; where there is so much smoke, there must be at least a little fire.[12] But even if one rejects all of Peirce's conclusions in this field, it is still possible to argue, I think, that the phenomenological method he delineated is an important part of philosophy, and can be pursued in the empirical and naturalistic spirit by which he was commonly motivated.

---

[12]It is worth recalling that Peirce himself disliked being told that his categories were entirely original products. In a letter to William James he remarks: "It rather annoys me to be told that there is anything novel in my three categories; for if they have not, however confusedly, been recognized by men since men began to think, that condemns them at once." (Quoted in Perry, *The Thought and Character of William James,* vol. II, p. 428.) In another place he sapiently observes that "originality is the last of recommendations for fundamental conceptions" (1.368).

V

INQUIRY IN LOGIC
Explicative Inference and General Semiotic

1. PEIRCE AS A LOGICIAN

IF we had to describe Peirce's vocation in a single word, the most adequate would be "logician." That was the title he preferred himself; and certainly, the study of logic was his grand passion which overshadowed all others. He liked to date his interest in the subject from his twelfth year, when he discovered Archbishop Whateley's *Logic* and mastered its contents in a few days. The book made an immediate appeal to his native "logical bent" which had previously found expression in other ways (cf. 4.533). His very first paper, privately printed and "distributed at the Lowell Institute, Nov. 1866," was entitled "Memoranda concerning the Aristotelian Syllogism." In it he undertakes to demonstrate that Kant was wrong in assuming that the reduction of all syllogisms to *Barbara* involves no logical principle that *Barbara* does not involve. By some closely knit analysis, Peirce shows that the second and third figures can only be reduced to the first if we assume a principle which is expressible syllogistically in the figures from which the reduction is made (cf. 2.792 ff.). About this time, he received from De Morgan a copy of his famous memoir on the logic of relatives, in which he found "a brilliant and astonishing illumination of every corner and every vista of logic" (1.562). Out of the study of this work, his own original researches grew. In addition to the purely formal aspect of logic, its applied or inductive side strongly attracted him; and it is hard to say in which of the two fields he did more significant work. When he began to write, the whole science of logic was in a torpid, unprogressive state, against which he never ceased to do battle. Its history since his death amply confirms the assessment he made of his own contributions. "I am as confident as I am of death," he wrote, "that Logic will hereafter be infinitely superior to what it is as I leave it; but my labors will have done good work toward its improvement" (2.198).

What I propose to discuss is Peirce's theory of logic as a mode of human inquiry. I shall not attempt to review his detailed contributions to formal logic; these will be mentioned only in so far as they are pertinent to the general theme of the discussion.[1] We have noted that the word "logic" is deliberately employed by Peirce in two senses. "In its narrower sense, it is the science of the necessary conditions of the attainment of truth" (1.444). This is often called "Critical Logic" or simply "Critic." It subdivides into the analysis of explicative or deductive inference on the one hand, and of ampliative or synthetic inference on the other. In its broader sense, logic is "the science of the necessary laws of thought, or, still better (thought always taking place by means of signs), it is general semeiotic, treating not merely of truth, but also of the general conditions of signs being signs" (*ibid.*). Since ampliative inference is a complete topic in itself, I shall postpone discussion of it until chapter VI. We are therefore left with two subjects requiring attention: (*a*) that portion of critical logic which deals with explicative inference; and (*b*) general semiotic. These will now be taken up in order.

A. THE ANALYSIS OF EXPLICATIVE INFERENCE

2. THE PRESUPPOSITIONS OF LOGIC

Before examining explicative inference at close range, there are one or two preliminary matters in need of comment. The first is the question to what extent logic involves any presuppositions. Peirce's opinion on this point was by no means uniform throughout his life, and varied with the changes in his conception of the general nature of logic. Where the discipline is construed in naturalistic terms, as reposing on positive facts, the presuppositions, while including the "prior" sciences of mathematics and phenomenology, are constituted mainly

[1] Excellent surveys of specific points in connection with Peirce's logical work will be found in C. I. Lewis, *Survey of Symbolic Logic* (Berkeley, Calif., 1918), chap. I, sec. 7; and W. V. Quine's reviews of volumes 2, 3, and 4 of the *Collected Papers*, in *Isis: Quarterly Organ of the History of Science Society*, vol. XIX (1933), pp. 220-29; vol. XXII (1934), pp. 285-97, 551-53.

by a number of pre-logical or common-sense beliefs which are more
or less indubitable. In later years, logic is made to depend ultimately
on ethics and esthetics. The determination of the *summum bonum*
and the discovery of what man ought deliberately to admire *per se,*
become foundational parts of the science. Since I take this position
to be a consequence of Peirce's transcendentalism, I shall discuss it in
that context. The naturalistic presuppositions, however, must be noted
here.

It will be remembered that Peirce regards mathematics as the
practice of necessary reasoning, whereas logic presents the theory of
such reasoning. Without the former, logic would be bereft of at least
half its subject-matter. It would have no illustrations of "precise,
necessary reasoning" to study. In that sense, at least, the science of
mathematics must be one of logic's presuppositions. Phenomenology,
too, must have something to contribute, inasmuch as the categories
it discovers, if they are genuinely universal, will inevitably find exemplification in the pattern of human reasoning. Peirce relates that they
did indeed serve him as a key wherewith to "unlock many a secret"
in the domain of logic (1.352). Lest it be thought that he is contra-
dicting himself here, we may recall that the principle which phenomenology adopts in its search for the categories, viz., that there are
only three irreducible types of relations, is a principle established not
by logical but by mathematical inquiry. Both mathematics and
phenomenology are held to be wholly independent of the theory of
reasoning, as are esthetics and ethics. Even logic itself "must contrive,
by hook or by crook, to work out its own salvation without a full pre-
acquaintance with its own discoveries" (2.120).

In what was to have been part of the second chapter of the "Minute
Logic," Peirce discusses conversationally with the reader a group of
opinions which are "almost certainly" entertained by anyone desiring
to study logic. These amount to a set of common-sense beliefs presupposed by the science. "In the first place, you would not wish to
study logic unless you intended to reason; and you doubtless hold the
purpose of reasoning to be the ascertainment of the truth" (2.125).
The conviction that there is such a thing as truth, in the sense that
"something is so—is correct, or just—whether you, or I, or anybody
thinks it so or not" (2.135), is a basic assumption of all logical inquiry.
Some eminent thinkers have sought to advance *a priori* arguments
against this conviction, urging the inconceivability of any truth apart
from thought about it. But, as Peirce shows, it is equally easy to invent

a priori arguments in favor of that assumption. The upshot of the matter is that "all such *a priori* arguments, whether *pro* or *con,* about positive fact are rubbish. This question is a question of fact, and experience alone can settle it." (2.137) The verdict of experience, as expressed in our common-sense convictions, is that truth is not something which depends upon our own private thought-processes. That is to say, the ideally complete set of stable beliefs attained by scientific inquiry (which is what we mean by Truth with a capital "T") does not result from any inquiry which you or I singly may happen to conduct.

Closely allied to the above are the opinions that truth can be *known,* at least in part, and that such knowledge is the product of reasoning. But since reasoning is fallible and may lead us astray, what we must be concerned with as students of logic is to find the criteria by means of which *sound* reasoning may be discriminated from unsound. For the former is the only kind which can provide us with genuine knowledge. Our concern here reflects a further presupposition, namely, our belief that reasoning is superior to intuition or any other uncritical method of settling opinion (2.129). Finally, we have a nest of closely related assumptions appertaining to the effects which we hope the study of logic will have on our own reasoning. We feel certain that we *do* reason and are conscious of so doing; that we have a rudimentary theory of the process; that our theory is wrong, or at least gravely defective; and that we can improve it by inquiry into logic—an exercise which ought in turn to improve our *practice* of reasoning. It is thus fairly clear "that a variety of facts are already assumed when the logical question is first asked" (5.369).

No elaborate reinterpretation of these statements is required to enable us to see that they conform to the general pattern of inquiry Peirce has sketched. For example, the initial problem which sets logical investigation in motion arises from the failure of our reasoning to lead consistently to stable opinions, and the incapacity of our existing theory of reasoning to account for this failure. Furthermore, the inquiry only gets under way because we have already taken for granted a number of indubitable beliefs, which may therefore be thought of as forming its vague, "ultimate premisses." Such beliefs are themselves not immune from revision. But genuine doubt about them can arise only in the course of inquiry, not antecedent to it (cf. 3.432). As in his other references to this subject, Peirce makes no attempt to catalogue all the presuppositions of critical logic. He merely singles out those that are most important (cf. also 2.18; 3.433).

3. LOGIC AND PSYCHOLOGY

Another preliminary matter that must be cleared out of the way is the connection between logic and psychology. Peirce's attitude here is unequivocal. "My principles absolutely debar me from making the least use of psychology in logic" (5.157). He is consistently hostile to thinkers like Sigwart, and the German logicians generally, who persist in mixing up the two disciplines. "The psychological question is what processes the mind goes through. But the logical question is whether the conclusion that will be reached, by applying this or that maxim, will or will not accord with the *fact*." (5.85) In other words, *how* we think is the concern of a special science which tries to discover the laws exemplified in the ways men relate their ideas. What the conditions are which determine that the results of our thinking sometimes agree with the facts, and sometimes disagree, is the concern of logic. Psychology can therefore quite properly regard thinking as a "physiological operation" governed by strict causal laws. Logic has to examine it as an operation amenable to control and correction. Unless we were convinced that it is so amenable, we would never embark on logical inquiry at all.

Peirce realizes, however, that "formal logic must not be too purely formal; it must represent a fact of psychology, or else it is in danger of degenerating into a mathematical recreation" (2.710). We must never fall into the error of believing that a symbolic calculus can encompass the whole theory of reasoning. Take the process which we represent abstractly as a syllogistic argument. Does our mind actually go through such a process? If we are asking whether the conclusion as a separate item in consciousness (e.g., an image) suddenly displaces two other items (the premises) after the manner of a syllogism, the answer will probably be in the negative—though the whole issue is shrouded in doubt. "But it is a matter of constant experience, that if a man is made to believe in the premises, in the sense that he will act from them and will say that they are true, under favorable conditions he will also be ready to act from the conclusion and to say that it is true. Something, therefore, takes place within the organism which is equivalent to the syllogistic process." (5.268) Yet this something may consist of a great many different ways of passing from the premises to the conclusion, so that the logical form of the syllogism would not correspond to any single psychological process.

Another aspect of the question is this. That which determines us, from given premises, to draw one conclusion rather than another, "is some habit of mind, whether it be constitutional or acquired. The habit is good or otherwise, according as it produces true conclusions from true premises or not; and an inference is regarded as valid or not, without reference to the truth or falsity of its conclusions specially, but according as the habit which determines it is such as to produce true conclusions in general or not." (5.367) Hence it is quite possible for us to feel a psychological impulse to accept a given conclusion on the basis of certain premises, when logic would condemn such acceptance as unwarranted. This would illustrate a "bad" habit of reasoning. As a matter of fact, we have very few of these. If it were otherwise, we should not survive long in the world. Broadly speaking, then, "we do generally reason correctly by nature" (5.365), because experience has taught us more reliable than unreliable habits.

How far may we be said to have a "natural instinct" for right reasoning? Peirce has little fondness for this manner of speaking, since it suggests an inherited disposition, not susceptible to modification. "There is probably no special instinct—using this word in a sense in which it shall embrace traditional as well as inherited habits—for rationality" (2.160). For one of the most obvious features of instincts is "their persistence when all the lights of reason are against them, and this whether they are true inherited instincts or merely traditional" (*ibid.*). But our common-sense ideas about reasoning do not have this feature. They are easily changed as a consequence of the study of logic. We are corrigible in this respect; and even welcome having our erroneous opinions put right. All that we can admit, therefore, is a natural capacity for reflection, which appears early in life, and receives "a severe training by its conclusions being constantly brought into comparison with experiential results" (2.3). In this sense we may speak of a natural instinct for right reasoning, for we mean simply such thinking as the business of a man's daily life requires him to do— a process which springs up spontaneously under the pressure of circumstances. Moreover, we all develop an "instinctive theory of reasoning," a *logica utens* as the scholastics called it, which we become aware of as soon as our attention is drawn in any degree to our inner life (2.186). It is because of dissatisfaction with our *logica utens* that we turn to the scientific study of reasoning, and arrive at a *logica docens* (2.204).

As might be expected, Peirce makes a sharp distinction between the judgment and the proposition, identifying the former with a psychological process of assent, and excluding it from the purview of logic. He thinks that those logicians, chiefly from the camp of absolute idealism, who regard the analysis of judgments as their primary task are complicating matters quite gratuitously. Indeed, when they go on to define propositions in the light of the results of their analysis, they are accounting for what is essentially clear in terms of what is obscure. "To explain the proposition in terms of the 'judgment' is to explain the self-intelligible in terms of a psychical act, which is the most obscure of phenomena or facts" (2.309 n.). The one feature of the judgment which is reasonably patent is that it permits us to entertain or to accept a proposition. "The judger seeks to impress upon himself the truth of a proposition" (2.252). Or, if we like, "a judgment is an act of consciousness in which we recognize a belief" (2.435). Note that Peirce does not say that the judgmental act *asserts* a proposition. This is because he regards assertion as a characteristic of propositions (2.436; 3.446), and hence brings it within the fold of logic. The analysis of its nature belongs to that part of the science which Peirce calls "speculative grammar" (3.430-432). Only indirectly, by virtue of its function of enabling us to accept propositions, does judgment become allied to assertion (cf. 5.30). But the latter is a logical, whereas the former is a psychological affair.

4. THE MAIN STEPS IN EXPLICATIVE INFERENCE

We must next describe the main steps in explicative or deductive inference. Such inference, we must remember, is "the conscious and controlled adoption of a belief as a consequence of other knowledge" (2.442). The first step is to bring together certain propositions which we believe to be true, but which, if the inference is a new one, we have not hitherto thought of in combination. To designate this procedure, Peirce adopts the term *colligation,* which was coined by Whewell.[2] Thus in the simplest case we have separate propositions *A* and *B;* and we then colligate them into the premisses of an inference. This operation is not itself inferential. If it were, we should have to say that the first conclusion to be drawn from the separate propositions *A* and *B* is the conjunctive proposition "*A* and *B.*" It may seem like hair-splitting to break up the reasoning

All men are mortal
All patriarchs are men
∴ All patriarchs are mortal

[2]Cf. *Novum organon renovatum,* chap. ii, sec. 4.

into the four steps

> All men are mortal
> All patriarchs are men
> All men are mortal and all patriarchs are men
>
> ∴ All patriarchs are mortal.

Yet the formation of the argument clearly hinges on the bringing together of the premisses. "The mere 'colligation of the facts,' to use Whewell's term, is a most important and difficult part of that whole operation which in its totality is called *reasoning*" (2.469 n.). "It is plain that colligation is half the battle in ratiocination" (4.45).

But what about immediate inference? It seems to be a type of argument in which colligation can play no part since there is just one premiss. Peirce's answer to this is that immediate inference is not a process of *reasoning* in the most characteristic sense of that term. For in immediate inference "the state of things expressed in the premiss is the same as the state of things expressed in the conclusion, and only the form of expression is changed" (3.169); while in genuine reasoning the conclusion expresses something other than what is expressed in the premisses. In 1867 he went so far as to declare categorically that "conversions and contrapositions are not inferences" (2.496). By 1893, however, he was prepared to recognize them as "formal inferences," that is to say, procedures which show how certain abstract forms of argument are connected (2.496 n.). What we should say, then, is "that every complete and *material* (in opposition to merely *formal*) argument must have at least two premisses" (3.170). Hence, every such argument involves colligation.

The next step in the process of inference consists of observing the colligated premisses, and discovering some hitherto unnoticed relation embedded in them. This step is closely akin to what takes place in mathematical reasoning, and like such reasoning, requires the presence of diagrams. The cardinal difference between the two cases is that whereas in mathematics the diagrams themselves constitute the subject-matter of the science, in logic they are simply the means of representing certain objective and non-diagrammatic facts. The mathematician has, therefore, a greater degree of freedom in handling his special symbols, precisely because they are "a creation of conventions," in a sense in which logical symbols are not. For the latter have to be so constructed as to represent accurately the structure of the argument being investigated, and hence the construction cannot be a wholly conventional affair. The observation which takes place in both sciences, however, is essentially the same.

One rather important consequence of Peirce's stress on the observational factor in logic deserves mention here. He was impressed by the extent to which man's visual sense predominates over his other conscious activities, and makes spatial relations one of the easiest things to grasp. This fact, he thought, could be exploited in the interests of logic if spatial diagrams or "graphs" were utilized in analyzing logical facts. Euler's treatment of the syllogism by means of circles provided a precedent for this; so Peirce undertook towards the close of his career to extend the Eulerian technique to cover all explicative reasoning. The first fruit of his efforts was the system of "entitative graphs" formulated about 1897 (cf. 3.468-491; 4.434). It developed rapidly into his *"chef d'œuvre"*—the elaborate scheme of "existential graphs" completed in 1903 (cf. 4.394 ff.). I have no intention of tackling the thorny details of this subject. But some reference to its general import seems appropriate in the present context.

The fundamental feature of the system of graphs is its representation of logical relations "by such spatial relations that the necessary consequences of these logical relations are at the same time signified, or can, at least, be made evident by transforming the diagram in certain ways" (4.347). This method of representation has only one aim: to facilitate the analysis of inference into its ultimate components, to enable us to observe the transformation of the premises into the conclusion "by a series of steps, each of the utmost possible simplicity" (4.429). The graphical technique is superior to the algebraic, Peirce believes, because, being constructed on spatial lines, it permits familiar steps in inference to be readily discerned and paves the way for the detection of less obvious steps. Even more explicitly than the algebraic calculus, does the method of graphs free logic from psychological entanglements. For the necessity with which the conclusion follows from the premises in explicative reasoning is shown to be not primarily a compulsion due to the way our minds work, but rather "a relation between the *facts* represented in the premises and the facts represented in the conclusion" (4.353). If we recognize the essence of thinking to be the process of inference, we can truly say that existential graphs "put before us moving pictures of thought" (4.8).

It is important to be clear about the things the method does not profess to accomplish. (*a*) There is no suggestion that graphs prove the validity of explicative reasoning. This was the "rather ridiculous" view F. A. Lange came close to holding (cf. 4.354). The fact of the matter is that the reason Eulerian diagrams, for instance, accurately represent syllogism, lies in a certain identical relation which obtains among the parts of the diagram and also among the parts of the syllogism. "Thus, as far as logical dependence goes, the validity of the syllogism and the property of the Eulerian diagram depend upon a common principle. They are analogous phenomena neither of which is, properly speaking, the cause or principle of the other." (4.355) (*b*) While it is true that the study of the method of graphs, and constant practice with it, will help us to train our minds in the ways of accurate thinking, "still that consideration has not had any influence in determining the characters of the signs employed" (4.424). (*c*) The system is not intended to serve as a universal language or calculus of reasoning. That is to say, it does not present an apparatus by means of which conclusions may be reached and problems solved with greater facility than by the existing systems of expression. The function of the graphs is not to enable us to pass with security at one bound over a series of difficult inferential steps. On the contrary, the object is to dissect the operations of inference into as many distinct steps as possible. (*d*) Finally, although the graphs possess an inherent interest on their own account, "yet the system is not intended for a plaything, as logical algebra has sometimes been" (*ibid.*).

One can hardly avoid the conclusion that in the end Peirce permitted his graphs to become just such a "plaything." The fascination they exerted led to a steady increase in their internal complexity, without any corresponding increase in their positive results (cf. 4.526). Hence, the student who is accustomed to the algebraic analysis of logic finds it hard to share Peirce's enthusiasm for his *"chef d'œuvre."* Some of the virtues he claims for it, such as that it permits for the first time the proper treatment of logical possibility and modality (4.579 ff.), or that it can take into account the temporal element, which is not an "extra-logical" affair as traditional logicians have held, but of great importance for the science (cf. 4.523), are given scarcely any concrete embodiment. Quite apart from that, however, the system of graphs gives the impression of being an extraordinarily cumbersome instrument. This may not be an indigenous feature of it. Perhaps with further refinement it might become a more impressive technique than the algebraic method. But the fact remains that, as Peirce has formulated it, it seems far inferior to logical algebra. To say this is in no sense to deny the validity of his insight that all inference has an observational phase which requires the presence of signs.

Having colligated the premisses and observed the graphical representation of them, we reach the concluding phase of inference. This is the performing of an experiment on the graph. As in mathematics, the experiment may be a purely mental one, or it may involve the actual manipulating of the lines, dots, etc., of the diagram with pencil or pen. A very few such experiments—in many cases a single one—will suffice to convince us of the truth of a general proposition expressing a relationship displayed in the graph. "Hence, the mind is not only led from believing the premiss to judge the conclusion true, but it further attaches to this judgment another—that *every* proposition *like* the premiss . . . *would* involve, and compel acceptance of, a proposition related to it as the conclusion then drawn is related to that premiss" (2.444). In other words, we make the judgment that what we observe in the colligated data conforms to a rule. This is the third and final step in inference.

When the reasoning in question is non-syllogistic, we find, Peirce contends, that the third stage is analyzable into two parts, which he calls *iteration* and *erasure*. "We first duplicate portions of it [the graph]; and then we erase portions of it, that is, we put out of sight part of the assertion in order to see what the rest of it is. We observe the result of this experiment, and that is our deductive conclusion." (5.579) Since the initial phase of colligation is presupposed, we may say that "three things are all that enter into the experiment of any Deduction—Colligation, Iteration, Erasure" (*ibid.*).

Not all deductive inference, however, has these components. For, Peirce holds, in elementary forms such as ordinary syllogism the iterative phase is lacking. "There is but one conclusion of any consequence to be drawn by ordinary syllogism from given premisses" (*ibid.*). The process of drawing the conclusion is a purely mechanical one which can be performed equally well by a machine. The principle underlying ordinary syllogism is excessively simple, and a logical machine is an instrument which operates on just such a principle which it applies in manifold and complex ways (2.59). The failure to recognize non-syllogistic types of inference has misled some logicians into thinking that a logical machine might be constructed to draw *all possible* deductive conclusions. "But this conception is not borne out by relative logic" (3.641). In the logic of relatives there are conclusions of different orders, "depending upon how much iteration takes place"

(5.579); and it is only the human mind which can determine in a given case the degree of iteration applied. The logic of relatives, therefore, constitutes a domain in which no logical machine would be adequate. Since any accurate description of explicative inference must embrace both syllogistic and non-syllogistic forms, Peirce does not insist on including iteration and erasure in his account. He concludes, therefore, that the essential stages are "colligation, observation, and the judgment that what we observe in the colligated data follows a rule" (2.444).

5. THE VALIDITY OF EXPLICATIVE INFERENCE

The next topic we must consider is Peirce's account of the grounds of validity of explicative inference. After what we have observed him saying in connection with mathematical demonstration, we shall scarcely be surprised to find that he offers no consistent theory of logical validity. It is not merely that his naturalism and his transcendentalism yield different doctrines, but even within the former of these positions diverse views make their appearance. We shall limit our attention here to the discussions that fall within his naturalism, beginning with his arguments against the German logicians.

In the second chapter of his projected "Minute Logic," Peirce contrasts at some length the English and the German conceptions of logical validity. He reviews several arguments which the German logicians employ to show that the correctness of a piece of inference must in the last analysis be certified by an appeal to a "feeling of rationality" or *Rechtsgefühl* (cf. 2.154-174). The arguments as stated seem woefully inconclusive, and Peirce has little difficulty in showing their weakness. He thinks they reflect that "subjectivity" which is so marked a characteristic of the German mind (2.162). In certain disciplines like mathematics, this subjectivity does little harm. In logic, however, its effect is lamentable, for "it causes appeal to be made to feeling, to prejudice, instead of to fact, and blocks any real advance" (*ibid.*).

Consider, for example, the attempt of the Germans to establish their doctrine by appealing to the affinity of Logic, Esthetics, and Ethics. All three, it is urged, are normative sciences which aim at setting up rules that need not, but ought to be observed. Now in esthetics, the excellence of the norms consists exclusively in their conformity to the natural judgment of the cultivated mind. The ultimate source of standards in morals must likewise be the nature of the human soul, whether these standards be regarded as a dictate of reason, or as a statement of that which constitutes man's happiness, etc. But since rationality is intimately related to taste and morals, within the field of the normative sciences, its criteria must also spring from a subjective source.

Peirce's objection to this argument is that in affirming such a close similarity among the three normative disciplines, it mis-states the facts. For morality is far more objective than taste; and taste, morality, rationality form a true sequence in that order. "So that rationality ought according to the true analogy to be purely objective; taste being purely subjective, and morals half subjective, half objective" (2.156). This is in line with what the English logicians have urged. Their view is that logical validity depends on objective considerations, not on any feeling of rationality.

Another argument which Peirce singles out for criticism is the one advanced by Sigwart in his *Logik*. According to it, the question of what is sound logic and what unsound *must* ultimately be determined by feeling, since if any other criterion is employed its correctness has to be justified by reasoning, and in this reasoning, antecedent to the establishment of any rational criterion, we have to rely upon *Gefühl*. Peirce's reply here is as follows. (i) If the doctrine were true, there could be no such thing as sincere reasoning that was bad, and logic, as the criticism of arguments and the determination of the good from the bad, could have no basis at all. Furthermore, he adds, "my sincere argument that Sigwart is wholly in the wrong would be a decision from which there would be no appeal" (5.87). (ii) Sigwart declares that the making of an inference depends on a certain feeling of logical satisfaction connected with the process. But in fact, "I never know the inference will afford me any such satisfaction except by a subsequent reflection after I have already drawn it. It may be that on recognizing the satisfaction the inference gives me I shall consider that as an additional reason for believing in it. But this is *another* inference which in its turn will afford a new gratification if I stop to reflect about it." (*Ibid.*) At best, then, our native sense of logicality can be no more than a tolerably strong argument in favor of the soundness of an inference. For "although no doubt the sense of logicality carries men right in the main, yet it very frequently deceives them" (*ibid.*).

Peirce goes on to suggest that what the Germans have taken to be an instinctive feeling of rationality is in reality a set of *habits* of thinking which are the effect of evidence vaguely apprehended by us in the past. These habits lead us to anticipate the future, and to appraise arguments in an immediate, and seemingly intuitive manner. "I believe," he observes, "that our natural judgments as to what is reasonable are due to thinking over, ordinarily in a more or less confused way, what would happen. We imagine cases, place mental diagrams before our mind's eye, and multiply these cases, until a habit is formed of expecting that always to turn out the case, which has been seen to be the result in all the diagrams. To appeal to such a habit is a very different thing from appealing to any immediate instinct of rationality." (2.170) The habit in question obviously rests on certain observed facts which the diagrams symbolize. It may therefore be regarded as the product of a subconscious inference, i.e. an operation which would be inferential if it were fully conscious and deliberate. Such a phenomenon is clearly not to be confused with any indigenous logical sense. The upshot of this whole matter, which Peirce thinks "a momentous question for logic," is that no instinctive or intuitive criterion of validity can be admitted.

Some people have taken the view that the grounds of logical validity lie, not in any subjective source, but rather in the three traditional "laws of thought." Any argument which conforms to the principles of identity, contradiction, and excluded middle must therefore be formally correct. Thus, it has been maintained that the principle of identity is the necessary and sufficient condition of the validity of affirmative syllogisms; and that the two other principles constitute the additional necessary and sufficient conditions for the validity of negative syllogisms. Any rules governing other types of explicative inference can be logically reduced to some one, or all, of the laws of thought.

Peirce's dissent from this view takes two forms: (1) he demonstrates that the validity of syllogistic reasoning depends not upon the laws of thought but upon quite different considerations; and (2) he contends that the principles of identity, contradiction, and excluded middle are in reality definitions of the meaning of "is" and "not" as used in logical discourse.

1. In a very lucid essay entitled "The Critic of Arguments," which appeared in the *Open Court* during 1892, Peirce demolishes the doctrine that syllogism presupposes the laws of thought as a condition of its validity. He shows that the one mood of universal affirmative syllogism, *Barbara*, depends not upon the principle of identity, but upon the fact that the relation expressed by the copula is *transitive*. The

form of an argument in *Barbara* is:

> Every *M* is *P*
> Every *S* is *M*
> ∴ Every *S* is *P*.

Now if we supplant the term *is* by *loves*, we get:

> Every *M* loves *P*
> Every *S* loves *M*
> ∴ Every *S* loves *P*.

"That this should be universally true, it is necessary that every lover should love what his beloved loves. A relation of which the like is true is called a *transitive* relation. Accordingly, the condition of the validity of *Barbara* is that the relation expressed by the copula should be a transitive relation." (3.408) The analogue of the principle of identity in the above example is that everybody loves himself. But plainly, the truth of this principle would not suffice to make the inference valid; nor would its falsity destroy the validity of the inference provided *loves* is a transitive relation. Consequently, the principle of identity is neither a necessary nor a sufficient condition of the truth of universal affirmative syllogisms.

Peirce goes on to prove that negative syllogisms likewise do not depend in any special way on the laws of thought. He makes his point by examining several of the simpler varieties, and showing wherein their validity consists. Thus, he takes the mood *Celarent* which can be formulated as follows:

> Every *M* is not *P*
> Every *S* is *M*
> ∴ Every *S* is not *P*.

Now the first thing to observe here is that the only relevant property of the negative is that of expressing a relation. For if we put, say, *injures* in the place of *is not*, we obtain

> Every *M* injures *P*
> Every *S* is *M*
> ∴ Every *S* injures *P*,

which is a perfectly valid inference, irrespective of the kind of relation *injuring* is. What about the property of the copula? Let us substitute *loves* for *is* in the minor premiss, so that we get

> Every *M* injures *P*
> Every *S* loves *M*
> ∴ Every *S* injures *P*.

If this is to be valid (still without reference to the kind of relation *injuring* is) it can only be on the principle that nobody loves anyone but himself. In other words, the relation expressed in the minor premiss must be reflexive, or as Peirce calls it, a *sibi-relation* (3.409). That alone is the condition of the validity of *Celarent*. And it is not a condition stated by the laws of thought.

Consider next the negative syllogism *Cesare* which has the form:

> Every *P* is not *M*
> Every *S* is *M*
> . ·. Every *S* is not *P*.

Substituting *fights* for *is not* we have:

> Every *P* fights *M*
> Every *S* is *M*
> . ·. Every *S* fights *P*.

This inference holds (i) because the fighting is with *every* member of the class fought, and (ii) because the relation expressed by *fights* implies its own converse, so that everything must fight whatever fights it. That is to say, (i) affirms that the predicate of any negative proposition is distributed, and (ii) affirms that the relation expressed by a universal negative proposition is symmetrical. The latter may be regarded as the analogue of the principle of contradiction; but it is clearly not identical in content with that principle.

"We see, then, that the principles of universal syllogism of the ordinary sort are that the copula expresses a *sibi-relation*, not that it expresses an agreement, which is what the principle of identity states, and that the negative is its own converse, which is the law of contradiction" (3.412). It follows from this that the laws of thought cannot be regarded as the three co-ordinate and sufficient laws of all reasoning (2.595).

2. Peirce does not suggest, of course, that the principles of identity, contradiction, and excluded middle have *no* bearing on the validity of inference. He takes the position that the principles are analytical or explicative propositions, concerned exclusively with symbols, not with real things (2.315). What they do is to define the meaning of the copula and the term *not*, i.e. they explain what kind of relation "is" and "is not" designate. In order to demonstrate that the laws of thought are thus really definitions, Peirce examines each of them successively.

The law of identity is customarily stated as "A is A." This formula does not, it is true, exhaustively define the meaning of the copula, but it does delimit the possibilities of interpretation. For instance, if we interpret "is" in a non-existential sense, "then the meaning of the formula is that no universal affirmative proposition having the same term as subject and predicate is false" (2.594). Or alternatively, the law of identity states "that the relation of subject to predicate is a elation which every term bears to itself" (3.407). If the copula be taken to imply existence, the meaning is either that no universal affirmative proposition is false in which the same term is both subject and predicate, provided that the term denotes any existing object, or that no universal affirmative proposition is false in which the subject and predicate are the same proper name of an individual. Now the exact meaning of the copula must in substance involve one or other of the above interpretations; "so that in any case the principle of identity is merely a part of the definition of the copula" (2.594).

The law of contradiction is traditionally given as "*A* is *B* and *A* is not *B* cannot both be true." Peirce re-construes this more briefly as "*A* is not not-*A*." This formula might be taken in three different senses:

first, that any term is in the relation of negation to whatever term is in that relation to it, which is as much as to say that the relation of negation is its own converse; second, that no term is in the relation of negation to itself; third, that every term is in the relation of negation to everything but itself. But the first meaning is the best, since from it the other two readily follow as corollaries (3.407).

The usual version of the principle of excluded middle is: "Everything is either *A* or not-*A*." To give this a form parallel to that of the law of contradiction, Peirce re-states it as "Not not-*A* is *A*." Here also there are three possible interpretations:

first, that every term, *A,* is predicable of anything that is in the relation of negation to a term which is in the same relation to it, *A;* second, that the objects of which any term, *A,* is predicable together with those of which the negative of *A* is predicable together make up all the objects possible; third, that every term, *A,* is predicable of whatever is in the relation of negation to everything but *A.* But, as before, the first meaning is to be preferred, since from it the others are immediately deducible. (*Ibid.*)

Peirce summarizes the defining role of the last two laws in the following way. He formulates them in quasi-Boolean terms, so that the law of contradiction reads: "Whatever is both *A* and non-*A* is nothing," and the law of excluded middle reads: "Everything is either *A* or non-*A*." Then he supposes a division of all ordered pairs of individuals in the universe into those having the form *A:A,* and those having the form *A:B.* In the light of this division, the meaning of the two laws can be accurately specified. "The principle of contradiction excludes from the relation 'not' all [pairs] of the form $A:A$. The principle of excluded middle makes the relation of 'not' to include all pairs of the form $A:B$." (2.598) Taken together, therefore, the principles define important logical features of negation.

Having made it clear that for Peirce the validity of explicative inference depends neither on an innate "logical sense" nor upon the traditional laws of thought, we must now proceed to his own positive views. As has already been remarked, these do not constitute one consistent doctrine. There seem, in fact, to be three different positions struggling for expression in his thought. They may be called (1) the *genetical*, (2) the *factual*, and (3) the *formal* accounts of logical validity. Actually, (1) and (3) receive much less emphasis than (2). But we must glance briefly at each of them in turn.[3]

1. An essential component of Peirce's naturalism is his evolutionary conception of man. Not only have men arisen from more primitive biological forms, but human knowledge has had a correlative development. It is therefore theoretically possible to write a natural history of knowledge, one chapter of which would embrace the evolution of logic as a type of human activity. Such a genetical account of the subject is implicit in Peirce's theory of inquiry. For, as we have noted, rational thought is held to have arisen in the course of the human animal's struggle to escape from a state of doubt and re-establish stable belief. Certain procedures of thinking prove themselves efficacious in this struggle, are repeated until they become fixed habits, and are eventually formulated by the logician as the principles of inference. The latter can accordingly be described as the result of the experience undergone by the race in the course of its evolution.

Now Peirce is usually scrupulous in separating the question of the genesis of logical principles from the question of their validity. Thus, in his review of Dewey's *Studies in Logical Theory*[4] he notes that the aim of the book seems to be the outlining of "a natural history of thought," which, if it can be worked out, "will undoubtedly form valuable knowledge." But to call such a natural history "logic" is, he says, "a suspicious beginning." It creates a misleading impression that the enterprise can give us a basis for differentiating sound from unsound reasoning. We know, however, that such a basis must consist of

[3] I am particularly indebted here to Justus Buchler's discussion in *Charles Peirce's Empiricism* (New York and London, 1939), pp. 192-200.

[4] *Nation*, vol. LXXIX (1904), p. 220.

normative principles; and normative principles cannot be obtained from a purely historical discipline. It follows that logic as the science of valid inference must never be confused with a genetic survey of thought.

Yet at times Peirce comes very close to accepting the doctrine which he here condemns. Some of his remarks suggest that the maxims of reasoning are logically sound *because* they have developed in the course of evolution as successful ways of establishing belief. Herein lies their power of compelling "catholic consent" in the long run (cf. 3.161). That is to say, certain forms of inference like syllogism must be accepted as valid (*a*) because they represent habits of thinking which have enabled men to arrive at stable beliefs, and (*b*) because they have won, or will in future win, universal acceptance. It should be added, in fairness to Peirce, that nowhere does he espouse the genetical doctrine in quite so bald a form as this. But he does occasionally use language which suggests implicit adherence to it.

2. A view advanced in the *Collected Papers* more frequently and explicitly than the above is the one Peirce attributes to "the English logicians." These thinkers hold that the validity of inference depends not upon any genetical considerations but upon the truth of the propositions which constitute the inference. Thus a deductive argument from premisses A and B to conclusion C is valid if, and only if, it is the case that C is *always* true when A and B are true. Likewise, if C is true on *most* of the occasions when A and B are true, the argument is sound as an induction. This doctrine recognizes that "every reasoning holds out some expectation. Either, for example, it professes to be such that if the premisses are true the conclusion will always be true, or to be such that the conclusion will usually be true if the premisses are true . . . or to make some other such promise. If the facts bear out that promise, then, say the English, the reasoning is good. But if the facts violate the promise, the reasoning is bad, no matter how deliberately human reason may have approved of it." (2.153) The science of logic is therefore an objective or positive inquiry which aims at discovering whether the facts necessarily accord with the professions of this or that inference. And the validity of a given inference will consist wholly in the presence of such an accord—not in any psychological appeal it may happen to have, or in its success as a means of fixing belief.

Peirce repeatedly affirms his allegiance to the English doctrine. A typical statement is the following, made in 1903. "Our inference is

valid if and only if there really is such a relation between the state of
things supposed in the premises and the state of things stated in the
conclusion. Whether this really be so or not is a question of reality,
and has nothing at all to do with how we may be inclined to think. . . .
If the entire human race were unable to see the connection, the argument would be none the less sound, although it would not be humanly
clear." (5.161)   For the English logicians, then, the central task is to
classify arguments into good and bad on the basis of the factual relations concerned.

How is logic able to progress with this task? By reason of two
things, declares Peirce. (i) Every inference is thought of, at the time
it is drawn, as one of a possible *class* of inferences (2.444); and (ii)
every such class is constituted in accordance with a rule which Peirce
calls its *leading principle* (3.164, etc.). When we reason, we are cognizant, however dimly, of proceeding in terms of a general rule (or
habit) which is applicable to all other reasonings of that type. The
investigation of the role of leading principles becomes, therefore, a
matter of prime importance for logic.

It is a mark of Peirce's insight that he addressed himself to this
question in one of his earliest papers. The opening paragraphs of the
essay "On the Natural Classification of Arguments" (1867) point out
that in every inference there is involved, besides the premises and the
conclusion, a judgment that if *such* propositions as the premises are,
are true, then a proposition related to them as the conclusion is, is true.
"The principle implied in this judgment, respecting a genus of argument, is termed the leading principle" (2.462). For instance, in the
syllogism

> Every man is mortal
> Enoch is a man
> . ·. Enoch is mortal

the leading principle is "If every *A* is *B* and *C* is *A* then *C* is *B*." Suppose the principle to be designated by *L,* and the premises and conclusion by *P* and *C* respectively. The reasoning may now be fully
expressed as

> *L* and *P*
> . ·. *C.*

But this is a new argument which must also have its leading principle,
L'; and so on. Hence, just as we cannot have an inference without
premises, so we cannot have an inference without a leading principle.

In his article on this subject in J. M. Baldwin's *Dictionary of Philo-*

sophy and Psychology (1902), Peirce distinguishes two classes of leading principles, *material* and *formal* (or *logical*). These may be illustrated very simply as follows. The conjunction of propositions

Enoch is a man

∴ Enoch is mortal

does not produce a necessary inference. But if we add its leading principle, "Every man is mortal," and assume this to be true, then the inference becomes necessary. As such, it has in turn the leading principle, *L*, which we have noted above. Now the statement "Every man is mortal" is called by Peirce a *material* leading principle, whereas "If every *A* is *B* and *C* is *A* then *C* is *B*" is a *formal* or *logical* leading principle. The difference between them is that the truth of the former is not implied in the premisses, while the truth of the latter is so implied. To illustrate the difference we need only construe the leading principle of the argument

Every man is mortal
Enoch is a man

∴ Enoch is mortal

intensionally as *nota notae est nota rei ipsius,* and record the result in a new argument

Nota notae est nota rei ipsius
Mortality is a mark of humanity which is a mark of Enoch

∴ Mortality is a mark of Enoch.

Here, the very same principle of the *nota notae* operates as a leading principle in terms of which the conclusion is drawn, "so that the last state of the argument is no more complete than the last but one" (3.166). We are consequently able to avoid an infinite regress in our analysis because the leading principle of the last argument is contained in its very premisses (2.466). Such is not the case, however, with a material leading principle.

What bearing has this on the question of validity? Unfortunately, Peirce leaves the issue in an unsettled state. The view which appears to be most in harmony with his factual criterion is that "a *valid* argument is one whose leading principle is true" (2.463), or, more precisely, one in which both premisses and leading principle are true (2.464). The attributing of truth to leading principles seems to presume (*a*) that they are genuine propositions, (*b*) that they assert observed facts of necessary connection between premisses of a certain kind and conclusions of a certain kind, and (*c*) that as principles of explicative reasoning they are themselves universal and necessary. Yet none of these points receive sufficient discussion, and often things are said which seem to controvert them.

3. It is in connection with other characterizations of leading principles that Peirce's *formal* conception of validity emerges. We may approach this by way of a comment which he made in a paper of 1893. He there speaks of leading principles not as true, but as "satisfactory." A satisfactory leading principle is one that "can only lead either from a false premiss or to a true conclusion . . . and whether it leads from false to false, from true to true, or from false to true, it is equally satisfactory" (4.69). Conversely, it will be unsatisfactory or "bad" if it leads from a true premiss to a false conclusion. For then the reasoner will be systematically misled, and "the whole purpose of logic" is to prevent just this (2.448). Peirce clearly has in mind here the familiar "extensional" definition of implication, according to which "if *p* then *q*" holds except where *p* is true and *q* false. An argument such as

> Every man has four legs
> Every giraffe is a man   (*p*)
>
> ∴ Every giraffe has four legs   (*q*)

is perfectly valid, despite the falsity of the premisses (*p*), since (*p*) does entail the conclusion (*q*). It is therefore not the case that a valid argument must have true premisses. If it be urged that at least the leading principle must be true, the reply can be made that if so, the word "true" means something quite different from what it means when applied to the conclusion. Hence the suggestion that the leading principle is better described as "satisfactory."

From the point of view of material content, then, a leading principle must be regarded as purely formal or "empty." It adds nothing to the premisses of the argument it governs because it makes no reference to matters of fact (3.168). Leading principles are, indeed, not genuine propositions, or at least are not genuine assertions. For "any assertion means merely how we would act under given circumstances," whereas a logical principle "means only what we would infer from certain premisses" (2.467 n.). Accordingly, "logical principles are merely rules for the illative transformation of the symbols of the particular system employed. If the system is essentially changed, they will be quite different." (2.599) Now a rule is not appropriately spoken of as "true" or "false." It is accepted or rejected, obeyed or violated. The only possible sense in which the word "true" could be applied to it would be "*supposed true* in order to sustain the logical validity of any argument" (3.168; italics mine). But this is tantamount to saying that logical principles are simply "truths by convention."

The conventional element in Peirce's logical theory appears most clearly at two points in his writing, in some of the early logico-mathematical papers and in the later work on existential graphs. Thus, in the essay of 1867, "Upon the Logic of Mathematics," he remarks apropos of the indemonstrability of logical principles, that if we consider them as "speculative truths" they are "absolutely empty and indistinguishable" (3.41). The sole thing they enunciate is the rules or maxims of inference. A similar conception arises in a paper of 1903 where he is dealing with the construction of a logical calculus.

We frame a system of expressing propositions—a written language—having a syntax to which there are absolutely no exceptions. We then satisfy ourselves that whenever a proposition having a certain syntactical form is true, another proposition definitely related to it—so that the relation can be defined in terms of the appearance of the two propositions on paper—will necessarily also be true. We draw up our code of basic rules of such illative transformations, none of these rules being a necessary consequence of others. We then proceed to express in our language the premisses of long and difficult mathematical demonstrations and try whether our rules will bring out their conclusions. (4.481)

The kinship between this view and the one advocated in our day by logicians such as Carnap[5] is apparent at a glance.

Peirce's "conventionalism," however, remains an inchoate side of his logic. He was far more interested in connecting leading principles with habits of thought than with linguistic or symbolic rules. This connection has two distinct aspects. (i) A leading principle may be regarded as the *active determination* or habit "within us" to draw a conclusion q from a certain premiss p. Whether the habit be constitutional or acquired is of no importance to logic (5.367). "The habit is logically good provided it would never (or in the case of a probable inference, seldom) lead from a true premiss to a false conclusion; otherwise it is logically bad" (3.163). (ii) A leading principle may be considered as the *articulation* of such a habit in a proposition which shall state that every proposition q, related in a given general way to any true proposition p, is true. It is the precise status of leading principles in this second sense—whether they are to be regarded as truths or merely as conventional maxims—that Peirce leaves unclarified.

[5]E.g. in his *Logical Syntax of Language* (London, 1937).

A more satisfactory result might have been reached had Peirce recognized that the meaning of "if p then q" required for explicative reasoning is not that of "material implication" but that of "entailment." As we have seen, he consistently interprets "if p then q" in the material sense to mean "either p is false or q is true."[6] But when, for instance, p stands for the premisses of a syllogism in *Barbara* and q stands for the conclusion, "if p then q" means that q "follows from" p, or that q is "deducible from" p. This relation between p and q is the one called "entailment"; and the inference *qua* explicative involves no reference to the truth or falsity of its constituent propositions. It is, moreover, a *necessary* inference precisely because a further proposition (the leading principle), which states that "p entails q," holds.

Now if we call this proposition an "entailment-statement," the question arises whether it "holds" in the sense of being (a) contingently true, or (b) necessarily true, or (c) accepted as a convention of linguistic usage.[7] Without presuming to settle the issue in a few lines, I may say that alternative (b) seems to me the only one capable of yielding an adequate account of logical validity. Hence, if logic rests on positive observations, as Peirce insists, we must literally "see" that the facts of entailment have to be formulated in entailment-statements that are necessarily true. We *know* this with certainty because of the evidence. The appeal to "logical evidence" at the formal level appears to be a *sine qua non* of rational thought.[8]

On the face of it this doctrine may seem wholly alien to Peirce's

[6]Peirce was, of course, familiar with other possible interpretations of the conditional. Thus, he mentions (3.441 ff.) the ancient dispute between Diodorus and Philo, in which the latter affirms while the former denies that "either not-p or q" expresses what is usually meant by "if p then q" (cf. M. Hurst, "Implication in the Fourth Century B.C.," *Mind*, n.s., vol. XLIV (1935), pp. 484-95). Although he subscribes to the Philonian view, Peirce is willing to admit that if the Diodoran were somewhat modified "it might prove the preferable one" (3.443).

[7]An interesting recent discussion of this question can be found in W. Körner, "On Entailment," *Proceedings of the Aristotelian Society*, n.s., vol. XLVII (1946-47), pp. 143-62; and in P. F. Strawson, "Necessary Propositions and Entailment Statements," *Mind*, n.s., vol. LVII (1948), pp. 184-200.

[8]Hans Reichenbach has made this point convincingly in his *Elements of Symbolic Logic* (New York, 1947), p. 184. Peirce himself seems to hint at something like this doctrine in a fragment of 1897 where he is discussing the process of "abstractive observation" employed in the study of signs. By this process we can reach "the truths which *must* hold good of all signs used by a scientific intelligence" (2.227). The contrast here is with the special sciences which merely concern themselves with what obtains contingently in the actual world. Logic as the science of signs has, therefore, a mode of observation which enables it to discover necessary formal relationships.

way of thinking. Yet I believe he might have espoused it without
being obliged to modify his theory of inference very drastically.
For the appeal to logical evidence is not an appeal to a subjective
Rechtsgefühl; nor is it necessarily incompatible with a naturalistic
conception of logic. We have seen that he was unable to avoid introducing a special "intuition" to account for the apodictic nature of
mathematical demonstration. But this could have been dispensed with
had he coupled the doctrine of logical evidence with the view that
mathematics has its roots in logic.

6. EXPLICATIVE INFERENCE AS ANALYTIC, DEDUCTIVE, AND NECESSARY

We may now pull together the threads of Peirce's discussion by
noting certain features of his characterization of explicative inference
as "analytic," "deductive," and "necessary." Although his use of these
expressions is by no means uniform, it provides some basis for a review
of essential points.

In general Peirce seems to employ "analytic" as a synonym for
"explicative" when he is thinking of this kind of inference in relation
to its contrary opposite, viz., synthetic or ampliative inference. All
arguments can be put into one or the other of these two classes
(2.680). The term "analytic" serves to indicate that in arguments of
the first class the conclusion is derived from an examination of the
premises, and elicits a hitherto unobserved relation contained in
them.[9] This type of inference is an extremely useful means of setting
our beliefs in order (5.392). But it in no way adds to our knowledge
of the real world. For such an addition we must turn to synthetic
inference, where "the facts summed up in the conclusion are not among
those stated in the premises" (2.680). Both kinds of reasoning depend
on observation. What "analytic" emphasizes is that in explicative reasoning our observation is directed upon that which has already been
affirmed or postulated by us, not upon extraneous data.

The word "deductive," on the other hand, often appears in places

[9]Peirce is insistent that his use of "analytic" has nothing in common with
Kant's use of the term. "What Kant calls an explicative, or analytical, judgment
is either no judgment at all, because void of content (to use his phrase), or else
it sets forth distinctly in the predicate what was only indistinctly thought (that is,
not actually thought at all) in the subject. In that case, it is really synthetic, and
rests on experience; only the experience on which it rests is mere internal experience—experience of our own imaginations." (2.451 n.) Hence, in Kant's
sense there is no such thing for Peirce as "analytic" inference (cf. 3.641).

where Peirce wishes to contrast explicative inference with the two subclasses of ampliative inference, viz., induction and abduction. These "three grand varieties" of reasoning have quite separate aims. Deductive inference is exclusively concerned with drawing the logical consequences of a hypothesis or set of hypotheses. Induction subjects the consequences to experimental test. Abduction generates the hypothesis in the first place as an explanation of certain facts. Each process is an important phase of the total pattern of inquiry. But deductive reasoning differs from the other two in being occupied with what is logically possible or impossible rather than with what is actual.

Explicative inference is spoken of as "necessary" to underline the fact that its conclusion *invariably* follows from the premises, and *must* so follow on pain of contradiction. The contrast here is with cases where the conclusion *may*, but need not, follow, i.e. with probable inference. Unfortunately, Peirce creates some confusion by talking about "probable deduction" as something to be differentiated from "necessary deduction" (cf. 2.267). We shall have to discuss this matter when we have examined Peirce's theory of probability. For the present it will be enough to remark that "probable deduction" sometimes signifies explicative inference, the propositions of which are about probability-relations, and sometimes a kind of ampliative or quasi-ampliative inference. In the former case the conclusions are just as "necessary" as in syllogism; so that "statistical deduction" (an expression that Peirce does often adopt) seems a more accurate designation.

A word may be said in conclusion about the relative importance which Peirce attaches to syllogism within the domain of explicative reasoning. Traditionally, of course, it was regarded as coextensive with that domain. Peirce's familiarity with the logic of relatives enabled him to avoid this mistaken notion. Yet he held that we can easily go to the other extreme and underrate the significance of syllogistic inference, "as many have done" (2.445). The fact seems to be that taken in a wide sense it represents one, but not perhaps the best, form in which necessary reasoning can be expressed (2.664). Furthermore, syllogism has a peculiar primacy because it exhibits an elementary feature of the relation of inclusion, viz., transitivity, by virtue of which whatever is included in something included in anything is itself included in that thing. "We thus get *Barbara* as the primitive type of inference" (2.710). Even if the universe were so fluid that nothing retained its individual identity long enough to be measured, yet, provided one portion remained enclosed within a second itself enclosed within a third, "a syllogism would be possible" (2.696). Critical logic could therefore operate in such a universe, though in a very elementary way.

B. GENERAL SEMIOTIC

7. LOGIC AND THE THEORY OF SIGNS

The view that logic should be conceived more broadly than as a criticism of arguments was first adumbrated by Peirce in his paper "On a New List of Categories" (1867). He had by this time proceeded from an intensive study of Kant to the works of the British Empiricists, Aristotle, and certain scholastic thinkers, notably Duns Scotus and William of Ockham (1.560). As a result, he found his early interest in symbolism strongly reinforced. Like Aristotle, he saw that symbols are the medium through which the rationality in the universe must be expressed and communicated. "The woof and warp of all thought and all research is symbols, and the life of thought and science is the life inherent in symbols; so that it is wrong to say that a good language is *important* to good thought, merely; for it is of the essence of it" (2.220). The subject-matter dealt with by the logician ought, therefore, "to embrace all the necessary principles of semeiotic" (4.9).

Once this extension of logic is made, an enormously complex body of facts comes into view. Prior to Peirce's day, these facts had never been systematically investigated, and he was thus forced to become the founder of a new discipline. "I am, as far as I know," he remarks, "a pioneer, or rather a backwoodsman, in the work of clearing and opening up what I call *semiotic,* that is, the doctrine of the essential nature and fundamental varieties of possible semiosis; and I find the field too vast, the labour too great, for a first-comer" (5.488). The difficulties of the task are reflected in the piecemeal, not to say obscure, character of much of his writing on the subject. Yet much of it is also both subtle and profound. Few initiators of a science have discerned its main features so accurately, or said as many important things about it.

My purpose is not to present an exhaustive account of Peirce's doctrine of signs. That would require a complete book in itself. I shall merely sketch the theory in outline, with such details as seem to cast further light on his theory of inquiry. General semiotic, we shall discover, brings into a striking focus many of his most characteristic ideas.

8. THE BRANCHES OF SEMIOTIC

To place the discussion in its proper setting, we may note first the major branches of logic conceived in this wider sense. They are, Peirce holds, (a) *Speculative Grammar* (also called "formal grammar," "pure grammar," "stecheotic," or "stoicheology"); (b) *Critical Logic* (also called "obsistent logic," "critic," or simply "logic"); and (c) *Methodeutic* (also called "speculative rhetoric," "formal rhetoric," "pure rhetoric," or "transuasional logic"). Precisely what is included in each of these divisions never appears with full clarity. Nor are their interrelations explored in any detailed manner. Broadly speaking, Speculative Grammar embraces the classification of signs, the analysis of their nature as signs, and the determination of the formal conditions which govern their *meaning* (1.191; 2.93). Critical Logic classifies, analyzes, and estimates the validity of one particular variety of sign, viz., arguments. Methodeutic "studies the methods that ought to be pursued in the investigation, in the exposition, and in the application of truth" (1.191). Each division depends on the findings of the one that precedes it, with Speculative Grammar drawing certain principles from Phenomenology.

Two comments may be made about this scheme. In the first place there is a slight doubt whether Peirce intended it to encompass *all* signs whatsoever, or merely that important subclass which he customarily referred to as "symbols." Thus, a typical pair of statements, one made in 1867 and the other in 1906, declare for the latter alternative (cf. 1.559; 4.9). Elsewhere (e.g., 1.191; 2.93), it is perfectly plain that the former alternative is adopted. Some of this ambiguity is undoubtedly due to his use, especially in early papers, of "symbol" as the equivalent of "sign." However, the pronouncement of 1906 explicitly affirms that Stecheotic, Critic, and Methodeutic are divisions within the "logic of symbols," not within the logic of "icons" or of "indices" (4.9).

The ambiguity here is not unconnected with a second point. Peirce holds that semiotic is the science of the *"necessary laws* of signs" (2.93; italics mine). Now such laws can only be those embodied in the *actual use* of signs in human thought and discourse. But in that case, symbols are the type of sign required. They constitute the sole vehicle of inference and communication. This was virtually admitted by Peirce when he remarked in 1867 that the laws of logic "hold good of any symbols, of those that are written and spoken as well as of those which are thought. They have no immediate application to likenesses or indices, because no arguments can be constructed of these alone, but do apply to all symbols." (1.559) Precisely how the "necessity" of such laws is to be established we have already discussed sufficiently. I think it is fair to say that if Peirce fails to give a satisfactory account of the necessity involved in explicative inference, he leaves us still more in the dark as to how that characteristic can attach to "the principles of semeiotic."

9. THE CLASSIFICATION OF SIGNS

In the remaining part of this chapter the salient features of Speculative Grammar will be reviewed. Its primary task is to formulate a working definition of a sign, and then to classify the major types of signs under suitable headings. An important principle is provided at the outset by Phenomenology. This science has shown that all phenomena whatsoever possess three aspects, specifiable under the categories of Firstness, Secondness, and Thirdness. We must therefore expect that signs will exhibit a large number of triadic properties, and subsequent investigation proves this to be the case. Thus, wherever we observe a sign, or *representamen* (in his early papers Peirce speaks of "representation"), we have "something which stands to somebody for something in some respect or capacity" (2.228). It is the subject of a triadic relation, involving the *sign* itself (e.g., a physical object, image, quality, thought, etc.), what the sign stands for (its *object*), and the equivalent sign or *interpretant* which the first sign creates in the mind of the person apprehending it. This second sign is the representation "to which the torch of truth is handed along." As such, it has *its* interpretant in turn; "and so on *ad infinitum*" (2.303). The most generalized form of this infinite series is identical with the on-going process of scientific thought.

The triadic character of every symbolic situation led Peirce to distinguish three divisions of signs: (1) the sign in itself, (2) the sign in relation to its object, and (3) the sign in relation to its interpretant (2.243). Since each of these is subject to the three categories, we obtain on further analysis the following trichotomies. Under (1) there occur the *Qualisign, Sinsign,* and *Legisign;* under (2) the *Icon, Index,* and *Symbol;* under (3) the *Rheme, Dicisign* or *Dicent Sign,* and *Argument* (2.244-252). While these are Peirce's most common designations, other names are occasionally used, with the result that one can never be sure whether some new facet of semiotic is being discriminated or whether an old aspect is simply being given a new label.

For our purpose, however, the above designations will be adequate.

By bringing another principle of phenomenology to bear on the three trichotomies, Peirce was able to divide all signs into ten *classes*. The principle in question is that whatever is a First determines only a First; whatever is a Second determines a Second or (degenerately) a First; and whatever is a Third determines a Third or (degenerately) a Second or a First (2.235). This yields the following scheme:

   (i) *First determining a First:* a Qualisign (e.g. any sensory quality such as "red").

  (ii) *Second determining a First:* an Iconic Sinsign (e.g. an individual diagram).

 (iii) *Second determining a First:* a Rhematic Indexical Sinsign (e.g. a spontaneous cry).

 (iv) *Second determining a Second:* a Dicent Sinsign (e.g. a weather-cock).

  (v) *Third determining a First:* an Iconic Legisign (e.g. a diagram apart from its factual individuality).

 (vi) *Third determining a First:* a Rhematic Symbol (e.g. a common noun).

(vii) *Third determining a Second:* a Rhematic Indexical Legisign (e.g. a demonstrative pronoun).

(viii) *Third determining a Second:* a Dicent Indexical Legisign (e.g. a street cry).

 (ix) *Third determining a Second:* a Dicent Symbol (e.g. an ordinary proposition).

  (x) *Third determining a Third:* an Argument (e.g. ordinary syllogism).

Peirce does very little more than list the above classes and make a few comments on the outstanding features of each. But the scheme as a whole shows how sensitive he was to the complexities of the semiotic process.

As he pursued his reflections, this sensitiveness increased rather than diminished. Thus, about 1906 he discovered that instead of just three trichotomies and ten classes of signs, there are in fact ten trichotomies and sixty-six classes of signs. Indeed, if we make the assumption (admittedly most improbable) that the ten trichotomies are wholly independent of one another, a theoretical total of 59,049 classes of signs can be derived (cf. 1.291)! These late developments were never worked out in detail by Peirce. They are dealt with most fully in his correspondence with Lady Welby, though even here the discussion is mainly concerned with the principles in the light of which the sixty-six classes of signs are differentiated.[10] These principles are not at all difficult to follow, as may be seen from a recent lucid exposition of them.[11] We shall not stop to examine them, however, but will turn instead to the more carefully elaborated scheme of the three trichotomies.

10. THE THREE TRICHOTOMIES OF SIGNS

Qualisigns, sinsigns, and legisigns. When we concentrate our attention on the nature of a sign in itself, quite apart from its object or interpretant, we find that it may be of three sorts. (*a*) It may be a sheer quality or appearance, in which case Peirce refers to it as a Qualisign or Tone (2.244; 4.537). A qualisign cannot operate symbolically, of course, until it is embodied; but this does not affect its character as a sign. (*b*) A sign may be an individual object or event. As such it is entitled a Sinsign or Token. Since it can only manifest itself through its qualities, it presupposes a qualisign, or more accurately, a group of qualisigns (2.245). (*c*) Finally, a sign may be a rule or law, in which case it is denominated a Legisign or Type. "This law is usually established by men. Every conventional sign is a legisign. It is not a single object, but a general type which, it has been agreed, shall be significant." (2.246) Just because it is general, a legisign can only function through an instance, or *replica,* of itself. But this replica must be a sinsign, which in turn involves qualisigns.

As illustrative of the above distinctions, Peirce considers the question "What is a word?" He points out that we mean something different when we say "the word 'the' occurs twenty times on this page" from what we mean when we say that twenty "thes" occur on the page. In the second case, we are really counting twenty sinsigns of the legisign "the" which does not, and could not possibly, appear on the page at all (4.537). It could not appear for the simple reason that "the word itself has no existence although it has a real being, *consisting in* the fact that existents *will* conform to it" (2.292). That is to say, it is a law or rule governing the production of sinsigns, each of which is a unique, unrepeatable instance of the legisign. The latter lays it down that whenever I write the word "the" in English, I shall make a mark

[10]This correspondence, which is to be included in volume 9 of the *Collected Papers*, is for the most part unpublished. Interesting portions of it are quoted, however, in C. K. Ogden and I. A. Richards, *The Meaning of Meaning* (4th ed., London and New York, 1936), Appendix D, sec. 6.

[11]Paul Weiss and Arthur Burks, "Peirce's Sixty-Six Signs," *Journal of Philosophy*, vol. XLII (1945), pp. 383-88.

similar to the one I have just made, or utter a sound similar to the one I have just uttered, and the two will be related by the convention according to which a certain mark stands for a certain sign in English. A legisign may obviously have all sorts of sinsigns. Thus, the word "the" may be written, spoken, typewritten, printed, carved on stone, etc. As for the qualisign, it is the mere quality of an appearance, and is not exactly the same throughout a second. It is therefore to a large degree indeterminate, whereas the sinsign is entirely specific.

Icons, indices, and symbols. This trichotomy occupied a place of peculiar importance in Peirce's thought. He discovered it in 1867, where it appears as the distinction between *likenesses, signs,* and *symbols* (1.558). These are spoken of as "three kinds of representations" considered in relation to the objects they represent. Likenesses refer directly to objects because of a common quality they share with them. Signs or indices refer to objects because of "a correspondence in fact." Symbols, "the ground of whose relation to their objects is an imputed character," are simply *general* signs. After 1885, Peirce not only replaced these designations with new ones, but was able to specify more precisely the relationships for which they stood. He was also perfectly clear that Icons, Indices, and Symbols constitute "the most fundamental division of signs" (2.275).

Turning to his mature doctrine, we find that the Icon, as its name suggests, is a literal image or facsimile. It is "a sign which refers to the Object that it denotes merely by virtue of characters of its own, and which it possesses, just the same, whether any such Object actually exists or not" (2.247). These characters simply happen to resemble those of the object. The icon excites "analogous sensations in the mind for which it is a likeness," but it lacks any dynamical connection with the object it represents (2.299). Another way of putting it is to say that icons represent only the *formal* aspects of things. "No pure Forms are represented by anything but icons" (4.544). Strictly speaking, since it is of the nature of an appearance, an icon "exists only in consciousness, although for convenience in ordinary parlance and when extreme precision is not called for, we extend the term *icon* to the outward objects which excite in consciousness the image itself" (4.447).

As examples of icons, Peirce mentions pictures, photographs, geometrical diagrams, algebraic formulae, and the ideographic signs employed in the writing of primitive cultures. All language, however, even the most developed, possesses an iconic element. This is owing to the likeness which can exist between the relations of the parts of the language and the relations of the parts of what is being symbolized. If, for example, we represent the relations of the various kinds of signs by the following brace:

$$\text{Signs} \begin{cases} \text{Icons} \\ \text{Indices} \\ \text{Symbols,} \end{cases}$$

we have used an icon. But the only respect in which it "resembles" what it signifies is that it shows the relations involved to be *as they really are* (2.282). A more familiar illustration of this iconic element in language occurs in similies, metaphors, and arguments from analogy. When we argue that because the planet Mars and the earth are alike in a great many respects, therefore Mars probably resembles the earth in being inhabited, we are employing the earth as an icon for Mars.

Clearly, then, an icon may be "like" its object in several ways. Peirce notes three in particular. (*a*) Where there is a resemblance in respect of simple qualities, as in the case of a photograph of a person, the icon is an *image*. (*b*) Where the relations of the icon's parts are matched by analogous relations of the object's parts, we have a *diagram*. The blueprint of a completed building is an obvious illustration. (*c*) Where there is no precise matching but a more general "parallelism" of relations or characters, we have an icon functioning as a *metaphor* (2.277).

From the point of view of knowledge and communication, icons have both strength and weakness. Their strong point consists in the fact that "the only way of directly communicating an idea is by means of an icon; and every indirect method of communicating an idea must depend for its establishment upon the use of an icon. Hence, every assertion must contain an icon or set of icons, or else must contain signs whose meaning is only explicable by icons." (2.278) Peirce calls the idea signified by the set of icons the *predicate* of the assertion. The weakness of this kind of sign is that "a pure icon alone can convey no positive or factual information; for it affords no assurance that there is any such thing in nature" (4.447). We cannot know that the subject of a given photograph exists simply by observing the photograph. The latter may be a composite production; or the person it depicts long since dead. The blueprint may represent a house that was never built. The reason for this state of affairs is that the icon merely informs us that its object is logically possible (4.531); but beyond that it cannot go. In order to ensure that the icon is brought into "a dynamical relation" with the actual world, it must be supplemented by an *index.*

This sign has three distinctive characteristics: (*a*) it bears no significant resemblance to its object; (*b*) it refers to single units, single collections of units, or single continua; and (*c*) it directs attention to its object by blind compulsion (2.306). There is an inseparable connection between the index and the object. "They make an organic pair, but the interpreting mind has nothing to do with this connection, except remarking it, after it is established" (2.299). If its object were removed, the index would immediately lose its character as a sign, though it would not lose that character if no interpreter of it were present. An index is always an existent individual, whether a thing or a fact. And since every individual must have qualities of some sort, it follows that an index may contain a Firstness, and so an icon, as a constituent part of it (2.283).

Indices are either genuine or degenerate. In the former case, the index is in dynamical (or causal) connection both with what it signifies and with the senses or memory of the person for whom it serves as a sign (2.305). On perceiving the index he is led directly to a cognition of the object. Hence the sign is "evidence for" the object or the event it represents. A bullet-hole is the index of the passage of a bullet; a plumb-bob is an index of a vertical direction; a weathercock is an index of the direction of the wind; a low barometer with moist air is an index of rain; the cry of "Hi!" uttered by the driver of a vehicle as a warning to a careless pedestrian to get out of the way is, in so far, an index (2.286-287; 2.304). In all these cases, there is a Secondness involved which is an "existential relation."

When the Secondness is "a reference," however, the index is degenerate. This is best illustrated by certain signs in language which serve as a substitute for gestures, and so relate our discourse to the real world. Since the most basic way of specifying the meaning of words is to *point out* what they designate, the utility of the index "especially shines where other signs fail" (4.544). Demonstrative pronouns such as "this" and "that" are indices. They cannot be significantly employed except to call attention to some item present to both speaker and listener (or writer and reader). "For they call upon the hearer to use his powers of observation, and so establish a real connection between his mind and the object" (2.287). It is clear that the real world cannot be distinguished from a fictitious world by any description. No language has any particular form of speech to show that what is being spoken of in any given case belongs to the domain of actual existence. "Nothing but a dynamic sign or index can distinguish it from fiction" (2.337).

One might be inclined to conclude from this that indices have exclusive reference to the domain of physical objects and events, and are unnecessary in mathematics and logic. But Peirce reminds us that these are observational sciences whose subject-matter consists of elements that can be recognized and identified as individuals. The imaginary constructions of the mathematician are, therefore, dealt with by means of indices, such as the letters *A, B, C*, etc., on a geometrical figure and the ordinary letters in algebra. Such signs "are absolutely indispensable in mathematics" (2.305). Formal logic also makes extensive use of indices in the "selective pronouns" or quantifiers which its propositions require. The universal quantifiers (*any, every, all, no, none,* etc.) are indexical because they mean "that the hearer is at liberty to select any instance he likes within the limits expressed or understood, and the assertion [Any S is P; No S is P] is intended to apply to that one" (2.289). The particular quantifiers (*some, a, a certain, few,* etc.) are likewise indexical because they mean that the speaker can point to an instance which establishes the truth of his assertion (Some S is P; Some S is not P). The important difference between the two cases is that when a person uses the "particular selective" he guarantees the existence of the required instance; whereas when he leaves the selection to another and no instance is found, his original statement is not disproved (2.523). Consequently, from "every" it is permissible to infer "some" provided only that there is some other premiss containing an index which guarantees that something exists.

The link between the genuine and the degenerate forms of the index is rather difficult to determine, since Peirce does not subscribe to an exclusively causal view of signs. All that his distinction seems to amount to is that just as we cannot have an effect without a cause, so we cannot employ an index unless there is something present to which we can refer. Thus, a bullet-hole is an index of the passage of a bullet, and the word "this" is an index in the proposition "this is where the bullet entered." But although the passage of the bullet is the cause of the bullet-hole, it is not the cause of "this." It is not even the cause of my uttering the proposition, though I could hardly do so meaningfully unless something were presented to me. The *description* of what is thus presented will, of course, require signs other than indices. For it is the great limitation of the latter that they cannot specify the qualities of the objects they denote (3.434). To accomplish this we need *symbols.*

"A *Symbol* is a sign which refers to the Object that it denotes by virtue of a law, usually an association of general ideas, which operates to cause the Symbol to be interpreted as referring to that Object" (2.249). This law is one established by men, and hence has a purely conventional origin. The fitness of a symbol to represent lies in the fact of there being a widespread habit or disposition to interpret it in a standard way. Because it is a law, the symbol *per se* is a legisign, which, as we have seen, functions always through sinsigns. Unlike the icon and the index, the symbol has no inherent connection with its object. Anything can be used to symbolize anything else; the one important thing is that notification be given that it *is* being so used. For by itself the symbol has no meaning. Its meaning is assigned by the human beings who interpret it, and if there were no interpretant the symbol would lose its character as a sign.

All written or spoken words, sentences, books, etc., are symbols. As such they are not particular existents but *types.* We can, for example, inscribe on a piece of paper the word "star," but that does not make us the creator of the word. Neither do we destroy the word if we erase what we have written. "The word lives in the minds of those who use it. Even if they are all asleep, it exists in their memory. So we may admit . . . that generals are mere words without at all saying, as Ockham supposed, that they are really individuals." (2.301) Furthermore, a symbol cannot by itself indicate any particular thing. It can only indicate a *kind* of thing. The symbols contained in the statement "the watermelon is a succulent fruit," do not specify any particular watermelon. In order to do this, an index must be employed. For the complete object of a symbol, i.e. its meaning, is of the nature of a law, and is consequently an *ens rationis.*

Summing up, we may indicate the relative importance of the three varieties of signs as follows. "The value of an icon consists in its exhibiting the features of a state of things regarded as if it were purely imaginary. The value of an index is that it assures us of positive fact. The value of a symbol is that it serves to make thought and conduct rational and enables us to predict the future." (4.448) To put it otherwise: icons aid us in getting knowledge about the formal or structural features of the world; indices enable us to know particular existents; and symbols provide the means of knowing kinds, classes, and laws. We must remember, of course, that in actual human inquiry these signs are blended, and therefore rarely function apart from one another.

Rhemes, dicisigns, and arguments. This trichotomy has to do with the way in which signs may be represented by their interpretants. It is not clearly delineated by Peirce, and one cannot be sure what each of the terms in it designates. A *dicisign* is described as a "double or informational" sign (2.309), composed of (*a*) a subject which is an index of a Second existing independently of being represented, and (*b*) a predicate which is an icon of a Firstness or quality (2.312). These two parts are represented by the interpretant as connected in such a way that if the dicisign has any object, the dicisign must be an index of a Secondness subsisting between the object and the Firstness or quality. In other words, the dicisign is a proposition, or "quasi-proposition" (2.309), which conveys some factual information to the interpretant. Yet logically, the dicisign is built on a more basic entity, the *rheme,* which is a sign "understood as representing such and such a kind of possible Object" (2.250). The rheme is "a blank form of proposition" (4.560). Thus, the formula "⸺ is a philosopher" does not express a proposition. But it will become a proposition (however nonsensical) when the blank is filled with a proper name. The formula is a possible assertion, providing a framework for a variety of propositions. The *argument,* on the other hand, is a complex symbol which for its interpretant is the sign of a law. It is a "triple or rationally persuasive" sign (2.309) composed of at least three dicisigns. Traditional syllogism, regarded as a formal regularity or law of inference, exemplifies it perfectly.

Peirce assures us that of these three classes of representamens, the dicisign "is, by all odds, the easiest to comprehend" (*ibid.*). It is doubtful, however, whether many readers will agree with him. For his remarks about this sign raise more questions than they settle. A few of the most pressing difficulties may be noted briefly in passing.

(*a*) Any sign which must be either true or false is a dicisign (2.310). This clearly makes it identical with a proposition expressed by a sentence in the indicative mood. Yet Peirce also declares that the dicisign "is equivalent to a grammatical sentence, whether it be Interrogative, Imperative, or Assertory" (4.538). If so, not only are truth or falsity inapplicable to many dicisigns, but they are not *necessarily* informational signs. A query such as "What time is it?" does not directly convey any information, nor is an order such as "Present arms!" either true or false.

(*b*) Peirce sometimes uses the term "proposition" in an extremely broad sense. It is generally distinguished from its verbal expression, the sentence. But more than that, it seems to have no intrinsic connection with sentences at all. For "a portrait with the name of the original below it is a proposition. It asserts that if anybody looks at it, he can form a reasonably correct idea of how the original looked." (5.569) This is hard to square with his previous description of the dicisign, since the subject of the above "proposition" is not an index but an icon (i.e., the portrait).

(*c*) To the extent that a dicisign is regarded as expressible in a sentence in the indicative mood, it appears to have a close affinity with an icon. The order of the words in such a sentence must have some conformity with the order of the elements in the fact being communicated. This conformity presupposes an iconic character in the signs employed. It is precisely "the arrangement of words in the sentence" that "must serve as *Icons,* in order that the sentence may be understood" (4.544). In other passages, however, Peirce quite explicitly denies that a proposition is an icon (2.251; 2.314). The reason he gives is that an icon provides no ground for the interpretation of it as referring to actual existence, whereas "a Dicisign necessarily represents itself to be a genuine Index, and to be nothing more" (2.310). Its object is always an existential fact or Secondness. Indeed, all propositions that are not indexical must be interpreted so as to lead to propositions that are; otherwise, they will be devoid of meaning. "Thus every kind of proposition is either meaningless or has a real Secondness as its object. This is a fact that every reader of philosophy should constantly bear in mind, translating every abstractly expressed proposition into its precise meaning in reference to an individual experience." (2.315) A more forthright statement of Peirce's naturalism could scarcely be found.

While it is true that a proposition is more accurately construed as an index than as an icon, it is also true that its verbal enunciation requires symbols. The proposition is stated in words or other conventional signs. In this sense we have to agree that a proposition is "a Dicisign that is a Symbol" (2.320). Now just because the dicisign receives linguistic expression, there is a danger that we shall consider as essential to the sign what is in reality a peculiar feature of a given language. The classic illustration of this error is the conclusion that the connection between the parts of the dicisign must be some form of the verb "to be." The traditional doctrine of the copula, leading to the view that the basic type of proposition is the categorical, has its source

in a peculiarity of Indo-European languages, viz., their marked differ-
entiation of common nouns from verbs (3.459). But the great majority
of languages have no general class names or adjectives that are not
conceived as parts of some verb. Consequently, "nothing like a copula
is required in forming sentences in such languages" (2.328). Peirce
therefore urges that on strictly logical grounds it is more satisfactory
to regard the *is* as an inseparable part of the class name, and to interpret the relation between the parts of the proposition in other than
categorical terms.

The proposal he makes (and it has momentous consequences for
his philosophy) is that the relation should be treated as a *conditional*.
Thus, "sinners are miserable" says in effect "if you take any sinner, you
will find he is miserable" (2.453). Similarly, *Socrates is wise* says that
there is an individual such that if he is Socrates, he is wise. Formally,
of course, complete equivalence exists between the hypothetical and
the categorical modes of statement, as Peirce effectively argued against
Schröder in 1896 (cf. 3.446). It is only from a wider perspective that
the hypothetical formulation is seen to be preferable. This wider perspective embraces the determination of the meaning of propositions
and their connection with the living process of thought. For Peirce
held that the essential function of the cognitive mind is the activity of
inference. "Hence, the illative relation is the primary and paramount
semiotic relation" (2.444 n.). A proposition is therefore really a derivative from an argument. It is simply "an argumentation divested of the
assertoriness of its premiss and conclusion. This makes every proposition a conditional proposition at bottom." (3.440; cf. 2.355)

Rhemes, dicisigns, and arguments, then, are related to each other
as follows. Semiotically, arguments are the fundamental way in which
signs are represented by their interpretants. From arguments, dicisigns
or propositions can be derived; and from dicisigns we can obtain
rhemes. For a "non-relative rhema" or "term" such as the expression
"—— is mortal," is "nothing but a proposition with its indices or subjects left blank, or indefinite" (3.440); just as "if he is a sinner then he
is miserable" is an argument minus any assertive element.

This brings us to the question of what Peirce means by "assertion"
—a matter to which he devoted a good deal of reflection, particularly
in later years. His first serious examination of it as a logical problem
occurred about 1895. Prior to that time he was content to say simply
that "a proposition asserts" (4.40), or that "any one proposition written down by itself is considered to be asserted" (4.13). By 1902 he was

more cautious. "Writing down a proposition *under certain circumstances* asserts it" (4.376; italics mine). The discovery of these circumstances was to be undertaken, he held, by combining two procedures:
(*a*) the direct observation of what is familiar to our experience of
assertions and seems to be inseparable from them; and (*b*) the deduction of what the nature of an assertion must be from the theory "that
truth consists in the definitive compulsion of the investigating intelligence" (2.333). In the latter procedure, of course, inquiry must be
completed by noting whether our deductions are or are not verified
by observation.

Such investigation shows that in every assertion we must have a
speaker and a listener. The listener does not need to be another individual actually present. He may have only a problematical existence,
as when a shipwrecked sailor seals a message in a bottle and casts it
into the sea. Indeed, the problematical "listener" may be within the
same person as the "speaker." In that case, the person is seeking to
impress upon *himself* the truth of some proposition, and we have a
situation where assertion is very closely allied to judgment, conceived
as a mental act (2.252; 5.29). The distinctiveness of an assertion, however, lies in its furnishing of evidence to the listener "that the speaker
believes something, that is, finds a certain idea to be definitively compulsory on a certain occasion" (2.335). By his utterance, the speaker
has performed an act which he realizes will render him liable to the
social (or moral) disapproval visited on the liar if the proposition
asserted is not true. The act is akin to laying a wager or appearing
before a notary to swear an affidavit (5.30-31). Furthermore, the
speaker nearly always wishes his hearer to experience a similar compulsion to accept the proposition. That is why he uses an index or a
group of indices as the subject of his utterance (2.336). Every assertion must therefore be a dicisign, but not every dicisign is an assertion.

While Peirce's position here is not wholly clear to me, I think it
embraces four main constituents. There is the individual act of consciousness or *judgment* which is simply a process of recognizing a
belief. There is the *assertion* which is a process of impressing on ourselves or our hearers the truth of our belief, i.e. its compulsiveness.
An assertion is consequently not a pure act of signification but has a
markedly volitional character (cf. 2.436). There is the *content* of what
we assert, i.e. the proposition or dicisign. It is a sign capable of being
asserted, a possible assertion. Finally, there is the *meaning* of the

proposition or other sign. This is a factor quite distinct from the previous three. No analysis of judgments, assertions, or propositions will throw any light on the widely different question of meaning. It is a matter which needs separate consideration.

11. THE PRAGMATIC INTERPRETATION OF SIGNS

The subject of meaning brings us to the heart and center of Peirce's logic. Not only do we encounter here his best-known doctrine—the pragmatic maxim—but we also find a watershed that divides his naturalism from an important side of his transcendentalism. The diverse constructions which can be put on his pragmatism epitomize the basic conflict in his thought. We shall first of all examine the maxim as a device for the scientific determination of the meaning of signs.

The earliest suggestion of the pragmatic doctrine appears in the review of Fraser's edition of Berkeley's *Works* (1871). In the course of analyzing the Berkeleyan argument that our inability to frame the idea of some element (e.g., matter) is a sufficient guarantee of the non-existence of that element, Peirce remarks: "A better rule for avoiding the deceits of language is this: Do things fulfil the same function practically? Then let them be signified by the same word. Do they not? Then let them be distinguished."[12] Although it is not mentioned by name, this is the pragmatic principle in a nutshell.

Seven years later, in the now famous essay "How to Make Our Ideas Clear" (1878), Peirce elaborates his doctrine in greater detail. Briefly, he intends it as an alternative to the traditional method of clarifying the meaning of ideas. According to the majority of philosophers from Descartes on, there are only two possible grades of clearness with respect to any idea: (i) the clearness derived from its familiarity, and (ii) the clearness derived from the abstract definition of it. On the basis of (i), an idea is held to be clear when it is "one which is so apprehended that it will be recognized whenever it is met with, and so that no other will be mistaken for it" (5.389). On the basis of (ii), the meaning of an idea is held to be clear "when we can give a precise definition of it, in abstract terms" (5.390). Peirce rejects both of these criteria as inadequate. The meaning of an idea is not necessarily clear because it is familiar; we can easily become at home with thoroughly confused notions which we never stop to analyze.

---

[12]*North American Review*, vol. CXIII (1871), p. 469. Peirce reports that he first used the *name* "Pragmatism" in 1873, though he "used to preach the principle" at a Metaphysical Club in Cambridge in 1871 (cf. 6.482; 6.490).

Neither is abstract definition a sound method of specifying meaning. For here we may simply correlate one empty symbol with others equally empty. Indeed, most of the confusion, disagreement, and lack of progress which characterize the history of philosophy, is traceable to these two modes of thought. Hence, "it is easy to show that the doctrine that familiar use and abstract distinctness make the perfection of apprehension has its only true place in philosophies which have long been extinct; and it is now time to formulate the method of attaining to a more perfect clearness of thought" (*ibid.*).

The new method which Peirce proposes requires that all abstract ideas or "intellectual signs" should give an account of themselves in terms of concrete experience and action. It is based on the conviction that the meaning of the abstract must be explained by reference to the concrete, and not *vice versa*. More specifically, the method affirms that what we mean by any concept, proposition, word, or other symbol, is what we can verify experimentally by some actual or possible operation or activity. "That is, the rational purport of a word or other expression, lies exclusively in its conceivable bearing upon the conduct of life; so that, since obviously nothing that might not result from experiment can have any direct bearing upon conduct, if one can define accurately all the conceivable experimental phenomena which the affirmation or denial of a concept could imply, one will have therein a complete definition of the concept, and *there is absolutely nothing more in it*" (5.412). Peirce observes that he learned this doctrine as a result of his early training in the laboratory. For if you argue with an experimentalist, "you will find that whatever assertion you may make to him, he will either understand as meaning that if a given prescription for an experiment ever can be and ever is carried out in act, an experience of a given description will result, or else he will see no sense at all in what you say" (5.411). The pragmatic method of clarifying the meaning of ideas is therefore simply the method by which all the successful sciences have reached the degree of certainty and precision which they possess. It is the scientific application of an older logical rule: "By their fruits ye shall know them."

Peirce gives an illustration of the way in which the method is used in science by considering how a logically minded chemist would explain the meaning of the symbol *lithium*.

He will tell you that if you search among minerals that are vitreous, translucent, grey or white, very hard, brittle, and insoluble, for one which imparts a crimson tinge to an unluminous flame, this mineral being triturated with lime or witherite rats-bane, and then fused, can be partly dissolved in muriatic acid; and if this solution be evaporated, and the residue be extracted with sulphuric acid, and duly purified, it can be converted by ordinary methods into a chloride, which being obtained in the solid state, fused, and electrolysed with half-a-dozen powerful cells, will yield a globule of a pinkish silvery metal that will float on gasolene; and the material of *that* is a specimen of lithium (2.330).

The distinctive feature of this definition, or precept, is that it tells us what the word *lithium* denotes by specifying what we must *do* in order to gain a perceptual acquaintance with the object of the word.

In its original form, the pragmatic maxim was stated as follows. "Consider what effects, which might conceivably have practical bearings, we conceive the object of our conception to have. Then, our conception of these effects is the whole of our conception of the object." (5.402) By 1905 Peirce had not merely re-christened his doctrine "Pragmaticism" (in protest against the misuse of "Pragmatism" by James and Schiller), but had re-formulated it thus: "*In order to ascertain the meaning of an intellectual conception one should consider what practical consequences might conceivably result by necessity from the truth of that conception; and the sum of these consequences will constitute the entire meaning of the conception*" (5.9). An alternative way of putting the same thing is to say that every theoretical judgment expressed in a sentence in the indicative mood is a confused form of thought, and needs to be translated into a practical maxim expressed in a conditional sentence having its apodasis in the imperative mood. Only if this translation can be effected does the original statement possess any meaning.

What exactly does Peirce mean by the "practical consequences" of a concept? Unfortunately, he never discusses this question in detail. From his various illustrations, however, it becomes apparent that he means the *class of operations* to which the concept gives rise, and the *sensible effects* which follow when the operations are carried out. For example, what is the meaning of the symbol "hard"? In the strict mineralogical sense it means "will resist the pressure of a knife-edge." Hence, when we say "a diamond is hard" the purport of our proposition is "if at any time you press a knife-edge against the diamond, you will experience resistance." This, and similar operations, prescribed by an unlimited series of conditional statements, constitute the *complete meaning* of "hard." The same is true *mutatis mutandis* of every symbol. Since what is involved here is a uniform sequence of occurrences, it is clear why Peirce defines a symbol as "a law or regularity of the indefinite future." It is also clear why he regards all propositions as having at bottom a conditional form.

The standard objection to this view is, of course, that properties like hardness belong to things *simpliciter*. A diamond which existed for several millenia at the bottom of the ocean and was then destroyed, would still have been hard even though no one subjected it to any pressure. The stone was "really" hard in its own right, quite apart from all human experience of it. Peirce's reply to this objection is that it employs language which is devoid of meaning.

We must dismiss the idea that the occult state of things (be it a relation among atoms or something else), which constitutes the reality of a diamond's hardness can possibly consist in anything but in the truth of a general conditional proposition. For to what else does the entire teaching of chemistry relate except to the "behavior" of different possible kinds of material substance? And in what does that behavior consist except that if a substance of a certain kind should be exposed to an agency of a certain kind, a certain kind of sensible result *would* ensue, according to our experiences hitherto. (5.457)

The position of the pragmaticist is precisely that nothing else than this can be *meant* by saying that an object possesses a property.

Peirce never made the mistake of supposing that the pragmatic maxim applied to all signs. He repeatedly restricts it to "determining the meanings of intellectual concepts, that is, of those upon which reasonings may turn" (5.8; 5.464; etc.). Only symbols, not icons and indices, are so interpretable. "Pragmaticism fails to furnish any translation or meaning of a proper name or other designation of an individual object" (5.429). Such an indexical sign has "meaning" in the sense that it performs a denotative function which is essential to every assertion. Because what is thus denoted must be present to both speaker and listener, there is no danger of an index being an empty sound or mark. But a symbol, just because it is a general sign, *is* exposed to this danger. Consequently, if it is to have a "rational purport" it must be construed pragmatically.

The point may be amplified slightly by noting what Peirce has to say about the "interpretants" of signs. The interpretant, it will be recalled, is the effect of the sign upon a person apprehending it.[13] Three

---

[13]In 1908 Peirce wrote to Lady Welby: "My insertion of 'upon a person' is a sop to Cerberus, because I despair of making my own broader conception understood." (Quoted in Ogden and Richards, *The Meaning of Meaning*, p. 288.) Peirce sometimes refers to the *interpreter* of a sign as "a Quasi-mind" (4.536). This question will be considered more fully below.

broad classes are distinguished. The first is the immediate or "emotional" interpretant (5.475; 4.572). It is the *feeling* produced in the interpreter on encountering a sign. This feeling can easily be confused with the sign's cognitive meaning, as when we think we understand an idea that is merely "familiar." Secondly, there is the dynamical or "energetic" interpretant. It is a *specific reaction* elicited by a sign, best illustrated by a spontaneous muscular effort like that which follows the hearing of such an indexical sign as "Present arms!" Peirce thinks this class should also embrace particular acts of mental effort or exertion directed upon our "inner world." Thirdly, there is the effect of a sign in establishing regular or habitual modes of response. Peirce calls this the final or "logical" interpretant (5.476; 4.536). Now every symbol or general concept has such a deliberately formed *habit* as its ultimate interpretant. For the meaning of a symbol lies in the class of actions designed to bring about certain perceptible effects. And these actions are precisely the "experimental habits" by which the course of future events can be predicted and controlled.

In its most incisive formulation, Peirce's pragmatism was a theory of meaning whose sphere of application was the domain of Speculative Grammar. Its only other important bearing, as will appear, was on the process of abduction. Within the context of his naturalism, the pragmatic doctrine was never put forward as a theory of truth or "a sublime principle of speculative philosophy" (5.18). It was rather the challenge of a thinker trained in the techniques of the laboratory to the Cartesian notion of "clear and distinct ideas," and to the view of the "seminary philosophers" that the meaning of concepts is to be determined by abstract definitions. Because it affirmed that intellectual signs mean only the experimentally verifiable consequences which follow from our acting upon them, pragmatism effectively linked theory with practice. It thus supplied one of the cardinal principles of a naturalistic philosophy. Peirce was convinced that the adoption of the maxim would put an end to those prolonged philosophical disputes where no observation of facts can bring about a settlement, and where each disputant claims to prove his opponents wrong. For pragmatism insists that meaning depends on operations that are public and repeatable. Its use will therefore promote general agreement by getting rid of ideas that have no publicly ascertainable import, i.e. ideas that are wholly subjective and private. The result will be the extension of scientific method into philosophy.

While the above represents the dominant emphasis of the pragmatic doctrine, there is a side of it which becomes absorbed into Peirce's transcendentalism. We find this towards the close of his career, when, for example, he speaks of pragmatism as yielding only "a relatively high degree of clearness," and professes to "prove" the pragmatic principle by showing it to be an implication of Synechism—a doctrine embodying "a still higher grade of clearness of thought" (5.3). But all that will require attention later.

It should be apparent, even from this brief review, that Peirce's semiotic is a science of enormous sweep and complexity. Logic thus conceived embraces nothing less than the total intellectual life of humanity. With such a panorama before him, the wonder is not that Peirce's work remains sketchy and incomplete, but rather that he was able to say so much that is pertinent and illuminating.

VI

INQUIRY IN LOGIC

Ampliative Inference

1. INTRODUCTION

A MOST important species of inference investigated by Critical Logic is that in which the conclusion does not follow from the premisses with necessity. Arguments of this sort are important because their conclusions amplify rather than explicate what is stated in the premisses. The latter constitute a ground for asserting certain additional facts in the conclusion, but do not entitle us to make the affirmation apodictically. All the empirical sciences use such reasoning. Without it, Idioscopy would not exist. Moreover, it is the only kind of reasoning that can add to our store of knowledge. Consequently, any survey of human inquiry must devote close attention to ampliative or synthetic inference.

This subject had a high priority among Peirce's studies. To it he brought his great analytic powers reinforced by wide experience in several experimental sciences. He was thus in a position, as we shall see, to make contributions of lasting value on a number of points. Yet here, as elsewhere, a systematic treatment is not to be expected. Nor must we look for uniform consistency in his discussions. What he has left us are piecemeal analyses in which profound insights and unresolved problems exist side by side.

The investigation falls naturally into two main sections in accordance with Peirce's subdivision of ampliative inference into (A) Induction, and (B) Abduction. Under the former heading the topic of probability will also be considered.

A. INDUCTION

2. THE THREE TYPES OF INDUCTION

A convenient approach to this subject is provided by Peirce's analysis of induction into three types or kinds. The first and weakest kind he calls "crude induction." This is most clearly exemplified in the familiar practice of generalizing about the trend of future events on the basis of past experience. It is practically the same as Bacon's "induction by simple enumeration." When, for instance, we conclude that *all* cases of cancer are incurable because every known case has proved to be so, or that there is no such thing as clairvoyance because no genuine case of it has ever been established, we are employing crude induction.[1] Such inferences manifestly purport to reach universal conclusions. Indeed, crude induction is the only kind of ampliative inference that purports to do this, since what is called "complete" or "perfect" induction is in reality a species of deduction. The obvious weakness of crude induction is that "if its conclusion be understood as indefinite, it will be of little use, while if it be taken definitely, it is liable at any moment to be utterly shattered by a single experience" (2.757). Hence its role in science can never be other than a minor one.

From the weakest kind of induction Peirce turns to the strongest which he terms "quantitative induction." This is concerned with investigating the "real probability" that a member of a given experiential class, say the *S*'s, will have a certain character, say that of being *P*. It presupposes that the subject-matter being investigated consists of denumerable units (6.526). When, for instance, we estimate the probability of a pair of dice turning up "sixes" on a given throw, or the probability of drawing a red counter from a bag containing a determinate number of red, white, and blue counters, we utilize quantitative induction. Stated formally, this means that we proceed by first collecting on scientific principles a fair sample of the *S*'s, taking due account in doing so of the intention of using its proportion of members that possess the predesignate character *P*, and being particularly careful not to include in our sample any of the *S*'s which gave rise to the original suggestion about the character *P*. It is then inferred that the proportion of *S*'s of the sample that are *P*, probably approximates,

[1] Since complete reliance on this method would lead an individual to dismiss peremptorily any suggestion that the future will *not* resemble the past, Peirce sometimes speaks of crude induction as a "Pooh-pooh Argument" (2.269). Cf. his amusing little "parable" in 2.757 n.

within a certain limit of approximation, to the proportion that are *P* among all the *S*'s of the class. From this it is easy to calculate the probability of any *given S* being *P*.

The remaining kind of induction stands midway between the other two in respect of both the security and the scientific value of its conclusions. Peirce calls it "qualitative induction."[2] "It consists of those inductions which are neither founded upon experience in one mass, as Crude Induction is, nor upon a collection of numerable instances of equal evidential values, but upon a stream of experience in which the relative evidential values of different parts of it have to be estimated according to our sense of the impressions they make upon us" (2.759). That is to say, in making a qualitative induction the investigator first deduces from a hypothesis as many experienceable consequences as he can conveniently put to the test. These constitute predictions that if the hypothesis were true the consequences would necessarily follow. In calling them predictions Peirce does not mean that they *must* relate to future events (though in most cases they actually do), but only that they must antecede the investigator's knowledge of their truth. Having made his predictions, the investigator proceeds to ascertain their truth or falsity through experimentation. He then attempts to estimate whether the evidence entitles him to regard the hypothesis (*a*) as proved, or (*b*) as well on the way toward being proved, or (*c*) as requiring a definite modification in the light of the new experiments, or (*d*) as not, strictly speaking, true, but nevertheless presenting some analogy to the truth in such a way as to suggest a better hypothesis, or (*e*) as so wide of the mark that it is unworthy of further attention. This kind of induction, Peirce contends, is of more general utility to the practicing scientist than either of the others.

3. SAMPLING

Now the foregoing types of inference have one important feature in common. They are all methods of reaching probable conclusions on the basis of "samples." They all presuppose, therefore, as a funda-

---

[2]Sometimes he speaks of it as an "abductory induction," because it involves an element of guess-work owing to the vagueness of the characteristics being investigated. "Suppose we wish to test the hypothesis that a man is a Catholic priest, that is, has all the characters that are common to Catholic priests and peculiar to them. Now characters are not units, nor do they consist of units, nor can they be counted, in such a sense that one count is right and every other wrong. Characters have to be estimated according to their significance. The consequence is that there will be a certain element of guess-work in such an induction; so that I call it an *abductory induction*." (6.526)

mental condition of their validity, that the samples are *representative* of the class from which they are drawn. What precisely does this mean? It means that every sample must be drawn at random. "That is to say, the sample must be taken according to a precept or method which, being applied over and over again indefinitely, would in the long run result in the drawing of any one set of instances as often as any other set of the same number" (2.726). The importance of this rule is obvious; the difficulty is to know how we are to carry it out in practice.

Peirce admits that he has no definite solution to offer here. He does point out, however, that two main sorts of obstacles confront the investigator. The first arises from what may be called "physical limitations," and is illustrated by cases where part of the subject-matter of investigation is inaccessible to our powers of observation. For example, if we want to know whether it will be profitable to open a mine in a certain area, we sample the ore in that region. But in advance of mining operations, we can obtain only what ore lies on or near the surface. Hence, any inductive conclusions made on the basis of this set of samples alone are bound to be weak, because the samples are not representative or "fair."

The second obstacle in the way of obtaining fair samples arises from the psychological limitations of the investigator. For no matter how honest and objective he may be, there is always a danger that his selection of samples will be biased. Unconscious assumptions, prejudices, and predilections may conspire to "cook" the evidence, in spite of every precaution. Since no infallible technique for avoiding this obstacle exists, sampling is rather an art than a science. No hard and fast rules can be laid down to guarantee its validity. The best that can be done, granted the *bona fides* of the investigator, is to abstract as far as possible from the peculiarities of the objects being sampled, and choose this or that one from motives wholly unconnected with those peculiarities. In other words, "the volition of the reasoner (using what machinery it may) has to choose S so that it shall be an *M*; but he ought to restrain himself from all further preference, and not allow his will to act in any way that might tend to settle what particular *M* is taken, but should leave that to the operation of chance" (2.696). This is quite possible, Peirce contends, because willing (like other operations of the mind) is a type of habit, and is therefore general and imperfectly determinate. Thus, for example, when I wish for a horse, it may be for some particular *kind* of horse, but it will rarely be for any particular one. For I merely will to act in a way of which I have a general conception; and so long as my action conforms to that conception, I do not care how it is further determined. Now in choosing the instance S, I can act in a way of which I have a general conception, viz. to select an M, "but beyond that there should be no preference; and the act of choice should be such that if it were repeated many enough times with the same intention, the result would be that among the totality of selections the different sorts of M's would occur with the same relative frequencies as in experiences in which volition does not intermeddle at all" (*ibid.*).

But what about cases where the class of things examined is indefinitely large, or even infinite in extent? Is it possible to obtain a random sample from such a class? Peirce replies that it is quite possible, provided the infinite class is characterized by some kind of *order*. Reiterating his definition of a random sample as one chosen according to a method that would in the long run yield any one instance as often as any other, he adduces the following ingenious example.

Conceive a cardboard disk revolving in its own plane about its centre, and pretty accurately balanced, so that when put into rotation it shall be about as likely to come to rest in any one position as in any other; and let a fixed pointer indicate a position on the disk: the number of points on the circumference is infinite, and on rotating the disk repeatedly the pointer enables us to make a selection from this infinite number. This means merely that although the points are innumerable, yet there is a certain order among them that enables us to run them through and pick from them as from a very numerous collection. In such a case, and in no other, can an infinite lot be sampled. (2.731)

As a matter of fact, Peirce adds, it is perfectly true to say that a finite lot can be sampled adequately, only if it can be regarded as equivalent to an infinite lot. For the random sampling of a finite class presupposes the possibility of selecting a sample, noting its characteristics, replacing it, and continuing this process indefinitely. Nothing must prevent samples from being chosen independently, or make it impossible for a sample that has been drawn once to be drawn again.

4. PREDESIGNATION

In addition to the requirement of fair sampling, inductive inference depends for its effective working on another operation, namely, the "predesignation" of the particular features of the subject-matter being examined. By this Peirce means that before the sampling of any class, say the M's, can be profitably undertaken, we must decide what the characteristic P is for which we propose to sample the class. It will not do to draw our samples first and *then* look for the respects in which they agree, because it will nearly always be possible to discover *some* points of agreement among them; and these points may be so trivial as to be unrepresentative of the class from which the samples were taken. "Suppose we were to draw our instances without the predesignation of the character P; then we might in every case find some recondite character in which those instances would all agree. That, by the exercise of sufficient ingenuity, we should be sure to be able to do this, even if not a single other object of the class M possessed that character, is a matter of demonstration" (2.737). Hence it is essential to specify beforehand, on the basis of our existing knowledge, the general character whose occurrence we are going to investigate.

Peirce presents several illustrations of the way in which failure to comply with the condition of predesignation leads to invalid inductions. One of the most interesting is based on a sample of eminent men whose names are selected at random from a biographical dictionary. Turning to pages 100, 300, 500, 700, and 900, he records the following names and dates which appear at the top of each page:

	Born	Died	
Francis Baring	1740	1810	Sept. 12
Vicomte de Custine . . .	1760	1794	Jan. 3
Hippostrates (of uncertain age)			
Marquis d'O.	1535	1594	Oct. 24
Theocrenes	1480	1536	Oct. 18

Now in violation of the rule of predesignation, we might, Peirce suggests, be tempted to make the following inductions:

1. Three-fourths of these men were born in a year whose date ends in a cipher. Hence about three-fourths of all eminent men are probably so born. But, in fact, only one in ten is so born.
2. Three eminent men out of four die in autumn. In fact, only one out of four.
3. All eminent men die on a day of the month divisible by three. In fact, one out of three.
4. All eminent men die in years whose date doubled and increased by one gives a number whose last figure is the same as that in the ten's place of the date itself. In fact, only one in ten.
5. All eminent men who were living in any year ending in forty-four died at an age which after subtracting four becomes divisible by eleven. All others die at an age which increased by ten is divisible by eleven. (1.96)

The wide margin of error in each of these inductive inferences arises from a failure to observe the rule of predesignation.

In the physical sciences, this rule takes the form of an emphasis on the need for the prediction of determinate effects *before* experimental verification takes place. Since, on Peirce's view, scientific inquiry always begins with some problem, the first step in trying to solve it is to entertain a hypothesis which will lead to a number of observable effects. The effects are forecast, and the predictions subsequently confirmed or falsified. Thus is the initial problem solved, or subjected to further inquiry. Peirce is therefore indicating his dissent from the view of scientific procedure which regards it as starting with the dispassionate collection of facts. His emphasis on predesignation is a reminder that facts are always selected because of their *relevance* to a particular problem in hand. They are never gathered indiscriminately. And it is only on the basis of pre-existing knowledge that their relevance or irrelevance can be determined. Hence, "when we get to the inductive stage, what we are about is finding out how much like the truth our hypothesis is, that is, what proportion of its anticipations will be verified" (2.755).

5. THE MEANING OF PROBABILITY

So far I have spoken of inductive inference as "probable," without stopping to say what Peirce means by that term. We have now reached a point where it is necessary to deal with this question. Induction and probability are so closely associated in his thought that it is impossible to treat one of them adequately except in relation to the other. Unfortunately, Peirce's discussion of probability is not always as clear or consistent as one could wish. Yet the subject was of perennial interest to him, as may be seen from the fact that his writings on it extend all the way from 1867 to 1910. In what follows, I shall sketch his theory of probability as succinctly as I can, and then try to show its bearing on induction.

It is a familiar fact that common discourse has made the word "probability" highly ambiguous. "We, all of us, use this word with a degree of laxity which corrupts and rots our reasoning to a degree that very few of us are at all awake to" (2.662). Thus in different contexts we talk about facts, events, beliefs, propositions, arguments, laws, etc., being "probable," although a moment's reflection must convince us that we cannot be employing the expression in the same sense throughout. Logicians have endeavored to bring some order into this chaos by giving probability an exact and uniform definition. But even here general agreement has proved hard to attain.

One of the simplest definitions connects probability with belief. Facts and events in the world are strictly determinate; but our beliefs about them have frequently to be based on partial evidence. When this is the case we lack certainty, and have to fall back on probability. The latter is therefore defined as "simply the degree of belief which ought to attach to a proposition" (2.673). Peirce, following Venn, refers to this as the "subjective" or "conceptualistic" view. Its purest manifestation is to be found in De Morgan's *Formal Logic,* though the "classical" formulation appears in Laplace and Quetelet. One of the implications of this interpretation is that where we have *no* evidence either for or against a given proposition, we may indicate the measure of our belief by the fraction ½ (since total belief is represented by 1 and total disbelief by 0). Complete ignorance, therefore, "where the judgment ought not to swerve either toward or away from the hypothesis," entitles us to assert a definite probability value (2.679).

Few writers, however, have been able to treat probability in purely subjective terms. For most beliefs, particularly in science, depend on evidence; so that upholders of the conceptualistic view are inevitably led to talk about the probability of *events* as well as of beliefs. Hence, although they may begin by defining the probability of an event as the reason we have to believe that it has taken place, "shortly after they state that it is the ratio of the number of cases favorable to the event to the total number of cases favorable or contrary" (2.673). On this basis the probability of throwing a six in a single toss of a die is

$\dfrac{1}{1+5} = \dfrac{1}{6}$. Such a definition presupposes the "thoroughly unclear idea" that the cases concerned are equally possible. But at least it does mark a step away from subjectivity by introducing an objective factor.

As might be expected, Peirce was opposed to the conceptualistic interpretation. He objected to it on the following counts.

1. In order to have any value at all, probability must express an external, public fact, and not a mere state of mind (2.677; 5.21). How otherwise can we account for the enormous practical success of those enterprises, both scientific and commercial, which base their procedure on probability calculations? Insurance companies, for example, solve their problems entirely in factual (i.e., statistical) terms. This can only mean that probability is not a matter of private conviction, but has some objective ground.

2. While the conceptualists are right in connecting the probability

of an event with the degree of our belief in it, they are wrong in thinking that the latter is what *uniquely defines* the probability. Consider
the following illustration. Suppose we have a large bag of beans from
which one has been secretly taken at random and hidden under a
thimble. We wish to form a probable judgment as to the color of that
bean; and so we begin drawing beans singly from the bag, looking at
them, throwing each one back, and mixing the whole collection well
before the next drawing. Now on the conceptualistic view, each drawing has a determinate effect on our belief about the hidden bean. If
the first twenty beans drawn should turn out to be black, a belief that
the hidden bean was black would attain considerable strength. But
suppose the twenty-first bean were white, and that we were to continue
drawing until we found that we had obtained 1,010 black beans and
990 white ones. According to the conceptualists, our belief that the
hidden bean is black should still preponderate slightly over a belief
that it is white (since an excess of twenty black should produce a
corresponding excess of belief). But this would not be the case were
we actually to conduct such an experiment. "We should conclude that
our first twenty beans being black was simply an extraordinary accident, and that in fact the proportion of white beans to black was
sensibly equal" (2.678). In other words, our belief would be that it
was an even chance that the hidden bean was black. This strongly
suggests that the probability of an event is not always proportional to
our belief in its occurrence; nor is the probability based on any single
set of observations.

3. What is the probability that the hidden bean is black, *before any
drawings whatever have been made?* On the conceptualist interpretation, it is ½, since we have no evidence one way or the other. This
doctrine Peirce regards as utterly indefensible. It amounts to an attempt to extract knowledge from ignorance (2.744). "When we have
no knowledge at all . . . there is no sense in saying that the chance of
a totally unknown event is even (for what expresses absolutely no fact
has absolutely no meaning), and what ought to be said is that the
chance is entirely indefinite" (2.677). The conceptualistic position
implies, moreover, that of all theories proposed for examination one-
half are true. "In point of fact, we know that although theories are not
proposed unless they present some decided plausibility, nothing like
one half turn out to be true" (2.744). The recognition that probability
must be a matter of fact makes it impossible for us to accept such *a
priori* determinations of it.

The view which Peirce himself favored is called nowadays the "frequency theory." He speaks of it as the "objective" or "materialistic" interpretation, taking the latter designation from Venn. Peirce was undoubtedly influenced by the *Logic of Chance*, which he reviewed in 1867,[3] but it is unlikely that its contentions were entirely new to him. In his paper on "The Doctrine of Chances" in 1878, he remarks: "The conception of probability here set forth is substantially that first developed by Mr. Venn, in his *Logic of Chance*. Of course, a vague apprehension of the idea had always existed, but the problem was to make it perfectly clear, and to him belongs the credit of first doing this." (2.651 n.) Fifteen years later, in 1893, he declared apropos of the subject, that his opinion "was fully made up before I saw the book. I do not think I learned anything from that except a classification of the philosophies of probability." (6.590) These pronouncements are not necessarily incompatible, as it is quite possible that Peirce had arrived at his central conception independently. The fact that he mentions Locke as the person who made the "first steps in profound analyses" of probability, suggests that he may have received his inspiration from sources older than his British contemporary.

Venn's doctrine makes probability a statistical ratio obtained by investigating events belonging to a series. Peirce agrees that "a probability is a statistical fact, and cannot be assumed arbitrarily."[4] He also agrees that it is a ratio. But he prefers in general not to speak of it as a property of *events*. "Some of the worst and most persistent errors in the use of the doctrine of chances have arisen from this vicious mode of expression" (2.651). The character of probability attaches rather to certain *inferences* or *arguments*, namely, to those which sometimes prove successful and sometimes not, and that "in a ratio ultimately fixed" (2.650). Peirce holds, as we have seen, that every argument belongs to a genus or class of arguments governed by a leading principle. The class in which true premises are *invariably* followed by true conclusions constitutes the class of necessary inferences. The class in which true premises are *sometimes* followed by true conclusions constitutes the class of probable inferences. The latter is what Locke has in mind when he declares a probable argument to be "*such as,* for the most part, carries truth with it."[5] Another way of

---

[3]Cf. *North American Review*, vol. CV (1867), pp. 317-21.

[4]*Ibid.*, p. 320.

[5]*Essay concerning Human Understanding*, Bk. IV, chap. xv, sec. 1. Quoted by Peirce in 2.649 and 2.696.

putting this is to employ the nomenclature of the medieval logicians who called the fact expressed by the premiss an *antecedent,* and that which follows from it its *consequent.* The leading principle, that every such antecedent is followed by such a consequent, they termed the *consequence.* "Using this language, we may say that probability belongs exclusively to *consequences* [i.e. to leading principles], and the probability of any consequence is the number of times in which antecedent and consequent both occur divided by the number of all the times in which the antecedent occurs" (2.669).

An argument is probable only in so far as it is a member of a class of arguments. The degree of probability which any given argument possesses can be expressed by a proper fraction whose numerator is the number of times the premisses and conclusion are true, and whose denominator is the number of times the premisses are true. This numerical value is ascertained empirically by statistical investigation (5.21). It "essentially refers to a course of experience" (5.169). But the course of experience is that which holds *in the long run,* so that the idea of probability "belongs to a kind of inference which is repeated indefinitely" (2.652).

It is clear that for both Venn and Peirce the fact of relative frequency lies at the heart of probability. Venn interprets it as the relative frequency of the occurrence of a given event within a series of events. Peirce takes it to be the relative frequency with which an argument yields true conclusions in the class of arguments to which it belongs. Actually, there is no fundamental difference between these two ways of formulating the matter, and a translation from one to the other can be readily effected. Hence, Peirce occasionally resorts to the language of events in discussing probability (e.g., in 3.19, 5.169, etc.), more for the sake of verbal economy than for anything else. He is quite well aware that such a mode of expression is elliptical, and may sometimes hinder the task of clarification and refinement.

Acceptance of the frequency interpretation entails several important corollaries. (i) Probability is *always* capable of being given a numerical value. It is "a kind of relative number" (2.657). Unless this condition is fulfilled, we are not in strict accuracy entitled to use the term at all. (ii) Probability cannot be predicated of events or arguments taken as isolated units. "An individual inference must be either true or false, and can show no effect of probability; and, therefore, in reference to a single case considered in itself, probability can have no meaning" (2.652). We ought not to talk about the "probability" of

Caesar having visited England, or the "probability" of fine weather tomorrow, if we mean *literally* to attribute that characteristic to the single occurrences. (iii) It is equally illegitimate on this view to talk about the probability of scientific theories and laws. "It is nonsense to talk of the probability of a law, as if we could pick universes out of a grab-bag and find in what proportion of them the law held good" (2.780). For science is engaged in investigating but one universe; and the presumption is that, since it is not chaos, it possesses a single determinate arrangement of facts, events, and laws.

These corollaries of the frequency interpretation run counter to popular usage. In everyday speech we do often refer to single events as "probable," and do so in a non-metrical sense. We also inquire about the probable truth of such doctrines as Newton's law of gravitation or Einstein's theory of relativity. For this reason, some writers, notably Keynes, have concluded that probability cannot be exhaustively analyzed in terms of relative frequencies.[6] Peirce never discusses this view in detail. But he would doubtless agree with von Mises that the inapplicability of the scientific definition of probability to popular discourse is not a valid objection to that definition.[7] No one objects to the scientific definition of "work" because it is utterly unlike the common-sense meaning of that word. Why, then, should an objection based on popular usage be made to the scientific treatment of probability? As a matter of fact, it is possible in certain cases to construe colloquial probability statements in scientific terms. "Thus, when an ordinary man says that it is highly probable that it will rain, he has reference to certain indications of rain—that is, to a certain kind of argument that it will rain—and means to say that there is an argument that it will rain, which is of a kind of which but a small proportion fail" (3.19). Whether *all* probability statements are capable of being translated in this manner is a question which is still being debated by the experts.

In his earlier papers Peirce refers to the ratio which represents the numerical value of a probability as something reached *in the long run*. But this way of speaking is not precise enough to serve the purposes of a mathematical treatment of probability, and in 1905 Peirce attempted a re-formulation. "When we say that a certain ratio will have a certain value in 'the long run,' we refer to the *probability-limit* of an endless succession of fractional values; that is, to the only possible value from

[6]Cf. J. M. Keynes, *A Treatise on Probability* (London, 1921), pp. 95 ff.
[7]Cf. R. von Mises, *Probability, Statistics and Truth* (London, 1939), pp. 6 ff.

0 to ∞ , inclusive, about which the values of the endless succession will never cease to oscillate; so that, no matter what place in the succession you may choose, there will follow both values above the probability-limit and values below it" (2.758). In other words, such a statement as "The probability of a thirty-year-old male surviving at least one year is .945" means that as statistical inquiry proceeds over a very long period, the results will be found more and more to oscillate about this value. If we were to plot the results on a graph, we should obtain a curve which is asymptotic to one of the co-ordinate axes of the graph.[8]

The most trenchant objection to this method of interpreting probability is that since the series of values involved is both *empirical* and *infinite*, we can have no grounds for selecting *one* value as the limit of the relative frequency, because we cannot foresee what the course of an endless future experience will be like. The point may be made in a slightly different way by means of a simple illustration.[9] On the frequency view, the proposition "The probability of obtaining heads with a symmetrical coin is ½," must be taken as a hypothesis which has been confirmed by a large number of empirical tests. Suppose we set out to substantiate the hypothesis by making 1,000 throws, and suppose that these all happen to turn up heads. We might then be tempted to reject the hypothesis as false. But such a sequence is quite compatible with our hypothesis, because the latter refers not to a finite number of throws but to an infinite number. The hypothesis specifies the limiting ratio of heads in an infinite class. But if so, the ratio can be maintained in the face of *any* empirical findings, for these must always be finite in extent. Consequently, statistical evidence can neither refute nor confirm it; and the same must hold true for every probability statement.

Something like this difficulty seems to have occurred to Peirce during the last years of his life. Commenting in 1910 on his writings, "after the lapse of a full generation," he remarks:

When I come to define probability [in the paper of 1878], I repeatedly say that it is the quotient of the *number* of occurrences of the event divided by the *number* of occurrences of the occasion. Now this is manifestly wrong, for probability relates to the future; and how can I say how many times a

[8]Cf. von Mises, *ibid.*, pp. 19 ff.

[9]See the monograph, *Principles of the Theory of Probability,* by Ernest Nagel, vol. I, no. 6, "International Encyclopedia of Unified Science" (Chicago, 1939), p. 51. This is one of the best brief presentations of the frequency theory in the literature. Another excellent general discussion is chapter x of C. I. Lewis's *An Analysis of Knowledge and Valuation* (La Salle, Ill., 1946).

given die will be thrown in the future? . . . It is plain that, if probability be the ratio of the occurrences of the specific event to the occurrences of the generic occasion, it is the ratio that there *would be* in the long run, and has nothing to do with any supposed cessation of the occasions. This long run can be nothing but an endlessly long run; and even if it be correct to speak of an infinite "number," yet $\frac{\infty}{\infty}$ (infinity divided by infinity) has certainly, *in itself*, no definite value. (2.661)

By way of overcoming this difficulty Peirce resorts to his concept of "habit." Thus to say that the probability is 1/3 that a die thrown from a dice box will turn up a number divisible by three, "means that the die has a certain 'would-be'; and to say that a die has a 'would-be' is to say that it has a property, quite analogous to any *habit* that a man might have" (2.664). In order that the full effect of the die's habit can be manifested, it is requisite that the die should undergo an endless series of throws from the box, and that the throws should be independent of one another. One cannot legitimately object that an endless series of throws is impossible, because the impossibility is merely physical (or physiological), not logical (2.666).

Every probability statement, then, refers to an objective property or "habit" belonging to a given subject-matter. Since a habit is not something which will necessarily hold in the future, probability statements are only approximately reliable. They are hypotheses which have received support from existing statistical data; but the ratios they assert are by no means absolute. Hence, a given probability statement can withstand minor deviations from the ratio it predicts. It does not need to be modified because a few exceptions arise from time to time, for the statement refers to an endless series. But modification is essential if wide deviations from the predicted ratio continue to occur as the total number of cases examined increases. In that event, empirical evidence points the way to a new and more adequate ratio.

The area in which the notion of probability is employed with most precision is that of the probability calculus. The calculus is a strictly mathematical discipline, manifesting the traits of deductive reasoning. "In any problem of probabilities, we have given the relative frequency of certain events, and we perceive that in these facts the relative frequency of another event is given in a hidden way. This being stated makes the solution. This is, therefore, mere explicative reasoning." (2.681) The calculus is thus purely formal and abstract. From certain propositions about probability values it derives other propositions about probability values as necessary conclusions. While Peirce recognizes the existence of such a discipline, he is not always careful to distinguish it from its application to empirical material. The interpretation of the calculus, rather than its formal elaboration, was the thing that interested him.

To summarize the main points in Peirce's analysis: (1) Probability does not belong primarily to beliefs or judgments. (2) It is an objective property of a certain type of argument, or more exactly, of the leading principle governing that type of argument. (3) The arguments it characterizes are those that sometimes yield true conclusions in the class of arguments to which they belong. (4) Probability defines the relative frequency with which those arguments occur. (5) It is therefore a ratio represented by a proper fraction whose numerator is the number of times the premisses and the conclusion are true, and whose denominator is the number of times the premisses are true. (6) Probability always has a numerical value. (7) It is therefore capable of being formalized in a calculus governed by precise rules. (8) Probability values are always ascertained empirically, i.e. statistically. (9) Probability thus belongs to inferences that are repeated indefinitely, so that the probability ratio is the limit of an endless succession of fractional values. (10) Probability cannot be predicated literally of isolated events or of scientific laws. (11) The property of a given subject-matter to which a probability statement refers may be interpreted as a "habit" of that subject-matter. (12) A probability statement is in effect a hypothesis supported by existing factual evidence. (13) As such it can never be completely confirmed, but must remain more or less approximate—though its adequacy increases as the number of supporting cases becomes greater.

It would be foolish to affirm that Peirce satisfactorily answers all the objections, or even the major objections, which have been directed against the frequency interpretation. In particular, I do not see how he can avoid the charge that his theory leads to an infinite regress of probabilities. Must that not be the case if every probability statement is itself only approximately (i.e., probably) true? Nor would I care to argue that Peirce has elaborated an internally complete theory, quite apart from extraneous objections. What impresses me most about his discussions is their sensitiveness to the manifold aspects of this difficult subject. They are particularly valuable, also, because they seek to formulate a doctrine of probability that is in harmony with the practice of the empirical sciences, to ground the doctrine in objective fact, and to state it in such a way that subsequent refinement has been not only possible but fruitful. The recent development of the frequency theory by men like von Mises and Reichenbach has stemmed in large measure from Peirce's pioneering.

6. PROBABILITY AND INDUCTION

Our next task is to trace the connection between this analysis of probability and induction. In doing so, we shall have to consider some of the formal aspects of probable (and statistical) deduction; and then try to see in what sense, if any, probability can be predicated of ampliative inference generally. Before beginning our discussion, however, we must examine the ambiguity in Peirce's use of the term "probable deduction" to which we have already called attention. Stated briefly, the ambiguity is this. (i) Sometimes "probable deduction" refers to a type of *necessary* reasoning in which the constituent propositions are about probability. It is regarded as a subclass of explicative reasoning, and occurs primarily, if not wholly, in the calculus. (ii) At other times, "probable deduction" is used as though it referred to a type of ampliative inference, or to a hybrid form partaking of characteristics of both explicative and ampliative inference. Illustrations of this duality of meaning will emerge in what follows.

The long, obscure paper which Peirce published in the Johns Hopkins *Studies in Logic* (1883) contains a treatment of the formal aspects of probable reasoning. He starts by giving an example of what he calls "simple probable deduction," which he compares with the singular syllogism in *Barbara*. Thus,

> About 2% of persons wounded in the liver recover,
> This man has been wounded in the liver;
>
> Hence there are 2 chances out of 100 that this man will recover.

Stated formally, this inference becomes

> The proportion ρ of the *M*'s are *P*'s,
> S is an *M*;
>
> It follows, with probability   , that S is a *P*.

On the other hand we have the singular syllogism,

> Every man dies,
> Enoch was a man;
>
> Hence, Enoch must have died.
>
> *or*
>
> Every *M* is a *P*,
> S is an *M*;
> Hence, S is a *P*.

The latter argument, according to Peirce, consists in the application of a general rule to a particular case. The former applies to a particular case a rule not absolutely universal, but subject to a known proportion of exceptions. "Both may alike be termed deductions, because they bring information about the uniform or usual course of things to bear upon the solution of special questions" (2.694). This rather sounds like the venerable error that deduction is a process of reasoning "from the general to the particular." One would have expected Peirce to say that both inferences are deductive because their conclusions follow apodictically from their premisses.

A closer scrutiny of the two modes of inference, however, brings to light certain important differences between them. (*a*) The only logical relation involved in necessary syllogism is that of class-inclusion or exclusion, whereas probable inference takes account of the proportion of one class which is contained in a second. (*b*) "A cardinal distinction between the two kinds of inference is, that in demonstrative reasoning the conclusion follows from the existence of the objective facts laid down in the premisses; while in probable reasoning these facts in themselves do not even render the conclusion probable, but account has to be taken of various subjective circumstances—of the manner in which the premisses have been obtained, of there being no countervailing considerations, etc.; in short, good faith and honesty are essential to good logic in probable reasoning" (2.696). Thus, in the example mentioned above, it is requisite not merely that S should be an *M*, but that it should be chosen as a *random instance* of *M*'s. (*c*) "The conclusions of the two modes of inference likewise differ. One is necessary; the other only probable." (*Ibid.*) The basic difference between syllogism and simple probable deduction, therefore, is that in the former we conceive such facts as are expressed by the premisses *always* to imply the fact expressed by the conclusion; while in the latter, we merely conceive that in reasoning as we do, we are following a general maxim that will *usually* lead us to the truth.

These comments are an illustration of the ambiguity mentioned at the beginning of the section. The inference which Peirce calls simple probable deduction is only "probable" in the sense that its major premiss and conclusion are *about* probabilities. But the conclusion is a necessary consequence of the premisses, quite apart from any existential facts to which they may or may not refer.[10] That is to say, the argument is a deduction. Everything that Peirce remarks about it

[10]Peirce seems to admit this *by implication*, as we shall see below.

would be true *if* the argument were of the following kind:

> About 2% of persons wounded in the liver recover;
> This man has been wounded in the liver;
> Hence, this man will recover.

Here we have an inference in which the conclusion is only probable on the basis of the premises—provided the latter are arrived at in accordance with the rules of "good faith and honesty." But this is obviously not a deductive inference.

Similar puzzling references occur in Peirce's article on "Syllogism" in J. M. Baldwin's *Dictionary of Philosophy and Psychology*. He takes for purposes of analysis the argument:

> The probability of throwing doublets with a pair of dice is 1/6,
> Different throws of pairs of dice are independent;
> Therefore, the probability of throwing precisely two doublets in 6 throws is just half that of throwing one doublet in 6 throws.

The exact meaning of the first premiss is interpreted thus: "we should square our actions on each single occasion to the fact that, taking throws of the dice as they occur in the course of experience, the ratio of the number of throws of doublets hitherto to the total number of throws hitherto would, if the course of experience were endless, become, after a time, permanently remote from every other ratio than 1:6, but would never become so from this ratio" (2.564). The second premiss means that no matter what segment of experience we take, each throw of the dice remains unaffected by any other throw. The "necessary conclusion" means that we should square our actions on every occasion to the principle that, taking an endless succession of different sets of six throws, just as they occur in the course of experience, the ratio of the number of sets containing two doublets to the number of sets containing one doublet will at length permanently depart from every other ratio than 1:2, and will not depart from this ratio.

Now Peirce contends that we have here an inference which is both necessary and probable. It is necessary because given the premises, the conclusion *must* follow in the long run. "Yet it is merely probable in this sense, that we cannot be sure that the number of sets of six throws containing just one doublet would be twice the number containing two doublets in a hundred trials, or in a million, or in any other fixed number. But what is certain is that any other ratio would eventually prove decidedly wrong, while 1:2 would not." (*Ibid.*)

This illustrates the same basic confusion as before, but with a slightly different emphasis. It might now be supposed that there are two kinds of "necessary" reasoning—strict deduction and reasoning which is necessary "in the long run." The above inference would come under the second category; hence it is both probable and necessary. But such a use of terms is both profoundly unsatisfactory, and incompatible with Peirce's judgment elsewhere (cf. 2.267). Necessary reasoning surely means reasoning which holds in *every* case. If so, we cannot legitimately talk about reasoning which will "eventually" be necessary, but is not so in any single instance or finite number of instances. Therefore, probable deduction ought to be a subclass of deductive reasoning which is necessary because it simply analyzes the probability statements involved. Peirce does occasionally speak of it thus. "Necessary inference may be applied to probability as its subject-matter; and it then becomes, under another aspect, probable inference. . . . This is probable deduction. It covers all the ordinary and legitimate applications of the mathematical doctrine of probability." (2.785) But there is no consistent adherence to such usage.

Returning to the Johns Hopkins paper, we find Peirce examining the following kind of argument:

> A little more than half of all human births are males,
>
> Hence, probably a little over half of all the births in New York during any one year are males.

Stated formally, this argument is:

> The proportion r of the M's are P's,
> S', S'', S''', etc., are a numerous set, taken at random from among the M's;
>
> Hence, *probably* and *approximately*, the proportion r of the S's are P's.

Peirce declares that we have here not mere probable inference, but *probable approximate* inference, the qualification being admittedly "a somewhat complicated one" (2.700). He speaks of the argument as "statistical deduction." Its fundamental principle is that the two proportions concerned—namely, that of the P's among the M's and that of the P's among the S's—are probably and approximately equal. "This principle justifies our inferring the value of the second proportion from the known value of the first" (2.702). But we can equally infer the value of the first from that of the second, if the first is unknown but the second has been obtained by empirical observation. In that case we get an argument having the following form:

S', S'', S''', etc., form a numerous set taken at random from among the M's,

The proportion ρ of S', S'', S''', etc., are found to be P's;

Hence, *probably* and *approximately,* the same proportion, ρ, of the M's are P's.

For instance, from a bag of coffee a handful is taken out and found to have nine-tenths of the beans perfect. Whence it is inferred that about nine-tenths of all the beans in the bag are probably perfect. This "inverted" statistical deduction Peirce declares to be a typical induction.

Before making a closer scrutiny of the relation between these two modes of inference, a word must be said about the connection between statistical deduction and probable deduction. Again the issue is a thorny one. Perhaps the clearest pronouncement occurs in a manuscript dated around 1903.

Probable Deductions, or more accurately, Deductions of Probability, are Deductions whose Interpretants represent them to be concerned with ratios of frequency. They are either *Statistical Deductions* or *Probable Deductions Proper.* A Statistical Deduction is a Deduction whose Interpretant represents it to reason concerning ratios of frequency, but to reason concerning them with absolute certainty. A Probable Deduction proper is a Deduction whose Interpretant does not represent that its conclusion is certain, but that precisely analogous reasonings would from true premisses produce true conclusions in the majority of cases, in the long run of experience. (2.268)

Thus, statistical deduction is analytic inference yielding necessary conclusions; whereas probable deduction is the hybrid form already noted, which is valid if the conclusion asserted "would be true, in the long run, in a proportion of times equal to the probability which this argument assigns to its conclusion" (2.781).

In the Johns Hopkins paper, however, such a distinction is not sustained. We have already noted the analysis given there of simple probable deduction, viz.,

The proportion ρ of the M's are P's,
S is an M;
It follows, with probability ρ, that S is a P.

Now in the case where S, instead of being a single M, is a numerous set of M's, this inference becomes a statistical deduction (2.698). Thus, to repeat:

The proportion r of the M's are P's,
S', S'', S''', etc., are a numerous set, taken at random, from among the M's;
Hence, probably about the proportion r of the S's are P's.

Both types of inference, therefore, involve the application of the same logical principles. But Peirce goes on to remark in a footnote:

The conclusion of the statistical deduction is here regarded as being "the proportion *r* of the *S*'s are *P*'s," and the words "probably about" [or "probably and approximately"] as indicating the modality with which this conclusion is drawn and held for true. It would be equally true to consider the "probably about" as forming part of the contents of the conclusion; only from that point of view the inference ceases to be probable, and becomes rigidly necessary, and its apagogical inversion is also a necessary inference presenting no particular interest. (2.720 n.)

In other words, statistical deduction *can*, by suitable modification of the conclusion, be interpreted as necessary inference. But its literal formulation requires the conclusion (like that of simple probable deduction) to be taken not as necessary, but as probable (cf. 2.621).

Thus, probable deduction and statistical deduction are said on the one hand to be distinct types of inference, and on the other hand to be essentially the same type, or at least to be derivatives of one another. In the former case, statistical deduction yields necessary conclusions, whereas probable deduction yields non-necessary conclusions (2.268). In the latter case, *neither* yields necessary conclusions (2.698 ff.). But probable deduction is also said to be a demonstrative argument of the sort which appears in mathematical treatments of probability (2.785). Part of the inconsistency here is doubtless due, as Buchler has suggested,[11] to the fact that Peirce employs "deduction" to cover both necessary and probable inference (cf. 2.267). But I think there is a corresponding failure to distinguish sharply between the logistic treatment of probability in a calculus, and the application of such a calculus to empirical data. The result is a muddle over the term "probable," as may be seen most obviously in regard to induction.

This brings us at long last to the question of the sense, if any, in which inductive reasoning is probable. Previous discussion has shown us that the exact definition of probability represents it as measuring a ratio of frequency in numerical terms. Now induction might be conceived as (1) probable in precisely this sense, (2) probable in a different sense, or (3) not strictly probable at all. Actually, each of

---

[11]*Charles Peirce's Empiricism* (New York and London, 1939), pp. 263-66. Buchler points out that Peirce's article on "Inference" in the *Century Dictionary* asserts that "explicative inference" and "necessary inference" are different, the latter being a subclass of the former.

these contentions can be found in Peirce—though ultimately, the third tends to take precedence over the others.

1. That induction is probable in a frequency sense is a view which appears early in Peirce's writings, and seems never to have been wholly abandoned. Significantly enough, it is indicated more by implication than by explicit statement; but its presence in an inchoate form can hardly be gainsaid. On this view, an inductive argument always "concludes a ratio of frequency" (2.369; 5.194). The frequency concerned registers the proportion of arguments yielding true conclusions within a given class of arguments. Now the class to which an induction belongs is the *class of all* inductions, i.e. the class of arguments whose leading principle is the inductive method. Since only a percentage of such arguments are sound, the probability of an induction is measured by a fraction whose numerator is the number of sound inductions, and whose denominator is the total number of inductions. Peirce declares that such a fraction will always be greater than ½, because induction is a process which "for the most part" leads to true beliefs. In any event, the fraction "evaluates an objective probability" (2.775), so that induction "might be called a statistical argument" (5.275).

An obvious objection to this view is that we can never ascertain the numerical value of the denominator in the fraction which specifies the objective probability in question. For if the phrase "the total number of inductions" means every *possible* induction, then we have a class which is infinitely large, and a determinate calculation of a probability ratio becomes impossible. If the phrase be taken to mean every induction that has been or will be made *in fact,* there is still no basis for a precise reckoning. Every theory which regards induction as probable in a frequency sense is bound to encounter this difficulty.

2. We have already noted Peirce's attempt in the Johns Hopkins paper to construe induction as an "inverted" statistical deduction. The latter, it will be recalled, was of the form:

> The proportion r of the M's are P's,
> S', S'', S''', etc., are a numerous set, taken at random from among the M's;
> Hence, *probably* and *approximately*, the proportion r of the S's are P's.

The result of inverting this inference, we saw, is the induction:

> S', S'', S''', etc., form a numerous set taken at random from among the M's,
> The proportion ρ of S', S'', S''', etc., are found to be P's;

Hence, *probably* and *approximately,* the same proportion, ρ, of the *M*'s are *P*'s.

Commenting on these arguments, Peirce makes the following important assertion:

The nature of the probability in the two cases is very different. In the statistical deduction, we know that among the whole body of *M*'s the proportion of *P*'s is ρ; we say, then, that the *S*'s being random drawings of *M*'s are probably *P*'s in about the same proportion—and though this may happen not to be so, yet at any rate, on continuing the drawing sufficiently, our prediction of the ratio will be vindicated at last. On the other hand, in induction we say that the proportion ρ of the sample being *P*'s, probably there is about the same proportion in the whole lot; or at least, if this happens not to be so, then on continuing the drawings the inference will be, not *vindicated* as in the other case, but *modified* so as to become true. The deduction, then, is probable in this sense, that though its conclusion may in a particular case be falsified, yet similar conclusions (with the same ratio ρ) would generally prove approximately true; while the induction is probable in this sense, that though it may happen to give a false conclusion, yet in most cases in which the same precept of inference was followed, a different and approximately true inference (with the right value of ρ) would be drawn. (2.703)

Thus, statistical deduction is "probable" in a frequency interpretation of that term. The ratio which its conclusion asserts is such that it will be substantiated more and more fully as investigation proceeds; "though the predicted ratio may be wrong in a limited number of drawings, yet it will be approximately verified in a larger number" (2.709). But induction is "probable" only in the sense that it is a *successful approximative process.* The ratio which its conclusion asserts will not be substantiated as investigation proceeds, but altered so as to represent more adequately the objective facts. "The ratio may be wrong, because the inference is based on but a limited number of instances; but on enlarging the sample the ratio will be changed till it becomes approximately correct" (*ibid.*). Both techniques concern themselves with ratios that are expressed mathematically. But the probability attaching to induction "is in every way different—in meaning, numerical value, and form," from that which belongs to statistical deduction (2.748).

3. During the latter part of his life, and particularly after 1883, Peirce dropped this double use of "probable," and, save for occasional lapses, restricted its range of application to relative frequencies in the strict sense. He was therefore obliged to deny that inductive reasoning

is probable at all.[12] Accordingly, we find him remarking in 1896 on the "absurdity" of the supposition that "induction renders the state of things asserted in the conclusion probable" (1.92). Six years later he writes that it "often is conceived, that induction lends a probability to its conclusion. Now that is not the way in which induction leads to the truth. It lends no definite probability to its conclusion." (2.780) A similar emphasis appears in 1903 when he criticizes Laplace and others for imagining that an "affirmative experience imparts a definite probability to a theory" (5.169). On the positive side, Peirce stresses the "approximative" capacity of induction as that which makes its conclusions "strong" or "valid." But the approximation is not so much to a determinate mathematical ratio (as was suggested in 1883); it is rather an approximation to the truth. "The validity of an inductive argument consists, then, in the fact that it pursues a method which, if duly persisted in, must in the very nature of things, lead to a result indefinitely approximating to the truth in the long run" (2.781). This remarkable property is due to the fact that through repeated application induction gradually eliminates its own errors, i.e. it is a "self-corrective" technique of inquiry. The development of this point will be undertaken in the following section.

7. THE JUSTIFICATION OF INDUCTION

One of the topics considered by every student of scientific method is the logical justification of induction. In science, inductive conclusions are accepted not only as accurate transcriptions of nature, but also as reliable guides to future occurrences. What is the rational ground for such an attitude? Peirce investigates this question in detail. He begins by criticizing effectively two types of justification that have been offered by logicians: (1) Laplace's Rule of Succession, and (2) Mill's principle of the Uniformity of Nature. We shall consider his remarks on each of these doctrines.

1. The principle referred to as the Rule of Succession, which is due primarily to the mathematician Laplace, has been employed to justify induction by linking it with a particular interpretation of probability. The rule offers a formula for estimating the probability of an event, which has occurred a certain number of times, occurring on the next occasion, given the appropriate circumstances. If, for instance,

---

[12]Traces of this denial are to be found as early as 1878. For example: "There is . . . a manifest impossibility in so tracing out any probability for a synthetic conclusion" (2.681).

we know that an event has occurred m times and failed to occur n times, under given circumstances, then the probability of its occurrence when those conditions are again fulfilled is $\dfrac{m+1}{m+n+2}$. Now if this rule were sound, it would obviously give a high probability to predictions based on cases where an event is known to have occurred a large number of times, and where no instance of its failure to occur is recorded. Thus (to use Quetelet's example) if I have observed the tide rise for 10,000 successive days, and know of no day that it did not rise, I am entitled to believe with a probability of $\dfrac{10,000+1}{10,000+2}$ that it will rise tomorrow. Since this fraction approaches very close to unity, the principle involved seems to offer a means of justifying induction by simple enumeration. For the larger the number of positive instances registered, the closer the procedure leads to certainty.

Peirce rejects this doctrine for several reasons.

(i) In the first place, he points out that it presupposes the subjective or conceptualistic interpretation of probability. For if we apply the formula to the case of a man who has *never* seen the tide rise, i.e., if m and n both equal 0, then the probability that it will rise the *first* time he observes it is ½. Such a solution involves the conceptualistic principle that there is an even chance of a totally unknown event. Where we have absolutely no evidence *pro* or *con*, the probability measure is always ½. But this doctrine has already been shown to be erroneous, because ignorance cannot entitle us to assert a probability ratio.

(ii) In the second place, the reasoning which yields the Laplacean formula depends on a highly questionable postulate, viz., the "equiprobability of ratios" with respect to unknown probabilities. According to this postulate, when the probability of an event is unknown, we may suppose all possible values of the probability between 0 and 1 to be equally likely *a priori*. Translated into the frequency interpretation, this is tantamount to saying that antecedent to empirical evidence, all frequencies are equiprobable. But "the latter proposition, though it may be applied to any one unknown event, cannot be applied to all unknown events without inconsistency" (2.746). Peirce tries to show where the inconsistency lies by means of an illustration. Suppose there are four possible occasions upon which an event can occur. Then all the frequencies indicated in the following table may be taken to be equiprobable (*Y* stands for an occurrence and *N* for a non-occurrence):

4 occurrences	3 occurrences	2 occurrences	1 occurrence	0 occurrence
Y Y Y Y	Y Y Y N	Y Y N N	Y N N N	N N N N
	Y Y N Y	Y N Y N	N Y N N	
	Y N Y Y	Y N N Y	N N Y N	
	N Y Y Y	N Y Y N	N N N Y	
		N Y N Y		
		N N Y Y		

Here there are 16 possible distributions of occurrences and non-occurrences.

Now consider the event which consists in a *Y* following a *Y*, or an *N* following an *N*. The various ways in which *this* event may or may not occur can be displayed thus.

3 occurrences	2 occurrences	1 occurrence	0 occurrence
Y Y Y Y	Y Y Y N	Y Y N Y	Y N Y N
N N N N	N N N Y	N N Y N	N Y N Y
	Y Y N N	Y N N Y	
	N N Y Y	N Y Y N	
	N Y Y Y	Y N Y Y	
	Y N N N	N Y N N	

Here again there are 16 possible distributions. Yet, Peirce argues, "it will be found that assuming the different frequencies of the first event to be equally probable, those of this new event are not so" (*ibid.*). But if both events are wholly unknown, the frequencies should be equiprobable in *both* cases. The inconsistency which our analysis has disclosed must therefore lead us to conclude that the postulate of the equiprobability of ratios is untenable, and the formula based upon it unsound.

(iii) It has sometimes been affirmed that the Rule of Succession depends rather on the assumption of the equiprobability of constitutions than on the equiprobability of ratios. Although these two doctrines have usually been regarded as equivalent (e.g. by Boole in his *Laws of Thought*), Peirce thinks they are slightly different. The equiprobability of constitutions can be illustrated most readily by referring to the calculation of so-called "inverse probability" ratios. For example, a ball is drawn from a bag known to contain 10 balls, and is found to be white. What is the probability of there having been only 1 white ball in the bag?[13] The solution of this problem requires the assumption

---

[13]Cf. J. Venn, *The Logic of Chance* (London, 1886), p. 180.

that all possible constitutions of the bag are equally probable. But the difficulty is that here again we have no evidence to warrant our assumption. It is purely gratuitous. Moreover, if we try to draw an analogy between this situation and the investigation of Nature, we shall find ourselves driven to the conclusion that all natural events are *independent*, just as the individual drawings from the bag, the successive tosses of a penny, or throws of a die, are independent. But in that case, "the occurrences or non-occurrences of an event in the past in no way affect the probability of its occurrence in the future" (*ibid.*). Accordingly, if we have found the order of Nature more or less regular in the past, this has been by a pure run of luck, like throwing a series of ten successive heads and ten successive tails with a penny; and we have absolutely no reason to believe that such a run of luck will continue. In short, we should have to assume "that Nature is a pure chaos, or chance combination of independent elements, in which reasoning from one fact to another would be impossible" (2.684; cf. 6.399). Such an assumption not only makes nonsense out of our practical activity, but also leaves inductive inference without a shred of rational justification.

In opposition to the Laplacean view, Peirce contends that it is meaningless to speak of the equiprobability of constitutions with respect to Nature as a whole. "The relative probability of this or that arrangement of Nature is something which we should have a right to talk about if universes were as plenty as blackberries, if we could put a quantity of them in a bag, shake them well up, draw out a sample, and examine them to see what proportion of them had one arrangement and what proportion another. But, even in that case, a higher universe would contain us, in regard to whose arrangements the conception of probability could have no applicability" (2.684).

Thus, both in its actual formulation and in its presuppositions, the Rule of Succession is inadequate, and fails to provide a valid method of justifying induction.

2. Since a number of his contemporaries were inclined to follow J. S. Mill's analysis of induction, it was natural that Peirce should devote some attention to the *System of Logic*. He prefaces his remarks with a tribute to the clarity and acumen of its author, who, as Hobhouse remarked, "wrote intelligibly enough to be found out."[14] Mill's natural candor, says Peirce, "led to his making many admissions with-

---

[14]L. T. Hobhouse, *The Theory of Knowledge* (London, 1896), p. ix.

out perceiving how fatal they were to his negative theories" (6.99). The consequence is that an attentive reader can detect in his exposition an unconscious wavering between three or four incompatible accounts of the justification of induction.

"The first (stated in Bk. iii, Ch. 3, Sec. 1) is [that] the whole force of induction is the same as that of a syllogism of which the major premiss is the same for all inductions, being a certain 'Axiom of the uniformity of the course of nature' (so described in the table of 'Contents'). This was substantially Whateley's theory of 1826." (2.761) Given the major premiss in that form, together with any minor premiss stating observed facts about particular instances, a valid inductive conclusion can, according to Mill, be drawn.

Against this theory Peirce urges the following objections. (i) The phrase "uniformity of nature," although it seems straightforward enough, is in fact highly ambiguous, and Mill attaches no univocal sense to it. If we take it to mean that nature is everywhere uniform, that as one part of it is, so is every other—the doctrine runs counter to observed facts. For "nature is not regular. No disorder would be less orderly than the existing arrangement. It is true that the special laws and regularities are innumerable; but nobody thinks of the irregularities, which are infinitely more frequent." (5.342) "In fact, the great characteristic of nature is its diversity. For every uniformity known, there would be no difficulty in pointing out thousands of non-uniformities." (6.100) Mill sometimes says he means by the uniformity of nature simply that when all the circumstances accompanying two phenomena are the same, they will be alike. "But taken strictly this means absolutely nothing, since no two phenomena ever can happen in circumstances precisely alike, nor are two phenomena precisely alike" (*ibid.*). The truth seems to be that *the* uniformity of nature is a conception to which no objective fact corresponds. Hence, it cannot be employed to justify induction.

In addition to this general criticism, there are a number of specific objections to Mill's first theory. (ii) He failed to recognize that an induction, unlike a formal demonstration, rests not only upon the facts observed, but also "upon the manner in which those facts have been collected." (2.766) (iii) Mill's doctrine is really designed to obliterate the distinction between deduction and induction. For while every valid syllogism is such that its conclusion is a necessary consequence of the premisses, induction never yields a necessary conclusion. To suppose the contrary is to construe induction as a kind of "disguised deduction."[15] (iv) The error in this is shown by the fact that whereas a syllogism does enrich our knowledge of the relations among ideas, it does *not* increase our information about the world. Kant drew attention to this in his remark that deduction only explicates but does not amplify our knowledge. Induction, however, *does* amplify our knowledge. The two modes of reasoning are therefore radically different. (v) The "inductive syllogism" proposed by Mill is formally fallacious, because its major premiss is so vague that the syllogism involves the fallacy of undistributed middle. For "all we really know of the general uniformity of nature is that *some* pairs of phenomena (an apparently infinitesimal proportion of all pairs) are connected as logical antecedent and consequent" (*ibid.*). (vi) The principle of the uniformity of nature cannot be a valid ground of induction, because (in spite of Mill's arguments to the contrary) the only way we can come to know the probable truth of the principle is by using induction. But this involves a circular inference. (vii) Lastly, the logical extension of the conclusion of a sound syllogism must be no greater than the extension of its minor premiss (when this is suitably stated). But in a true induction the conclusion cannot fulfil such a requirement.

Having disposed of Mill's first theory, Peirce turns to a second, which he says appears most clearly in book III, chapter IV, section 2 of the *System of Logic*. The gist of the second theory is "that induction proceeds *as if* upon the principle that a predicate which throughout a more or less extensive experience has been uniformly found to be true of all the members of a given class that have been examined in this respect may, with little risk, be presumed to be true of every member of that class, without exception; and that while it is not necessary that the inductive reasoner should have this principle clearly in mind, the *logician,* whose business it partly is to explain why inductions turn out to be true, must recognize the fact that nature is sufficiently uniform to render that *quasi* principle true, and must recognize that [nothing] else renders induction a safe and justifiable procedure" (2.761). In effect, this theory is little more than the old maxim that we must judge the future by the past, which Mill elsewhere attacks as misleading. Here, however, he seems to utilize it surreptitiously as a logical guarantee of induction.

Peirce agrees that Mill's second theory does describe the procedure

---

[15]Cf. B. Russell, *The Principles of Mathematics* (Cambridge, 1903), p. 11 n. "What is called induction appears to me to be either disguised deduction or a mere method of making plausible guesses."

followed by the mind in making crude inductions. As a psychological account of how we think in such cases, it is tolerably adequate. Moreover, the principle of the theory also sufficiently explains how it is that we encounter so many opportunities to draw crude inductions as we do (provided, of course, we interpret it as meaning not that future history will *repeat* past history, but that under sufficiently similar conditions future history will *closely resemble* past history). But the moment we seek to apply this theory so as to justify, or exhibit the validity of even crude induction (to say nothing of the other kinds) it lays itself open to all the objections levelled against the first theory. "For this second theory . . . differs from the first merely in not allowing, as essential to induction, that it should have any of such force as it might derive from employing the uniformity of experience as a premiss. Now this point of difference cannot confer upon induction as explained by the second theory any validity that it would not have if it were explicable by the first theory." (2.767)

Mill's third theory, according to Peirce, manifests itself in book III, chapter III, section 3 of his treatise. Here he appears to admit that nature as a whole is not absolutely uniform, and that variety is a far more dominant feature of it. Such uniformity as exists is "a mere tissue of partial regularities," each consisting in the fact that some classes of objects show a greater and some a less tendency to resemble all of their members in respect to certain lines of characters. Whoever realizes this, Mill adds, "knows more of the philosophy of logic than the wisest of the ancients," and has "solved the problem of induction." Curiously enough, although this theory was original with Mill, his implied disparagement of the "ancients" was somewhat ill advised. For, as Peirce points out, a quarter of a century after his remark, Gomperz published what remained of a papyrus from Herculaneum, in which the Epicurean Philodemus, the teacher of Cicero, propounded a theory of the validity of induction almost identical with that of Mill.

The endeavor to ground induction on the special uniformities present in nature is, Peirce grants, superior to the other theories in two respects. First, it removes a large part of the vagueness attaching to the general principle of uniformity; and in some cases makes the special uniformity entail a merely probable conclusion, thus rendering the refutation of the theory, on the ground that induction does not conclude apodictically, considerably more difficult. Secondly, it is undeniable that the special uniformities in nature *do* help to strengthen or weaken inductive conclusions.

By way of amplification, Peirce mentions four types of uniformities which are of importance to the scientific reasoner. (*a*) There is the case where the members of a class possess a greater or less general resemblance in regard to a certain line of characters. "Thus, the Icelanders are said to resemble one another most strikingly in their opinions about general subjects. Knowing this, we should not need to question many Icelanders, if we found that the first few whom we met all shared a common superstition, in order to conclude with considerable confidence that nearly all Icelanders were of the same way of thinking." (6.98) (*b*) There is the case where a character has a greater or less tendency to be present or absent throughout the whole of a group of classes, or with respect to all the species of a genus. Since black is more often a generic character than white, it is safer to conclude that all crows are black than it is to conclude that all swans are white. (*c*) There is the case where a certain set of characters may be intimately connected so as to be usually all present or all absent in certain kinds of objects. Thus, the different chemical reactions of gold are so inseparable that a chemist need only obtain one of them in order to be confident that the body under examination will show every reaction of gold. (*d*) Finally, there is the case where "an object may have more or less tendency to possess the whole of certain sets of characters when it possesses any of them" (2.743). Suppose we know about a certain individual that whatever political party he belongs to, he is likely to embrace without reserve the entire creed of that party. We shall only need to know some of his political opinions, in order to infer with great confidence the remainder. The knowledge of the truth or falsity of any of these kinds of uniformities is bound to strengthen or weaken our inductive inferences. Hence Mill's third theory does state correctly *part* of the argument for very many inductive conclusions.

Nevertheless, this theory cannot be regarded as wholly adequate. For, Peirce insists, "these special uniformities (such, for example, as that every chemical element has the same combining weight, no matter from what mineral or from what part of the globe it has come), have only become known by induction, often only by elaborate investigations, and are not logical principles; so that they need to be stated as premisses when the argument is to be set forth in full" (2.768). But this creates the same problem that arose in connection with the principle of the uniformity of nature—namely, how can a logical justification for such premisses be found? The difficulty appears insurmountable. It indicates quite plainly that the problem cannot be successfully resolved in the terms laid down by Mill.

What, then, is the true guarantee of the validity of induction? Peirce's opinion on this question changed considerably throughout his career. In early writings, where he is much concerned with tracing the formal relations between deduction and induction, he seeks to justify the latter by showing that it is reducible to the former. An illustration will help to clarify his procedure. Suppose we are confronted with a bag containing a number of beans, the color of which we wish to discover. We draw out a handful at random, and find all the beans in it to be white. We may then conclude that all the beans in the bag are white. This gives us an inductive argument which can be formulated thus:

> These beans are from this bag,
> These beans are white;
> Therefore, all the beans in this bag are white.

But these same propositions can be rearranged so as to produce a valid deductive argument.

> All the beans in this bag are white,
> These beans are from this bag;
> Therefore, these beans are white.

The fact that such rearrangement is possible proves that our original induction is valid. For the "central characteristic and key to induction is, that by taking the conclusion so reached as major premiss of a syllogism, and the proposition stating that such and such objects are taken from the class in question as the minor premiss, the other premiss of the induction will follow from them deductively" (5.275). Thus, by "inverting" a deductive syllogism, we can produce a corresponding induction, or *vice versa*. This holds true irrespective of the figure and mood of the syllogism concerned (2.512; 2.619 ff.).

The same theme appears in the Johns Hopkins essay of 1883, but with certain modifications. Peirce now insists that only a *statistical* deduction can be made to yield a corresponding induction. "The inversion of *ordinary* syllogism does not give rise to an induction" (2.718). It is in this context that he presents the example already quoted several times, of the derivation of a typical induction from a statistical deduction. The significance of the derivation continues to lie in the fact that it enables us to test the correctness of our ampliative inference. For there is but one rule to be followed in order to make valid and strong inductions, "namely, that the statistical deduction of

which the Induction . . . is the inversion, must be valid and strong"
(2.715). In its capacity as a validating form of inference, a statistical
deduction is spoken of as an "explanatory" syllogism. Hence, "in order
that an induction . . . should have any validity at all, it is requisite
that the explanatory syllogism should be a valid statistical deduction"
(2.718; cf. 2.723).

On this view, deductive reasoning is obviously taken as the basic
variety. It is the touchstone for all other kinds of inference, in much
the same way as the first figure of the syllogism was in Aristotelian
logic. As his ideas developed, Peirce came to recognize the extreme
artificiality of such a view. Writing in 1902 he confesses that his youthful papers were "too much taken up in considering syllogistic forms
and the doctrine of logical extension and comprehension, both of
which I made more fundamental than they really are" (2.102). Not
only that, but in many cases where scientific inductions are made, it is
quite impossible, because of lack of knowledge, to arrive at a corresponding statistical deduction. This would mean that a large class of
inferences in science must be theoretically untestable—a conclusion
highly unsatisfactory in view of the practical successes to which such
inferences have led.

We have observed that Peirce ultimately became convinced that
the distinctive thing about induction was its reliability as a method of
inquiry. "In the case of analytic inference we know the probability of
our conclusion (if the premises are true), but in the case of synthetic
inferences we only know the degree of trustworthiness of our proceeding" (2.693). The true guarantee of the validity of induction, therefore, arises from the fact that it is a "method of reaching conclusions
which, if it be persisted in long enough, will assuredly correct any
error concerning future experience into which it may temporarily lead
us. This it will do not by virtue of any deductive necessity (since it
never uses all the facts of experience, even of the past), but because
it is manifestly adequate . . . to discover any *regularity* there may be
among experiences." (2.769) Its adequacy here arises from a *self-
corrective* power which enables it gradually but inevitably to get rid
of its own errors (5.575 ff.).[16] This self-corrective tendency is in turn
due to the fact that induction is based on samples drawn at random
from the subject-matter under investigation, and that each sample is

---

[16]This is "one of the most wonderful features of reasoning and one of the
most important philosophemes in the doctrine of science, of which, however, you
will search in vain for any mention in any book I can think of" (5.575).

free to turn up with the same relative frequency. Consequently, the objective constitution of the subject-matter *must ultimately reveal itself*, if scientific inquiry is unchecked.

Another way of putting the matter is to say that induction is concerned with finding out how often within a specific set of events certain conditions will, in the long run of experience, be followed by a result of a predesignate description. The inquirer proceeds to note the results as members of this set of events present themselves in experience; and finally, when a considerable number of instances have been observed, he infers that the general character of the whole endless succession of similar events in the course of experience will be approximately of the character observed.

For that endless series must have some character; and it would be absurd to say that experience has a character which is never manifested. But there is no other way in which the character of that series can manifest itself than while the endless series is still incomplete. Therefore, if the character manifested by the series up to a certain point is not that character which the entire series possesses, still, as the series goes on, it must eventually tend, however irregularly, towards becoming so; and all the rest of the reasoner's life will be a continuation of this inferential process. This inference does not depend upon any assumption that the series will be endless, or that the future will be like the past, or that nature is uniform, nor upon any material assumption whatever. (2.784)

The self-corrective power of induction is the necessary and sufficient guarantee of its success.[17]

Although the above statement represents Peirce's opinion in its mature form, some interesting anticipations of it are to be found in earlier papers. Thus, his essay on the "Grounds of Validity of the Laws of Logic" (1868), maintains that the justification of induction involves two questions. (i) Why are the majority of inductions which men make borne out by the course of events? (ii) Why have men not been fated to light always upon the small proportion of worthless inductions? The answer to these questions hinges on the fact that inductive reasoning requires samples to be drawn from a class of items.

---

[17]"Thus it is that inquiry of every type, fully carried out, has the vital power of self-correction and of growth. This is a property so deeply saturating its inmost nature that it may truly be said that there is but one thing needful for learning the truth, and that is a hearty and active desire to learn what is true. If you really want to learn the truth, you will, by however devious a path, be surely led into the way of truth, at last. No matter how erroneous your ideas of the method may be at first, you will be forced at length to correct them so long as your activity is moved by that sincere desire." (5.582)

But what we mean by the word "class" can only be specified by refer-ring to concrete experience. This is a necessary implication of the pragmatic method of ascertaining meaning. Hence, the members of any class are by definition the same as all that are to be known. It follows that "in the long run any one member of a class will occur as the subject of a premiss of a possible induction as often as any other, and, therefore, the validity of induction depends simply upon the fact that the parts make up and constitute the whole" (5.349). The basic prerequisite is that classes should be objectively real and their mem-bers completely knowable. Peirce adds that it is better not to talk about the majority of inductions being true, but to say rather that in the long run they approximate to the truth (5.350). All we can be sure of in a given instance is that we are pursuing a technique which ulti-mately gets rid of its own errors. Clearly, then, "a sufficiently long succession of inferences from parts to whole will lead men to a knowl-edge of it, so that in that case they cannot be fated on the whole to be thoroughly unlucky in their inductions" (5.351).

This conclusion is supported, according to Peirce, by the fact that the opposite assumption leads to a self-contradictory result. For sup-pose men were *not* able to learn from induction. This could only be because as a general rule when they had made an induction the order of nature (as it appears in experience) would undergo a change. In such a universe the order would depend on how much men knew about it. "But this general rule would be capable of being itself discovered by induction; and so it must be a law of such a universe, that when this was discovered it would cease to operate" (5.352). But this second law would also be capable of discovery. Hence in such a universe there would be nothing which would not sooner or later be known; and it would possess an order capable of discovery by a sufficiently long course of reasoning. "But this is contrary to the hypothesis, and there-fore that hypothesis is absurd" (*ibid.*).

We have seen that for Peirce the paradigm of induction is repre-sented by the situation in which an urn containing a collection of multi-colored balls is sampled to ascertain the proportion of the colors present. But it may be objected that in this situation the assumption is always made that the subject-matter has a *determinate character*. Therefore, if Peirce's interpretation be correct, an equivalent material assumption must underlie every inductive inference. The result is that in place of postulating the "uniformity of nature," the present scheme requires us to postulate that nature in all its phases is characterized by *some kind* of uniformity. But how does this differ in principle from Mill's much-maligned procedure? Is it not exposed to exactly the same criticism?

To this objection Peirce makes the following reply. It is not necessary for the inductive reasoner to assume that nature is characterized by some determinate order or regularity, *because it could not in fact be otherwise*. Whatever exists must exemplify at least a minimal degree of order. An existent state of complete disorder or "chaos" is a material impossibility. "Chaos is pure nothing" (5.431). Moreover, the larger and more diversified the collection of items being investigated, the greater will be the number of its constituent uniformities. Peirce endeavors to indicate why this must be so by means of another illustration.

If upon a checker-board of an enormous number of squares, painted all sorts of colors, myriads of dice were to be thrown, it could hardly fail to happen, that upon some color, or shade of color, out of so many, some one of the six numbers should not be uppermost on any die. This would be a regularity; for, the universal proposition would be true that upon that color that number is never turned up. But suppose this regularity abolished, then a far more remarkable regularity would be created, namely, that on every color every number is turned up. Either way, therefore, a regularity must occur. Indeed, a little reflection will show that, although we have here only variations of color and of the numbers of the dice, many regularities must occur. And the greater the number of objects, the more respects in which they vary, and the greater the number of varieties in each respect, the greater will be the number of regularities. (5.342)

Consequently, in a universe of such extraordinary magnitude and complexity as ours, the number of regularities (although vastly less than the irregularities) is nevertheless indefinitely large. However, it is quite unnecessary for induction to *presuppose* anything of this sort. The basic fact that *any* existential subject-matter must be ordered, and that random sampling will eventually disclose its order, is all that is required. The conception of a universe in which inductive inference should consistently yield false conclusions belongs to the realm of fancy.

Does this mean that induction is an entirely presuppositionless technique? Peirce does not make any such claim. As we have seen, he admits that the process of obtaining random samples is always a precarious one. In any given instance, it may err very seriously; and there is even the possibility that it is generally fallacious, because of some mysterious and malign connection between the mind and the universe—

such as the possession by objects of an unperceived character which influences the will toward choosing or rejecting them. "I grant, then, that even upon my theory some fact has to be supposed" to make induction a valid process; "namely, it is supposed that the supernal powers withhold their hands and let me alone, and that no mysterious uniformity or adaptation interferes with the action of chance" (2.749). However, Peirce contends, this negative assumption is quite different from the sort of thing postulated by Mill. The principle of the uniformity of nature was designed to serve as a major premiss from which the conclusions inferred by induction could be deduced. But Peirce's assumption is precisely the denial of any major premiss from which the falsity of inductive conclusions could in general be deduced. In short, the validity of induction does not depend on the presence of any *particular* order in the world. All that is necessary is the presence of some kind of order; and that this must be a characteristic of our world follows from the fact that the latter exists.

The question naturally arises whether Peirce offers adequate grounds for accepting the above doctrine. So far as I can see, he does not. In the last analysis, his appeal is to the criterion of inconceivability. We cannot imagine a world, he declares, in which inductive inference would be systematically misleading, i.e. a world totally devoid of order.[18] Although this may be true in the sense that we cannot imagine the details of such a world, nevertheless Peirce has sufficiently stressed the fact that "inconceivability" is no proper guarantee of truth or falsity. It cannot serve as the ground for the doctrine in question. One might, of course, take the position suggested by Professor C. I. Lewis, that "a certain minimal order is prescribed *a priori* in our recognition of the real."[19] But this line of thought is never pursued by Peirce; and for Professor Lewis it seems to mean little more than adopting the regulative maxim "that there must be some order in any given area of reality." It seems clear, then, that Peirce's doctrine that order is a necessary attribute of existence remains a methodological postulate which the inductive reasoner has to adopt; and is thus a material assumption about the constitution of nature.

Among many other points which might be discussed, two may be singled out for comment in bringing this section to a close. It seems

[18]Yet elsewhere he himself admits that the "universe might be all so fluid and variable that nothing should preserve its individual identity," so that "no measurement should be conceivable." In such a universe, "probable inference could not be made" (2.696).

[19]Cf. *Mind and the World-Order* (New York, 1929), p. 353.

to me that Peirce fails to show how it is possible to obtain truly fair or representative samples from an indefinitely large class of items. For it is surely the case that if the amount of independent variety characterizing such a class is indeterminately great, or even too great to be investigated with the scientific techniques at man's disposal, he may *never* obtain representative samples, no matter how long he carries on the process. Hence it appears as though some further assumption, such as the existence of a limit in a rapidly converging series of variations, or the existence of a finite number of characters and classes in nature, is required if our procedure of sampling is to yield us representative instances. Closely connected with this is another point. Peirce continually speaks of induction as a process within the continuum of inquiry, that will inevitably approximate to truth "in the long run." But is not the qualifying phrase "in the long run" far too vague as it stands to provide the scientific reasoner with a basis for deciding precisely when his conclusions are beginning so to approximate? For the "long run" may be so long, that the samples examined at any given stage in the inquiry are absurdly inadequate and unreliable. But how is the inductive reasoner to know this? Or what grounds can he find for attaching a determinate degree of probability to any of his generalizations?

Despite these adverse considerations, Peirce's account of induction has many sound features. Not only does it portray with fidelity the actual method used by a scientist in conducting his investigations, but it also avoids a number of old theoretical pitfalls by its emphasis on the central role of sampling and on the self-corrective character of the total process. That he had "solved the problem of induction," I do not suppose Peirce would have claimed. For he observes in 1905 that after actively studying the problem for half a century, he still hopes "to detect errors and omissions in my views, even if others do not confer upon me the benefits of such amendments" (2.760). Yet Reichenbach is surely correct in saying that Peirce's views "mark the first forward step towards a solution of this problem" since it was pointed out by David Hume.[20]

[20]See his essay in *The Philosophy of John Dewey* (Evanston and Chicago, 1939), p. 187. Royce accepted Peirce's account of induction as essentially correct. Cf. *Encyclopedia of the Philosophical Sciences*, vol. I, *Logic* (London, 1913), pp. 82-88. Professor D. C. Williams in his *The Ground of Induction* (Harvard University Press, 1947) also seems to have drunk deep of the Peircean spring. Cf. pp. 196-200.

B. Abduction

8. THE GENERAL CHARACTER OF ABDUCTION

The second kind of ampliative inference is referred to variously by Peirce as Abduction, Presumption, Retroduction, or Hypothesis.[21] For the sake of simplicity only the first of these designations will be employed in what follows. Broadly speaking, abduction is a term which covers "all the operations by which theories and conceptions are engendered" (5.590). The most important manifestation of abduction is the process of arriving at scientific hypotheses. Peirce takes the view that this process is essentially inferential. Its form is:

> The surprising fact, *C*, is observed;
> But if *A* were true, *C* would be a matter of course,
> Hence, there is reason to suspect that *A* is true.

Such a process is inferential because it is subject to certain conditions. That is to say, the hypothesis "is adopted for some reason, good or bad, and that reason, in being regarded as such, is regarded as lending the hypothesis some plausibility" (2.511 n.). Furthermore, "*A* cannot be abductively inferred, or if you prefer the expression, cannot be abductively conjectured until its entire content is already present in the premiss, 'If *A* were true, *C* would be a matter of course'" (5.189).

9. ABDUCTION AND INDUCTION

The specific features of abduction can best be brought out by contrasting it with induction. Just here, however, we find in Peirce two distinct emphases.

1. In his earlier papers, induction and abduction are treated as independent forms of inference. They are distinguished by the fact that "the former infers the existence of phenomena such as we have observed in cases that are *similar*," while the latter "supposes something of a different kind from what we have directly observed, and frequently something which it would be impossible for us to observe directly" (2.640). For in induction all we do is to generalize from a number of cases of which something is true, and infer that the same thing is probably true of a whole class. We conclude that facts *like* those observed are true in cases not examined (2.636). This does not involve the postulation of elements different in kind from those that

---

[21]He suggests that this is what the twenty-fifth chapter of Aristotle's second *Prior Analytics* imperfectly described as ἀπαγωγή (2.776).

have already come under our scrutiny. But in abduction we pass from the observation of certain facts to the supposition of a general principle which, if it were true, would *account for* (i.e. explain) the facts being what they are. We thus conclude the existence of something quite different from anything empirically observed, something that is in the majority of cases empirically unobservable. Thus induction may be said to be reasoning from particulars to a general law; abduction, reasoning from effect to cause. "The former classifies, the latter explains" (*ibid.*).

Explanatory hypotheses may be of widely different kinds, and Peirce alludes to at least three varieties in the course of his writing.[22] (i) There are hypotheses which refer to facts unobserved when the abduction is made, but which are nevertheless *capable* of having been observed by the investigator. For instance, on discovering a heap of white beans near a bag containing only white beans, we adopt the hypothesis that the heap came from the bag (2.623). This supposition accounts, at least in part, for the beans being where they are; it "explains" their presence. (ii) Then there are hypotheses which refer to facts not only unobserved but physically incapable of being observed by the investigator. This is the case with all hypotheses about the past. "Fossils are found; say, remains like those of fishes, but far in the interior of the country. To explain the phenomenon, we suppose the sea once washed over this land." (2.625)   (iii) Finally, there are hypotheses which refer to entities which in the present state of knowledge are both factually and theoretically incapable of being observed (e.g. molecules, electrons, the luminiferous ether, etc.). These are, of course, scientific hypotheses *par excellence*, and their explanatory function is of the highest importance.

As an illustration of the third class, Peirce mentions the kinetic theory of gases. It is devised to explain certain simple formulae, the chief of which is Boyle's Law. This law asserts that if air or any gas be placed in a cylinder with a piston, and if its volume be measured under the pressure of the atmosphere, say fifteen pounds per square inch, and then if another fifteen pounds per square inch be placed on the piston, the gas will be compressed to one-half its bulk, and in similar inverse ratio for other pressures (2.639). This law is entirely the result of inductive generalization from particular instances. It is what physicists call an *empirical formula*. "Such formulae, though very useful as means of describing in general terms the results of observa-

[22]Cf. Buchler, *Charles Peirce's Empiricism*, pp. 131-32.

tions, do not take any high rank among scientific discoveries" (2.637).
Now the hypothesis which has been adopted to account for Boyle's
Law is that gases consist of small, solid particles (molecules) at great
distances from each other (relative to their dimensions) and moving
with great velocity, without sensible attractions or repulsions, until
they happen to approach one another very closely. Once this is admitted, it follows that when a gas is under pressure what prevents it
from collapsing is not the incompressibility of the separate molecules,
which are under no pressure at all, since they do not touch, but the
pounding of the molecules against the piston. The more the piston
falls, and the more the gas is compressed, the nearer together the molecules will be; and the greater number there will be within a given
distance of the piston; and the more frequently any given molecule
will strike it. This explains Boyle's Law. And because the hypothesis
has received support from other investigations into the mechanical
theory of heat, it stands high on the list of reliable explanatory principles.

It is clear that on the above view abduction and induction are
separate forms of inference. "Generally speaking, the conclusions of
Hypothetic Inference cannot be arrived at inductively, because their
truth is not susceptible of direct observation in single cases. Nor can
the conclusions of Inductions, on account of their generality, be
reached by hypothetic inference." (2.714) Abductive reasoning is,
moreover, a less reliable procedure than induction. For the hypothesis
problematically inferred always stands a chance of being completely
wrong; and in many cases the fallaciousness may be difficult, if not
impossible, to detect. Hence, "hypothesis is a weak kind of argument"
(2.625). Even in this early formulation, however, Peirce was not prepared to make an absolute separation between the two forms of inference. He points out that induction can easily pass over into abduction,
if it is stretched sufficiently beyond the limits of our observation. Now
"it would be absurd to say that we have no inductive warrant for a
generalization extending a little beyond the limits of experience, and
there is no line to be drawn beyond which we cannot push our inference; only it becomes weaker the further it is pushed" (2.640). Induction, therefore, shades gradually into abduction, so that they may
be conceived as occupying opposite ends of the continuum of ampliative inference.

2. In papers written after 1900, Peirce tended to shift his emphasis
so that abduction and induction, while remaining distinguishable types

of inference, become closely interlinked. It is now asserted that every inductive conclusion was at some prior time the conclusion of an abduction. For the latter "furnishes the reasoner with the problematic theory which induction verifies" (2.776). Abduction is thus "the provisional adoption of a hypothesis because every possible consequence of it is capable of experimental verification" (1.68). Induction consists in starting from a theory previously recommended by abduction, deducing from it a number of consequences, and then observing whether the predicted consequences are substantiated by experimental tests (cf. 2.755, 2.775, 5.170, etc.). Or again, "Induction is an Argument which sets out from a hypothesis, resulting from a previous Abduction, and from virtual predictions, drawn by Deduction, of the results of possible experiments, and having performed the experiments, concludes that the hypothesis is true in the measure in which those predictions are verified, this conclusion, however, being held subject to probable modification to suit future experiments" (2.96). Abduction is consequently "the only kind of reasoning that supplies new ideas, the only kind which is, in this sense, synthetic" (2.777).[23] It *suggests* the theories which induction subsequently verifies by reference to a large number of random samples (6.100).

This second position may, I think, be taken to represent Peirce's mature judgment on the matter. Accordingly, he does not hold that abduction differs from induction in going beyond what is directly observed, because this is a characteristic of induction as well. Indeed, *all* knowledge "must involve additions to the facts observed" (6.523). Hence, it is rather the *degree* to which the two processes go beyond the directly observed that distinguishes them. Neither is there any ground for holding that abduction explains, whereas induction only describes or classifies. Explanation is now seen to be the result of the two procedures operating together. A fact is explained when (*a*) it is exhibited as a necessary consequence of other facts asserted in a hypothesis, and (*b*) when the hypothesis has received a substantial amount of inductive confirmation. That is to say, "a scientific explanation ought to consist in the assertion of some positive matter of fact, other than the fact to be explained, but from which this fact necessarily follows; and if the explanation be hypothetical, the proof of it lies in the experiential verification of predictions deduced from it as necessary consequences" (6.273). If we wish to retain the traditional usage and say that description reveals the "how" of an event while explanation re-

---

[23]"All the ideas of science come to it by way of Abduction" (5.145).

veals its "why," we shall have to add that "the distinction between the 'Why' of the hypothesis and the 'How' of induction is not very great" (2.717).

10. THE CHOICE OF HYPOTHESES

What are the general conditions which determine the choice of hypotheses? In the simplest kind of situation, the stimulus is provided when the investigator finds himself confronted with some puzzling or surprising occurrence or set of occurrences. On examination, he notices a character or relation among them which immediately evokes a conception with which his mind is already stored, so that a theory is suggested which would explain (that is, render necessary) the occurrences. He accordingly accepts that theory so far as to give it a prominent place among ideas which merit further scrutiny. It may be objected at this point that his conclusion hardly appears to be the product of reasoning. Is the investigator not free to examine whatever theories he likes? Not at all, Peirce replies. "If he examines all the foolish theories he might imagine, he never will (short of a miracle) light upon the true one" (2.776). He has therefore to make a selection from the indefinitely large number of hypotheses at his disposal; and to be adequate, his selection must be governed by certain well-defined criteria. The latter are authoritative because they have emerged from, and have been validated by, the actual history of successful scientific inquiry. The logician's job is to state them as precisely as possible.

Of primary importance in Peirce's estimation is the principle of Ockham's razor—*Entia non sunt multiplicanda praeter necessitatem*.[24] The meaning of this principle is explained as follows.

Before you try a complicated hypothesis, you should make quite sure that no simplification of it will explain the facts equally well. No matter if it takes fifty generations of arduous experimentation to explode the simpler hypothesis, and no matter how incredible it may seem that the simpler hypothesis should suffice, still fifty generations are nothing in the life of science, which has all time before it; and in the long run, say in some thousands of generations, time will be economized by proceeding in an orderly manner, and by making it an invariable rule to try the simpler hypothesis first. (5.60)

But what precisely is meant by the expression "simpler hypothesis"? In his early writings, Peirce took this to mean *logical* simplicity; so

---

[24]Peirce is careful to point out that he approves of Ockham's razor merely "as a sound maxim of scientific procedure" (5.60). Nevertheless, he declares elsewhere that the principle is also one which "ought to guide the scientific metaphysician" (6.535).

that the preferable hypotheses were those containing the smallest number of independent types of elements, i.e. those which added least to what has been observed. Subsequent reflection on the history of science, however, convinced him that this interpretation was less than half the truth. "It was not until long experience forced me to realize that subsequent discoveries were every time showing I had been wrong ... that the scales fell from my eyes and my mind awoke to the broad and flaming daylight that it is the simpler Hypothesis in the sense of the more facile and natural, the one that instinct suggests, that must be preferred" (6.477). Not logical but *psychological* simplicity is what Ockham's razor requires of a hypothesis. "I do not mean that logical simplicity is a consideration of no value at all, but only that its value is badly secondary to that of simplicity in the other sense" (*ibid.*). The reason for this unusual way of construing Ockham's razor will manifest itself below.

Peirce stresses certain other criteria to which every sound hypothesis should conform. (*a*) A very important one is that the hypothesis should be "such that definite consequences can be plentifully deduced from it of a kind which can be checked by observation" (2.786). A hypothesis should only be admitted if it yields a number of predictions that can be tested experimentally. One of the advantages of observing the maxim of Ockham's razor is that "the simplest hypotheses are those of which the consequences are most readily deduced and compared with observation; so that, if they are wrong, they can be eliminated at less expense than any others" (6.532). The converse of this requirement is, of course, that a hypothesis on which no verifiable predictions can be based should never be accepted (5.599). Peirce sometimes speaks of this as the "principal rule" of abduction. It is closely connected, as we shall see, with his doctrine of pragmatism. (*b*) Every hypothesis should be distinctly put as a question, before making the observations which are to test its truth (2.634). It "ought, at first, to be entertained interrogatively" (6.524). (*c*) In making predictions on the basis of a hypothesis we should not restrict ourselves to a particular set which we know antecedently will be fulfilled. Our choice of predictable consequences should be a random one. (*d*) Lastly, the failures as well as the successes of our predictions must be honestly noted. "The whole proceeding must be fair and unbiased" (2.634). This implies a refusal to permit subjective elements to determine the selection of one's hypotheses. One ought to maintain "ethical neutrality." "I myself," Peirce asserts, "would not adopt a hypothesis, and would not even take it on probation, simply because the idea was pleasing to me" (5.598). Abduction can have nothing to do with "wishful thinking" or the "will to believe."

In one of his last papers, the important "Note on the Doctrine of Chances" (1910), Peirce suggests a threefold classification of hypotheses under the headings *plausible, likely,* and *probable.* These distinctions relate to the degree of reliability possessed by the propositions concerned. A *plausible* hypothesis is one which (*a*) has not yet been tested, (*b*) accounts adequately for the phenomena which it was devised to explain, and (*c*) recommends itself for further investigation. A *likely* hypothesis is one which (*a*) has not yet been tested, (*b*) accounts adequately for the phenomena in question, and (*c*) "is supported by such evidence that if the rest of the conceivably possible evidence should turn out upon examination to be of a *similar* character, the theory would be conclusively proved" (2.663). More briefly, a likely hypothesis is one which "falls in with our preconceived ideas" (1.120). It is sometimes called nowadays an "antecedently probable" hypothesis, i.e., one which has a measure of likelihood with respect to all known facts other than the special set of facts it is put forward to explain. A *probable* hypothesis, finally, is one that has survived the process of testing to the extent that a large number of its empirical consequences have been verified. Inductive investigation has established with a high degree of probability that the hypothesis will hold true in the long run. This means that it is practically certain—if we understand by a "long run" an endless series of trials (2.664).

Summarizing and re-stating the main points of this discussion, we have the following conditions which every adequate hypothesis should fulfil. (i) It should provide the answer to the problem that generated the inquiry, i.e. it should "account for the facts." (ii) It should be the simplest hypothesis available. (iii) It should yield a large number of verifiable predictions which can be readily put to the test. (iv) These predictions should be such that it is always possible for them to be falsified, and hence for the hypothesis itself to be disproved.

11. ABDUCTION AND PERCEPTUAL JUDGMENTS

Just as there is continuity between induction and abduction, so, according to Peirce, there is continuity between abduction and the basic propositions of scientific reasoning, perceptual judgments. "Abductive inference shades into perceptual judgment without any sharp line of demarcation between them" (5.181). As we saw above, a perceptual judgment is a rapid, uncontrollable cognition which characterizes or interprets a percept. It offers a kind of instantaneous theory as to the nature of the data; and in this respect it is similar to the "flash of insight" whereby a hypothesis is suggested to the mind of a scientific investigator. So swift and unconscious is the process of perceptual judgment, that the interpretation of the data has the appearance of being actually given in perception. Thus, for example, in the case of the well-known unshaded outline figure of a pair of steps seen in perspective, we seem at first to be looking at the steps from above. "But some unconscious part of the mind seems to tire of putting that construction upon it," and suddenly we seem to see the steps from below as an overhanging cornice. This in turn changes, and we see the steps in their original arrangement. The perceptual judgment and the percept itself keep shifting from one general aspect of the figure to the other repeatedly. The first time we encounter this illusion, it seems as completely beyond the control of rational criticism as any percept is. But after many repetitions, the illusion wears off, becoming first less decided, and ultimately ceasing altogether. "This shows that these phenomena are true connecting links between abductions and perceptions" (5.183). Peirce expresses the relation involved here by saying that perceptual judgment is the "limiting case" of abductive judgment (5.186). That is, in the former we have a continuous series of what, discretely and consciously performed, would be abductions. If this were not so, we should expect to find our perceptual experience devoid of interpretational elements. But it is in fact permeated with such elements; and that is conclusive evidence of the continuity which exists between abduction and perceptual judgment. Yet the two are not identical, and it is therefore important to form a clear idea of how they differ. "The only symptom by which the two can be distinguished is that we cannot form the least conception of what it would be to deny the perceptual judgment. . . . An abductive suggestion, however, is something whose truth *can* be questioned or even denied." (*Ibid.*) In other respects the processes are akin. Thus, the connection between the epistemological and the logical aspects of scientific investigation is guaranteed for Peirce by the fact that perceptual judgments, abduction, and induction can be shown to dovetail into one another.

12. PRAGMATISM AND ABDUCTION

Abduction has, for Peirce, a close and significant connection with pragmatism. Since the former is the process of formulating explanatory hypotheses, and the latter is the method whereby meaningful propositions are distinguished from meaningless, it is not hard to see that from one point of view pragmatism is simply the "logic of abduction." "That is, pragmatism proposes a certain maxim which, if sound, must render needless any further rule as to the admissibility of hypotheses to rank as hypotheses, that is to say, as explanations of phenomena held as hopeful suggestions" (5.196). For according to the pragmatic maxim (*a*) only those hypotheses which permit of experimental verification may be validly entertained, and (*b*) if two or more hypotheses yield the same practical consequences, then their logical import is identical, no matter how much their verbal expression may differ. The propositions which the maxim admits, all philosophers would agree ought to be admitted; while, on the other hand, it cannot exclude any proposition which ought to be considered. For all it asks is that proposed hypotheses should have some empirically testable effects. The criterion it applies does not rule out the highest flights of imagination, provided this imagination ultimately alights upon a possible practical effect (*ibid.*). In other words, the criterion is not *a priori* and formal, but *a posteriori* and scientific. This is exactly what one would expect of a doctrine born and bred in the laboratory. Its intimate connection with abduction is therefore not surprising.

13. THE JUSTIFICATION OF ABDUCTION

The problem of justifying abduction was taken by Peirce in his early writings to be exactly the same as that of justifying induction. It was simply a question of reducing any given abductive inference to a corresponding deduction. If the latter turned out to be valid, the correctness of the abduction was guaranteed; if not, the abduction was incorrect. Thus, to take a variation on a theme already familiar: I enter a room where there are a number of bags containing different kinds of beans, and discover upon a table a handful of white beans. After some searching I find that one of the bags contains white beans only. I at once infer as a reasonable hypothesis that this handful was taken out of that bag (2.623). The abduction involved is:

> All the beans in this bag are white,
> These beans are white;
> Therefore, these beans are from this bag.

By reversing the position of the minor premise and conclusion we obtain the valid deductive syllogism:

> All the beans in this bag are white,
> These beans are from this bag;
> Therefore, these beans are white.

This proves that our abduction is sound; for "just as induction may be regarded as the inference of the major premiss of a syllogism, so hypothesis may be regarded as the inference of the minor premiss, from the other two propositions" (5.276). In both cases, however, the touchstone of validity is the fact of reducibility to a valid deduction.

Paralleling the development of his thought on induction, we find Peirce declaring in 1883 that it is reducibility to a valid *statistical* deduction that certifies the correctness of an abductive argument. Consider the following, which Peirce calls "*Statistical deduction in depth*" (2.705).

> Every *M* has, for example, the numerous marks *P'*, *P''*, *P'''*, etc.,
> *S* has an *r*-likeness to the *M*'s;
> Hence, probably and approximately, *S* has the proportion *r* of the marks *P'*, *P''*, *P'''*, etc.

Such a mode of inference is "clearly deductive"; and when *r* = 1, it can be reduced to *Barbara*. Corresponding to it, we have the abduction:

> *M* has the numerous marks *P'*, *P''*, *P'''*, etc.,
> *S* has the proportion *r* of the marks *P'*, *P''*, *P'''*, etc.;
> Hence, probably and approximately, *S* has an *r*-likeness to *M*. (2.706)

For instance, we know that the ancient Mound-builders of North America present, in all those respects in which we have been able to make the comparison, a limited degree of resemblance to the Pueblo Indians. Consequently, it is a reasonable hypothesis that in *all* respects there is about the same degree of resemblance between these races. Since this type of argument is simply the inversion of a valid statistical deduction, its soundness can be taken as established.

What Peirce here considers an abduction is, I think, quite different from anything previously mentioned. Instead of being simply "the probational adoption of a hypothesis" (2.96), the above argument is an "induction of properties," or a kind of argument from analogy. Indeed, Peirce himself admits that in an extended sense of the word "induction," "this argument is simply an induction respecting qualities instead of respecting things. In point of fact *P'*, *P''*, *P'''*, etc., constitute a random sample of the characters of *M*, and the ratio *r* of them being found to belong to *S*, the same ratio of all the characters of *M* are concluded to belong to *S*." (2.706) However, in actual practice, this kind of argument differs quite sharply from induction, owing to the impossibility of counting qualities as one counts individual things. The objects referred to in induction are always capable of being enumerated, whereas qualities (e.g. colors, odors, etc.) fall into categories so general that they permit of a continuous range of variation. Hence, the numerical specification of such characters is not possible. If they are to be estimated at all, it must be by some other method than counting.

A much more satisfactory analysis of "argument from analogy" is given in 2.733, and we may mention it briefly in passing. Peirce contends that analogical argument is a complex process, involving both explicative and ampliative inference. A concrete illustration of it would be the following. We know that of the major planets, the Earth, Mars, Jupiter, and Saturn revolve about their axes; and we conclude that the remaining four, Mercury, Venus, Uranus, and Neptune, probably do the same. Our reasoning here is that the Earth, Mars, Jupiter, and Saturn constitute a random sample of a natural class of major planets, and we conclude inductively that all members of the class rotate on their axes. But since Mercury, Venus, Uranus, and Neptune share, so far as we know, all the properties of this natural class, we conclude by abduction and deduction that they too rotate on their axes. Stated formally the argument is:

S', S'', S''', etc., are samples of the X's,	Every X is, for example, P', P'', P''', etc.,
S', S'', S''', etc., are found to be R's;	Q is found to be P', P'', P''', etc.;
Hence, inductively, every X is an R.	Hence, hypothetically, Q is an X.

Hence, deductively, Q is an R.

Analogical inference thus consists of an induction and an abduction followed by a deduction. Peirce's illustration is a particularly felicitous example of the way in which induction, abduction, and deduction are interwoven in the total pattern of scientific inference.

In his mature writings on the justification of abduction, Peirce abandoned this highly formal approach, and treated the matter from the standpoint of two main problems: (1) that of justifying the use of hypotheses as principles of explanation, against the proponents of extreme positivism and phenomenalism; and (2) that of accounting for the fact that scientists have been so relatively successful in hitting upon true theories about nature. Both the utilization and the achievements of abductive inference call for special discussion.

1. Peirce was well aware of the kind of criticism that would be levelled at abduction by thinkers like Comte, Poincaré, and Pearson. For these men, in common with the majority of positivists, embraced a "descriptive" theory of science, according to which the function of hypotheses was rigidly limited, and relegated to a minor role. Broadly speaking, they subscribed to the doctrine that hypothetical inferences are essentially fictitious in the sense that they never refer, or at least can never be known to refer, to constitutive features of the world. A hypothesis to which observed data give rise does not specify any objective process or quality in nature. It has no correlative object. It is simply a conceptual device for stimulating and directing the discovery of further data. For this reason, hypothetical constructions ought to be used sparingly by scientists and philosophers. Indeed, Comte goes so far as to contend that no hypothesis is admissible which is not capable of verification by direct observation.[25] On such a view, unperceived elements would have to be rigorously excluded from scientific knowledge.

While he expresses admiration and respect for the theories of Comte and Poincaré, Peirce is unable to accept what they have to say about hypothetical inference. He sees in their remarks another reflection of the nominalism which has vitiated so much of modern thought. Generality or Thirdness is an ineluctable part of the cosmos. Consequently, the scientific laws suggested by abduction and confirmed by induction cannot be fictional, but are genuine ingredients of nature. Furthermore, those people who hold that scientific hypotheses are purely symbolic constructions having no counterpart in the outer world are logically committed to the denial of the uniformity of nature, and hence "ought to abstain from all prediction" (5.210).[26] But this would not only make scientific investigation impossible; it would also make nonsense of all practical activity. Such a position could not be

---

[25]Cf. *Cours de philosophie positive* (Paris, 1869), 28me leçon.

[26]In his review of Pearson's *Grammar of Science* (*Popular Science Monthly*, vol. LVIII (1901), pp. 296-306), Peirce criticizes the author for arguing that prediction has no place in scientific inquiry, since the latter is confined to a description of sense-impressions. "Nothing is more notorious than that this method of prediction . . . has proved the master-key of science; . . . Professor Pearson does not say that he would permit generalization of the facts. He ought not to do so, since generalization inevitably involves prediction." The review closes with an amusing dialogue between a realistically minded sailor and a disciple of Professor Pearson, in which the weakness of extreme phenomenalism is acutely exposed.

consistently maintained by any philosopher in the course of his ordinary life.

If recourse be had to Comte's dictum that we may admit only those hypotheses which refer to what is directly observable, the reply is that this leads to fantastic consequences. For instance, it would forbid an archeologist who uncovers a deposit of ancient arms and utensils to suppose that they were either made or used by any human being, since no such beings could ever be detected by direct observation. "The same doctrine would forbid us to believe in our memory of what happened at dinner-time to-day," and "with memory would have to go all opinions about everything not at this moment before our senses. You must not believe that you hear me speaking to you, but only that you hear certain sounds while you see before you a spot of black, white, and flesh color; and those sounds seem to suggest certain ideas which you must not connect at all with the black and white spot." (5.597) In short, this whole doctrine reduces to an extreme phenomenalism, and leads ultimately to "solipsism of the present moment." Hence, no philosopher who is in earnest about his job of analyzing the practical and theoretical achievements of science can take the doctrine seriously.

There is some vacillation on Peirce's part over the question whether abduction has or has not an unrestricted range of application, i.e. whether it is possible to devise an explanatory hypothesis for literally *everything* in the universe.

(i) On the one hand, he continually insists that we must never regard any facts as absolutely incapable of being explained. "Nothing justifies a retroductive inference except its affording an explanation of the facts. It is, however, no explanation at all of a fact to pronounce it *inexplicable*. That, therefore, is a conclusion which no reasoning can ever justify or excuse." (1.139) Moreover, by supposing a phenomenon to be inexplicable, we "set up a barrier across the road of science," and thereby prevent any further attempts to comprehend the phenomenon (6.171). This violates the first rule of reason which warns us not to "block the way of inquiry" (1.135). Just here abduction makes contact with Peirce's metaphysical doctrine of Synechism or continuity. For, as will be manifest later, synechism operates in part as "a regulative principle of logic, prescribing what sort of hypothesis is fit to be entertained and examined" (6.173). The hypotheses it favors are those involving true continuity; while it rejects those containing "inexplicable ultimates" of any kind. These statements seem to imply that the abductive procedure has no determinate limits. Hence, there can never be the slightest excuse for supposing the universe to contain inscrutable factors.

(ii) On the other hand, as we have noted, it is an essential part of Peirce's philosophy that certain features of the universe *are* irreducible, and therefore abduction cannot apply to them. In his phenomenology, the categories of Quality and Fact are of this nature. So are the categories of Feeling and Reaction. It is unreasonable to try to account for "that utterly inexpressible and irrational positive quality" which the color *red* has (5.92). Nor should one try to find an explanation for the "isolated aggressive stubbornness and individual reality" of facts (1.405). Their "hereness and nowness" are *sui generis.* "Why this which is here is such as it is; how, for instance, if it happens to be a grain of sand, it came to be so small and so hard, we can ask; we can also ask how it got carried here; . . . but why ɪᴛ, independently of its general characters, comes to have any definite place in the world, is not a question to be asked, it is simply an ultimate fact" (*ibid.*). Equally inexplicable are feelings and thoughts in their immediacy (5.289), and the phenomena of indeterminacy and variety. "Why one definite kind of event is frequent and another rare, is a question to be asked; but a reason for the general fact that of events some kinds are common and some rare, it would be unfair to demand" (1.405). If all births took place on one day of the week, or if there were always more on Sundays than on Mondays, it would be perfectly legitimate to employ abduction to render this intelligible. But that births happen in about equal proportions on all days of the week requires no particular explanation. The truth is, Peirce contends, that only facts of a general or orderly nature need to be accounted for; hence this is the area in which abduction operates. "We must look forward to the explanation, not of all things, but of any given thing" which enters into a uniform sequence of events (*ibid.*). It is in regard to such items that the assumption of absolute inexplicability is never warranted.

2. There remains the problem of accounting for the remarkable success which abduction has achieved in leading to true theories about nature. The issue here arises, according to Peirce, for the following reason. It is beyond any reasonable doubt that man possesses a number of true scientific doctrines. The fact that he is able to predict and control so many natural events is sufficient evidence of this (5.591). But every such doctrine owes its origin to an abductive inference. The most firmly established scientific principle was once a hypo-

thesis in the mind of some investigator. Now, how is it that in the relatively short time man has been studying nature, he has been able to arrive at *so many true theories?* "You cannot say that it happened by chance, because the possible theories, if not strictly innumerable, at any rate exceed a trillion—or the third power of a million; and therefore the chances are too overwhelmingly against the single true theory in the twenty or thirty thousand years during which man has been a thinking animal, ever having come into any man's head" (*ibid.*). Consider, for example, a physicist who comes across some new phenomenon in his laboratory. How does he know but that the conjunction of the planets may have something to do with it, or that it may be connected with some obscure geological process on the other side of the globe, and so on? Think of the multitude of possible hypotheses which he might entertain, of which only one is true. And yet, after two or three, or at the very most a dozen guesses, he hits pretty nearly on the correct explanation. If it were simply a matter of chance, he would not have been likely to do so in the whole time that has elapsed since the earth was solidified (5.172). But, it may be contended, astrological and magical hypotheses were resorted to at first, and it has been only by degrees that we have learned certain general laws of nature in consequence of which the physicist looks for the explanation of his phenomenon within the four walls of the laboratory. This may be granted; but even so, the basic problem remains, namely, how is it that in the comparatively brief history of science, such a large number of true theories have been selected from the infinity of possible ones?

According to Peirce, the most reasonable supposition is that man has come to the investigation of nature with *a special aptitude* for choosing correct theories (2.753; 5.173; 6.531; etc.). "It seems incontestable therefore that the mind of man is strongly adapted to the comprehension of the world; at least, so far as this goes, that certain conceptions, highly important for such a comprehension, naturally arise in his mind" (6.417). This facility is not a mysterious dispensation from heaven, but is derived from his instinctive life through the process of evolution. Its source lies mainly in the instincts connected with the need of nutrition and with sexual reproduction (1.118; 5.603; etc.). From the former, primitive man derived the germ of his ideas of force, matter, space, and time. The necessity of procuring food compelled him to become a kind of "applied physicist." The "knowledge" thus acquired, while excessively narrow and inchoate, was also essentially sound. It *had* to be, in order to possess any survival-value. The result was that "our innate mechanical ideas were so nearly correct that they needed but slight correction. The fundamental principles of statics were made out by Archimedes. Centuries later Galileo began to understand the laws of dynamics, which in our times have been at length, perhaps, completely mastered." (2.753)   The instincts connected with sexual reproduction, on the other hand, have furnished all animals like ourselves with some virtual knowledge of their fellows. From these "instinctive ideas about human nature" the anthropological sciences (including the moral sciences) have slowly developed. Here again, the ideas were broadly reliable, for upon them depended the survival of the race.

Thus, the achievements of abductive inference are due to the fact that the human intellect is peculiarly adapted to the comprehension of the laws of nature. This adaptation is in turn a derivative from man's instinctive life. If he did not have the gift, which every other animal has, of a mind adjusted to his requirements, not only would he be devoid of knowledge, but he could not have maintained his existence for a single generation (5.603). But because certain general features prevail throughout the universe, and because the investigating mind is itself a product of this universe, the same general features are incorporated in man's own nature. For we should never forget "to how great a degree it is true that the universe is all of one piece, and that we are all of us natural products, naturally partaking of the characteristics that are found everywhere through nature" (5.613). Consequently, "it is somehow more than a mere figure of speech to say that nature fecundates the mind of man with ideas, which, when those ideas grow up, will resemble their father, Nature" (5.591).

In view of this justification of abduction it becomes clear why Peirce interprets Ockham's razor to mean that we should choose hypotheses which are simple in the sense of being spontaneously appealing to the investigating mind. For the chances are in favor of such hypotheses being sound rather than otherwise. It is not suggested, at least in the naturalistic phase of Peirce's thought, that instinctive preferences should be accepted as true without being put to the test. Nor is it implied that they always turn out to be true. In the immediacy of their occurrence, they are merely guesses; and it is quite possible for us to guess incorrectly on the first few occasions. But in the long run, "before very many hypotheses shall have been tried, intelligent guessing may be expected to lead us to the one which supports all tests, leaving the vast majority of possible hypotheses unexamined" (6.530). This is the foundation on which abductive inference rests.

Writing in the *Monist* in 1893, Peirce remarked: "I was brought up in an atmosphere of scientific inquiry, and have all my life chiefly lived among scientific men. For the last thirty years, the study which has constantly been before my mind has been upon the nature, strength, and history of methods of scientific thought." (6.604) The fruits of that study, which we have now reviewed, must lead us to agree with the judgment of John Dewey, that "to have grasped in its totality the significance of scientific method, and to have applied it to a restatement of traditional logic, is . . . an achievement whose importance will stand out more and more as the years go by."[27]

[27]*New Republic,* January 30, 1935, p. 338.

VII

METAPHYSICAL INQUIRY

1. PEIRCE'S ATTITUDE TO METAPHYSICS

"VERILY, metaphysics is the Paris of the intellect: no sooner do the most scrupulously severe reasoners find their feet on this ground than they give the loosest reins of license to their logic." This picturesque observation made by Peirce in the course of a review[1] of Sylvester's *Collected Mathematical Papers*, is peculiarly applicable to his own metaphysical efforts. Even the most sympathetic student cannot help noticing a decline in the quality of his thinking when he turns to this subject. Indeed, his attitude towards its worth as a cognitive enterprise shows a marked ambivalence. In the context of his naturalism, the attitude takes the form of either overt antipathy, or the attempt so to define metaphysics as to make it a discipline capable of using the scientific method of inquiry. In the context of his transcendentalism, metaphysics becomes a form of *a priori* speculation on first and last things. As a matter of fact, the results of this speculation constitute the larger portion of his published work in the field, and will concern us in Part Two. For the present we shall devote ourselves to discussing those aspects of his metaphysics which are broadly naturalistic.

When he looked at the various historical examples of metaphysics, and contrasted their pretensions with their achievement, Peirce, like Kant, was profoundly unimpressed. The discipline, he says, has been "a mere arena of ceaseless and trivial disputation" (6.5). Worse still, it has been pursued in a spirit the very contrary of that of wishing to learn the truth. Aping the science of geometry, it has sought to embody the ideal of rigid demonstration from self-evident principles (1.400). But in fact, "the demonstrations of the metaphysicians are all moonshine" (1.7). They are "so many systems of rummaging the garret of

[1]In the *Nation*, vol. LXXIX (1904), p. 203.

the skull to find an enduring opinion about the Universe" (5.382 n.).
Little wonder, then, that right down to the present metaphysics has
remained "a puny, rickety, and scrofulous science" (6.6).

Two main reasons are suggested by Peirce for this situation. The
first is that metaphysics is trying to accomplish the impossible. The
"knowledge" it seeks is beyond the reach of human cognition because
it is wholly unverifiable. Take, for instance, assertions regarding the
immortality of the soul. They are quite incapable of any kind of confirmation. Even if true, such assertions could be verified by the asserter
only after he had gone out of business as a metaphysician! But the
pragmatic maxim has already shown that when a sign has no humanly
verifiable consequences, it is devoid of meaning. Hence, the maxim
serves to warn us "that almost every proposition of ontological metaphysics is either meaningless gibberish—one word being defined by
other words, and they by still others, without any real conception ever
being reached—or else is downright absurd" (5.423). Such propositions
are not about the universe or about "being *qua* being." They are
"primarily and at bottom thoughts about words, or thoughts about
thoughts" (5.294). In short, to a scientific philosopher metaphysics is
a subject "the knowledge of which, like that of a sunken reef, serves
chiefly to enable us to keep clear of it" (5.410).

The other reason for the retrograde condition of the subject was
advanced by Peirce in the latter part of his career. The trouble with
metaphysics is that the wrong sort of people pursue it. We cannot lay
the blame on its excessive abstractness, for mathematics, an eminently
progressive science, far surpasses it in this respect. Nor does the difficulty lie in the fact that metaphysics traffics in unobservables. "This is
doubtless true of some systems of metaphysics, though not to the
extent that it is supposed to be true" (6.2). For that matter, many of
the things dealt with by the special sciences are beyond the reach of
direct observation. "We cannot see energy, nor the attraction of gravitation, nor the flying molecules of gases, nor the luminiferous ether,
nor the forests of the carbonaceous era, nor the explosions in nerve-
cells. It is only the premisses of science, not its conclusions, which are
directly observed." (*Ibid.*) No; the chief cause of the backwardness
of metaphysics is that its leading professors have been theologians.
These gentlemen, trained in the seminary, are quite incapable of treating the subject in a scientific spirit. Not only do they lack the experimental cast of mind, but they are "inflamed with a desire to amend the
lives of themselves and others" (1.620). This has made it impossible

for them to undertake a disinterested pursuit of truth. Consequently, in their hands metaphysics has become "the most powerful of all causes of mental cecity" (5.499).

But it does not follow that the enterprise must remain an unscientific one. At any rate the pragmaticist is not committed to any such conclusion. "So, instead of merely jeering at metaphysics, like other prope-positivists, . . . the pragmaticist extracts from it a precious essence, which will serve to give life and light to cosmology and physics" (5.423). He performs the extraction "by proceeding modestly, recognizing in metaphysics an observational science, and applying to it the universal methods of such science, without caring one straw what kind of conclusions [he reaches] or what their tendencies may be, but just honestly applying induction and hypothesis" (6.5). Only in this way can the fruitless disputes of the past be eliminated, and the science placed on the solid road of progress.

2. THE SUBJECT-MATTER OF SCIENTIFIC METAPHYSICS

The question now arises what the subject-matter of scientific metaphysics must be. In the first place, its "attitude toward the universe is nearly that of the special sciences . . . from which it is mainly distinguished by its confining itself to such parts of physics and of psychics as can be established without special means of observation" (1.282). Peirce does not go into further detail here. But if we take note of his casual comments, we find the following areas suggested as being in need of metaphysical scrutiny: (i) the fundamental assumptions, i.e. concepts and principles, of the special sciences; (ii) the implicit metaphysics which "every man of us has," and which is constituted by the common-sense beliefs forced upon us by ordinary life; (iii) the broad conclusions of the physical and psychical sciences, which require to be "unified" or incorporated into a single, coherent scheme of ideas; and (iv) the most general features of reality and real objects (1.129; 1.229; 1.186; 6.6). Of these, (i), (ii), and (iii) presuppose a careful observation of scientific and common-sense knowledge, while (iv) involves an observation of phenomena, like that performed by phenomenology. But where the latter science draws no distinction between reality and fiction, metaphysics of necessity does so.

In actual practice Peirce concentrated mainly on the fourth of these areas. His naturalistic metaphysics therefore became a quest—somewhat fitfully pursued—for the ultimate categories in terms of which whatever in the universe we denominate "real" can be interpreted. The successful formulation of such categories would result in a set of "hypotheses" having a maximum degree of generality, and leading to a multitude of inductively verifiable consequences. Since they are more inclusive than the notions used in the special sciences and in ordinary life, metaphysical categories have philosophical priority with respect to those notions. Their formulation consequently achieves, at least in part, the objectives implicit in (i), (ii), and (iii) above. At no time, however, did metaphysics ever become for Peirce the primary division of philosophy. It remained subordinate to both phenomenology and normative science (particularly logic) from which it derived essential aid.

In one respect the subordination of metaphysics to other branches of philosophy worked in favor of Peirce's transcendentalism, since it provided him with a basis for "deducing" the categories of reality *a priori*. It was in this connection that he liked to declare his allegiance to the tradition of Aristotle and Kant, with its recognition of the primacy of logic over metaphysics. Yet it seems possible to interpret that doctrine so as to make it compatible with his naturalism. For he can be taken to mean—and some of his actual analysis supports this—that phenomenology and logic contribute not a set of axioms to metaphysics, but important regulative principles as well as ideas likely to prove fruitful in the search for categories. In other words, metaphysics, like every scientific inquiry, begins with a problem, viz., that of discovering the supremely general features of all that is real. As its first step, it entertains certain hypotheses which can be put to the test, and these are most reasonably drawn from phenomenology and logic. Similarly, its procedural principles must come from an attested source; otherwise invalid conclusions may be drawn. That is why logic occupies so pre-eminent a position. Throughout the inquiry, however, crucial significance attaches to the observational confirmation of the categories being sought. The situation, in short, is like that noted in the case of the empirical side of his phenomenology. The conclusions reached are equally tentative and subject to modification in the light of further evidence.

A possible source of misunderstanding should perhaps be dealt with at this point. According to the present study, the conflict of naturalism and transcendentalism in Peirce may be appropriately called a "metaphysical" one. For the conflict stems from the two incompatible sets of assumptions outlined in the opening chapter;

and these assumptions were spoken of as "metaphysical" because of their peculiarly basic role in his thought. Peirce himself, however, adopts a different usage for this term. Consequently, we must distinguish between *two* sorts of metaphysics which his work contains. On the one hand, there is what we may call his *implicit* metaphysics, consisting of the aforementioned assumptions whose influence can be detected throughout his work, but which are never overtly taken account of by him. On the other hand, there is his *explicit* metaphysics, consisting of all the doctrines presented by him under that title. His explicit metaphysics is subordinated to his logic and phenomenology. His implicit metaphysics is foundational to his total philosophy, including both these disciplines. Furthermore, since the bifurcation in his basic assumptions gives rise to a cleavage in all the major aspects of his thought, his implicit metaphysics on its naturalistic side gives rise to a corresponding kind of explicit metaphysics. A parallel relation is also present within his transcendentalism. The present chapter will consider only the naturalistic aspect of his explicit metaphysics.

Now we have seen that unlike phenomenology, metaphysics confines itself to the study of phenomena in so far as they are "real." The next task, therefore, is to discover what Peirce means by that expression. Our best plan will be to take the expression in its substantival form, and consider how he employs the term "reality" in relation to the cognate terms "being" and "existence." We shall find the latter two used with a fair degree of uniformity. But the use of "reality" is somewhat irregular.

In his writings prior to 1890, Peirce means by "being" the totality of possible objects of thought or discourse. The notion is not arrived at "by observing that all things we can think of have something in common, for there is no such thing to be observed. We get it by reflecting upon signs—words or thoughts." (5.294)   The principal sign involved is the copula of the proposition. In the statements "A griffin *is* a winged quadruped," and "Man *is* a rational animal," the conception of *being* expresses the logical fact that both verbs perform the same function of joining the predicate to the subject. No additional property of men or griffins is implied beyond what is explicitly stated. If we decide to speak about something "possessing being," all we can mean is that the item concerned *may be* referred to in a genuine proposition. "The conception of being, therefore, plainly has no content" (1.548). It is an abstract, logical notion of no interest to metaphysics.

The totality of that which is actual constitutes "existence." Whatever exists is individual, and in dynamic or brute interaction with all other individuals of the same universe (3.613; 5.429; 6.336). Not only are there different kinds of existence (1.433), but at least two different grades of it. The "lower" grade is made up of the sheer actuality of particular qualities; the "higher" grade comprises those dyadic relations which an object has with every other object in the same domain. Existence *per se* is not intelligible. It is experienced, rather than cognized, as the brute, irrational insistency or Secondness of individual things.

Now Peirce sometimes uses "reality" as a synonym for "existence" in the above sense. This is apparent, for example, when he states that "the percept is the reality," and that "the most immediate judgment concerning it is abstract" (5.568). Again, he remarks that "reality is altogether dynamic, not qualitative. It consists in forcefulness." (2.337) Secondness is predominant in it (1.325). Aristotle failed to strike the nail squarely on the head when he suggested that singulars are known by sense. It would have been more accurate to say that a singular is known by the compulsion which characterizes experience. "For the singular subject is real; and reality is insistency. That is what we mean by 'reality.' It is the brute irrational insistency that forces us to acknowledge the reality of what we experience, that gives us our conviction of any singular." (6.340)

On other occasions, however, Peirce is perfectly clear that "*reality* and *existence* are two different things" (6.349). They are distinguishable because in addition to action which is merely forceful and sporadic, there is regular action or law in the world. By virtue of regular action things persist; and it is just this persistence, independent of human thought, which makes them real. "Reality, then, is persistence, is regularity" (1.175). Peirce occasionally talks as though absolutely no reference to human thought were involved in the definition of "reality." Thus he says: "I define the *real* as that which holds its characters on such a tenure that it makes not the slightest difference what any man or men may have *thought* them to be, or ever will have *thought* them to be . . .; but the real thing's characters will remain absolutely untouched" (6.495). Perhaps such statements can be so construed as to make them accord with his more usual view that reality "is a cognitionary character" (5.503). At any rate, we know he held that what is real, while it stands in complete independence of the thought of any particular person, is wholly dependent on the final opinion reached by the community of scientific minds. Apart from inquiry, "reality" is a meaningless expression. For "what anything really is, is what it may finally become to be known to be in the ideal state of complete information" (5.316; cf. 5.311, 2.650, etc.). We may therefore conclude that where existence is a matter of Secondness only, "reality is an affair of Thirdness as Thirdness, that is, in its mediation between Secondness and Firstness" (5.121).

Peirce refers to being, existence, and reality as the "three Universes of Experience" (6.452). He also calls them the "three modes of being" (6.342), or monadic, dyadic, and triadic being (6.343). The members of the first universe are "possibles," those of the second universe "facts," and those of the third universe "laws" or "necessitants." The interrelation of the three domains appears to be that existence is a special mode of reality, which is in turn a special mode of being. For among the objects of possible discourse are to be found those which are what they are independently of any assertion about them, and among the latter objects are to be found those which are absolutely determinate, individual, and unique (6.349).

When, therefore, Peirce says "metaphysics is the science of Reality" (5.121), he means that its subject-matter embraces all phenomena which exhibit regular action or law. The metaphysician studies such phenomena by abstracting as far as possible from their qualitative and existential aspects, and concentrating on their Thirdness (5.124). His primary concern is to discover the categories which give the most adequate account of things from this perspective. Since phenomena can be conveniently subdivided into (*a*) those commonly spoken of as "physical," (*b*) those commonly spoken of as "mental" or "psychical," and (*c*) phenomena of Space and Time, metaphysics becomes the analytical study of each of these regions in respect of its pervasive and enduring features. I shall now attempt to give an account of Peirce's fragmentary researches.

3. THE METAPHYSICAL ANALYSIS OF PHYSICAL PHENOMENA

The category of chance. An obvious question for the metaphysician to ask in connection with the laws of the physical world is whether they govern every single phenomenon without exception, or whether we must admit an element of indeterminacy in things. Various thinkers from the time of Aristotle onwards have affirmed that chance is a constitutive feature of the universe. On the other hand, the whole tradition of modern science has been hostile to such a doctrine. Determinism or necessitarianism has been the scientific orthodoxy; and a good many philosophers have been led to accept it without question. Peirce was convinced, however, that the orthodox view was an unverifiable dogma, "a loose inference from the discoveries of science" (1.403). And conversely, he held that absolute chance, regarded as a hypothesis, is supported by sufficient evidence to render its probability very high.

Peirce first undertook to refute necessitarianism in an article carried by the *Monist* in 1892. The essence of the doctrine he takes to be "the common belief that every single fact in the universe is precisely determined by law" (6.36). From this it follows, as Laplace argued, "that the state of things existing at any time, together with certain immutable laws, completely determine the state of things at every other time" (6.37). Now what reasons are there for thinking such a belief to be true? According to Peirce, it must be justified on one of three grounds. Either (i) it is a *necessary postulate* of scientific inference, or (ii) it is an *a priori principle,* or (iii) it is an *empirical generalization.* But none of these possibilities stand up under critical analysis. They all involve fallacious assumptions which it is the business of the scientific metaphysician to expose.

Take, first of all, the view that strict determinism is a necessary postulate of science. This, says Peirce, is clearly not *proof* that determinism actually is true. For to postulate a proposition is merely to *hope* that it is true; and unless it can ultimately be verified by experience we have no way of ascertaining its truth or falsity. That is to say, a postulate of scientific inference is the formulation of a material fact which we are not entitled to assume as a premiss, yet whose truth is requisite to the validity of inference. "Any fact, then, which might be supposed postulated, must either be such that it would ultimately present itself in experience, or not. If it will present itself, we need not postulate it now in our provisional inference, since we shall ultimately be entitled to use it as a premiss. But if it never would present itself in experience, our conclusion is valid but for the possibility of this fact being otherwise than assumed, that is, it is valid as far as possible experience goes, and that is all that we claim." (6.41) Moreover, the whole idea that postulates are involved in inductive reasoning belongs to a mistaken conception of logic. For induction consists in inferring the constitution of a class from the constitution of samples drawn at random from that class. The validity of the inference depends on the fact that continued sampling leads us progressively nearer and nearer to the true state of affairs. Such a procedure "manifestly involves no postulate whatever" (6.40).

But the advocate of necessitarianism may seek to rest his case on *a priori* considerations. He may say (*a*) that the very notion of absolute chance is inconceivable; or (*b*) that although barely conceivable, it is rationally unintelligible; or (*c*) that the exact regularity of the world is a universal and natural belief confirmed by experience. None of these contentions strike Peirce as convincing. "They received such a socdolager from Stuart Mill in his examination of Hamilton, that holding to them now seems to me to denote a high degree of imperviousness to reason" (6.48). Mill pointed out once for all the error involved in thinking that an inconceivable proposition must be false. Inability to conceive is a purely subjective phenomenon. Hence an argument based on it is powerless to prove that chance is non-existent (6.51). As far as the second *a priori* objection is concerned, it is incapable of being either sustained or dismissed on purely logical grounds. The only way of telling whether the doctrine of absolute chance is intelligible or not is to define accurately what we mean by it and then turn to experience for a verdict. Much the same can be said of the third *a priori* objection. The sole way of settling the question whether the exact regularity of the world is a universal belief confirmed by experience is through empirical observation. And, of course, it is quite possible that a belief may be generally accepted at a given time without being in the least degree true.

The determinist is thus obliged to rest his case on empirical considerations. Surely, he may say, it is undeniable not only that there are reliable uniformities discoverable in everyday experience, but that the laboratory scientist is continually verifying these uniformities with precision. The scientist's whole procedure depends on the existence of invariant laws of nature which operate in identically the same manner everywhere. To this Peirce replies that he does not deny the existence of *large* regularities in the world. What he does deny is that we have any evidence for supposing these regularities to be perfect and exact. Certainly, it is not possible to *observe* their exactitude in the laboratory.

Try to verify any law of Nature, and you will find that the more precise your observations, the more certain they will be to show irregular departures from law. . . . To one who is behind the scenes, and knows that the most refined comparisons of masses, lengths, and angles, far surpassing all other measurements, yet fall behind the accuracy of bank accounts, and that the ordinary determinations of physical constants, such as appear from month to month in the journals, are about on a par with an upholsterer's measurements of carpets and curtains, the idea of mathematical exactitude being demonstrated in the laboratory will appear simply ridiculous. (6.46; 6.44)

Physical laws, then, as Peirce's contemporary Boltzmann was also urging, are not mechanical but *statistical* regularities.

In opposition to strict determinism, and as an amplification of this statistical view, Peirce argues (i) that chance is an observationally verifiable element in the world, and (ii) that the recognition of chance does not abrogate the governance of events by law. We shall take up these points in reverse order.

A common error of the necessitarians is the confusion of law with causality. Since chance involves the absence of a cause, they conclude that there must *ipso facto* be an absence of law. Peirce insists, however, that causality is a relation which holds between *facts* which are abstracted portions of events. Hence a causal relation may be absent, and yet the events themselves may still be subject to law. In order to understand this, let us note what is normally done in establishing the presence of causality. A ball comes to rest after traversing a rough surface. This is an event having an enormous number of discriminable aspects. One of these, abstracted and represented in a true proposition, is the fact that the ball has ceased to move. What is the cause of this fact? To obtain an answer we must locate another fact (e.g., the roughness of the surface) by abstracting another portion of the total event in a true proposition. If this second proposition, together with an established law of nature, syllogistically implies the first proposition, then the abstracted part of the event represented in the second proposition is the cause of the abstracted part of the event represented in the first proposition (6.67). We have, in other words, applied abduction to the discovery of a causal relation. Suppose after extended inquiry we could find no fact related in the above manner to the first fact specified. We should then regard the latter as contingent. But it would not in the least follow that the total event of which it is a part was not governed by law.

Peirce applies this distinction to the analysis of a well-known example used by Boethius to support necessitarianism. A boat is wrecked in a lake, and one part is carried down one river while the remaining part is carried down a second river. After many miles the rivers flow together; whereupon the two parts of the boat are dashed against one another. Now that seems like a fortuitous event if there ever was one. Yet, says Boethius, the currents forced the parts to move just as they did, so that no chance was really at work. The laws of nature operated rigorously throughout. Peirce's reply to this is worth quoting in full.

True, the existential events were governed by law. But when we speak of *chance*, it is a question of *cause*. Now it is the ineluctable blunder of a nominalist, as Boethius was, to talk of the cause of an event. But it is not an existential *event* that has a cause. It is the *fact*, which is the reference of the event to a general relation, that has a cause. The *event*, it is true, was governed by the law of the current. But the *fact* which we are considering is that the two pieces that were dashed together had long before belonged together. That is a fact that would not happen once in ten thousand times, although when you join to this fact various circumstances of the actual event, and so contemplate quite *another* fact, it would happen every time, no doubt. . . . The example is a very good one as showing that the causal necessitation of more concrete *fact* does not prevent a more prescinded, or general, *fact* of the same event from being quite fortuitous. (6.93)

A genuinely scientific metaphysics must therefore admit that plenty of contingency is to be observed in the world. Common sense is perfectly right in speaking of "coincidences." Just at the moment I sneeze, a man in Tibet whistles. That fact is wholly a matter of chance; though the separate events are in each case governed by law. Likewise, every throw of dice is a denotative instance of contingency. No invariant laws can be made to account for the *fact* that on a given occasion a pair of sixes turned up rather than some other possible combination. It is again a matter of chance. If it be objected that in all such cases "chance" is only a name for causes unknown to us, since each die moves under the influence of mechanical laws, Peirce retorts that "it is not these laws which made the die turn up sixes; for these laws act just the same when other throws come up. The chance lies in the diversity of throws; and this diversity cannot be due to laws which are immutable. The diversity is due to the diverse circumstances under which the laws act." (6.55)   Thus, all the specificity and variety of things is an exemplification of chance; and the theory based on the recognition of this Peirce calls "Tychism." It is a theory which frankly admits that "when we gaze upon the multifariousness of nature we are looking straight into the face of a living spontaneity" (6.553).

From the standpoint of Peirce's naturalism, the category of chance may be regarded as a protest against the empirically unwarranted theory of determinism, an anticipation of a statistical conception of law, and an analysis of the proper relation between law and efficient causality. In each case the arguments stay exclusively within the confines of the observable and the verifiable. Consequently, they conform to the program laid down for a scientific metaphysics. What happens to the category when Tychism becomes part of a speculative cosmology is, of course, another story.

The category of continuity. The study of phenomena in their Thirdness leads the scientific metaphysician to a second category, that of continuity. The haze of obscurity surrounding Peirce's exposition of this idea makes a precise comprehension of it difficult. But at least three aspects of it seem relevant to his naturalism: (*a*) continuity as a regulative principle in the natural sciences, specifying what kind of conceptions should be favored as candidates for the status of laws; (*b*) continuity as an expression of the fact that inexactitude necessarily attaches to the statement of every law; and (*c*) continuity as an observable feature of all mental action. Reserving discussion of (*c*) for the next section, we will here consider (*a*) and (*b*) together.

Peirce became impressed with the importance of continuity as a result of his reflection on the procedure of the physical sciences. In his paper on "The Doctrine of Chances" (1878), he remarks that not only do these sciences become exact when quantitatively treated, but their progress is vastly accelerated when they make use of the notion of *continuous* quantity. This notion turns out to be "the direct instrument of the finest generalizations," because it resolves all differences into differences of degree. So useful does it prove, that "it is perpetually introduced even where there is no continuity in fact, as when we say that there are in the United States 10.7 inhabitants per square mile, or that in New York 14.72 persons live in the average house" (2.646). In such instances continuity is a convenient fiction of the sort that science often employs.

When he came to write the article on continuity ("Synechism") for J. M. Baldwin's *Dictionary of Philosophy and Psychology* in 1902, Peirce stressed the regulative function of the idea almost exclusively. He declared that it is "not an ultimate and absolute metaphysical doctrine" but a regulative principle of logic, prescribing what sort of hypothesis is fit to be entertained (6.173). The hypotheses whose fitness it guarantees are those which avoid making any reference to "inexplicable ultimates." For to suppose a thing inexplicable is not only to relegate it to the domain of mystery. It is also to place a barrier across the road to further inquiry; and a philosophy which encourages this commits "the one unpardonable offence in reasoning" (1.136). Peirce admits, as we have observed, that every phenomenon possesses certain inexplicable and ultimate aspects in its Firstness and

Secondness. What the "synechist" does, however, is to use these as a basis for generalization, "since it is only so far as facts can be generalized that they can be understood" (6.173). And "true generality is, in fact, nothing but a rudimentary form of true continuity" (6.172).

In the light of the above, it may be said that to treat continuity as a metaphysical category is a wilful misrepresentation of Peirce's view. He has told us quite clearly that it is a maxim of *logic,* and that is how it ought to be construed. The answer to this objection is, I think, plain. If the only hypotheses allowed in science are those involving true continuity, then their inductive validation will result in *laws* which will also be characterized by continuity. Hence it will be a constitutive feature of all the laws of science. But scientific metaphysics is precisely the study of such features. Therefore, continuity is a proper metaphysical category.

How does Peirce interpret the details of this category? His analysis of it makes use of material from two regions, pure mathematics and direct experience. With regard to the former, we shall limit our attention to such points as are philosophically important. Stated broadly, Peirce's chief contribution here consists in arguing forcibly for the Aristotelian thesis that a continuous series is not a collection of discrete items such as *points,* but is rather a general possibility of endless further determination of parts. Points are non-existent, even "ideally," save as breaches of continuity.

Peirce's thought only gradually moved towards this conclusion. The first intimation of it appears in his paper "The Law of Mind" (1892). During the discussion, he has occasion to consider the definitions of continuity suggested by Aristotle, Kant, and the German mathematician, Cantor. According to Cantor, continuity is a property of a series which is *concatenated* and *perfect.* "By a concatenated series, he means such a one that if any two points are given in it, and any finite distance, however small, it is possible to proceed from the first point to the second through a succession of points of the series each at a distance, from the preceding one, less than the given distance" (2.121). The series of rational fractions arranged in order of their magnitude has this property. "By a perfect series, he means one which contains every point such that there is no distance so small that this point has not an infinity of points of the series within that distance of it" (*ibid.*). Such a property is possessed by the series of numbers between 0 and 1 capable of being expressed by decimals in which only the digits 0 and 1 occur.

Now Peirce admits that the foregoing definition includes every series that is continuous. Yet he thinks it has certain serious defects. "In the first place, it turns upon metrical considerations; while the distinction between a continuous and a discontinuous series is manifestly non-metrical. In the next place, a perfect series is defined as one containing 'every point' of a certain description. But no positive idea is conveyed of what all the points are. . . . Cantor's definition does not convey a distinct notion of what the components of the conception of continuity are." (6.121) The core of this objection seems to be that *points* and *continuity* are incompatible ideas.

A similar objection holds in connection with Kant's definition of continuity as consisting in the fact that between any two points of a series a third may be found.[2] While this does express one simple property of a continuum, "it allows of gaps in the series" (6.122). If, for example, from the whole series of rational fractions we remove ¼ and ½ together with all the fractions intermediate between these in value, this makes a gap in the series. Yet it remains true of the series thus mutilated, as it was of the unmutilated series, that if any two fractions which belong to it are given, a fraction of intermediate value can be found to belong to it. Finally, Aristotle's definition of a continuum as that whose parts have a common limit,[3] while it is correct so far as it goes, is like Kant's definition, one-sided. It specifies a necessary but not a sufficient condition of continuity. However, if we combine the two definitions we reach a satisfactory conception of a continuous series. As Peirce puts it, such a series possesses both *Kanticity* and *Aristotelicity!*

More than a decade after his paper on "The Law of Mind," Peirce expressed profound dissatisfaction with its discussion of continuity. He calls it "my blundering treatment . . . the crudest of my struggles with such subjects" (6.174; 6.182). His considered opinion was that he had misinterpreted the import of Kant's definition of continuity—as Kant himself had done! For what that definition properly implies is that a continuous line, for instance, contains no points until its continuity is broken by points being marked or otherwise specified. "In accordance with this it seems necessary to say that a continuum, where it *is* continuous and unbroken, contains no definite parts; that its parts are created in the act of defining them and the precise definition of them breaks the continuity" (6.168). Hence, what Cantor talks about

[2]*Critique of Pure Reason*, A169 = B211; A659 = B687.
[3]*Metaphysics* 1069a. 5.

is a *pseudo-continuum* (6.176). A real continuum has no actually existing parts, but only an inexhaustible potentiality for being divided into parts. Thus a continuous line contains an infinity of point-places, at each of which a point *could* be located. But these places, since they are mere "possibles" without determinate existence, are not individuals. In essence, therefore, Aristotle was right when he insisted that a continuous series is not a collection of discrete items.

This later analysis obviously squares with Peirce's mature view on cognate matters. Phenomena are discontinuous in so far as their existence is concerned, i.e. *qua* facts or individuals. Phenomena are continuous in so far as their reality is concerned, i.e. *qua* laws or generals. For "continuity and generality are two names for the same absence of distinction of individuals" (4.172). And both names designate an important attribute of physical laws.

Yet when we ask *exactly* how a given law is characterized by continuity, the answer is far from clear. Take Newton's third law of motion. In what sense is it "continuous"? Does Peirce mean simply that the statement, "To every action there is an equal and opposite reaction," makes no reference to the specific actions to which it applies? Or does he mean that just as a line is continuous because it has "room" for any multitude of points whatsoever, so the law is continuous because it can have any multitude of instances whatsoever? Continuity certainly involves infinity "in the strictest sense" (1.166). And of course an infinity of instances no more constitutes a law than an infinity of points constitutes a line. Or again, does Peirce mean that continuity attaches to the law in the sense that when we try to state it with absolute precision, we find that it tends to "merge" with other laws? The merging here might conceivably be an overlapping which would render it progressively more difficult to determine the boundaries of particular laws as the refinement of formulation continued. Consequently, an element of vagueness necessarily attaches to the statement of every law. This would make Synechism the metaphysical correlate of Fallibilism. "For fallibilism is the doctrine that our knowledge is never absolute but always swims, as it were, in a continuum of uncertainty and of indeterminacy" (1.171).

There is no doubt about this last consideration being *part* of what is intended by the category of continuity. Whether the other considerations mentioned are also intended must remain problematic. The fact of the matter is that Peirce was quite unable to keep his discussion of continuity on the modest level of scientific metaphysics.

Its speculative possibilities as "the master-key which . . . unlocks the arcana of philosophy" (1.163), proved too tempting. In the latter role, as will appear, the notion becomes a central component of his trans-cendentalism.

The category of evolution. The third category of scientific meta-physics is dealt with in an even more fragmentary manner than the other two. Here again, the speculative employment of the idea greatly overshadows its treatment in an "observational" context. The program of scientific metaphysics would seem to call for a careful definition of evolution, and a demonstration that it is required to account for a pervasive feature of reality. Such a discussion, falling within the con-fines of the experientially verifiable, is scarcely more than adumbrated by Peirce. He does, however, present (1) a brief analysis of evolution as a biological conception, (2) a criticism of Spencer's philosophical generalization of this conception, and (3) some suggestions as to what an appropriate metaphysical version of evolution ought to include. We shall review these in order.

1. Peirce was a warm defender of the biological theory of evolution. When Darwin's work first appeared, he was immediately impressed, regarding its statement of the evolutionary doctrine as "a thoroughly scientific generalization" based on researches that were "minute, sys-tematic, extensive, strict" (1.33). In his Smithsonian lecture of 1900 he remarked that it was his "inestimable privilege to have felt as a young man the warmth of the steadily burning enthusiasm of the scientific generation of Darwin."[4] Yet he never became a Darwinian in the sense of accepting *The Origin of Species* as a full and final account of things. Indeed, by 1893 he could say of this work that "to a sober mind its case looks less hopeful now than it did twenty years ago" (6.297). Not that he ever had doubts about the general fact of evolution. The evidence in its favor was far too weighty. His doubts centered on Darwin's explanation of the precise way in which evolu-tion had taken place. Here he felt unable to commit himself to any single view.

The result was that he considered three theories relevant to the understanding of how organic species had evolved (1.104). The first was Darwin's theory, with its postulation of fortuitous variations and their transmission through reproduction, operating in the struggle for existence so as to favor the survival of certain types. The second theory

[4]*Smithsonian Institution Reports* (Washington, 1900), p. 694.

was Lamarck's. According to it, "the development of species has taken place by a long series of insensible changes, but . . . those changes have taken place during the lives of the individuals, in consequence of effort and exercise, and . . . reproduction plays no part in the process except in preserving these modifications" (6.16). The third theory was that of "cataclysmal evolution." Much evidence exists that alterations in species have not been gradual but sudden. These mutations have, furthermore, been correlated with evidence of rapid changes in the physical environment. It is therefore reasonable to infer that such changes have functioned as causal agents in evolution. This inference seems to be called for by "some of the broadest and most important facts of biology and paleontology" (6.17). At any rate, cataclysmal evolution calls attention to the occurrence of "breaks" in the history of living forms.

Now Peirce thinks that while "all three of these modes of evolution have acted," it is probable that "the last has been the most efficient" (1.105). By 1906 he was speaking of the new doctrine of mutations as the "theory which I have *always* insisted must be the way in which species have arisen" (6.498). His preference here was dictated by the conviction that both Darwinian and Lamarckian theories were too mechanistic to provide a satisfactory interpretation of the facts.

2. The same conviction led him to be sharply critical of Spencer's "philosophy" of evolution. He was not unsympathetic to the sweeping application of the evolutionary idea which that philosophy made. On the contrary he agreed that the Darwinian principle "is plainly capable of great generalization" (6.15). What he repudiated was Spencer's assumption that evolution must be explained in purely mechanical terms. He was especially contemptuous of the chapter in *First Principles* where evolution is shown to be a consequence of the law of the conservation of energy. This, he observes, is not only mathematical nonsense, but it convicts the author of being "a man who will talk pretentiously of what he knows nothing about" (6.554).

Let us turn to the evidence, Peirce suggests, and see whether we can discover the central feature of evolution. Take it in the limited biological sense first. Consider the life of an individual animal or plant. Go on from there to examine the succession of forms shown by paleontology. Take it in a much wider sense so as to include the development of a mind. "Glance at the history of states, of institutions, of language, of ideas . . . the history of the globe as set forth in geology . . . what the astronomer is able to make out concerning the changes of stellar systems. Everywhere the main fact is growth and increasing complexity" (6.58). Evolution, in short, means nothing but *growth* in the broadest sense of the word (1.174). It is the general process of diversification or increase in variety.

Now this is precisely what a mechanical principle such as the law of the conservation of energy cannot explain. For the essence of such a law is that "whatever changes can be brought about by forces can equally happen in the reverse order (all the movements taking place with the same velocities, but in the reverse directions), under the government of the same forces" (6.554). All operations governed by mechanical laws are so reversible. But growth is intrinsically irreversible. "Boys grow into men, but not men into boys" (*ibid.*). The process is unidirectional. It follows that growth is not explicable in terms of mechanical laws, "even if they be not violated in the process of growth" (6.14). Spencer's "evolutionary" philosophy, then, rests on a wholly fallacious foundation.

Among other objections mentioned by Peirce, we may note his charge that Spencer is only "a half-evolutionist." For in seeking to "deduce" the phenomena of evolution from "the persistence of force," what Spencer is really doing is denying that evolution is a fundamental feature of reality. He is explaining it away in terms of that which does *not* evolve. Philosophy, however, "requires thoroughgoing evolutionism or none" (*ibid.*). If we admit the notion at all (and it is hard to see how a philosophy could reject it completely), we must be prepared to make it metaphysically ultimate.

3. The concept of evolution implied in the above criticisms, partial as it is, foreshadows the ideas of later thinkers such as Bergson, Alexander, and Whitehead. In common with these men, Peirce was convinced that empirical evidence obliged the metaphysician to recognize (*a*) that change or becoming is a primary aspect of reality; (*b*) that the most important form of change is development or growth; (*c*) that growth cannot be understood in purely mechanical terms; (*d*) that it is a unidirectional process involving "creativity" or the "emergence of novelty"; and (*e*) that the facts entitle us to extend the category of evolution, thus conceived, beyond the domain of the biological to the interpretation of physical, social, and historical phenomena. It would be erroneous, of course, to suggest that Peirce advocated a doctrine of emergent evolution. The most we can say is that the naturalistic elements in his thought were tending in that direction. There are various illustrations of this, not the least interesting being

his remarks on the "evolution" of standards of weights and measures, and on the "evolution" of scientific ideas (cf. 1.106 ff.). Such remarks show how far ahead of his time he was in assessing the influence of Darwin on philosophy.

4. THE METAPHYSICAL ANALYSIS OF PSYCHICAL PHENOMENA

The other main task of scientific metaphysics is the analysis of psychical phenomena in respect of their reality. Before proceeding with this subject, two general comments must be made. (*a*) Peirce in general wished to avoid using the term "psychical" to designate a mental substance or stuff. He repudiated "the Cartesian idea of the mind" (5.128), and agreed with James and Schiller that there is probably no "consciousness" different from "a visceral or other external sensation" (6.485). The distinction between the physical and the psychical is not an ontological but an empirical one. (*b*) A metaphysical analysis of mind must not be confused with any psychological inquiry. Psychology is a division of idioscopy, a special science concerned with discovering truths which cannot be established by ordinary observation. It rests on the science of logic, and aims at the quantitative statement of its results. Metaphysical investigation has for its subject-matter data "well-known even if little noticed, to all grown men and women, that are of sound minds" (5.485). The *psychical* truths which it seeks are not only quite distinct from psychological truths, but are validated at a different level of experience.

On the former of the above points, Peirce's thought remained steady throughout his life. He stayed consistently within the anti-Cartesian camp. The positive side of his "metaphysics of mind," however, manifests some development. This may be described broadly as a shift from an exclusively cognitive view of psychical phenomena to one which takes account of the elements of feeling and action as well. That is to say, in his early papers mind is identified with the logical process of interpreting signs. Later it is conceived as an organic process, directly manifested in feeling and having a teleological function in relation to behavior. The elucidation of these matters will require a review of Peirce's critique of Cartesianism, and a sketch of the alternative doctrine he proposed.

At the center of the Cartesian view of mind lies the principle (well expressed, for example, by Bergson in the opening sentence of *Creative Evolution*) that the object we know best is our individual self. I am most certain of my own existence as a thinking substance. This is the principle which Peirce undertook to refute in his paper of 1868 entitled, "Questions concerning Certain Faculties Claimed for Man." His attack is directed against two alleged faculties, (1) that of intuitive self-consciousness or self-knowledge (5.225), and (2) that of introspection (5.244). In arguing against each of these Peirce takes for granted the intrinsically temporal character of awareness which makes it a process rather than a state, and the common-sense distinction between phenomena that are "external" and phenomena that are "internal." The details of these assumptions are clarified as the argument advances.

1. That we do have knowledge of the self is not a matter of dispute. The question at issue is whether such knowledge is immediate, or whether it is the result of inference. Do we, or do we not, have an intuitive power of self-consciousness? For an answer the scientific metaphysician turns to the factual evidence. If, he argues, there were any such power, we should expect to see it emerging very early in the life of the individual. But in fact, as Kant pointed out, children come very late to the use of the common word "I." This, taken in conjunction with the unmistakable signs of thought in young babies, strongly suggests, though of course it does not prove, that they lack self-consciousness. Furthermore, the gradually increasing use of the first personal pronoun can be correlated with a gradual growth of self-consciousness. Peirce outlines the stages involved here, beginning with the baby's awareness of its own body, of other bodies, of language, and then through language, of its own ignorance. "A child hears it said that the stove is hot. But it is not, he says; and, indeed, that central body [his own] is not touching it, and only what that touches is hot or cold. But he touches it, and finds the testimony [of others] confirmed in a striking way. Thus, he becomes aware of ignorance, and it is necessary to suppose a *self* in which this ignorance can inhere." (5.233) Such dawning self-consciousness is reinforced by the recognition of another fact, namely, that certain things are private and valid only for one body. "In short, *error* appears, and it can be explained only by supposing a *self* which is fallible" (5.234). It is therefore unnecessary to postulate an intuitive knowledge of the self. We come to know it by inference from the facts of ignorance and error.

There is just one formal argument in this connection which Peirce thinks worth refuting. It runs as follows. (i) We are more certain of our own existence than of any other fact. (ii) A fact which is more certain cannot be inferred as a conclusion from a less certain fact as premiss. Hence, (iii) our own existence cannot have been inferred from any other fact. Peirce admits (i) but denies (ii), which he says is founded "on an exploded theory of logic." A conclusion cannot be more certain than *some* one of the facts which support it. Yet it may easily be more certain than *any* one of those facts. "Let us suppose for example, that a dozen witnesses testify to an occurrence. Then my belief in that occurrence rests on the belief that each of those men is generally to be believed upon oath. Yet the fact testified to is made more certain than that any one of those men is generally to be believed." (5.237)   In the same way, a grown person finds his own existence supported by *every other fact*, and therefore more assured than any one of those facts. This is quite consistent with his own existence having been established inferentially.

2. Not only do we lack immediate knowledge of the self, but there is not even a direct perception of particular states of the self. Metaphysical analysis discloses no good reasons for supposing a power of introspection. Peirce phrases his argument here in terms of the contrast between the external and the internal "worlds," and contends that what is internal is arrived at by inference from what is external. We must, I think, regard "internal" in this context as a synonym for "mental." This is strongly suggested by his frequent assertion that there is no immediate awareness of the psychical as such (1.250; 1.253; etc.). On the other hand, such an interpretation is consistent with a different use of "internal" which enables him to say later that we do directly observe objects of our inner world—these being logical signs or meanings not in themselves psychical. The denial of introspection, then, seems to be primarily the denial that any purely mental datum can be found.

There are three kinds of phenomena commonly regarded as mental because of their uniquely subjective character, viz., sensations, emotions, and volitions. Yet a little reflection shows, according to Peirce, that each of these arises in connection with a judgment about external phenomena. Consider, for example, a sensation of redness. It is no doubt partly determined by internal conditions, so that some knowledge of the mind can be gleaned from an examination of it. "But that knowledge would, in fact, be an inference from redness as a predicate of something external" (5.245). We are first cognizant of red things, and only afterwards do we discover sensations. What about emotions? They do not seem to arise as predicates of objects, but seem rather to be referable to the mind alone. Not so, replies

Peirce. When a man feels anger, for instance, his emotion consists in his saying, "this thing is vile, abominable, etc." It is a sign of returning rationality when he says, "I am angry." All emotions are thus, at the outset, predications concerning some object or situation (cf. 5.292). "The chief difference between this and an objective intellectual judgment is that where the latter is relative to human nature or to mind in general, the former is relative to the particular circumstances and disposition of a particular man at a particular time" (5.247). As for the sense of willing or volition, it is nothing but the power of concentrating attention, of abstracting. "Hence, the knowledge of the power of abstracting may be inferred from abstract objects, just as the knowledge of the power of seeing is inferred from colored objects" (5.248). The upshot is that no valid reasons exist for believing either that mental phenomena are "given" or that we have a power of introspection.

Additional light is shed on these criticisms by taking note of Peirce's own doctrine of mind. In his papers of 1868 he argues that the given element from which our notion of the mind is derived is a process of cognition taking place in accordance with the laws of valid inference (5.267; 5.279). When we begin to reflect we find this process already going on, and we must therefore accept it as our datum. Now the "stuff" of the process consists of signs. If it were possible to "freeze" the process at an instant, we should discover that the entire phenomenal content of consciousness "is a sign resulting from inference" (5.313). Of course, such a sign would be devoid of meaning, and would remain a simple, unanalyzable feeling. "No present actual thought (which is a mere feeling) has any meaning, any intellectual value; for this lies not in what is actually thought, but in what this thought may be connected with in representation by subsequent thoughts; so that the meaning of a thought is altogether something virtual" (5.289).[5] Now this continuous activity of interpreting signs is the reality of mind. Herein lies "man's glassy essence." Accordingly, "just as we say that a body is in motion and not that motion is in a body we ought to say that we are in thought and not that thoughts are in us" (5.289 n.).

This position has one important consequence for Peirce's naturalism. It leads to the conclusion that the major factor in the development of mind has been language. To the use of words and allied signs the human spirit owes its evolution. Conversely, as the human spirit has

[5] In 1905 Peirce singled out this passage as containing the germ of the pragmatic doctrine (cf. 5.504 n.).

evolved, language has become more subtle and more influential. "Man makes the word, and the word means nothing which the man has not made it mean, and that only to some man. But since man can think only by means of words or other external symbols, these might turn round and say: 'You mean nothing which we have not taught you, and then only so far as you address some word as the interpretant of your thought.' In fact, therefore, men and words reciprocally educate each other." (5.313)   So intimate is the relationship that Peirce can go on to say that "the word or sign which man uses *is* the man himself" (5.314). Thus my language is the sum total of my *self* as distinct from my physical body. Because of this Peirce once playfully remarked that the physician is a privileged individual, since every time he examines a tongue he looks at the very organ of personality![6]

Yet the excessive emphasis Peirce lays on the inferential or logical function of mind (owing no doubt to the strong Kantian element in his thought at this stage) leaves his naturalism in a volatile condition. There are even traces of a movement towards a rationalistic idealism of the Hegelian variety. This appears, for example, in the suggestion that man should recognize his animal organism as "only an instrument of thought," and should see that his self-identity springs from "the *consistency* of what he does and thinks" (5.315). Our ostensible awareness of our physical bodies is reduced to a phase of cognition. For the awareness is either a sensation or an emotion, and each of these, as has been indicated, is but a component of judgmental acts. To put the matter in terms of his own later doctrine, Peirce shows a decided tendency in his papers of 1868 to reduce the Firstness and Secondness of psychical phenomena to their Thirdness. The correction of such one-sidedness, in so far as it advances his naturalistic metaphysics of mind, must now be considered.

We may approach this subject by way of a distinction which crops up frequently after 1893. It is the doctrine of the "two worlds" which every sane man inhabits. One of these is the outer world of percepts, the other the inner world of fancies (5.487). They are "directly distinguishable by their different appearances" (5.474), but the most reliable way of determining them is by experimentation (4.87). Over the objects of the inner world (i.e., the linguistic signs or "ideas") we have a great deal of control. They can be altered at will by a certain non-muscular effort, and they exert a comparatively slight compulsion

[6]R. B. Perry, *The Thought and Character of William James* (Boston, 1935), vol. II, p. 107.

on us. Over the objects of the outer world (i.e., the physical things and events) we have very little control. They can only be modified to a limited extent, and that by muscular effort alone. Hence they are full of irresistible compulsions for us. In the inner world man's power is virtually absolute. In the factual world "we are masters, each of us, of his own voluntary muscles, and of nothing more" (1.321). By means of them man is able to adapt his behavior to the demands of the environment. The chief role of thought and ideas is to facilitate this adaptation by enabling him to alter his habits when the need arises. Here the presence of the inner world serves him well, since it permits the reiteration "in fancy" of possible lines of conduct. New habits are thereby set up; and these, although not yet incorporated in his musculature, have the power to influence his actual behavior in the outer world, "especially, if each reiteration be accompanied by a peculiar strong effort that is usually likened to issuing a command to one's future self" (5.487).

This doctrine obviously puts the emphasis on the purposive rather than on the logical function of mind. The logical function is still essential, but it remains ancillary to action. That is why Peirce can say that final causation is the *modus operandi* of mind (cf. 1.250; 1.269). It is also why he insists that the final logical interpretant of a sign is not another sign but a habit, i.e. a certain kind of behavior (5.491). This conclusion proved important because it enabled him to relate the cognitive and the non-cognitive sides of man's nature without surrendering the insights provided by his study of semiosis. For habits are unique in being at once general (which is a necessary requirement of a logical interpretant) and a form of doing (which is non-intellectual). Through them the process of interpreting signs can be connected with action, and theory linked with practice.

Another significant result is that habit can be defined physiologically in terms of a property of the nervous system (cf. 1.390). Such a definition need introduce "not one word about the mind. Why should it, when habits in themselves are entirely unconscious, though feelings may be symptoms of them, and when consciousness alone—i.e. feeling— is the only distinctive attribute of mind?" (5.492) In other words, habits are organic functions, while mind or consciousness in its immediacy is simply "a congeries of feelings" (5.493). Yet consciousness is no more epiphenomenon—"though I heartily grant," Peirce adds, "that the hypothesis that it is so has done good service to science." The real function of consciousness is to facilitate self-control and the formation of habits. Without it, "the resolves and exercises of the inner world could not affect the real determinations and habits of the outer world" (*ibid.*).

Peirce's doctrine now begins to look like this. The total content of experience at any instant is describable in at least two ways. On its external side it is a percept or sign. On its internal side it is a feeling or group of feelings. If we stick to what is empirically discernible, we can find no basis for an ontological distinction of the physical and the psychical. We may indeed speak of feeling as "exclusively mental" (5.492), provided we do not mean to affirm the existence of a special kind of "stuff" differing completely from what external observation reveals. The sole justification for speaking thus is that feeling has precisely the sort of *unity* which will account for our sense of individuality, our awareness of being a person at each moment of time. We cannot attribute this unity to any purely physiological source, Peirce thinks. All we can say is that "it is the metaphysical nature of feeling to have a *unity*" (6.229). And we can say further that "feelings coordinated in a certain way, to a certain degree, constitute a person" (6.585; cf. 6.270).

But in addition to the feeling which occurs at each instant, there are action and thought, which function along the time series. Action, because of man's physical constitution, tends to become embodied in habits that keep him in stable equilibrium with his environment. Thought, as the semiotic process, performs in collaboration with feeling the office of reconstructing these habits when the environment makes that necessary. Such reconstruction is possible because thought commands the inner world of linguistic and other signs. These can be manipulated in manifold ways, and so give rise to new habits which will be adequate to changed situations. Since action and thought should be included along with feeling in the full definition of personality, we must conclude that personality "is not a thing to be apprehended in an instant. It has to be lived in time." (6.155)

The developmental character of personality or mind is seen in the fact that "thinking is carried on as a dialogue" (5.506). "Your self of one instant appeals to your deeper self for his assent. Consequently, all thinking is conducted in signs that are mainly of the same general structure as words." (6.338)   Even in solitary meditation, each judgment you make is an effort to press home on your self of the immediate future, and of the general future, some truth (5.546). If we ask Peirce point-blank whether the particular signs employed in this inner dialogue *are* the thought, the answer is: "Oh, no; no whit more than the skins of an onion are the onion. (About as much so, however.)" (4.6) To use another analogy: the matter of thought is signs in the sense in which the chessmen constitute the matter of a game of chess.

To what extent do psychical phenomena as above described illustrate the metaphysical categories of chance, continuity, and evolution? Peirce offers no discussion of this question. The rough outline of an answer may, however, be constructed in the light of his general doctrine and of certain detached comments which he makes.

If it be agreed that freshness, spontaneity, and unpredictability are descriptive marks of the contingent, then feeling must be admitted to fall under the category of chance. For at each moment the content of consciousness has a uniqueness, a distinctive "flavor," utterly incapable of being anticipated and quite unrepeatable once it has occurred. This *quale* is a directly discernible feature of feeling; and, phenomenologically, constitutes its Firstness. One aspect of the reality of psychical phenomena is therefore specifiable in the first metaphysical category.

Another directly observable feature of consciousness is its continuity (6.182). Prior to 1890, Peirce held this to be simply the process of "mediation" or thought (5.289). Thus, in 1878 he remarked that "thought is a thread of melody running through the succession of our sensations" (5.395). Later he attributed the continuity to the "coalescing" of present feelings with immediately preceding and immediately succeeding feelings. Consciousness shows itself directly as a "stream." This is where the second metaphysical category finds exemplification. As will shortly appear, there is an intimate connection for Peirce between the continuity of consciousness and the nature of time.

The category of evolution is illustrated in Peirce's developmental conception of the individual psyche. From infancy to maturity a growth takes place through a series of "selves," each one carrying a step further the expansion of knowledge and the reorganization of habits, when the latter is necessary. A more general illustration of the category appears in the fact that along with the evolution of biological phenomena must be taken the evolution of psychical phenomena. Here there has been a development from the simple to the complex. Evolution thus applies to the growth of mind in the widest sense. It is worth noting, as relevant to Peirce's naturalism, that just as he held the scientific evidence to point to the origin of man somewhere in the past history of the evolutionary process, so he concluded that the evidence points to man's ultimate disappearance from the cosmos in the remote future. "The existence of the human race, we may be as good as sure, will come to an end at last. For not to speak of the gradual operation of causes of which we know, the action of the tides, the resisting medium, the dissipation of energy, there is all the time a certain danger that the earth may be struck by a meteor or wandering star so large as to ruin it, or by some poisonous gas." (5.587) With the extinction of all living beings, the universe will be left without any intelligence whatever (5.357).

The foregoing has, I trust, made clear the strongly naturalistic elements in Peirce's metaphysics of mind. These elements were a consequence of his "just honestly applying induction and hypothesis" to psychic phenomena. It would obviously be absurd to say that he had a well-rounded doctrine, or that satisfactory solutions are provided to even the major problems in the field. Thus, for instance, on the vexed question of the nature of thought, he sometimes talks like a behaviorist, and one might be tempted to conclude that he was prepared to identify thinking with bodily responses of a linguistic kind.[7] At other times he seems to be arguing that thought is an activity having an irreducible status of its own. It is not analyzable into bodily responses, though without a physiological basis it could not exist, any more than the onion could exist without its skins. Yet how thought in this second sense acts on things, as it indubitably does, remains a mystery. We cannot at present make even a promising guess about its solution (cf. 5.106).

Again, when Peirce speaks of feeling as "mental," it may be questioned whether he is not in fact opening the door to the much criticized Cartesianism. The full import of this becomes apparent in his transcendentalism, where feeling is made the basis of a panpsychistic ontology. According to that doctrine, what common sense takes to be matter is really an inchoate form of mind. Everything in the universe is at bottom a mode of the psychical, and has its own immediate "feeling." But what is this save a seizing of the mental horn of the Cartesian dilemma, plus a denial that the other horn exists? When we learn, further, that part of the purpose of panpsychism is to cut the ground from under materialism, we may properly conclude that feeling involves a good deal more than simply "visceral or other sensations." It seems likely that we have here another illustration of the influence of Peirce's transcendentalism on his naturalism.

[7] Cf. C. W. Morris, *Signs, Language and Behavior* (New York, 1946), p. 289.

5. THE METAPHYSICAL ANALYSIS OF SPACE AND TIME

Both physical and psychical phenomena imply the presence of the two pervasive elements of space and time. These are taken vaguely by common sense to be media "in" which everything is located. Special sciences such as physics and mathematics work some refinements on the common-sense view, but only so far as is necessary for practical purposes. It is the metaphysician's duty to investigate space and time with respect to their reality. Now Peirce, unfortunately, never settled down to a systematic performance of this task. Consequently, his ideas on the subject have a perfunctory quality which often leaves important issues hanging in mid air. Many of his remarks show symptoms of the basic cleavage in his thought. Thus, there is on the one hand a tendency to relegate space and time to a subordinate status, and to exhibit them as the products of an "evolution" which is purely speculative in character. This is one phase of his "Cosmogonic Philosophy." On the other hand, Peirce's naturalism takes space and time seriously, and treats them as realities having a solid observational basis. The results of the latter approach must now occupy us.

Space. It is usual to separate the "space" we perceive when, for example, we open our eyes, from the "Space" we conceive when, for example, we think about the extent of the solar system. While fully recognizing the difference here, Peirce became convinced very early that no spatial datum entirely free from interpretational elements can be found. Visual space is not something given, but is rather a consequence of *judging* in the light of certain signs directly presented to us.

The evidence for this conclusion is partly psychological, partly anatomical. If, for example, a person of normal vision shuts one eye, he can see with the other a roughly oval expanse completely filled with patches of color. Yet we know that each eye has a blind spot caused by the junction of the optic nerve and the retina. A simple experiment mentioned in every psychological text-book enables a person to discover the presence of his own blind spots. "It follows that the space we immediately see (when one eye is closed) is not, as we had imagined, a continuous oval, but is a ring, the filling up of which must be the work of the intellect" (5.220). Furthermore, our ostensible perception of depth, or the third dimension, is really the result of inference. As Berkeley conclusively argued in *A New Theory of Vision,* since the retina is a surface at right angles to the line of sight, there is no physiological means of registering a sensation of the distance to a visually perceived object. Depth, then, cannot be something literally seen, but must be something *judged*.

As a matter of fact, the functioning of our eyes alone cannot account for the two-dimensional field of vision. For we know that the retina is not a continuous surface. It is composed of innumerable nerve-needles pointing towards the light; and only the extreme tips of the nerve-needles are sensitive to stimuli. The distances which separate the nerve-needles from one another are large relative to the area of each nerve-needle. "Now, of these points, certainly the excitation of no one singly can produce the perception of a surface, and consequently not the aggregate of all the sensations can amount to this" (6.416). Even if we were to suppose that each nerve-point conveys the sensation of a little colored expanse, the result of their combined action would be just a collection of spots, not a continuous surface (5.223). What we seem obliged to conclude, therefore, is that the relations subsisting between the excitations of different nerve-points are signs which we interpret in terms of the hypothesis of space (6.416).

The above consideration, however, gives us no warrant for rushing to the conclusion that visual space is "purely mental." Peirce can quite consistently hold that it is something observable, since for him all observation involves a judgmental component. At this level, space is a hypothesis reached by the simplest kind of abductive inference from percepts. Hence we incline instinctively to the view that it must have three dimensions (1.403). Only when through reflection we extend the hypothesis far beyond the region of direct observation, do we realize the possibility of additional dimensions (1.249; 2.732). Conceptual time offers a sharp contrast here, since it seems to be necessarily one-dimensional (1.273).

How does Peirce conceive Space taken in its most inclusive sense? First of all, he agrees completely with Newton as against Leibniz, that it is a real entity (5.530; 5.496). Space is no mere appearance or confused idea; it is an irreducible feature of the cosmos, and cannot be dissolved away by any *tour de force* of thought. But to pronounce it real is not to say that it is an existing thing. For existing things are reacting individuals, whereas Space "is that form of intuition in which is presented the law of the mutual reaction of those objects whose mode of existence consists in mutually reacting" (6.82). In short, we have to do here with an entity possessing the mode of being of a *law*. The latter is imposed on all objects as a necessary condition of their coexistence and interaction (1.488).

Particular observed spaces exhibit no breaks or gaps in their spatiality, but are perceptually continuous. It therefore seems reasonable to conclude that the metaphysical category of continuity applies to Space. Hence, Space forms a true continuum (6.212; 1.170). This means that it is without singularities, and that the spaces which compose it are not distinct identities (6.82). Similarly, "no collection of points, no matter how abnumerable its multitude, can in itself constitute Space" (1.319). As a continuum, it embodies the conditions of positional possibility; a limitless number of places can be located within it. Consequently, Space is something general, since continuity and generality are alternative names for the same absence of distinction of individuals (4.172).

Although it is a continuum, the whole nature and function of Space refer to the reacting objects affected by it. These can be treated as particles occupying points of space. In the light of this, Peirce formulates a number of principles which may be abridged as follows. (i) Particles are entirely independent of their spatial determinations, though their reactions are not so. (ii) Each particle occupies a single point of Space, and no two particles occupy the same point at the same instant. (iii) All laws of reactions among particles presuppose another continuum besides Space, viz., Time. (iv) In the absence of any reactions, an isolated particle is not so determined that it must adhere to its place. It merely remains subject to the general conditions of Space and Time. (v) Since reaction is an intrinsically dual or dyadic relation, and since Space is a law whose prescriptions are conditions of reactions, it follows that these prescriptions are necessarily dual. From this principle Peirce derives several corollaries. The most important are: (*a*) that all forces are between pairs of particles, (*b*) that two places in the path of an isolated particle being given, the law of Space determines all others, and (*c*) that except for the qualities of the particles themselves, it is the pure spatial determination which prescribes what the reaction of one particular particle on another shall be; i.e. the force between two particles depends solely upon their qualities and their places at the instant. (vi) Since reaction is a symmetrical relation, Space functions as the law of reciprocal interactions. Generalizing all this, we may conclude that "the continuity of Space so acts as to cause an object to be affected by modes of existence not its own, not as participating in them but as being opposite to them" (6.84).

The foregoing principles entitle us, Peirce thinks, to affirm certain others of an even more sweeping sort. Thus, from (i) we may deduce the conclusion that "matter must consist of Boscovichian atomicules, whatever their multitude may be" (6.82). The relativity of place implicit in (iv), together with the fact that different motions are quantitatively comparable in an absolute sense, obliges us to posit another object, placed in Space, to which all motion is referred. This "is the firmament, or Cayley's absolute" (*ibid.*; cf. 1.504, 4.145). Like Space it partakes of the nature of law, and is also continuous. Since every motion is determined by it, we must conclude "that it is a locus which every straight line cuts, and because space is a law of twoness only, and for other reasons, every straight line must cut it in two points. It is therefore a real quadratic locus, severing space into two parts, and the space of existence must be infinite and limited in every direction." (6.82)   Finally, there is some ground for inferring from the fact that the law presented by Space is perfectly general, that "every motion must admit of receiving the same kind of changes as every other." If this be granted, Peirce claims to be able to prove ("though the demonstration is far too long to give") that the number of dimensions of Space "ought to be just 4" (*ibid.*).

However fanciful, and even absurd, some of these deductions may appear in the light of present-day physics, we have to remember that Peirce was thinking within the framework of classical mechanics as commonly interpreted at the end of the nineteenth century. Despite his speculative predilections, he was no incompetent dabbler in physical theory, but was thoroughly familiar with its details.[8] Furthermore, his whole discussion is presented as a *hypothesis* about the ultimate character of Space (cf. 6.83). Many of the consequences of the hypothesis were, he believed, shown to be true by empirical observation. Others were in the nature of predictions capable of being confirmed or refuted by subsequent inquiry. Whatever the results, then, at least the method employed was one which stayed close to the requirements of a scientific metaphysics.

Time. As in the case of Space, there is a well-known distinction between "time" which is experienced directly and "Time" which is conceived abstractly. Peirce takes note of this distinction when he observes that the Time which appears in mathematical analyses differs

---

[8]Cf. 6.238 ff. It is worth noting that Peirce saw quite clearly in 1892 the inadequacy of the notion of "impenetrability" in connection with atoms and molecules (cf. 6.243).

radically from the time we perceive. The former "is an arbitrarily supposed object in some respects analogous . . . to the instantaneous condition of the water of some river whose water should be perfectly homogeneous" (6.325). That is to say, the mathematician constructs an abstraction, or frames a hypothesis, which, however much it may have been occasioned by experience, is *per se* determined exclusively by the conditions of consistent thought. It is therefore "a mere possibleness," not an existent like the imagined state of the river. The mathematician does not have to worry his head about the relation between his "purely arbitrary hypothesis" and what is perceptually experienced. This is a problem which falls into the lap of the metaphysician. For he is concerned with the reality of Time, not with fictitious constructions.

Now the primordial element in our experience, without which we should not have the idea of time at all, is that of transience or passage. We live our entire lives in the present; but whenever we ask what the content of the present instant is, our question comes too late. Before we can even articulate it, that particular instant has gone and another has taken its place. This gives the absolute present an occult quality, an inscrutability, which makes it curiously baffling to the intellect. Yet the fact of transience cannot be denied without absurdity (1.310; 2.85; 5.289; 5.459). It is customary to express the fact by saying that "time flows" (2.710; 6.128). But such a manner of speaking has its dangers, because it tempts us to think of time as though it were an existing object or thing. The analogy of the Heraclitean river, which comes so naturally to mind, is full of pitfalls for the unwary.

From the fact of transience or passage the relations "before" and "after" are derived. A very little thought enables us to judge that moment A preceded moment B, and hence that B succeeded A. These relations, taken in conjunction with the processes of recollection and anticipation, give rise to the distinction of past and future. We then note that time appears to have a one-dimensional quality (1.273). It "flows" in a single direction only—from past to future. But since this description goes beyond anything we directly experience, the question arises as to its legitimacy. Are there good grounds for holding that past and future, together with the unidirectional flow, belong to real Time? Or should these aspects be taken to depend upon the peculiar constitution of the human mind, so that real Time has nothing corresponding to them?

Although the textual evidence is not conclusive, it strongly suggests that Peirce subscribed to the latter alternative. Thus, he refers to the contrast between past and future as being "merely subjective," not only in regard to our knowledge of time but in regard to "*real Time*" (6.96). Even "a moderate appreciation of Kant's argument," he thinks, should enable us to see that this is true. Again, he declares the whole procedure of investigating the past and the future to be different from the problem of real Time (6.387). On the other hand, "one of the most marked features about the law of mind is that it makes time to have a definite direction of flow from past to future" (6.127). The asymmetrical relation of having temporal priority seems to be absent from the realm of physical events, where the "law of energy" is supreme. Here "there is no more distinction between the two opposite directions in time than between moving northward and moving southward" (*ibid.*). In pure dynamics, for instance, "the law of energy amounts to this, that the instantaneous accelerations of the motions of particles depend solely upon the relative positions of those particles" at the same instant; and what follows after depends "upon what now is, in the same way precisely, and is calculated by the same laws, as what went before depends upon what now is" (6.387). Thus, the directional flow of time, if not a wholly psychological affair, is at least not a dynamical one.

From the standpoint of human knowledge and action, however, the distinction of past and future is enormously important. "The Past consists of the sum of *faits accomplis,* and this Accomplishment is the Existential Mode of Time. For the Past really acts upon us, and *that* it does not at all in the way in which a Law or Principle influences us, but precisely as an Existent object acts." (5.459) Hence the past is fixed, determinate, actual. It works upon the future which it can only know "so far as it can imagine the process by which the future is to be influenced" (1.493). The future itself is not actual but potential (2.148). Everything it will contain is either destined, i.e. necessitated already, or undecided, i.e. possible. By its very definition it is endless and can never be completed. When we make assertions about past events, an inevitable reference to the future is involved. For the truth or falsity of such assertions is determinable only through what subsequent researches may bring to light (6.96; 5.543).

Reflection on one type of statement about the past, viz., assertions based on memory, led Peirce to the conclusion that real Time is probably continuous. His argument on this point "takes off" from two previously admitted facts—that all our experience occurs in the present, and that the present is characterized by transience. Now when we have knowledge of past events, certain memory data must be given to us in the present. But before we can interpret these data they have ceased to be present and are now past! How can this paradox be resolved? In one of two ways, Peirce suggests. Either my knowledge of the past is an illusion, in which case I shall be reduced to a "solipsism of the present moment"; or, I must say that the past is not known by inference but in some other way. While the solipsistic alternative is not theoretically refutable, it will be practically refuted, Peirce thinks, if we can give the other alternative a workable meaning (1.168).

The meaning suggested is the affirmation that we have an immediate consciousness of the past.

But if we have an immediate consciousness of a state of consciousness past by one unit of time and if that past state involved an immediate consciousness of a state then past by one unit, we now have an immediate consciousness of a state past by two units; and as this is equally true of all states, we have an immediate consciousness of a state past by four units, by eight units, by sixteen units, etc.; in short we must have an immediate consciousness of every state of mind that is past by any finite number of units of time. But we certainly have not an immediate consciousness of our state of mind a year ago. So a year is more than any finite number of units of time in this system of measurement; or, in other words, there is a measure of time infinitely less than a year. Now, this is only true if the series be continuous. Here, then, it seems to me, we have positive and tremendously strong reason for believing that time really is continuous. (1.169)

Reduced to bare essentials, this argument states that if time consisted of discrete instants "nobody could have any memory" (4.641).

The evidence, then, supports a belief in the continuity of real Time. This excludes any such thing "as an absolute *instant*, or absolutely definite before-and-afterness relatively to all other instants," within Time itself (6.326). Instants are merely possible points where the continuum might be broken (6.182). In other words, an instant comes about as a consequence of some brute existential fact related to time. It follows that the immediate present introduces discontinuity into the temporal continuum. The actual instant, although not entirely independent of all others, has sufficient individuality to produce a breach of continuity (6.86).

It might be thought that the above fact constitutes a blemish in the nature of Time. But this would be a complete mistake. For "time, as the universal form of change, cannot exist unless there is something to undergo change" (6.132). That is to say, from the point of view of existence, Time is a *law*, and as a law it must subject something to its governance. What it governs, of course, is the series of real events that "take place," or have dates, in real Time (1.492). In order to elucidate this, Peirce proceeds to specify the distinctive properties of an event.

Suppose a chemist mixes two yellowish solutions, and obtains one that is blue. This event, like every other, can be defined as "an existential junction of incompossible facts" (*ibid.*). For the mixture's being yellow and therefore not blue is a fact. It is likewise a fact that the mixture is blue and not yellow. These two facts are contradictory since they cannot both be true of precisely the same logical subject. But they can be true of the same subject existentially because of the law of time. Moreover, the locus of their actualization is the single event. Accordingly, "we may say that for an event there is requisite: first, a contradiction; second, existential embodiments of these contradictory states; third, an immediate existential junction of these two contradictory existential embodiments or facts, so that the subjects are existentially identical; and fourth, in this existential junction a definite one of the two facts must be existentially first in the order of evolution and existentially second in the order of involution. We say the former is earlier, the latter later in time." (1.493)

But the event considered as a "junction of states" is a rather puzzling entity. It is neither a subject nor an attribute of a subject. What mode of being, then, does it have? The best answer Peirce can devise is that an event is an *"existential quasi-existence,"* i.e. an approximation to existence where contraries can be united in a single subject (1.494). Phillip's being drunk and Phillip's being sober are only intelligible because Time makes the Phillip of today different from the Phillip of yesterday. The instantaneous Phillip who can be both drunk and sober has a potential being which does not quite amount to existence. Time as a law, therefore, governs events wherein "that which is existentially a subject is enabled to receive contrary determinations in existence" (*ibid.*).

A word may be said about the probable genesis of man's conceptions of Space and Time. Peirce thinks it likely "that they are the results of natural selection" (6.418). This is suggested by their great utility even to the humblest intelligence. Without them, no animal could seize his food or accomplish other actions necessary for the preservation of the species. Would instinct not suffice to guarantee such things? Only for brief periods, Peirce contends. For instinct is helpless in the face of novel situations such as the course of evolution is constantly bringing about. An animal whose mechanical conceptions did not break down in these situations would obviously have an immense advantage in the struggle for life. Hence, "there would be a constant selection in favor of more and more correct ideas of these matters" (*ibid.*). In this way knowledge of the fundamental laws of Space and Time would be gradually attained.

6. SCIENTIFIC METAPHYSICS AND COSMIC DESIGN

Has scientific metaphysics anything to say about the problem of design in the universe? At least it can try to state the problem accurately. The whole issue hinges, according to Peirce, on whether the material universe is of limited extent and finite age, or is boundless in Space and Time. In the former case, "it is conceivable that a general plan or design embracing the whole universe should be discovered, and it would be proper to be on the alert for some traces of such a unity" (6.419). Since the presence of design suggests a designer, the hypothesis of a creator or governor of the world would naturally arise here. On the other hand, if the universe is infinite, "the attempt to find in it any design embracing it as a whole is futile, and involves a false way of looking at the subject. If the universe never had any beginning, and if in space world stretches beyond world without limit, there is no *whole* of material things, and consequently no general character to the universe, and no need or possibility of any governor for it." (*Ibid.*)

Now this problem can only be significantly dealt with in the light of such fragmentary evidence as we possess. A final settlement of it is out of the question; and, of course, all *a priori* methods of attacking it are worthless. What sort of conclusion, then, does the available evidence suggest? As far as Space is concerned, we can observe no more than a finite amount of it even with the most powerful telescopes. Yet we do not discover anything that justifies the positing of an outer limit or boundary. "As to time, we find on our earth a constant progress of development since the planet was a red-hot ball; the solar system seems to have resulted from the condensation of a nebula, and the process appears to be still going on" (6.420). We lack any evidence regarding the state of the universe prior to the nebulous stage. But we also lack any evidence for an absolute beginning of things or for a first moment of Time.

In view of the above, it might seem sensible to adopt a policy of agnosticism. But Peirce thinks there is a "scientific presumption" that the unknown parts of Space and Time are like the known parts. We may therefore reasonably conjecture that the vast panorama of terrestrial evolution, the cycle of life and death in all development, can be found in other solar systems, "that as enormous distances lie between the different planets of our solar system, relatively to their diameters, and as still more enormous distances lie between our system relatively to its diameter and other systems, so it may be supposed that other galactic clusters exist so remote from ours as not to be recognized as such with certainty" (6.421). These are admittedly weak inductions. Their sole recommendation is that "they are the presumptions which, in our ignorance of the facts, should be preferred to hypotheses which involve conceptions of things and occurrences totally different in their character from any of which we have had any experience, such as disembodied spirits, the creation of matter, infringements of the laws of mechanics, etc." (*ibid.*).

The upshot is that "the universe ought to be presumed too vast to have any character" (6.422). Its apparently unbounded extent in Space and Time makes all talk about the beneficence, justice, or wisdom of Nature sound a little silly. The only examples of these attributes we know "are of a most limited kind—limited in degree and limited in range" (*ibid.*). Hence, even within the domain of observable fact, theories which affirm the presence of design or purpose should be treated critically. The first question we should ask about them is whether the relations they embody "are susceptible of explanation on mechanical principles, and if not they should be looked upon with disfavor as having already a strong presumption against them" (6.423). In the past, examination has generally exploded all such theories without much difficulty.

Faced with the inability to establish cosmic design on philosophical grounds, some minds will inevitably have recourse to mystical doctrines. Since these persons have no recognized logic of induction, "they cannot be driven from their belief" (6.425). But the scientific metaphysician has no concern with the ineffable raptures of mysticism. For him the best that can be done is to advance certain hypotheses "not devoid of all likelihood, in the general line of growth of scientific ideas, and capable of being verified or refuted by future observers" (1.7).

PART TWO

Peirce's Transcendentalism

which obvers
doctrinesis no

VIII

TRANSCENDENTAL ELEMENTS
in Mathematics, Logic, and Phenomenology

1. INTRODUCTION

THE transcendental aspect of Peirce's thought is made up of all the beliefs which he affirms on grounds other than those of scientific method. Such beliefs are not fixed by the process of abduction, deduction, and induction. Instead, they are established by at least two other methods. The first involves an appeal to feeling, sentiment, or "instinct," in connection with beliefs about "matters of vital importance." The second involves the use of *a priori* modes of reasoning to arrive at conclusions which go far beyond what is observationally verifiable. Scientific method places primary emphasis on the objective reference of beliefs, i.e. on their determination by that which is external to the investigating intelligence. The other two methods stress respectively (*a*) the subjective and anthropomorphic, and (*b*) the speculative and abstractly systematic, in the attainment of philosophical knowledge.

It is more difficult to give a coherent account of Peirce's transcendentalism than it is of his naturalism. The former is not only a less powerful aspect of his thought; it is also much less sharply exemplified. Peirce's predilection for vague and oracular language when writing in the transcendentalist vein (cf. the essay "Evolutionary Love") is a constant source of perplexity. Moreover, since the two methods mentioned above are never made the subject of a detailed discussion, their presence has to be inferred from the occurrence of certain doctrines which obviously run counter to his naturalism. The fact that these doctrines loom steadily larger as we pass from his philosophy of mathematics through logic and phenomenology to metaphysics, ethics, and theology, obliges us to give considerably more space to the last three topics than to the first. In the present chapter, the transcendental elements in his views on mathematics, logic, and phenomenology will be reviewed. As a prelude, however, it will be necessary to say something further about the rivals to the scientific method of fixing belief.

Peirce's espousal of evolutionism led him, as it did his younger contemporary Bergson, to entertain an exaggerated respect for the adaptation achieved by lower animals to the conditions of their existence. "Docilely allowing themselves to be guided by their instincts into almost every detail of life, they live exactly as their Maker intended them to live. The result is, that they very rarely fall into error of any kind, and *never* into a vital one." (1.649) The contrast with man in this respect is profound. He is constantly making mistakes and getting into difficulties. Indeed, it is thus that he becomes aware of his individual selfhood. Now it is tempting to attribute the difference here to the fact that man seeks to govern his conduct by rational thought, whereas the lower animals cannot do so. If such a conclusion be drawn, a further consequence readily follows, namely, that where practical action is concerned, instinct is a much more dependable guide than reason.

This is the general theme which Peirce elaborates in a lecture of 1898 entitled "Philosophy and the Conduct of Life"—the first of a series on "Detached Ideas on Vitally Important Topics." Representing himself as "an Aristotelian and a scientific man," he proceeds to condemn "with the whole strength of conviction the Hellenic tendency to mingle philosophy and practice" (1.618). For philosophy is "nothing more than a branch of science" (1.663), and as such is concerned exclusively with theory. Its task is the disinterested pursuit of the truth. Whenever a man proceeds to inquire into some question for an ulterior purpose "such as to make money, or to amend his life, or to benefit his fellows, he may be ever so much better than a scientific man, if you will . . . but he is not a scientific man" (1.45). Science has nothing at stake on any temporal venture, but is in pursuit of eternal verities (5.589). It might even be defined as "the study of useless things" (1.76). Certainly, it has no advice to give on practical issues, and is completely divorced from action (1.637). As one of the sciences, then, philosophy is powerless to assist in the conduct of life.

It follows from this line of thought that belief must be something beyond the pale of science. For we only believe a proposition we are prepared to act on. "*Full belief* is willingness to act upon the proposition in vital crises, *opinion* is willingness to act upon it in relatively insignificant affairs" (1.635). But the propositions accepted by a science are not intended as a basis for action. No scientific man would ever think of risking his life on them. At best they are mere opinions, highly tentative and fallible, whose function is to advance the process of theoretical inquiry. Practical conduct obliges us to banish every doubt from our minds. Scientific investigation, on the other hand, puts a premium on doubt, and is ceaselessly endeavoring to prove the worthlessness of its provisional opinions (6.3). The scientist is ready and happy to jettison them when experience so demands. "There is thus no proposition at all in science which answers to the conception of belief" (1.635).

Not only is science useless in practical affairs and "matters of vital importance," but reason in any form is to be eschewed as unreliable. When a man attempts "to reason out his plans from first principles . . . in at least nine such cases out of every ten, he blunders seriously, even if he manages to escape complete disaster" (2.176). The wise procedure is to rely entirely on instinct in the practical conduct of life, for "instinct is all but unerring; but reason in all vitally important matters is a treacherous guide" (6.86). Peirce thinks it safe to say that reason is "more than a thousand times as fallible" as instinct (2.176). No wonder, then, that the latter is in fact the basis on which most men conduct their daily lives.

Now instincts appear in consciousness as sentiments or instinctive beliefs. These constitute "the substance of the soul" (1.628). Yet as soon as we try to formulate our sentiments in conceptual terms, we find that they are extremely vague. "Nevertheless, our instinctive beliefs involving such concepts are far more trustworthy than the best established results of science" (6.496). Even logic supports this conclusion, demonstrating "in the clearest manner that reasoning itself testifies to its own ultimate subordination to sentiment" (1.672). The prescription of reason is that we ought to follow the dictates of instinct when such a policy answers our immediate requirements. In short, where the greatest affairs of life are at stake, "the wise man follows his heart and does not trust his head" (1.653).

This conclusion is similar to the position taken by many of the New England Transcendentalists, within whose orbit of influence Peirce was raised (cf. 6.102). Their stress on the spontaneous deliverances of the spirit led to a romantic exalting of feeling and sentiment at the expense of rational thought. It is but a short step from that doctrine to the view that thought has no bearing of any kind on action; and Peirce occasionally takes such a step. Reason, he contends, is supreme only in matters of theory; sentiment is supreme in practical affairs. Between these domains there is an irreconcilable opposition. "The two masters, *theory* and *practice,* you cannot serve" (1.642). The contrast with the naturalistic side of his thought is obvious here. No longer is it the case that beliefs must be fixed by the method of science before they can be accepted as reliable, for science has nothing to do with belief. No longer can it be said that "logicality in regard to practical matters . . . is the most useful quality an animal can possess" (5.366), for logic must always bow the knee to sentiment in such matters. No longer is it unqualifiedly true that "every proposition that is not pure metaphysical jargon and chatter must have some possible bearing upon practice" (5.539), for none of the propositions of science have any such bearing. Throughout the course of man's life, theory and practice function, or should function, quite independently of each other.

It is true that Peirce modifies this doctrine to the extent of admitting that "theory is applicable to minor practical affairs" (1.637). He even agrees that a remarkable man in a remarkable situation might, in default of a familiar rule of thumb, reason his way out (2.176). But most men at most times rely quite properly on their instincts. Only when something extraordinary occurs do they indulge in rational thought, and then merely in order to bring instinct to bear on the novel situation. That is to say, "reason is a mere succedaneum to be used where instinct is wanting" (6.500). This seems to be the main point Peirce wants to make. Of the various departments of the soul, reason is the most superficial and fallible, whereas instinct "is deep and sure" (1.647).

The bifurcation thus established has far-reaching consequences which will emerge as we proceed. An immediate implication would seem to be that the concerns of practice are much more important than the concerns of theory. Once the two domains are divorced, there is always a temptation to elevate one above the other in this way. Yet as the discussion of "vitally important topics" approaches a close, it becomes clear that Peirce considers theory to be of immeasurably greater significance than practice. For what, after all, are "practical matters"? They are the things I as an individual—or you—set the highest store by when the demands of the self are paramount. But in fact you and I are ephemeral beings. "Our deepest sentiment pronounces the verdict of our own insignificance" (1.673). Accordingly, our private affairs are of all things the veriest trifles, and *"vital importance . . . a very low kind of importance, indeed"* (1.647). Not in the contemplation of such topics, but rather in the contemplation of "the great cosmos of ideas to which the sciences belong" is man to find his supreme occupation. "To sum it up, all sensible talk about vitally important topics must be commonplace, all reasoning about them unsound, and all study of them narrow and sordid" (1.677).

This line of thought leads easily to the conclusion that the realm of theory is the only "real" world. The ideas which constitute it are "Platonized," or treated as entities having a status and efficacy of their own, quite apart from individual human minds. Interest then attaches to the "objective logic" found to obtain among these ideas, or imported into them by means of *a priori* premises. Such a logic can then be "read off" in the guise of a cosmology purporting to be a factual account of how the universe evolved. Since the ideas concerned are not checked by outer experience and practice, their content is likely to become more and more subjective. Traits which can only be discerned empirically in human personality are generalized so as to apply to the whole cosmos. At the same time, experience and practice, being obtrusive aspects of the world, are "idealized" or "intellectualized" in order to bring them into conformity with the line of thought pursued. The result is that experience comes to be interpreted as something intrinsically "mental"; while practice is reduced to a phase of a process directed towards an ideal end or *summum bonum*. These are the further themes of Peirce's transcendentalism which must now be elucidated.

3. MATHEMATICS AND THE REALM OF IDEAS

It will be remembered that the philosophy of mathematics outlined in Part One follows broadly the tradition of Kant. Mathematics is interpreted as a construction of the human mind. We make the truths involved by producing appropriate diagrams and observing the relations embodied therein. Now Peirce frequently uses "Platonic" language when he designates these relations, calling them "eternal forms" (1.648), and "pure forms" (4.118). This might be regarded as simply a manner of speaking, perfectly consistent with his naturalism, were it not for the fact that there are cognate expressions which point to a different doctrine. Such expressions make it fairly clear that he intended the phrase "eternal forms" to be taken in considerably more than a Pickwickian sense.

Suppose we ask a number of mathematicians about the subject-matter of their science. We will find, Peirce contends, that the majority subscribe to a kind of Platonism. The typical mathematician believes himself to be concerned with what is eternal; and "the eternal is for him a world, a cosmos, in which the universe of actual existence is nothing but an arbitrary locus. The end that pure mathematics is pursuing is to discover that real potential world." (1.646) Peirce was strongly attracted to this view. Thus, he insists that while the mathematician does "create *for himself*" the ideas with which he deals, he does not create them absolutely. In their purity they are eternal beings of the Inner World (4.161). The same is true not only of mathematical, but of all scientific ideas. Peirce even goes so far as to hint that "the soul's deeper parts" are somehow in contact with these realities, which must ultimately emerge upon its surface. "In this way the eternal forms, that mathematics and philosophy and the other sciences make us acquainted with, will by slow percolation gradually reach the very core of one's being . . . because they are ideal and eternal verities" (1.648).

Such a doctrine will seem fantastic only to the people who imagine that an idea has to be connected with a brain, or has to inhere in a soul. But this notion "is preposterous: the idea does not belong to the soul; it is the soul that belongs to the idea. The soul does for the idea just what the cellulose does for the beauty of the rose; that is to say, it affords it opportunity." (1.216) Indeed, we must go further and affirm that these eternal forms have the power to work themselves out in physical and psychical results. "They have life, generative life" (1.219). Hence, the statement: "Truth crushed to earth shall rise again," is not just a poetic fancy. It expresses a literal fact. The ideas of Truth and Right are the most powerful forces in the cosmos, "to which every knee must sooner or later bow or be broken down" (1.217). If it be objected that this will come about only when men decide to guide their lives by these ideas, Peirce replies that the objection puts the cart before the horse. For the ideas "have a power of finding or creating their vehicles, and having found them, of conferring upon them the ability to transform the face of the earth" (*ibid.*). An extreme Platonist could hardly put the matter more forthrightly.

Having reached this position, it is not surprising that Peirce should want to back water a little. His naturalism re-asserts itself to the extent of eliciting certain modifications of these excessive claims for ideas. In the first place, he disavows any suggestion that they can call new matter into existence. Such a contention "would be pure intellectualism, which denies that blind force is an element of experience distinct from rationality, or logical force" (1.220). In the second place, he admits that an idea must undoubtedly be embodied (or ensouled) in order to attain complete being. "If, at any moment, it should happen that an idea . . . was quite unconceived by any living being, then its mode of being . . . would consist precisely in this, namely, that it was about to receive embodiment (or ensoulment) and to work in the world" (1.218). It would have potential being, or being *in futuro.* The contrast here is with matter, which if it were to be deprived of the governance of ideas, would lapse into utter nothingness. In other words, matter devoid of ideas is sheer nothing; but ideas without matter are potential being. This reinforces the correctness of the view that *an,* if not *the,* ideal world is "in some sense the only real one" (3.529).

The attribution of "power" to ideas, which I take to be a distinctive feature of Peirce's transcendentalism, also appears in connection with his treatment of universals. Some reference has already been made to this point. Generals are declared to be not merely real, but *"physically efficient"* (5.431). Peirce considers such a doctrine to be warranted by the most obvious facts of experience. The illustration he gives is therefore worth noting. "No sane man doubts," he contends, "that if I feel the air in my study to be stuffy, that thought may cause the window to be opened. My thought, be it granted, was an individual event. But what determined it to take the particular determination it did, was in part the general fact that stuffy air is unwholesome, and in part other *Forms.* . . . So then, when my window was opened, because of the truth that stuffy air is malsain, a physical effort was brought into existence by the efficiency of a general and non-existent truth." (*Ibid.*) One not already committed to the view that ideas have a power of their own might argue that the cause of the opening of the window was a muscular effort, not a thought in the mind. True, this effort was in turn due to a belief possessed by me, and human beliefs can produce physical effects precisely because the beliefs are habits of action. If we take the terms "idea" and "universal" to designate the logical content of belief, then we are observationally entitled to assert that *ideas in individual human minds* may have causal efficacy. But there is no observational warrant for saying that ideas *per se* have any such power. Peirce's espousal of the latter notion "*literally*," as he puts it in a letter to Mrs. Ladd-Franklin,[1] can only be a consequence of his transcendentalism.

A similar situation exists in regard to the subclass of universals called "scientific laws." They are affirmed to be "really operative in nature" (5.101), and it is evident that Peirce sometimes understands this to mean that the laws *compel* or *force* events to occur in the manner they do. Again, one of his illustrations is instructive.

With overwhelming uniformity, in our past experience, direct and indirect, stones left free to fall have fallen. Thereupon two hypotheses only are open to us. Either

1. the uniformity with which those stones have fallen has been due to some mere chance and affords no ground whatever, not the slightest for any expectation that the next stone that shall be let go will fall; or

2. the uniformity with which stones have fallen has been due to some *active general principle*, in which case it would be a strange coincidence that it should cease to act at the moment my prediction was based upon it. (5.100).

Peirce holds, of course, that "every sane man will adopt the latter hypothesis" (5.101). Yet it is by no means clear why our choice should be restricted to just two hypotheses, each representing an extreme position. Peirce himself elsewhere provides a third alternative which is a middle road between radical nominalism and immoderate realism. This is the view that a formula expressing a well-attested scientific law is not simply a convenient fiction, but actually "*corresponds to,* a reality" (5.96). It does not follow that such a reality must be endowed with a special "activity" or "power" of its own. Peirce seems to speak in extreme terms mainly on the occasions when he is tacitly or explicitly identifying the laws of nature with "habits." He thinks, for instance, that the phenomenon of a man winding his watch every night and the phenomenon of a stone falling require the same sort of explanation. Hence, just as we attribute the regularity of the man's behavior to a habit which "makes" him wind his watch daily, so we should attribute the descent of the stone to a habit which "makes" it fall each time (cf. 5.99). This anthropomorphic mode of interpretation will be considered below in connection with Peirce's transcendental version of the categories.

Returning to his philosophy of mathematics, there is one other matter that must be touched on, namely, the sharp separation of mathematics from logic. This, it will be recalled, finds expression in the view (*a*) that mathematics is the practice, whereas logic is the theory of deduction; (*b*) that mathematics is the prior discipline, both temporally and logically; and (*c*) that it has its own "instinctive" or "intuitive" criterion of validity, which is wholly independent of logical criticism. Now it seems to me that such a doctrine can be plausibly attributed to the influence of Peirce's transcendentalism. For, as we have suggested, an important facet of the latter is the divorce of theory from practice. Each of these is regarded as an autonomous dimension of human experience. Moreover, a common consequence of such a dichotomy is the "elevation" of one member at the expense of the other. When, therefore, Peirce declares that mathematics is the highest form of reasoning, vastly superior to and much more evident than logic; and when he denies that the reasoning of the mathematician must conform to the principles of logic (cf. 4.243), he is surely thinking in the transcendentalist vein. The appeal to a special "mathematical intuition" is entirely out of harmony with his naturalism. It is also quite unnecessary in the light of his own analysis. If logic is the theory *of* deduction, then surely the rules which it formulates must be *applicable to* deduction, and hence to mathematics as a form of deductive thinking. The distinction between the two disciplines is not that one is "higher" than the other, but that they are concerned with totally different universes of discourse. To use the scholastic terms favored by Peirce himself, mathematics moves in first intentions, while logic treats of second intentions as applied to first (1.559; 2.548). The validity of mathematical reasoning, therefore, like that of every other kind, depends upon principles discovered by the logician.

4. LOGIC AND THE *SUMMUM BONUM*

This brings us to the place where we must examine the impact of Peirce's transcendentalism on his logical doctrine. In another letter to Mrs. Ladd-Franklin, dated "Thanksgiving Day, 1902," he makes a revealing statement about his opinions of twenty years before. "In those days I knew very little about logic, and did not even thoroughly understand upon what logic is based. I was not in possession of the proof that the science of logic must be based on the science of ethics, although I more or less perceived that sound reasoning depends more on sound morals than anything else."[2] The acceptance of this "proof" led Peirce to advocate the view (*a*) that logic is not a science of fact

---

[2]*Ibid.*, p. 717.

but a normative science, and (*b*) that it presupposes as a necessary condition of its existence the findings of ethics and esthetics, i.e. the determination of the *summum bonum*.

The roots of the above doctrine can be traced as far back as 1868. In a paper of that year, Peirce points out a consequence of his view that logic in the widest sense is a method of inquiry which will on the whole approximate to the truth. The consequence is "that no inference of any individual can be thoroughly logical without certain determinations of his mind which do not concern any one inference immediately" (5.354). If he permits an overruling personal interest to dominate his thinking, his position will be like that of an insurance company which assumed one risk greater than the sum of all its others. In neither case is there any security. Once the reasoner, for example, allows a limited number of samples to assume disproportionate significance, his inductive conclusions will inevitably deviate from the truth. For induction is only a valid procedure when based on random sampling in which all possible facts are coequal. Hence, "logic rigidly requires, before all else, that no determinate fact, nothing which can happen to a man's self, should be of more consequence to him than everything else. He who would not sacrifice his own soul to save the whole world, is illogical in all his inferences, collectively. So the social principle is rooted intrinsically in logic." (*Ibid.*)

Such "self-identification of one's own interests with those of the community" would completely guarantee private logicality, were it not for one consideration. There are no reasons for believing the community ever will reach the state of perfect knowledge in terms of which truth is defined. As far as any evidence is concerned, it cannot be proved that at some future date all living beings in the universe, and therefore all intelligence, may not be obliterated. The moral Peirce draws from this is typical of his transcendentalism. What reason cannot substantiate must be "fixed" by an appeal to sentiment. Our belief in the ideal community can therefore be grounded only in "a transcendent and supreme interest," which by its very nature "is unsusceptible of any support from reasons. This infinite hope which we all have (for even the atheist will constantly betray his calm expectation that what is Best will come about) is something so august and momentous, that all reasoning in reference to it is a trifling impertinence." (5.357) The best reason can do is to show the sentiment to be an "indispensable presupposition" of scientific inquiry.

Ten years later, Peirce repeats the same theme with a slight elaboration. He puts forward not one but three sentiments, namely, "interest in an indefinite community, recognition of the possibility of this interest being made supreme, and hope in the unlimited continuance of intellectual activity, as indispensable requirements of logic" (2.655). Of these, the first is the most important, since without it probable inference would remain highly precarious. Logic "inexorably requires that our interests shall *not* be limited. They must not stop at our own fate, but must . . . reach, however vaguely, beyond this geological epoch, beyond all bounds." (2.654) If we feel inclined to raise our eyebrows at such a doctrine, we must remember, Peirce says, that (*a*) logic takes its origin in the struggle to escape doubt; (*b*) this struggle, since it terminates in action, must begin in emotion; and (*c*) the only cause of our adopting reason is that the other methods of removing doubt fail on account of the social impulse (2.655). Why, then, should we be surprised to learn that social sentiment is presupposed in reasoning? Peirce professes much interest in the similarity between his three logical sentiments and "that famous trio of Charity, Faith, and Hope, which, in the estimation of St. Paul, are the finest and greatest of spiritual gifts" (*ibid.*). If the New Testament is not a text-book of the logic of science, it is nevertheless profoundly relevant to an understanding of that subject!

By the time he came to elaborate his classification of the sciences, Peirce had ceased to talk in Kantian terms about "indispensable presuppositions" (cf. 2.113). He now placed logic among the normative sciences in such a position as to make it subordinate to ethics and esthetics. This was not, he believed, the result of any arbitrary decision. It was dictated by a deeper penetration into the nature of the disciplines themselves. Logic, he came to believe, is not just a compendium of rules which ought to be, but need not be followed. "It is the analysis of the conditions of the attainment of something of which purpose is an essential ingredient" (1.575). The thinking studied by the logician is deliberate or self-controlled, i.e. directed so as to be in conformity with an ultimate purpose or ideal (1.191; 1.573). Consider what happens in the normal course of a scientific inquiry. When we set up an experiment to test a theory, or when we imagine an extra line to be inserted into a geometrical diagram to settle some question, we perform voluntary acts which our logic approves. But "the *approval* of a *voluntary act* is a *moral* approval" (5.130). Hence, our *logica utens* is a species of morality (5.108); and our *logica docens* will be incomplete without an appeal to ethics.

Another way of putting the matter is this. Right reasoning must be such as will be conducive to our ultimate aim. Can the logician ignore the question of what that aim is? Peirce holds that he cannot, for otherwise an ideal of reasoning would be lacking, and there could be no norms of inference. "It seems to me," he observes, "that the logician ought to recognize what our ultimate aim is. It would seem to be the business of the moralist to find this out, and that the logician has to accept the teaching of ethics in this regard." (1.611) Such teaching will constitute a doctrine of the *summum bonum;* and it will be established not by scientific inquiry, but by having recourse to feeling or sentiment. If it be objected that the only relevant aim here is the logician's, which is the limited one of analyzing the conditions for the attainment of truth, Peirce replies that this "is nothing but a phase of the *summum bonum*" (1.575). In short, a faith springing from the human heart underlies all logic, and enables it to shine forth "with all its native nobility. . . . Our final view of logic will exhibit it (on one side of it) as faith come to years of discretion" (2.118).

It is hardly necessary to expatiate on the contrast between the above position and Peirce's naturalism. To put it baldly, his naturalism regards scientific method, concretely applied, as the proper subject-matter of logical theory. *Truth* and *reality* are defined in terms of that method, which is *de facto* the only dependable way of fixing our beliefs. His transcendentalism, on the other hand, seeks to make inquiry dependent on an ultimate aim or purpose, in some manner common to all mankind. It has obviously to be determined by a different method of fixing belief, viz., the appeal to feeling. Hence, the disciplines concerned with the determination of ultimate aims, i.e. ethics and esthetics, must be "sciences" in a very special sense. The problem created here will be considered in detail at a subsequent point in the discussion.

Even within his transcendentalism, however, the connection Peirce tries to establish between logic and the *summum bonum* seems to me quite vague. At times, he restricts himself to arguing that a reasoner must possess certain moral attributes if his inquiry is to yield solid results. "In induction a habit of probity is needed for success: a trickster is sure to play the confidence game upon himself. And in addition to probity, industry is essential. In the presumptive choice of hypotheses, still higher virtues are needed—a true elevation of soul." (1.576) This implies that a man of honor will be a more accurate reasoner than a rogue—a conclusion which might not be supported by an observation of the facts! Peirce refuses to go to the length of saying that every logical fallacy is a sin. But it is not clear why this further implication could not be drawn from his doctrine. It may be mentioned, incidentally, that he elsewhere points out how "in more ways than one an exaggerated regard for morality is unfavorable to scientific progress" (1.50). For morality encourages the conservatism of those "gentlemen" who always look askance at any new view or even any free inquiry. Consequently, in a country where "there is a large class of academic professors who are provided with good salaries and looked up to as gentlemen, scientific inquiry must languish. Wherever the bureaucrats are the more learned class, the case will be still worse." (1.51).

Apart from such considerations of morality, Peirce seems to have in mind another connection between logic and the *summum bonum*, which can be stated briefly as follows. Rational inquiry, because of its self-corrective capacity, is slowly leading men towards an ideally complete set of stable beliefs (i.e., the Truth). This "general drift in the history of human thought" which will produce "one catholic conclusion," is in the direction of man's highest good. To advance the cause of Reason, by making the world more reasonable, is the categorical imperative for every individual. So transcendent is this ideal that by comparison with it all private concerns pale into insignificance. "Let our hearts murmur 'blessed are we' if the immolation of our being can weld together the smallest part of the great cosmos of ideas to which the sciences belong" (1.670; cf. 1.615). Such is the faith of the logician.

As might be expected, the pragmatic maxim is also brought into subservience to the *summum bonum*. In its naturalistic setting, the maxim appeared as a method for determining the meaning of abstract ideas by specifying their experimental consequences. The effectiveness of this procedure sprang from the fact "that man is so completely hemmed in by the bounds of his possible practical experience, his mind is so restricted to being the instrument of his needs, that he cannot, in the least, *mean* anything that transcends those limits" (5.536). Since all his symbols have a conventional origin, they are nonsensical when used to refer to something allegedly lying beyond "conceivable human occasions" (5.532). Ideas are the vehicles of man's diverse purposes, and so find significant expression in his purposive activity. This doctrine, however, tends to disappear under the influence of the notion that there is but *one* ultimate purpose ingredient in the actions of mankind. The ideal end of "concrete reasonableness" towards which the whole creation moves becomes the goal of the pragmatic maxim. It cannot be expected that pragmatism should provide the highest grade of clearness of thought, for this is only to be found in the conception of the *summum bonum* (5.3).

Now I should like to suggest that the above shift in the interpretation of the pragmatic doctrine was due to a change in Peirce's view of the nature of human action. In the naturalistic phase of his philosophy action is conceived as bodily movement, muscular effort, or doing; a brute process which, while not itself rational, is capable of becoming so in the sense that it can be controlled and directed by thought. When this occurs, we have purposive behavior, which is a union of thought and action. Each of these is an essential ingredient. In the transcendental phase of his philosophy, on the other hand, Peirce tends to equate action with habit. Being general, habit is then treated as something *wholly* intelligible. Such an "idealization of action" produces a conception bearing little resemblance to the procedure of experimentation carried on in the sciences. For that procedure requires the component of muscular effort or doing which is quite irreducible to the process of thinking. At the risk of overstating the contrast here we may say that his naturalism construes action as Secondness, while his transcendentalism construes it as Thirdness. There is undoubtedly a connection between the latter doctrine and his speculative cosmology, which represents the final state of the cosmos as one of perfect rationality (cf. 6.33). Apparently, the evolution of the universe involves the "absorption" of Firstness and Secondness by Thirdness!

While the evidence for this interpretation is perhaps not conclusive, many comments Peirce makes appear to support it. Thus he insists that a good pragmaticist "adores . . . not the sham power of brute force . . . but the creative power of reasonableness" (5.520). This power is expressed in the evolutionary process whereby the existent comes more and more to embody those generals which are "destined" to triumph over all (5.433). Hence, sheer bodily exertion or the exercise of strength can be of no importance to the pragmaticist, for "material action is the mere husk of ideas." The difficulty Peirce found with James's position was that it "appears to assume that the end of man is action—a stoical axiom which, to the present writer at the age of sixty, does not recommend itself so forcibly as it did at thirty" (5.3). In his reaction against this doctrine, Peirce frequently talks as though the end of man were *thought*. But of course it is quite unnecessary to make one process ancillary to the other. When Peirce urges that "the end of thought is action only in so far as the end of action is another thought," he is advocating a sounder view. Theory exists for the sake of practice and practice for the sake of theory; and both for the sake of the concrete process of human living. Quite apart from this, however, it seems clear that where pragmatism ceases to be a method for the logical clarification of ideas and becomes a means of subserving an absolute, rational good, a decided shift in doctrine has taken place. It was this aspect of Peirce's transcendentalism which so strongly influenced the "Absolute Pragmatism" of Royce.[3]

5. EXPERIENCE AND PHENOMENOLOGY

What I have called the "idealization of action" has a counterpart in another theme which crops up at various points in the *Collected Papers*. This may be designated the "idealization of experience," that is, the treatment of experience as a cognitive construct. In order to bring out its full import, I propose to consider it vis-à-vis the interpretation of experience characteristic of his naturalism. Since perhaps no other single notion provides as crucial a testing-ground for the consistency of a philosophy, such a discussion will serve to throw the conflicting tendencies into relief from a new perspective.

1. Within the naturalistic context, Peirce speaks of experience as "the enforced element in the history of our lives" (5.581). It is that which we are compelled to accept because it involves "a brute bearing down of any will to resist it" (4.172). Hence, experience manifests a concrete duality (5.539), a sense of something reacting against us, the shock of an alien non-ego making its impact on the ego (2.139; 5.52). The sharpest illustration of this duality is the phenomenon of surprise. Consequently, "experience" is a name we apply to contrasts or sudden changes in our perception. "We experience vicissitudes, especially" (1.336).

As thus delineated, experience is "destitute of anything reasonable" (4.172). It is simply the action on us of the external world, the world of fact (1.321). For "we have *direct experience of things in themselves*. Nothing can be more completely false than that we can experience only our own ideas. That is indeed without exaggeration

[3]Quotations in this paragraph for which no references are given may be found in R. B. Perry, *The Thought and Character of William James* (Boston, 1935), vol. II, pp. 424-25. Cf. also p. 222. Evidence of the influence of Peirce on Royce can be found in the Preface to *The Problem of Christianity* (New York, 1913), and in vol. II of that work, *passim*.

the very epitome of *all* falsity." (6.95)   Psychologically, of course, this direct action of things gives us percepts, which may therefore be said to constitute experience proper, "that which I am forced to accept" (2.142). But there is nothing distinctively "mental" about percepts; they appear under a physical guise (1.253). Experience, then, may be said to acquaint us with facts—those determinate, irrational particulars whose occurrence *hic et nunc* is a matter of brute force (1.435).

Such experience is wholly non-cognitive. Yet precisely this non-cognitive experience is the *source* of all our knowledge. "All the creations of our mind are but patchworks from experience" (6.492). At the most elementary level, as we have seen, knowledge is obtained by describing the percept in a perceptual judgment. These two things, however, differ *toto caelo*. "The percept . . . is not itself a judgment, nor can a judgment in any degree resemble a percept" (5.54). The sole justification for a perceptual judgment is that it turns out to be useful, i.e. it enables us to guide our future actions (1.538). Experience provides "the evidence of the senses"; knowledge begins with "a sort of stenographic report of that evidence, possibly erroneous" (2.141).

Not only is experience the source of our knowledge, but it provides the only reliable *test* of knowledge. This was for Peirce its most important function. He had studied his Kant too thoroughly ever to accept the contention of traditional empiricism that the genesis of our knowledge is what matters. "Far be it from me to enunciate any doctrine of a *tabula rasa*" (5.50). The mind has a power to originate hypotheses, and the chief cognitive function of experience is to confirm or confute them. Accordingly, both the experimental activity and the observations whereby the consequences of a hypothesis are tested, constitute a "deliberate yielding of ourselves to that *force majeure*" of experience (5.581). This is the sense in which it is our only teacher.

2. The other account which I find in Peirce produces a different sort of picture. Instead of being a name for our direct contact with particulars, "experience" is now used as a synonym for "knowledge" or "cognition." "*Experience* means nothing but just that of a cognitive nature which the history of our lives has forced upon us" (5.539). It is "that determination of belief and cognition" (2.138), the "*information*" (1.537) or "resultant ideas" (4.318), which we have been compelled to accept. The "compulsion" involved here must therefore be a rational not an irrational affair. When he is thinking in this context, Peirce speaks of perceptual facts, rather than percepts, as being that

which is forced upon us. For the percept is an individual event happening *hic et nunc,* in the immediate present. But since the immediate present is an infinitesimal interval of time (6.110), its content must be wholly ineffable. Before any *experience* can occur, memory must come into operation and give us a perceptual fact. "A perceptual fact is a memory hardly yet separated from the very percept"; yet it is unlike the percept in being slightly generalized, i.e. it is a cognition. Over this process of forming perceptual facts we have no control (5.115). They must be accepted for what they are—the ineluctable first premises of our knowledge. Perceptual facts produced by the activity of memory, are what we mean by the term "experience."

The upshot of this approach is the view that experience is the result of the functioning of mind. "By experience must be understood the entire mental product" (6.492). In at least two places he even declares that our *percepts,* too, are "mental constructions" (2.141) or "the results of cognitive elaboration" (5.416). However, he may have been thinking here of perceptual facts, rather than percepts proper. Be that as it may, it seems clear that what I have called "the idealization of experience" is a well-marked tendency in Peirce. If systematically developed, it can only lead to a form of rationalistic idealism similar to that of Hegel. This was, indeed, one of the directions in which Peirce's transcendentalism drew him.

The contrast between the two versions of experience can be sharpened by relating them to the categories of his phenomenology. When writing in the naturalistic vein, Peirce seems to hold that experience is wholly an affair of Secondness. Thus, in 1903 he wrote to William James: "The practical exigencies of life render 'secondness' the most prominent of the three [categories]. This is not a conception, nor is it a peculiar quality. It is an experience. It comes out most fully in the shock of reaction between ego and non-ego. . . . All the *actual* character of consciousness is merely the sense of the shock of the non-ego upon us."[4] There is not the slightest suggestion of a cognitive element here. Nor is it implied that the non-ego is in any way akin to the ego. Experience is simply actuality, the compulsiveness of the world of fact or individual existence.

On the other hand, Peirce sometimes takes "experience" in a much wider sense as the *immediate cognitive whole* within which all three categories are contained. "I analyze experience," he says, "which is the

[4]Quoted in Perry, *The Thought and Character of William James,* vol II, p. 429.

cognitive resultant of our past lives, and find in it three elements. I call them *Categories.*" (2.84) This means that while the sense of compulsion (Secondness) "accompanies every experience whatever" (2.22), it is not *identical* with experience, for the latter also includes quality (Firstness) and law (Thirdness). From such a standpoint, Peirce finds it easy to agree with the teaching of that "king of modern thought" Immanuel Kant. Thus in 1890 he declares:

How is the extraordinary prominence of these conceptions [the categories] to be explained? Must it not be that they have their origin in the nature of the mind? This is the Kantian form of inference, which has been found so cogent in the hands of that hero of philosophy; and I do not know that modern studies have done anything to discredit it. . . . A man must be a very uncompromising partisan of the theory of the *tabula rasa* to deny that the ideas of first, second, and third are due to congenital tendencies of the mind. (1.374)

With experience transformed into a mental product and the categories into the result of the intellect's functioning, we have moved well along the road to transcendentalism.

It is in this connection that Peirce stresses his "deduction of the categories" from the mathematical principle which limits the irreducible types of logical relation to three. Instead of serving as a hypothesis which the student of phenomenology can subject to inductive examination, the principle becomes a premiss from which an important conclusion is inferred. Once he grasps the proof that relations can only be monads, dyads, and triads, the student can rest secure in the "knowledge" that "beyond the three elements of Firstness, Secondness, and Thirdness, there is nothing else to be found in the phenomenon" (1.347). This *a priori* doctrine is rendered all the more secure if it is combined with the view that experience is "the entire mental product." For then the phenomenologist does not have to reckon with the vagaries of something which presents itself *ab extra,* and which might therefore upset any categorial scheme by exhibiting in the future wholly novel traits. The domain of his investigation is circumscribed by what his own mind has produced. The ubiquitous features he descries in experience may be confidently affirmed to be the ultimate and irreducible categories of phenomena. This seems to be the position to which Peirce's transcendentalism inevitably commits him.

6. ANTHROPOMORPHISM AND THE CATEGORIES

A further consequence of the above position is to be found in certain anthropomorphic expressions which Peirce uses to specify the content of his categories. That he did not intend such expressions to be taken figuratively is apparent from his defense of "anthropomorphism" as a mode of thought proper to the sciences. Part of what he means by this has been explained in connection with the justification of abduction. The course of evolution has implanted in man's mind certain rudimentary notions which accord with the broad facts of the natural world. These notions have formed the nucleus of scientific hypotheses, and account for the fact that out of the multitude of possible ideas we have been able to hit upon so many whose truth has been established. Looking at the matter from the standpoint of the investigator, we may say, therefore, that "every scientific explanation of a natural phenomenon is a hypothesis that there is something in nature to which the human reason is analogous" (1.316). In this sense, not only are all our conceptions "anthropomorphic," but we should *prefer* ideas which have that quality as scientific working hypotheses (5.47 n.).

A much broader significance is attached to "anthropomorphic thinking" when Peirce is seeking a warrant for his transcendentalism. Here he is interested not in working hypotheses, but in truths derived from the "affinity of the human soul to the soul of the universe," or the "affinity between the reasoner's mind and nature's" (5.47; 1.121). This relationship, accepted as literal fact, becomes the basis for projecting human traits far and wide throughout the natural world. The projection is speculative, of course, since it does not entail consequences that can be validated observationally. The ideas concerned are espoused because they are anthropomorphic, not because they have been tested. Peirce makes no bones about stating his belief in the propriety of this procedure. "In the light of the successes of science," he remarks, "to my mind there is a degree of baseness in denying our birthright as children of God and in shamefacedly slinking away from anthropomorphic conceptions of the universe" (1.316). The effect of this belief on the categories of his phenomenology will now be noted.

Firstness has been represented as the category which designates the purely qualitative aspect of phenomena—sheer quality, considered in abstraction from everything else. The subclass of phenomena constituting the domain of psychology exemplifies the category in the element of feeling. So much his naturalism has made tolerably clear. But Peirce often speaks of "qualities of feeling" as being that which constitutes Firstness (cf. 1.304; 1.531). It is difficult to know what this expression means, unless we construe it in the light of his panpsychism.

For he tells us that, "for example, this or that red is a feeling" (1.310), and that sense-qualities in general are feelings (6.198). Again, he declares that "a *quality* is a consciousness. I do not say a *waking* consciousness—but still, something of the nature of consciousness. A *sleeping* consciousness, perhaps." (6.221) If we restrict our attention to colors what we have is always "a tridimensional spread of feelings" (6.132). I take it, then, that "qualities of feeling" must be roughly synonymous with "kinds of feeling," since the phrase is used to designate such things as "the color of magenta, the odor of attar, the sound of a railway whistle, the taste of quinine," etc. (1.304). The phrase is employed, I suggest, because of Peirce's transcendentalist conviction that all phenomena are at bottom psychical.

A certain amount of anthropomorphic language also occurs in connection with Secondness. This category is said to denote the element of "struggle" in phenomena (1.322; 5.45). Since it likewise specifies individual existence or factuality, we might infer that particulars have a power of "struggling" with one another. Peirce himself affirms just that. "The fact fights its way into existence" (1.432); it has "brute fighting force, or self-assertion" (1.434). Consider an individual atom. It exists "not at all in obedience to any physical law which would be violated if it never had existed, nor by virtue of any qualities whatsoever, but simply by virtue of its arbitrarily interfering with other atoms. . . . We can hardly help saying that it blindly forces a place for itself in the universe, or wilfully crowds its way in." (1.459) That these animistic expressions are to be understood quite literally is clear from Peirce's accompanying comments (cf. 5.46 ff.), as well as from his statement that he does not conceive atoms to be "absolutely dead" (6.201).[5]

"The third category of elements of phenomena consists of what we call laws when we contemplate them from the outside only, but which when we see both sides of the shield we call thoughts" (1.420). Now thoughts are something *general;* they can also be produced and grow. Hence the term "habit" fits them perfectly. But the striking feature of this term is its very wide applicability. It denotes "such a specialization, original or acquired, of the nature of a man, or an animal, or a vine, or a crystallizable chemical substance, or anything else, that he or it will behave . . . in a way describable in general terms upon every

[5]However, in his "tough-minded" moments Peirce admits that "we observe no life in chemical atoms. They appear to have no organs by which they could act." (1.459)

occasion . . . that may present itself of a generally describable character" (5.538). The result is that habit can be regarded as a pervasive dimension of phenomena. It ceases to be just an exemplification of Thirdness in the region of physiology or psychology, and becomes co-extensive with the category itself.

There can be little doubt that Peirce's anthropomorphic treatment of the categories, scrappy as it is, serves as a prolegomenon to his transcendentalist metaphysics. Having suggested that the most general traits of what appears are "First, Feelings; Second, Efforts; Third, Habits" (6.201), he has opened a road for his panpsychistic ontology and his speculative cosmology of evolution. It would be a mistake to suppose that his procedure here was a carefully formulated policy. The most one can say is that the procedure is implied by many of his remarks, but can only be elicited clearly when an attempt is made to reconstruct the "logic" of his transcendentalism. Our next task must be to survey the metaphysical "system" in which this logic culminated.

IX

TRANSCENDENTAL METAPHYSICS

1. ON SYSTEMATIC COMPLETENESS IN PHILOSOPHY

THE opposing tendencies in Peirce are well illustrated by a pair of statements which he made on the subject of constructing a philosophical system. Writing in the *Nation* in 1893 he remarked: "But systematic completeness, as Hegel's own system well shows, is about the idlest decoration that can be attached to a philosophy. The great desideratum for a philosophy, its indispensable condition, was first stated by . . . Auguste Comte; that is to say, a philosophy to be fruitful, must be 'positive'—it must lead to unmistakable consequences comparable in great detail with observation."[1] Yet five years later he was meditating on the procedure to be adopted in erecting "a philosophical edifice that shall outlast the vicissitudes of time," a theory like that of Aristotle, "so comprehensive that, for a long time to come, the entire work of human reason . . . shall appear as the filling up of its details" (1.1). Opinions regarding the feasibility of such an enterprise may differ. But one can scarcely deny that in seeking to undertake it Peirce had to resort very frequently to an *a priori* mode of thought. Not otherwise could the beliefs involved be "fixed."

When the system-building mood was on him, Peirce gave the freest possible rein to his constructive imagination. There was, in fact, something of the mystic in his nature—a not uncommon attribute of those with strong mathematical and logical powers. Nevertheless, it was in the employment of these powers that he found his vocation. The development of his system was an avocation. That his speculations were tempered at certain points by his naturalism is quite undeniable. Thus, he speaks of them as a "conjecture as to the constitution of the universe" (1.7), a "guess at the riddle" (1.354). They are put forward in

[1]*Nation*, vol. LVIII (1893), p. 34.

a spirit of "contrite fallibilism," and purport to be hypotheses whose consequences can be checked observationally by the widest possible range of facts. This moderate attitude, however, tends to get eclipsed when the interests of his architectonic are in the ascendant. Then, the "high priori" style of thinking is supreme.

At various times Peirce toyed with the question of classifying the different systems of metaphysics. One of his efforts in this direction appears briefly in the lectures on pragmatism of 1903. The classification is based on the three categories, its subdivisions being determined by what ones "each system admits as important metaphysico-cosmical elements" (5.77). The result is a sevenfold scheme which can be summarized as follows.

Category or categories admitted	Historical examples
(i) Firstness (Qualities of Feeling) only	Condillac and the Associationalists
(ii) Secondness (Reactions) only	Helmholtz
(iii) Thirdness (Thought-Habits) only	Hegelianism of all shades
(iv) Firstness and Secondness only	Ordinary nominalism
(v) Firstness and Thirdness only	Berkeleyanism
(vi) Secondness and Thirdness only	Cartesianism, Spinozism, and Leibnizianism
(vii) Firstness, Secondness, and Thirdness	Platonism, Aristotelianism, Kantism, Reid's philosophy, and Peirce's

Peirce recognizes that this is a somewhat "artificial classification," and that subdivision (vii) in particular ought to be further analyzed. Yet even as it stands, the scheme is "not without its utility." At the very least it serves to orientate Peirce's thought with respect to the major philosophical traditions.

The most significant feature of this classification is its assumption that the categories formulated by phenomenology and logic are directly applicable to metaphysics. From that assumption flow a great many consequences of importance for Peirce's transcendentalism. For once the position is adopted that "metaphysics consists in the results of the absolute acceptance of logical principles not merely as regulatively valid, but as truths of being" (1.487); and when, in addition, "being" is understood to signify "the sum-total of what is real," the way is paved for deducing an ontology and a cosmology. Thus we can say in advance "that the universe has an explanation, the function of which, like that of every logical explanation, is to unify its observed variety. It follows that the root of all being is One." (*Ibid.*) Metaphysics, then, must espouse some variety of monism. This entails not only the demonstration of the basic homogeneity of things that appear diverse perceptually, but also the presentation of a theory as to how the totality of being came to be. "Metaphysics has to account for the whole universe of being. It has, therefore, to do something like supposing a state of things in which that universe did not exist, and consider how it could have arisen." (6.214) Since the theory must show how time developed, along with everything else, the sequence delineated can only be "an objective logical sequence" (*ibid.*). One sometimes gets the impression that even in the midst of his strictly logical inquiries, Peirce was keeping his weather eye open for their application to his ontology and cosmology (cf. 3.487).

Another classification of metaphysical systems is restricted to those which affirm the reality of change or movement. Here there are three possibilities, designated by Peirce "elliptic, parabolic and hyperbolic" philosophy, or "Epicureanism, Pessimism and Evolutionism." According to the first of these, change has no absolute starting-point, no terminus, and no direction. "The development of the universe is like the increase of an angle, so that it proceeds forever without tending toward anything unattained" (6.27). This is the general contention of materialism. According to the parabolic or pessimistic view, there is a definite drift to the cosmos as a whole, but its absolute end is "the very same nothingness from which it advances" (6.582). Finally, the hyperbolic or evolutionary philosophy holds that the whole universe is "approaching in the infinitely distant future a state having a general character different from that toward which we look back in the infinitely distant past" (1.362). Here "reason marches from premises to conclusion," and "nature has [an] ideal end different from its origin" (6.582). The considerations which led Peirce to reject the first two positions and accept the third will emerge as we proceed.

It is thus determined *a priori* that the system of metaphysics which we adopt must take its fundamental conceptions from logic, since "to found logic on metaphysics is a crazy scheme" (2.168). Hence, the three categories will be considered ultimate modes of being; but the final interpretation of being, given by both ontology and cosmology, must be monistic. Since philosophy's explanation of anything is always an account of its derivation (6.581), the crown of the system will be a cosmological doctrine.

2. NEUTRALISM, MATERIALISM, AND IDEALISM

Three traditional forms of ontological monism are recognized by Peirce (6.24). He calls them (i) *Neutralism,* which regards the basic "stuff" of the cosmos as neither physical nor psychical but neutral, the laws of matter and mind being derivations therefrom; (ii) *Materialism,* which states that matter and its laws are primordial, "psychical" phenomena being derived and special; and (iii) *Idealism,* which considers mind and its laws to be basic, "physical" phenomena being derived and special. These are the only metaphysical positions that need to be taken seriously, he thinks, for Cartesian dualism "will hardly find defenders to-day" (*ibid.*).

Nowhere does Peirce give us a careful examination of these alternatives. Thus, he tosses neutralism aside as "sufficiently condemned by the logical maxim known as Ockham's razor, i.e. that not more independent elements are to be supposed than necessary" (*ibid.*). This maxim is one which ought to guide the scientific metaphysician in all his deliberations (6.535). Neutralism sins against it because "by placing the inward and outward aspects of substance on a par, it seems to render both primordial" (6.24). The only important contenders in the field, then, are idealism and materialism.

In order to appreciate Peirce's appraisal of materialism, we must bear in mind that he regards it as inseparable from mechanistic determinism. The theory has for him two parts. It states (*a*) that nothing really exists save matter, feelings being just the way matter appears to itself; and (*b*) "that the Whole is governed by mechanical forces that are determined by the state of things at the instant they act, without any reference to a purpose of bringing about any determinate state of things in the future" (6.274). This doctrine has the great virtue of simplicity. It adheres admirably to the conditions laid down by Ockham's razor. And it cannot be absolutely refuted. Nevertheless, there are weighty reasons why we ought to prefer the counter-doctrine of idealism. The whole issue must therefore be examined a little more closely.

A favorite contention of the materialists is that their doctrine underlies the procedure of all the special sciences. This, as it stands, is an extremely vague statement. Suppose we try to make it precise by saying that materialism is a working hypothesis adopted by every scientific investigator. Now a working hypothesis, declares Peirce, is a problematic proposition from which can be deduced definite conse-

quences which the inquirer can test by comparing them with observations. But if so, it obviously becomes absurd to say that an astronomer,
a physicist, or a chemist is engaged in testing the consequences of
materialism. "For even if materialism be false, nobody doubts that the
phenomena with which those men deal are the same as if it were true."
The situation is identical for the geometer, the historian, the economist,
the student of jurisprudence, etc. In fact the only investigators to
whom the question of materialism is relevant, and who use it as a
working hypothesis, are a certain class of biologists and a certain class
of psychologists. The doctrine finds favor with them because it provides a simple basis for experimentation. Yet "even now, there are
eminent biologists who hold that the hypothesis is refuted, and at
least half the psychologists are of the same opinion—and this, although
the question is whether the facts *can be made to fit* that hypothesis.
Were the question simply whether the facts seem on the whole to be
favorable or unfavorable to materialism, the vote against it would, of
course, be larger."[2]

The most difficult problem which materialists have to face arises
from the ostensible difference between the action of mind and the
action of matter. For the laws of matter are entirely mechanical and
blind. They admit of no teleology, prescribing merely that in given
relative positions the motions of particles shall have given accelerations. But mind does not act blindly. It incessantly pursues ends or
purposes. Materialists must, therefore, either declare that this is a
delusive phenomenon, or they must show how teleological action can
be a secondary effect of non-teleological action. The former course
obliges them to fly in the face of the most patent facts of observation.
The latter course presents an assignment which no materialist has so
far been able to complete satisfactorily. Furthermore, "the fact that
our knowledge of the future is of so different a kind from our knowledge of the past seems to be hopelessly in conflict with materialism;
since the laws of mechanics, as they are now understood, make the
dynamical relation of the past to the future exactly the same as that
of the future to the past" (6.274). In other words, we know the past
as something wholly determinate and fixed. We also know the future
to be partly indeterminate and rich with possibilities. But in the
philosophy of materialism such a contrast does not occur, for the
simple reason that everything is believed to be necessitated.

[2]The quotations in this paragraph, as well as its central line of thought, are
taken from Peirce's review of D. G. Ritchie's *Darwin and Hegel*, in the *Nation*,
vol. LVII (1893), p. 394.

This brings us to the point where the most damaging argument can be advanced against materialism. Tychism has already shown that a belief in necessitarianism is quite unwarranted. The evidence for the conformity of events to the rule of law entitles us to say that there is "a wonderful degree of approximation, and that is all" (1.402; cf. 6.36, etc.). Strict determinism has no observational basis even in the advanced sciences; and the *a priori* arguments for it are worthless. On the contrary, when we honestly take note of various obtrusive features of our world, such as the general prevalence of growth and variety, we find the hypothesis of a real indeterminacy in things quite irresistible. But the moment we admit that chance is an objective constituent of the universe, materialism collapses. For without the postulate of necessitarianism a materialistic philosophy is bereft of its foundation.

So far, there is little to distinguish Peirce's analysis of materialism from the sort of thing that might properly come within the purview of "scientific metaphysics." The doctrine has been rejected because it fails to find support in empirical fact. But we should remember that this whole discussion rests on the *a priori* principle that an ontology must be either materialistic or idealistic. Our choice is limited to one of these forms of monism. Consequently, the elimination of materialism is at the same time the substantiation of its opposite. "The one intelligible theory of the universe is that of objective idealism" (6.25). Thus, tychism becomes an important means of establishing a transcendentalist doctrine. "By supposing the rigid exactitude of causation to yield . . . we gain room to insert mind into our scheme, and to put it into the place where it is needed, into the position which, as the sole self-intelligible thing, it is entitled to occupy, that of the fountain of existence" (6.61).

In what form does mind thus occur? Primarily, as feeling. For "wherever chance-spontaneity is found, there in the same proportion feeling exists. In fact, chance is but the outward aspect of that which within itself is feeling." (6.265) Now we have seen that Peirce considers the qualitative aspect of things, their Firstness as such, to be a denotative example of contingency. Accordingly, it is easy for him to conclude that "the qualities of outward sense are excited by something psychic without us" (1.311). Instead of wondering how dead matter can excite feelings in the mind, it is better to deny outright that this is possible. After all, the new discoveries in physics have revealed how very little we know about the inner constitution of matter. It seems quite unaccountable that a minute difference in the speed of vibration of particles should produce such a marked difference of quality as that between deep vermilion and violet blue. May the trouble not lie in our representing those vibrations too abstractly, in purely quantitative terms? At any rate, Peirce declares his preference for the view "that it is a psychic feeling of red without us which arouses a sympathetic feeling of red in our senses" (*ibid.*). Our experience of Firstness is therefore, as Whitehead would say, a "feeling of feeling."

Peirce recognizes one of the implications of the above doctrine to be that the psychical must be extended in space. To justify this, he advances some speculations based on the data of biology. If we observe an extremely simple living organism, say, an amoeba, we note that in the absence of any stimulus the whole is quiescent and rigid. A place on it is now irritated. Immediately an active motion is set up which gradually spreads to other parts. In this action, no relation to a nucleus or other unitary organ can be discerned, for the amoeba is a mere amorphous continuum of protoplasm. Nor is there anything resembling a wave-motion. The activity does not advance to new parts at the same rate that it leaves old parts. Rather, in the beginning it fades at a slower rate than that at which it spreads. Two closely related conclusions seem to follow: first, that the motion in question is feeling; and secondly, that the feeling moves continuously through space. Or, as Peirce puts it: "Whatever there is in the whole phenomenon to make us think there is feeling in such a mass of protoplasm—*feeling*, but plainly no *personality*—goes logically to show that that feeling has a subjective, or substantial, spatial extension, as the excited state has" (6.133). To the objection that we find no clear evidence for the spatiality of feelings in the very domain where this ought to be most apparent, namely, our own inner experience, Peirce returns the answer that "we must not tax introspection to make a phenomenon manifest which essentially involves externality" (*ibid.*).

In his paper of 1892 on "Man's Glassy Essence," the hypothesis that protoplasm not only feels, "but exercises all the functions of mind" (6.255) is turned into an argument for the psychical nature of matter. After cataloguing the major properties of protoplasm, Peirce seeks to explain some of them in terms of "the excessively complicated constitution of the protoplasm molecule" (6.256). Fortunately, it is not necessary for us to puzzle out all the obscure details of his discussion. We merely have to note how he treats the two properties of habit-taking and feeling. The former ultimately resists being explained in molecular terms, and obliges him to fall back on the assumption of "a primordial habit-taking tendency" (6.262).

But what is to be said of the property of feeling? If consciousness belongs to all protoplasm, by what mechanical constitution is this to be accounted for? The slime is nothing but a chemical compound. There is no inherent impossibility in its being formed synthetically in the laboratory, out of its chemical elements; and if it were so made, it would present all the characters of natural protoplasm. No doubt, then, it would feel . . . and unless we are to accept a weak dualism, the property must be shown to arise from some peculiarity of the mechanical system. Yet the attempt to deduce it from the three laws of mechanics, applied to never so ingenious a mechanical contrivance, would obviously be futile. It can never be explained, unless we admit that physical events are but degraded or undeveloped forms of psychical events. (6.264)

We seem to have here a curious inversion of the former argument against materialism. It now appears that the materialists are quite justified in espousing mechanistic conceptions. The trouble is that they do not draw the full implications of those conceptions. For materialists stop at the point where they have purely physical mechanisms on the one hand and the admitted occurrence of feeling on the other. All they can do, therefore, is to suppose that certain complex mechanisms have the power to feel. But this is "a monstrous absurdity" (6.285), "as repugnant to scientific logic as to common sense" (6.24). What they *should* conclude is that they are not considering something purely physical, but something whose substance is inherently psychical. This conclusion would inevitably lead them away from the doctrine of universal determinism. "Thus, we see that the idealist has no need to dread a mechanical theory of life. On the contrary, such a theory, fully developed, is bound to call in a tychistic idealism as its indispensable adjunct." (6.265)

Peirce has no wish to deny an objective basis for the ostensible difference between the behavior of mind and the behavior of matter. That is why he often refers to the latter as a "degraded" or "undeveloped" variety of the former. The degradation involved is affirmed to be due to the fact that the feelings which constitute "dead matter" are almost completely subject to the rule of habit (6.585). The resulting induration causes bodies to act with a peculiarly high degree of mechanical regularity or routine (6.277). The spontaneity native to feeling has been reduced to proportions so minute that we cannot detect it in our ordinary dealings with such things as tables, chairs, stones, etc. Yet we must suppose that a residue of spontaneity remains.

Hence, "what we call matter is not completely dead, but is merely mind hidebound with habits" (6.158).

3. OBJECTIVE IDEALISM AND CONTINUITY

So far we have been considering Peirce's version of objective idealism mainly in relation to tychism. To bring out certain other aspects of the doctrine, we must now turn to its connection with synechism or the principle of continuity. In the present context, synechism appears as a vital metaphysical truth. No longer is it merely the regulative maxim discussed in chapter VII, but a principle affirmed on speculative grounds to be constitutive of the cosmos. Although in these matters Peirce's exposition only allows us to see through a glass, darkly, we must do the best we can to reconstruct his position.

The first region characterized by continuity is that of the qualities of feeling. For "we can hardly but suppose that those sense-qualities that we now experience, colors, odors, sounds, feelings of every description, loves, griefs, surprise, are but the relics of an ancient ruined continuum of qualities, like a few columns standing here and there in testimony that here some old-world forum with its basilica and temples had once made a magnificent *ensemble*" (6.197). The development of the human mind over a long period of time has gradually extinguished all but a few qualities, which therefore appear disconnected and disparate (6.132). Originally, however, they formed a genuine continuum. Indeed, it is very likely, Peirce adds, that they *still* do so, and that our inability to perceive the merging of qualities arises from the specialized functioning of our sense-organs (1.418). "Probably, were our experience of them not so fragmentary, there would be no abrupt demarcations between them, at all" (*ibid.*). This conclusion is reinforced by the knowledge that feelings, since they have spatial extension, coalesce in a continuous manner. For space itself is continuous, and whatever is capable of uniformly pervading a region of it must also have that property (6.134). Accordingly, "when any particular feeling is present, an infinitesimal continuum of all feelings differing infinitesimally from that is present" (6.132).

The other area in which synechism finds exemplification is that of ideas. When we examine any idea, we find, Peirce observes, that it has three constituent parts. "The first is its intrinsic quality as a feeling. The second is the energy with which it affects other ideas, an energy which is infinite in the here-and-nowness of immediate sensation, finite and relative in the recency of the past. The third element is the

tendency of an idea to bring along other ideas with it." (6.135) Now
continuity seems to be involved (*a*) in the fact that "past" ideas produce effects in the present, (*b*) in the process of "spreading" whereby
an idea becomes generalized, and (*c*) in the process of communication
whereby ideas literally "pass" from mind to mind. It is by no means
easy to discover exactly what Peirce means here. But something like
the following appears to have been intended.

Suppose we take the word "idea" to mean an event in an individual
consciousness. It is then clear "that an idea once past is gone forever,
and any supposed recurrence of it is another idea" (6.105). But if so,
the original event must be utterly unknowable, because it is completely
cut off from what comes after it. Such a conclusion, implying as it
does the delusiveness of all memory-knowledge, cannot be accepted
by a sane man. We must therefore admit that a past idea can also be
present. Or, in less paradoxical language, we must admit that the idea
"cannot be wholly past; it can only be going, infinitesimally past, less
past than any assignable past date" (6.109). No idea, then, has a
"simple location" in the time series.[3] It cannot be confined to an isolated event in some consciousness, but is an *entity* extending from the
past into the future. That is why it may produce effects in the present,
though first entertained long ago. All this is possible, of course, because
continuity likewise attaches to time and consciousness.

We are again within the orbit of the transcendental doctrine that
ideas have a "power" and "life" of their own, quite apart from any
human mind. For they are now said by Peirce to *become* continuous
by a process of "spreading" (6.137) which is native to them. In the
process, "they lose intensity, and especially the power of affecting
others, but gain generality and become welded with other ideas"
(6.104). This seems to be how they "grow." The only meaning I am
able to attach to such a view depends on the forbidden assumption
that ideas are merely events in individual minds. Thus (to hazard an
illustration), the sight of a rose gives rise to the idea "pink." That idea
has great intensity because it denotes the actual shade of color before
me. Later, my memory of the color grows dim, and the intensity of the
idea lessens. Yet I continue to say that "pinkness" belonged to the rose,
i.e. I have no inclination to think of it as having been pale yellow.
My judgment is therefore concerned with the general idea of pinkness,
which calls up in my mind a continuous series of many other generals

[3]Cf. C. I. Lewis, *Mind and the World-Order* (New York, 1929), p. 151.

(color, fragrance, etc.). The original idea asserts itself so feebly that I am unable any longer to isolate it from those to which it has become "welded." While this example gives some empirical content to Peirce's view, it would probably not please him. He would continue to insist on the *literal* truth of the principle "that wherever ideas come together, they tend to weld into general ideas; and wherever they are generally connected, general ideas govern the connection" (6.143).

The same emphasis appears in his treatment of the process whereby ideas pass from mind to mind. Synechism requires a continuity of feeling among minds to be operative in order that the passing may take place (6.158). To "understand" this, we must remember three things. (i) "A person is not absolutely an individual" (5.421), but a continuous series of individuals or "selves" stretching through time. At each moment, all that exists is a unity of feeling, with its inevitable tendency to spread. (ii) Because of this a "man's circle of society (however widely or narrowly this phrase may be understood), is a sort of loosely compacted person, in some respects of higher rank than the person of an individual organism" (*ibid.*). Hence, just as feelings may flow from one part of an organism to another, so they can flow from mind to mind within the "super-personality" of the group. (iii) "Every general idea has the unified living feeling of a person. The consciousness of a general idea has a certain 'unity of the ego' in it, which is identical when it passes from one mind to another. It is, therefore, quite analogous to a person; and, indeed, a person is only a particular kind of general idea." (6.270) Such is the interpretation which Peirce's transcendentalism led him to give of the doctrine that "man is a sign." Certain further consequences of this will be noted at a later point in the chapter.

The speculative use of the principle of continuity enabled Peirce to preserve the monism which he believed every metaphysical system must exhibit. Synechism prevented his objective idealism from becoming a monadology of any kind. Hence, as we should expect, the category of Secondness or individual existence is given little recognition here, since it involves discontinuity. There is even a suggestion of its outright denial, as when Peirce refers to "*synechism,* or the doctrine that all that exists is continuous" (1.172). Not only are ideas characterized by continuity, but "*all things* so swim in continua" (1.171). Neither domain contains entities which have simple location. For in the physical world, "a thing may be said to be wherever it acts; but the notion that a particle is absolutely present in one part of space and absolutely absent from all the rest of space is devoid of all foundation" (1.38). "We may suppose that one portion of matter acts upon another because it is in a measure in the same place" (1.170).[4] This extension of continuity to Secondness virtually destroys the category. Particular existents can no longer be indiscerptible components of the universe. They become transitory phases or "moments" of the process of cosmic evolution—a fate similar to that which befalls the individual in all forms of Hegelianism. How such a consequence comes about we must now indicate.

4. COSMIC EVOLUTION

Both tychism and synechism, according to Peirce, imply an evolutionary cosmology (6.102; 1.175). Tychism enables us to see the inadequacy of materialism, and therefore to rule out the possibility of elliptical philosophy or Epicureanism. Synechism enables us to eliminate the parabolic or pessimistic view. "For once you have embraced the principle of continuity, no kind of explanation of things will satisfy you except that they *grew*" (1.175). The parabolic standpoint denies any genuine growth in the cosmos. Its contention is that dust returns to dust, ashes to ashes. We are thus left with hyperbolic philosophy or Evolutionism as the only intelligible position. This commits us to the belief in an absolute goal for the development of the cosmos different from its absolute starting-point. The latter must be something "in its own nature not requiring explanation nor admitting of derivation" (6.581). The stopping-point must be "where the process of reason and nature is perfected" (*ibid.*). And the principle of movement must be assumed to be universal.

The first part of the project, then, consists in imagining a state of things in which the universe did not exist, and showing how it could have arisen. The intention is nothing less than that of explaining how evolution *ex nihilo* is possible. But since time is among the phenomena to be accounted for, "we have to suppose a state of things before time was organized" (6.214). The sequence to be traced is not in its initial

---

[4]Since Peirce gave expression to this doctrine as early as 1890, he may be said to have anticipated both Bergson and Whitehead in regard to it. The roots of the doctrine lie, of course, in the work done on electromagnetic phenomena by Faraday and Maxwell about the middle of the nineteenth century. The phrase "simple location" is' due to Whitehead. The astonishing similarity between many of the latter's conceptions and those of Peirce is well brought out in James Feibleman's *Introduction to Peirce's Philosophy* (New York and London, 1946), pp. 459 ff.

stages a temporal one at all. It is an objective logical sequence. Hence, such expressions as "before," "after," "arising," etc., used in connection with the primordial phase of cosmic development, must not be taken in a literal, historical sense. They are employed merely for the sake "of the commodity of speech" (*ibid.*). Furthermore, the objective logic to be elaborated cannot be identical with the logic which governs deductive inference. Like time, the latter is something which has evolved (6.193). We shall, therefore, be concerned in the beginning with a special kind of "evolutionary" logic. Finally, the starting-point, before the universe existed, "was not a state of pure abstract being. On the contrary it was a state of just nothing at all, not even a state of emptiness, for even emptiness is something." (6.215) We commence with pure zero.

Why not say that we commence with non-being? Because, Peirce replies, non-being involves the idea of negation. Negation means otherness; and "other" is merely a synonym for the ordinal numeral "second." "As such it implies a first; while the present pure zero is prior to every first" (6.217). The matrix of the universe is, indeed, *potential* being—absolutely undefined and unlimited possibility, unbounded freedom. But it cannot be described as non-being.

Is the matrix a state of pure Firstness? Peirce seems to waver on this point. The above quotation would lead us to believe that the category is derivative rather than primordial. The "pure zero of not having been born" is *prior* to every first. This, indeed, appears to be stated quite definitely in a passage which accounts for the earliest phase of the cosmological story. "Thus the zero of bare possibility, by evolutionary logic, leapt into the *unit* of some quality. . . . Unbounded potentiality became potentiality of this or that sort." (6.220) The same sequence is implied by his diagram of the evolutionary process. A chalk line is drawn on a clean blackboard which represents the original vague potentiality. The resulting whiteness is then described as a Firstness, "a springing up of something new" (6.203). Here the category emerges from that which in itself lacks all categorial features.

But this line of thought did not wholly satisfy the demands of Peirce's idealism. Hence he suggests occasionally that the starting-point of the cosmos *was* a state of sheer Firstness, "a chaos of unpersonalized feeling" (6.33). Now although such chaos must have been "pure nothing" (5.431), it was so only from a physical standpoint. "Yet it was not blank zero; for there was an intensity of consciousness

there, in comparison with which all that we ever feel is but as the
struggling of a molecule or two to throw off a little of the force of law
to an endless and innumerable diversity of chance utterly unlimited"
(6.265). On this view, the *fons et origo* of being is not a quasi-mathe-
matical zero, but something essentially psychical. There is undoubtedly
a connection here with Peirce's theological belief that the world was
created by God (cf. 1.362). That doctrine will be considered in the
next chapter.

Whether the primal condition of the universe be taken as psychical
or non-psychical, it was at any rate for Peirce a non-existent state of
utter indeterminacy, devoid of all individuality, compulsion, and law.
Such a state, he thought, could properly serve as the starting-point,
because it can neither be derived from nor explained in terms of anything more ultimate. But surely, it may be objected, to trace everything back to chance is not to give an intelligible account of it?
Genuine explanation must show how phenomena are derived from
laws, not from contingency. That, Peirce retorts, is the typical error
of a necessitarian. The latter is content when he has reached a fundamental law or set of laws concerning which nothing further can be
said. Yet ordinarily we regard a law or uniformity as something that
needs to be accounted for. "That a pitched coin should sometimes turn
up heads and sometimes tails calls for no particular explanation; but
if it shows heads every time, we wish to know how this result has been
brought about. Law is *par excellence* the thing that wants a reason."
(6.12) But the only possible explanation is to show how laws have
evolved "out of pure chance, irregularity, and indeterminacy" (1.407).
Sound logic will revolt against any other procedure (6.60).

The next question is, what necessarily resulted from this primordial
state of things? "The only sane answer is that where freedom was
boundless nothing in particular necessarily resulted" (6.218). It was
just here that Hegel made his biggest blunder. He failed to see that
although the whole universe must be regarded as rational, it does not
follow "that it is *constrained* to be as it is by the logic of events; for
the logic of evolution and of life need not be supposed to be of that
wooden kind that absolutely constrains a given conclusion. The logic
may be that of the inductive or hypothetic inference." (*Ibid.*) This
"may be" becomes a "must be," Peirce holds, when we recognize how
impossible it is that the qualitative aspect of phenomena should be a
necessary consequence of abstract being. How, for example, can the
fact that red is sensibly different from blue be *deduced* from any-

thing? It is surely just a contingent fact, due to a primary abductive inference (made, presumably, by the universe!), whose form was:

> Something is possible,
> Red is something;
> ∴ Red is possible. (6.220)

By a similar inference blue was established as a determinate possible; and likewise with all the other qualities. Had Hegel been less enamoured of Thirdness, his objective logic might have contained some account of the qualitative and factual aspects of things. As it was, he wholly neglected the place of Firstness and Secondness in the cosmos (cf. 5.79).

Yet Peirce's own objective logic fails to carry him very far. Like Plato, he has ultimately to desert logic and have recourse to myth.

Our conceptions of the first stages of development, before time yet existed, must be as vague and figurative as the expressions of the first chapter of Genesis. Out of the womb of indeterminacy we must say that there would have come something, by the principle of Firstness, which we may call a flash. Then by the principle of habit there would have been a second flash. Though time would not yet have been, this second flash was in some sense after the first, because resulting from it. Then there would have come other successions ever more and more closely connected, the habits and the tendency to take them ever strengthening themselves, until the events would have been bound together into something like a continuous flow. . . . But Secondness is of two types. Consequently besides flashes genuinely second to others, so as to come after them, there will be pairs of flashes, or, since time is now supposed to be developed, we had better say pairs of states. . . . This is the first germ of spatial extension. . . . Pairs of states will also begin to take habits, and thus each state having different habits with reference to the different other states will give rise to bundles of habits, which will be substances [i.e., things]. (1.412-414)

But we need not prolong the fantasy. It is perfectly clear that the same speculation which has derived qualities of feeling, reactions, habits, continuity, time, space, and substances, can produce anything else that may happen to be required.

Curiosity will perhaps lead us to ask how the realm of ideas or Platonic forms fits into all this. Are we to assume that it also is subject to the process of development? Peirce's reply is in the affirmative. If we are going to espouse a hyperbolic philosophy "we must think that not merely the existing universe, that locus in the cosmos to which our reactions are limited, but the whole Platonic world, which in itself is equally real, is evolutionary in its origin, too" (6.200). Moreover, just as we do not regard the evolution of the actual world as finished, so we ought not to balk at the conclusion that "the very Platonic forms themselves have become or are becoming developed" (6.194). Even "eternal objects" are susceptible of growth.

The general situation envisaged, then, is this. From the vantage point of the present we can look back to a point in the infinitely distant past when there was nothing but utter indeterminacy. We can also look forward to a point in the infinitely distant future when there will be no contingency at all but a complete reign of law. "At any assignable date in the past, however early, there was already some tendency toward uniformity; and at any assignable date in the future there will be some slight aberrancy from law" (1.409). Now the reason why laws have arisen is that things have a native tendency to take on habits. Once an atom, or molecule, or any other object, has acted in a given manner, it is more likely than not to continue to act thus in future. This habit-taking tendency is therefore continually on the increase. The cosmos is proceeding uniformly in the direction of greater and greater order.[5] Remembering that ontologically the nature of things is psychical, the goal of their development will consist in "an absolutely perfect, rational, and symmetrical system, in which mind is at last crystallized in the infinitely distant future" (6.33).

One final constituent of Peirce's cosmology must be specified. This is the power of Love or ἀγάπη, which is "the great evolutionary agency of the universe" (6.287). Chance and habit-taking alone are insufficient to account for the development of the cosmos. In order to explain growth, particularly the growth of concrete reasonableness, we must declare it to be due to love. Peirce does not relate in detail how love performs its office. We are left to draw our own conclusions from such passages as the following.

Suppose, for example, that I have an idea that interests me. It is my creation. It is my creature; for . . . it is a little person. I love it; and I will sink myself in perfecting it. It is not by dealing out cold justice to the circle of

[5]It may be of interest to note that the verdict of present-day physics is just the opposite of this. Thus Schrödinger, in explaining the statistical character of physico-chemical laws, points out that natural events tend to pass from a better ordered to a less ordered state in accordance with the Second Law of Thermodynamics. "The statistical theory provides an intelligible explanation of the fact that the course of natural events follows a definite direction which cannot be reversed. The explanation consists in regarding the uni-directional tendency as a development from a better-ordered to a less-ordered state (in every single case) of the atomic aggregation involved. . . . We do not wish to assert any more than that the *total balance* of disorder in nature is steadily on the increase." *Science and the Human Temperament* (London, 1935), pp. 34-39.

my ideas that I can make them grow, but by cherishing them and tending them as I would the flowers in my garden. The philosophy we draw from John's gospel is that this is the way mind develops; and as for the cosmos, only so far as it is yet mind, and so has life, is it capable of further evolution. (6.289)

To express the primacy of love in his cosmology, Peirce sometimes calls the latter *Agapism.*

As a slight elaboration, let us contrast the agapistic theory of the growth of ideas with two other positions. Some people hold that thought develops by slight departures from habitual conceptions, such departures being wholly contingent and unconstrained either by external circumstances or by the force of logic. The result will be certain new ideas which in turn become habitual. Peirce speaks of this doctrine as *tychasm.* If, however, we believe that although new ideas may be adopted without foreseeing whither they tend, yet their character is rigidly determined either by causes outside the mind (e.g., environmental changes) or by logical developments of ideas already accepted, our doctrine may be called *anacasm.* This is the position of Hegel. In contrast to both of these doctrines,

the agapistic development of thought is the adoption of certain mental tendencies, not altogether heedlessly, as in tychasm, nor quite blindly by the mere force of circumstances or of logic, as in anacasm, but by an immediate attraction for the idea itself, whose nature is divined before the mind possesses it, by the power of sympathy, that is, by virtue of the continuity of mind; and this mental tendency may be of three varieties, as follows. First, it may affect a whole people or community in its collective personality, and be thence communicated to such individuals as are in powerfully sympathetic connection with the collective people. . . . Second, it may affect a private person directly, yet so that he is only enabled to apprehend the idea, or to appreciate its attractiveness, by virtue of his sympathy with his neighbors, under the influence of a striking experience or development of thought. The conversion of St. Paul may be taken as an example of what is meant. Third, it may affect an individual, independently of his human affections, by virtue of an attraction it exercises upon his mind, even before he has comprehended it. This is the phenomenon which has been well called the *divination* of genius; for it is due to the continuity between the man's mind and the Most High. (6.307)

The last remark points us again in the direction of Peirce's theology. For agapism, as we shall discover, is a metaphysical version of his belief that evolution is the progressive unfolding of God's purpose in creation, and that the *summum bonum* is identical with God completely revealed. Before going on to these topics, there are several other points that must be noted.

5. INDIVIDUAL AND SUPER-INDIVIDUAL PERSONALITY

I take it to be a distinctive feature of every monistic metaphysics, whether non-idealistic as in the case of Spinoza or idealistic as in the case of Hegel, that it relegates the individual person to a minor place in the system. Particular selves, like all other particulars, are mere appearances, transitory manifestations of a higher Reality. Yet since idealistic monism frequently construes this Reality itself in terms of personality, the further we advance from the isolated self through groups of selves towards the community, the more fully do we find personal traits exemplified. Thus, for example, the "will" of the state may be regarded as a truer manifestation of the ultimate character of the universe than the will of any one of its citizens. A natural correlate of this view is the conception of the state as a kind of "organism," which is metaphysically more real than the persons who dwell in it.

Traces of such ideas have already cropped up in Peirce's transcendentalism, but it is now time to take explicit cognizance of them. His strong hostility to nominalistic individualism often made him go to the opposite extreme and affirm that the separate self is a snare and a delusion. "The most balsamic of all the sweets of sweet philosophy is the lesson that personal existence is an illusion and a practical joke. Those that have loved themselves and not their neighbors will find themselves April fools when the great April opens the truth that neither selves nor neighbor selves were anything more than vicinities; while the love they would not entertain was of the essence of every scent." (4.68) The individual man "so far as he is anything apart from his fellows, and from what he and they are to be, is only a negation" (5.317). Nothing could be more absurd than to subscribe to a metaphysics which attributes ultimate reality to persons.

But we may go further. Just as we know that a vast multitude of cells constitutes every human being, so we may infer that human beings in their turn are "mere cells of the social organism" (1.673). If so, it is reasonable to assume that society has a super-personality, for in the case of the individual, consciousness is simply a kind of "public spirit among the nerve-cells" (1.354). Consequently, *"esprit de corps,* national sentiment, sym-pathy, are no mere metaphors. None of us can fully realize what the minds of corporations are, any more than one of my brain cells can know what the whole brain is thinking. But the law of mind clearly points to the existence of such personalities." (6.271) Peirce suggests that there are many ordinary observations which might provide evidence of the influence of such greater persons upon individuals. He even offers an observation from his own experience. "When the thirty thousand young people of the society for Christian Endeavor were in New York," he reports, "there seemed to me to be some mysterious diffusion of sweetness and light" (*ibid.*). That it should have been so is not remarkable if we take seriously the doctrine that feelings and ideas spread in a continuous manner. Since according to the agapistic philosophy, this process is forever increasing, we ought in the future to find many more signs of corporate personality. The societies for psychical research would be well advised to devote themselves to discovering such signs, rather than seeking evidence for the far weaker phenomenon of telepathy (*ibid.*).

The view that personal existence is an ephemeral affair, and the conception of evolution as a process which is moving inexorably towards an unlimited community embodying concrete reasonableness and creative love, provide the basis for Peirce's ethics. In it, as we shall find, the evolutionary goal is equated with the *summum bonum*. The importance of the latter notion for his transcendentalism generally can scarcely be exaggerated. Only by reference to the notion do other ideas take on an intelligible meaning (2.116). Even *being* must be defined in such a way that "the modes of being" will be "elements of co-operation toward the *summum bonum*" (2.118). It will be fitting to consider these modes of being in closing our review of his metaphysical system.

6. ACTUALITY, POSSIBILITY, AND DESTINY

We mentioned in chapter VII, section 2, that Peirce used the term "being" prior to 1890 as a synonym for the unlimited universe of human thought or discourse. Being is the totality of the thinkable. It is therefore the most abstract of all conceptions, obtained by reflecting on the manner in which signs are used. That view I took to be consonant with his naturalism, according to which "abstract terms . . . are only a device for expressing in another way the meaning of concrete terms" (6.620). This quotation, incidentally, comes from a letter written by Peirce in 1868 to W. T. Harris, editor of the *Journal of Speculative Philosophy,* on the subject of the Hegelian theory of being. Harris published it with a prefatory note in which he remarked that it seemed to him "the most profound and compendious statement of the anti-speculative standpoint . . . that we have yet seen."[6] The same

[6]*Collected Papers of Charles Sanders Peirce,* vol. 6, p. 436.

standpoint underlies Peirce's declaration of 1902 that every abstractly expressed proposition must be translatable in terms of individual experience, or else be pronounced meaningless (2.315). Clearly, such an approach could only assign to being the status of a logical conception.

In the transcendental part of his philosophy, however, Peirce treats being ontologically. The term ceases to be merely an *ens rationis* and is objectified as something quite separate from any individual's thought. That is to say, it takes on the connotation which is elsewhere reserved for "reality." In certain passages the two terms are employed interchangeably. Thus, he tells us that "in addition to actuality and possibility, a *third* mode of reality must be recognized in that which, as the gypsy fortune-tellers express it, is 'sure to come true,' or, as we may say, is *destined*" (4.547). A few paragraphs later he refers to "the different Modes of Being: Actuality, Possibility, Destiny (or Freedom from Destiny)" (4.549). The hypostatization of being was a consequence, I think, of his "firm belief," which apparently became fixed after 1903, that there are real possibilities (4.580). This belief in turn is part of his extreme realism with regard to ideas. We may elaborate the matter briefly by examining the three modes of being.

It will perhaps be granted that whereas a naturalistic philosophy must regard the possible as defined in terms of the actual, a transcendentalist philosophy usually considers the actual as derived from the possible.[7] At any rate, there is no doubt that Peirce's transcendentalism adopts the latter position. "Possibility evolves the actuality" (1.453), for we must suppose "that the existing universe, with all its arbitrary secondness, is an offshoot from, or an arbitrary determination of, a world of ideas, a Platonic world" (6.192). The actual is but a fragment of the possible (3.527), and the possible is *real* even though it may not happen to be actualized. Consider, for instance, "the being of a feeling, in itself, unattached to any subject." Such a feeling is "merely an atmospheric possibility, a possibility floating *in vacuo,* not rational yet capable of rationalization" (6.342). Every quality *per se* is eternal, independent of time and of any realization (1.420). It is a general, or quasi-Platonic essence, wholly impervious to change. From the boundless domain of possibility which is both objective and real (5.527), the world of actual existence is derived.

---

[7] Whether these be equally defensible positions is another matter. See J. Loewenberg, "Possibility and Context," *University of California Publications in Philosophy,* vol. XVII (1934), pp. 79-105.

This approach leaves the world of existence in that volatile state to which attention has already been called. Particular things have no independent status in the system. Starting with eternal possibilities, actuality is produced by Secondness, i.e. by reaction and opposition. Yet the individual things which result are strangely effete. "No reaction among individual things can create one of those things nor destroy it; for before its existence or after it there would not be anything to react. So that the fountain of existence must be sought elsewhere." (1.460) In the case of a material body, the qualities are related to the "matter" accidentally, and this relation does not change the qualities. It merely imparts existence to them. Their mode of being remains that of real possibilities. "But the *matter*, on the other hand, has no being at all except the being a subject of qualities. This relation of really having qualities constitutes its *existence*. But if all its qualities were to be taken away, and it were to be left quality-less matter, it not only would not exist, but it would not have any positive definite possibility—such as an unembodied quality has. It would be nothing at all." (1.527) Furthermore, the existence of things consists in their regular behavior (1.411). Hence, apart from what is general either as possibility or as law, there is nothing else to be found in the actual. "All, therefore, that we perceive or think, or that exists, is general" (3.93 n.).

The third mode of being, destiny, has two aspects. Its narrower aspect is fate, which comprises all those future events which are necessitated already. Such events are "sure to come true, and can nohow be avoided." This is what we have in mind when we say that "we are all fated to die" (5.407 n.). It does not follow that every single incident in our lives between now and the moment of our death is rigidly determined. Fate is not identical with deterministic necessity (6.592). Rather, "*fate* is that special kind of *destiny* by which events are supposed to be brought about *under definite circumstances* which involve no necessitating cause for those occurrences" (4.547 n.). In the wider sense, destiny includes both fate and freedom. The latter is the contingent element which belongs to every future. Hence, destiny indicates that certain things are "sure to come about although there is no necessitating reason for it. Thus, a pair of dice, thrown often enough, will be sure to turn up sixes some time, although there is no necessity that they should. The probability that they will is 1: that is all." (*Ibid.*) In like manner, it is destined that cosmic evolution shall move toward its ultimate goal, and that man, "with all his miserable littlenesses," shall become "gradually more and more imbued with the Spirit of God, in which Nature and History are rife" (5.402 n.).

Peirce's metaphysical "system" makes one think of an enormous jig-saw puzzle in which a large number of the pieces are missing. The broad outline of the scene can be discerned, but the connection between various parts remains obscure. Thus, it is not clear whether he intended the modes of being to have precedence over the categories of his cosmology. This would seem to follow from the fact that ontology is the first division of metaphysics in his classification of the sciences. Yet we have seen that the realm of possibility is itself the product of evolution (6.200), and that the whole of reality has developed literally *ex nihilo*. On the face of it Peirce's Platonism and his Evolutionism do not fit together easily. Again, what precisely *are* the cosmological categories? Mind, matter, and evolution? Or, chance, continuity, and habit-taking? Or, tychism, synechism, and agapism? Or, chance, law, habit, and love? These are just a few of the more obvious questions that come to mind. Whether any light will be shed on such difficulties by Peirce's ethics and theology, we shall now see.

X

ETHICS AND THEOLOGY

1. ETHICS AND MORAL PRACTICE

PEIRCE did not take the subject of ethics seriously until late in his career. He reports that prior to 1883 all he knew of it was derived from a text-book by Jouffroy, studied while an undergraduate at Harvard, from Kant, and from "a wooden treatise by Whewell" (5.111). The result was that he at first refused to consider ethics as a theoretical science at all, and classed it among the practical arts. About the time he was forty, he began to read the works of the great moralists, whose fertility of thought he found "in wonderful contrast to the sterility of the logicians" (*ibid.*). The various ethical systems interested him, but he still had doubts whether they were concerned with anything more than the guidance of life (2.198). Not until 1899 did he reach the conclusion that ethics was a normative science of profound importance. He now saw it as "one of the very subtlest of studies" (2.120), "a most entrancing field of thought but soon broadcast with pitfalls" (5.36). Despite this, however, the subject received no extensive treatment at his hands. His views on it are scattered throughout the *Collected Papers*, and appear for the most part in the context of other discussions.

To commence our survey of these views, we may note the sharp separation he makes between ethics and moral practice. Virtuous conduct is not something which any of the "heuretic sciences" can undertake to specify (1.573). Their attention is devoted exclusively to the discovery of truth, not to the laying down of rules for action. Here, as elsewhere in his transcendentalism, Peirce maintains the divorce of theory from practice. Indeed, prior to his admitting ethics among the sciences, he occasionally deplored the whole enterprise of reflecting on morality. "When men begin to rationalize about their conduct, the first effect is to deliver them over to their passions and produce the

most frightful demoralization, especially in sexual matters" (1.57).
For the prevailing system of sexual rules, like the *mores* generally, "is
an instinctive or sentimental induction" summarizing the experience
of the race (1.633). It should therefore be a practically infallible guide
to each individual. "To be a moral man is to obey the traditional
maxims of your community without hesitation or discussion" (1.666).
Morality is inevitably and necessarily conservative. Accordingly, in
so far as we seek to reason out an explanation for it, we shall either
be encouraging immorality or we shall be doing what is superfluous.
"Ethics, then, even if not a positively dangerous study, as it sometimes
proves, is as useless a science as can be conceived" (1.667).

The most reliable guide to right living is the voice of conscience.
It is a subconscious part of the soul produced by the experience of
generations of human beings, and altered only with the greatest slow-
ness from age to age. Though not absolutely identical in different
individuals, it is hardly distinct in them, and constitutes "a sort of community consciousness, or public spirit" in the depths of their nature
(1.56). The deliverances of conscience are direct, forceful, and practically infallible (1.248; 1.365). Their compulsiveness is well illustrated
in the horror felt by all normal people at the thought of incest (2.171).
Despite the fact that this feeling or sentiment is unaccompanied by
any sense of evidence, it would be sufficiently strong to prevent a
person from practicing incest if he were foolish enough to think the
action justified by some new code of morals. It would be "disagreeable
to him to incur the sting of conscience" (1.604).

From this source springs our sense of obligation. Everybody agrees
that in following the dictates of his conscience a man acts rightly, even
though his conduct might have been different had certain aspects of
the case not escaped him. "This is because right and wrong are held to
be, in the ultimate analysis, subjective. It is every man's duty to en-
lighten his conscience as much as possible. Conscience itself requires
him to do that. But still, when all is done that circumstances permit,
it is his duty to act conscientiously." (2.153) Peirce does not, therefore, regard the distinction of right and wrong as a fundamental
problem for ethics (2.198). In practice it is not a problem at all, since
the verdict of conscience is always clear. Nor does the analysis of conscience fall within the domain of ethics. It belongs mainly to the
science of psychology (1.577).

In order, then, to avoid disrupting the moral practice of the community, we must not reason about that practice "except in a purely

speculative way" (1.50). If we remain exclusively on a theoretical plane, we can do no damage, and may even benefit ourselves intellectually. "As long as ethics is recognized as not being a matter of vital importance or in any way touching the student's conscience, it is, to a normal and healthy mind, a civilizing and valuable study" (1.669).

That Peirce was not altogether happy about this diremption is plain from certain comments he makes. Thus he admits that "the faculty of effective self-criticism" is essential to preserve the distinction between innocent and guilty conduct (1.604). Men of the purest intentions sometimes commit actions at variance with their own moral principles because they have never thought about the ethical implications of such actions (2.153). Most striking of all is the fact that "morality is a hardening agent. It is astonishing how many abominable scoundrels there are among sincerely moral people. The difficulty is that morality chokes its own stream. Like any other field, more than any other, it needs improvement, advance. Moral ideas must be a rising tide, or with the ebb foulness will be cast up. But morality, doctrinaire conservatist that it is, destroys its own vitality by resisting change, and positively insisting, This is eternally right: That is eternally wrong." (2.198) The appropriate remedy would seem to lie in a continuous rational criticism of prevailing moral beliefs. But Peirce's transcendentalism will not permit him to accept that remedy. "Clear as it seems to me that certain *dicta* of my conscience are unreasonable . . . yet I trust to its authority emphatically rather than to any rationalistic morality" (2.177). Ethics and moral practice must remain forever separated.

2. THE SUBJECT-MATTER OF ETHICS

How may we most adequately describe the subject-matter of ethics as a purely theoretical science? Peirce's answer is that it *"is the study of what ends of action we are deliberately prepared to adopt"* (5.130). We begin with the fact that there is voluntary or self-controlled conduct, and that this implies the presence of certain goals which are sought. The first task ethics undertakes is to survey such goals with a view to determining which one is fit to be supreme, i.e. to be the *summum bonum*. For "life can have but one end," and it must be ethics which defines this (2.198). A second task is the formulation of a theory of the conditions which govern the relation of action to an ideal. This, Peirce suggests, is not so much an assignment for pure ethics as for what he calls *practics* (1.573). The difference here seems to be that

practics investigates the conformity of conduct to *any* ideal, whereas
"in so far as ethics studies the conformity of conduct to an ideal, it is
limited to a particular ideal, which, whatever the professions of moralists may be, is in fact nothing but a sort of composite photograph of
the conscience of the members of the community" (*ibid.*). There seem,
then, to be three issues in need of discussion: (*a*) the various possible
ends of action; (*b*) the general conformity of action to those ends;
and (*c*) the determination of the end which is supreme above all
others. We shall take up each of these in turn.

To pass in review every one of the general classes of things which
anybody could accept as an ultimate end of conduct is obviously a
gigantic project. Its magnitude is not lessened by the circumstance
that the only method available to the investigator is that of direct self-
interrogation. But such a method produces no infallible results. "On
the contrary, consciousness may be set down as one of the most men-
dacious witnesses that ever was questioned. But it is the only witness
there is; and all we can do is to put it in the sweat-box and torture
the truth out of it, with such judgment as we can command." (1.580)
Since empirical verification is quite impossible here, we shall presumably recognize "the truth" in some intuitive manner when we encounter it. The nearest Peirce came to completing this project in his
published writings is a passage which occurs near the beginning of
his review of Pearson's *The Grammar of Science* in 1901. It seems
worth quoting in full.

A man may act with reference only to the momentary occasion, either from
unrestrained desire, or from preference for one desideratum over another,
or from provision against future desires, or from persuasion, or from imita-
tive instinct, or from dread of blame, or in awed obedience to an instant
command; or he may act in accordance with some general rule restricted
to his own wishes, such as the pursuit of pleasure, or self-preservation, or
good-will toward an acquaintance, or attachment to home and surroundings,
or conformity to the customs of his tribe, or reverence for a law; or, becoming a moralist, he may aim at bringing about an ideal state of things definitely conceived, such as one in which everybody attends exclusively to his
own business and interest (individualism), or in which the maximum total
pleasure of all beings capable of pleasure is attained (utilitarianism), or in
which altruistic sentiments universally prevail (altruism), or in which his
community is placed out of danger (patriotism), or in which the ways of
nature are as little modified as possible (naturalism); or he may aim at
hastening some result, not otherwise known in advance than as that, whatever it may turn out to be, to which some process seeming to him good must
inevitably lead, such as whatever the dictates of the human heart approve

(sentimentalism), or whatever would result from every man's duly weighing before action, the advantages of his every purpose (to which I will attach the nonce-name, *entelism*), or whatever the historical evolution of public sentiment may decree (historicism), or whatever the operation of cosmical causes may be destined to bring about (evolutionism); or he may be devoted to truth, and may be determined to do nothing not pronounced reasonable, either by his own cogitations (rationalism), or by public discussion (dialecticism), or by crucial experiment; or he may feel that the only thing really worth striving for is the generalizing or assimilating elements in truth, and that either as the sole object in which the mind can ultimately recognize its veritable aim (educationalism), or that which alone is destined·to gain universal sway (pancratism); or, finally he may be filled with the idea that the only reason that can reasonably be admitted as ultimate is that living reason for the sake of which the psychical and physical universe is in the process of creation (religionism).[1]

Faced with such an embarrassment of riches some generalization is quite imperative. Peirce was therefore prepared two years later to distinguish the following broad classes of ends: (i) those that are individual and subjective, e.g. a feeling of pleasure; (ii) those that are social and objective, e.g. the preservation of the race; and (iii) those that have the kind of being possessed by a law, e.g. the rationalizing of the universe (1.590). The next task is to discover which of the three classes contains an end that is genuinely ultimate. It must be something we would deliberately choose as desirable *per se*, without any ulterior consideration (1.579; 5.130). That is to say, it will be the answer to the questions: "What am I prepared deliberately to accept as the statement of what I want to do, what am I to aim at, what am I after? To what is the force of my will to be directed?" (2.198) Even if our discussion produces no final result at this stage, it may serve to eliminate certain alternatives.

Let us first query consciousness regarding individual pleasure or self-satisfaction. Suppose it were possible to satisfy each desire the instant it occurred. Is this an objective which due reflection would recommend for our pursuit? Peirce thinks that consciousness will reply with an emphatic negative (1.583). A person who tried to live in accordance with such an extreme form of hedonism could not maintain his sanity. He would be like the infant in the nursery-tale upon whom a malevolent fairy pronounced the curse that during his entire life whatever wish he conceived should be immediately gratified. Perhaps a less extreme form of egoistic hedonism might not suffer from this defect. But Peirce contends that it would still prove unacceptable.

[1] *Popular Science Monthly*, vol. LVIII (1901), pp. 298-99.

It is not "in the nature of man to be perfectly satisfied to make his personal comfort his ultimate aim" (5.130). No matter how refined the pleasure sought may be, a life lived for this alone "will be pronounced by every experienced person to be inevitably destined to miss the satisfaction at which it aims."[2]

The preservation of the race, interpreted in the widest sense, seems *prima facie* to be a worthy goal for all human effort. What higher aim can an individual have than that of preserving the welfare and stability of society? Yet consciousness may object that it is always proper to ask *why* society should be preserved, i.e. to demand a *reason* for it. If so, it cannot qualify as an ultimate end of action, for this by definition requires no reasons to be given on its behalf. Moreover, society and the human race are notoriously ephemeral when looked at from the perspective of history. Hence, "to demand that man should aim at the stability . . . of society at large, or at the perpetuation of the race as an *ultimate* end, is too much. The human species will be extirpated sometime; and when the time comes the universe will, no doubt, be well rid of it."[3] To base one's life on anything so transient would be to build on sand.

We are thus forced to the conclusion that the supreme aim of action cannot be particular or temporal. It must be general. This alone will enable it to possess the stability and permanence appropriate to the highest good. But since the total cosmos is evolving, "almost everybody will now agree that the ultimate good lies in the evolutionary process in some way. If so, it is not in individual reactions in their segregation, but in something general or continuous." (5.4) When we have reached this point in the argument, however, we have gone as far as ethics alone can take us. For ethics "merely tells us that we have a power of self-control, that no narrow or selfish aim can ever prove satisfactory, that the only satisfactory aim is the broadest, highest, and most general possible aim; and for any more definite information . . . [it] has to refer us to the esthetician, whose business it is to say what is the state of things which is most admirable in itself regardless of any ulterior reason" (1.611). The *summum bonum* can only be fully defined with the aid of esthetics or the science of ideals.

Before proceeding to this question, we may glance briefly at the enterprise which Peirce labelled *practics*. It is described as "the theory of the conformity of action to an ideal" (1.573), and is declared to be

[2]*Ibid.*, p. 299.
[3]*Ibid.*

the proper mid-normative science, between esthetics and logic. In this particular passage Peirce refuses to identify the mid-normative science with ethics, because, he says, the latter "involves the theory of the ideal itself, the nature of the *summum bonum*" (*ibid.*). Hence, he also calls practics *antethics*, or "that which is put in place of ethics, the usual second member of the trio" (*ibid.*). I think we may reasonably surmise that he was uncertain at this point whether the theory of the ideal should belong to esthetics proper, or whether it is a task for the special discipline of "pure ethics," which is quite different from practics. He may have been doubtful whether the definition of the ideal is a normative concern at all, for he states quite categorically in 1.577 that *What is good?* is a pre-normative question, and that "pure ethics, philosophical ethics, is not normative but pre-normative." When, however, he came to the conclusion that the determination of the *summum bonum* is the responsibility of esthetics, he was able to reinstate ethics as the mid-normative science. In that case, what is the function of practics?

One thing at any rate seems to be clear. Practics has nothing to do with the guidance of conduct. It is not akin to casuistry, which specifies what ought to be done in given circumstances where we are faced with a moral choice. For casuistry, while it "might be made at once extremely entertaining and positively useful," is merely an art, whereas practics is a theory. In the latter the objective is not instruction but cognition.

Beyond this we have to guess at Peirce's meaning since he does not dilate on the subject-matter of practics. I have therefore conjectured that its field is the whole range of voluntary action, which it surveys with an eye to discovering what conditions, if any, govern the conformity of all such acts to an ideal. Practics, for instance, calls attention to the remarkable parallelism between logical and moral activity (cf. 1.606). It points out that just as in morality we consider a certain line of conduct fine in itself, so in logic a certain hypothesis appeals to us because of its intrinsic attractiveness. Again, we want our conduct to be consistent, and likewise with our deductive inferences. Finally, we take into account the general effect of thoroughly carrying out our ideals in practice. "Just so certain ways of reasoning recommend themselves because if persistently carried out they must lead to the truth. The parallelism, you perceive, is almost exact." (1.608) If my conjecture here is right, practics would be a more general investigation than either logic or ethics. The findings of both these sciences would be relevant to it, for the principles of sound inference and of good conduct have to do with the conformity of action to a standard. But it is idle to speculate further on precisely what Peirce may have meant this investigation to include.

3. ESTHETICS, ETHICS, AND THE *SUMMUM BONUM*

The determination of the ultimate good, according to Peirce, obliges us to pass from the domain of ethics to that of esthetics. This is one of the most curious, and from our point of view one of the most significant, turns in his transcendentalist argument. By means of it he bases his doctrine of the *summum bonum* on an appeal to feeling, and thus removes it from the domain of scientific inquiry. Furthermore, since esthetics is the foundation on which ethics is reared, and ethics is surmounted in its turn by logic, the whole edifice of the normative sciences has an anti-naturalistic significance. Here again we see how his transcendentalism is able to make use of the *a priori* principle that the sciences have an order which is shown in the "dependence" of each one on the results of its predecessors.

When he became convinced of the primacy of esthetics among the normative sciences, Peirce felt embarrassed by his lack of familiarity with the discipline. He admits that he is "lamentably ignorant of it" (2.120), and like most logicians has "pondered that subject far too little" (2.197). It is interesting to find, however, that the first philosophical work he ever studied—at about the age of sixteen—was Schiller's *Aesthetische Briefe*, which he "undertook to expound" to his "dear friend, Horatio Paine" (*ibid.*). At that time he read various other works in the field. But as his devotion to logic increased, esthetics fell into the background and was completely neglected for almost half a century. He was therefore unable to deal with it confidently when he became persuaded of its importance (cf. 2.198).

A certain doubt existed in his mind whether esthetics is a normative science at all. Schleiermacher, in whose school the word "normative" was invented, restricted it to logic and ethics, and Peirce thinks there is much to be said for this view. "For that which renders logic and ethics peculiarly normative is that nothing can be either logically true or morally good without a purpose to be so. . . . On the other hand, a thing is beautiful or ugly quite irrespective of any purpose to be so. It would seem, therefore, that esthetics is no more essentially normative than any nomological science." (1.575) Yet the doctrine of the categories provides a strong reason for grouping the three disciplines under one heading. Logic is clearly concerned with Thirdness and ethics with Secondness. Esthetics, then, must be concerned with Firstness. It is the purely qualitative aspect of phenomena which furnishes the data for the initial normative science.

In support of this contention, Peirce rejects the definition of esthetics as the science of beauty. "The conception of beauty is but the product of this science, and a very inadequate attempt it is to grasp what it is that esthetics seeks to make clear" (2.199). Much more illuminating is the view that all three normative sciences aim at distinguishing good from bad. Logic does so in regard to the representations of truth, ethics in regard to efforts of will, and esthetics in regard to objects in the immediacy of their presentation (5.36). Peirce admits that "good" and "bad" are not very happy terms for the items discriminated in the third domain. The Greek καλός, he thinks, might be better. Consider the issue in the light of our general problem. "Ethics asks to what end all effort shall be directed. That question obviously depends upon the question what it would be that, independently of the effort, we should like to experience. But in order to state the question of esthetics in its purity, we should eliminate from it, not merely all consideration of effort, but all consideration of action and reaction, including all consideration of our receiving pleasure, everything in short, belonging to the opposition of the *ego* and the *non-ego*. . . . Using καλός, the question of esthetics is, What is the one quality that is, in its immediate presence, καλός?" (2.199). Or, what is the state of affairs most admirable in itself? (1.611).

The reader may well wonder at this point how we are to go about answering such a question. There appears to be just one procedure available, namely, to appeal to those whose taste is most discriminating. For in esthetics "the excellence of the norm consists exclusively in its accordance with the deliberate and natural judgment of the cultured mind" (2.156). This judgment springs directly from feeling, and can be given no further justification. It is as ultimate as that famous appraisal made by the student who wrote "I do not love thee Doctor Fell." Since taste is "purely subjective," we cannot expect it to conform to the kind of objective standard found in logic (*ibid.*).

That Peirce was ill at ease in this position is shown by the one brief attempt he made to rescue the esthetic good from pure subjectivity. His attempt took the form of a definition, according to which any object having a multitude of parts so related to one another as to impart a positive, simple, immediate quality to their totality, is, in so far, esthetically good, no matter what the particular quality of the total may be. "If that quality be such as to nauseate us, to scare us, or otherwise to disturb us to the point of throwing us out of the mood of esthetic enjoyment, out of the mood of simply contemplating the embodiment of the quality—just, for example, as the Alps affected the people of old times, when the state of civilization was such that an impression of great power was inseparably associated with lively apprehension and terror—then the object remains none the less esthetically good, although people in our condition are incapacitated from a calm esthetic contemplation of it" (5.132). But this suggestion, as Peirce himself perceived, involves the denial of positive esthetic badness. "And since by goodness we chiefly in this discussion mean merely the absence of badness, or faultlessness, there will be no such thing as esthetic goodness" (*ibid.*). If so, the distinction between that which is esthetically better and that which is esthetically worse will also have to go by the board. We shall be simply left with innumerable varieties of esthetic quality.

Peirce never developed this "objective" approach at greater length. To have done so would have necessitated a drastic revision in his view of the relation between esthetics and ethics, and perhaps of the normative sciences generally. Hence, his more usual position was the "subjective" one in which the admirable ideal is determined by the immediate judgment of mature and refined human beings. This ideal has "the only kind of goodness that such an ideal *can* have; namely, esthetic goodness. From this point of view the morally good appears as a particular species of the esthetically good." (5.130) Being rooted in Firstness, or feeling, the notion of the *summum bonum* has an ultimacy that is unassailable.

What, then, does esthetics propose as the most satisfactory ideal? Simply the growth of Reason or Noῦs—that agency which manifests itself in the human mind, in mind's development, and in the evolution of the cosmos. "The one thing whose admirableness is not due to an ulterior reason, is Reason itself comprehended in all its fulness, so far as we can comprehend it" (1.615). Such an ideal has the permanence which springs from the fact that it can never be wholly realized. Even the simplest general idea requires for its fulfilment that events should come to pass. But all that ever can have come to pass must fall short of entirely fulfilling its requirements. This is because the very meaning of a general term is identical with an unlimited series of conditional predictions. Moreover, the being of "the General, of Reason, *consists* in its governing individual events. So, then, the essence of Reason is such that its being never can have been completely perfected. It always must be in a state of incipiency, of growth. . . . The creation of the universe, which did not take place during a certain busy week in the year 4004 B.C., but is going on to-day and never will be done, is this very development of Reason. I do not see how one can have a more satisfying ideal of the admirable than the development of Reason so understood." (*Ibid.*).

Now "the instant that an esthetic ideal is proposed as an ultimate end of action, at that instant a categorical imperative pronounces for or against it" (5.133). In the case of the ideal just outlined the verdict is, of course, a whole-hearted affirmative. To the objection that this manner of speaking savors too much of Kant, whose position is known to be inadequate, Peirce replies that he does not think very highly of the logic of those who profess to refute that position. However, it is unnecessary to agree with Kant in every detail. The important point is that once conscience, through the categorical imperative, has put its seal of approval on an ideal, the latter is placed "beyond all possible criticism, except the quite impertinent criticism of outsiders" (*ibid*). Since the development of Reason is the aim adopted here as ultimate, ethics must declare the ideal of conduct to be that of making the world more reasonable. Our duty is to execute our little function in the process of creation, by helping Reason to extend its dominion wherever we can (1.615). In short, the answer to the question, What is the chief end of man? is: "To actualize ideas of the immortal, ceaselessly prolific kind" (2.763).

Suppose some person or group of persons refuses to accept this ideal and espouses another. Have we the right to brand their refusal a dereliction of duty, and their principles of conduct immoral? Certainly not, Peirce replies. "It would be monstrous for either party to pronounce the moral judgments of the other to be BAD. That would imply an appeal to some other tribunal." (2.151) Ethical norms are *consequent* upon the adoption of an ultimate aim. We may condemn them for being incompatible with that aim, but for nothing else. Peirce believes there is reason to hope that debate may lead men to modify their ideals "up to complete accord. Should it turn out otherwise, what can be said except that some men have one aim and some another?" (*Ibid.*) Ethics will perhaps always be a theatre of discussion, "for the reason that its study consists in the gradual development of a distinct recognition of a satisfactory aim" (4.243).

Is the view of morality as in the last resort a matter of esthetic judgment not simply old-fashioned hedonism? On the contrary, Peirce insists, it is "directly opposed to hedonism" (5.111). The latter doctrine defines the good in terms of pleasure and the evil in terms of pain. But for Peirce the good is that which the cultivated mind feels to be intrinsically attractive, and the evil that which it feels to be repulsive. The difference between the two positions is this. Instead of regarding pleasure and pain as basic, Peirce considers them to be feelings attaching themselves to, and excited by, other feelings. Thus, for example, a toothache is painful. But we must distinguish between the quality of feeling of the toothache, and the feeling of pain which *accompanies* it. Pain is a symptom of a feeling which repels us; pleasure a symptom of a feeling which attracts us. We may say, therefore, that "esthetic good and evil are . . . what would be pleasure or pain to the fully developed superman" (5.552). In other words, "the good is the attractive—not to everybody, but to the sufficiently matured agent; and the evil is the repulsive to the same" (*ibid.*). This is far removed from a hedonistic ethics.

The *summum bonum,* then, pronounced by esthetics to be most admirable in itself, and further accepted by ethics as the ultimate goal for action, is the promotion of "concrete reasonableness." This ideal is identical with the on-going process of cosmic evolution which is destined in the infinitely remote future to culminate in perfect rationality and the universal rule of law. Since each individual who recognizes the ideal has an obligation to act in such a way as to advance the cause of reason, logic becomes the means through which he performs his duty. Yet, as we have seen, he cannot be consistently logical unless he identifies his interests with those of an unlimited community. Such identification must be coupled with a clear recognition that the unlimited community will never in fact be realized. For the human race is but a transitory phenomenon in the evolution of the cosmos, a mere stage on the way towards the final goal. While the individual *qua* logician may need to base his procedure on the "hope" that the community will last beyond any assignable date, the individual *qua* moral agent finds his supreme command in a conception of duty which "completes" his personality "by melting it into the neighboring parts of the universal cosmos. . . . In fulfilling this command, man prepares himself for transmutation into a new form of life, the joyful Nirvana in which the discontinuities of his will shall have all but disappeared." (1.673)

An easy transition from Peirce's ethics to his theology is provided by several remarks he makes on the status of evil in the universe. For the individual, "the only moral evil is not to have any ultimate aim" (5.133). If a person embraces an aim which cannot be consistently pursued it must be judged bad, but the person himself is foolish rather than evil. From the point of view of the universe, however, evil is nothing positive. It is simply a deficiency of the love which lies at the center of the evolutionary process. Just as darkness is the defect of light, "so hatred and evil are mere imperfect stages of ἀγάπη and ἀγαθόν, love and loveliness" (6.287). Furthermore, when we admit that profoundest of all metaphysical truths which declares God to be Love, we see that imperfection is a necessary part of creation. "For self-love is no love; so if God's self is love, that which he loves must be defect of love; just as a luminary can light up only that which otherwise would be dark" (*ibid.*). This is the "everlasting solution" of the problem of evil which Henry James senior presented in his *Substance and Shadow: An Essay on the Physics of Creation.* Not only is evil necessary to God, it is also necessary to man. In struggling against it man performs his highest duty, and so develops his character. He has therefore good reason to "bless God for the law of growth with all the fighting it imposes upon him," and to recognize in evil "one of the major perfections of the Universe" (6.479).

4. THEOLOGY AND RELIGION

It is difficult to know how one should interpret many of Peirce's remarks on religion. Often they seem to be statements of private and personal beliefs rather than of studied philosophical conclusions. We have it from his own lips that he was attracted to philosophy "not for its teaching about God, Freedom, and Immortality," but for what it might be able to tell him about cosmology and psychology (4.2). We know, too, that he considered philosophy a "pure Heuretic Science, even less concerned, for example, about practical religion, if possible, than religion ought to be about it" (5.517). On the other hand, he made "religious metaphysics" one of the sub-orders of metaphysics proper (1.192), and became increasingly interested in it as his life drew to a close. Thus he refers in 1909 to "the book about God and religion upon which I have been at work for several years, and hope to write" (6.346). The sound procedure, then, is probably to assume that his ideas in this field, desultory as they are, represent a positive doctrine, and not simply a confession of faith.

Such an approach promptly discloses the same cleavage that we
have observed elsewhere in Peirce's transcendentalism. The theory and
practice of religion are totally divorced from one another. Religious
practice is grounded in the spontaneous feeling of "the sensible heart."
Its foundation "is a sort of sentiment, or obscure perception, a deep
recognition of a something in the circumambient All," which if a man
seeks to express it, "will clothe itself in forms more or less extravagant"
(6.429). In contrast with this, stand the various theologies or philosophies of religion upon which so much stress is mistakenly laid. They
are not, and should not be regarded as, matters of vital importance
(1.665). It is the height of folly to permit them to affect one's religious life, "as if any genuine religion could come from the head instead of from the heart" (*ibid.*). Of course, for the man who has had
no immediate "stirring of the spirit," no religion is as yet possible. In
that case "the only worthy course is to wait quietly until such experience comes," since "no amount of speculation can take the place
of experience" (1.655).

Peirce goes on to argue that an emphasis on creeds and dogmas
is a sure sign of the enfeeblement of religion. This condition is encouraged by those priests who insist on the acceptance of certain
formulas as essential for every participant in their denomination. Such
a practice substitutes the husk of religion for its heart, and may very
well render irreligious the persons who cannot believe the formulas
(6.427). Hence, "all those modern books which offer new philosophies
of religion, at the rate of one every fortnight on the average, are but
symptoms of the temporary dissolution of the Christian faith" (1.659).
How much sounder was the position of a man like Duns Scotus, that
metaphysics has nothing to say either one way or the other on any
religious question! Conversely, how absurd to think, as the "utterly
religionless" Boethius did, that philosophy can provide any genuine
consolation! The last part of his famous work, like every philosophical
treatise on this topic, "is a mere diet of bran for the hungered soul"
(*ibid.*).

It is from the Gospels that the religious sentiment draws its proper
nourishment. For the New Testament "is certainly the highest existing
authority in regard to the dispositions of heart which a man ought to
have" (2.655). The teaching of Jesus does not consist in "a lot of metaphysical propositions" (6.440), but in the presentation of the Way of
Life. The essence of this way of life is simply the practice of the law of
love. "As far as it is contracted to a rule of ethics, it is: Love God, and

love your neighbor" (6.441). If it be objected that such a doctrine is
not distinctively Christian, since it was anticipated by the early Egyp-
tians, by the Buddhists, the Stoics, and Confucius, the reply is that this
gives Christians all the more reason to regard their doctrine as possessing the ear-mark of divine truth, "namely, that it was anticipated
from primitive ages. The higher a religion the more catholic." (6.442)
Christianity, then, gives the purest expression to the ideal of the sensible heart—that of a world "united in the bond of a common love of
God accomplished by each man's loving his neighbor" (6.443-).

Now although religion has its origin in feeling, it "only comes to
full flower in a great church coextensive with a civilization" (*ibid.*).
This is because, like every species of reality, religion is a social or
public affair. A church is necessary, first, to form a powerful army
"to put down the principle of self-seeking, and to make the principle
of love triumphant" (6.448); and secondly, to enable individuals to
weld themselves together "in one organic, systematic perception of the
Glory of the Highest" (6.429). Neither of these functions is performed,
Peirce holds, by any existing churches, where the emphasis is on
observance of ritual and conformity to creed. Consequently, "a great
catholic church is wanted" (6.443). Yet men ought to hesitate before
planning to establish such an institution *de novo*. Even if it were possible to do so, would they not be wiser to devote their energies to
reforming the institution that already has such a large measure of
the truth in it? "Doubtless, a lot of superstition clings to the historical
churches; but superstition is the grime upon the venerable pavement
of the sacred edifice, and he who would wash that pavement clean
should be willing to get down on his knees to his work inside the
church" (6.447). Above all, no man ought to be alienated by the particular brand of theology promulgated by a particular body of priests.

Am I to be prevented from joining in that common joy at the revelation of
enlightened principles of religion which we celebrate at Easter and Christmas because I think that certain scientific, logical, and metaphysical ideas
which have been mixed up with these principles are untenable? No; to do
so would be to estimate those errors as of more consequence than the
truth—an opinion which few would admit. People who do not believe
what are really the fundamental principles of Christianity are rare to find,
and all but these few ought to feel at home in the churches. (6.427)

5. SCIENCE, THEOLOGY, AND RELIGION

The purifying of religion and the reforming of the church can only
be accomplished, Peirce contends, by taking a leaf from the book of

science. This is what we ought to learn from the prolonged conflict between science and the theologically dominated religion of the past. The roots of this conflict lie in certain sharply contrasted attributes which we shall do well to note. Four of these are particularly significant.

1. The motivation of the typical scientist is diametrically opposed to that of the typical theologian. The former has an intense desire to find things out, and so is eager to subject his "beliefs" to the most rigorous scrutiny. The theologian, however, wants to confirm himself in his existing beliefs, most of which he adopted early in life. His main desire seems to be to protect these beliefs from further examination, as though he were unsure whether they could survive it. This suggests that theology "derives its initial impulse from religious wavering" (6.3). If the theologian were really firm in his convictions he would welcome the most searching inquiry into them.[4]

2. Since positive science rests on experience, it renounces all title to theoretical infallibility. Approximation is the fabric out of which scientific knowledge is formed. But theology has been intent on affirming its dogmas to be absolute truths. The "blight of cocksureness" has descended upon it. Theologians have consequently opposed the principle of fallibilism as antagonistic to religion (1.151). Probability may be the guide to life in science, they say, but religion requires certainty.

3. The leading conception of science is that of continuity (1.62). By means of this the finest generalizations are secured (2.646). Scientists are ever on the look-out for evidence of connecting links between diverse classes of facts. Theologians, on the contrary, find it necessary to establish "hard lines of demarcation, or great gulfs, contrary to all observation, between good men and bad, between the wise and foolish, between the spirit and the flesh" (1.40). Having done so, they consider their principal business to be that of making men feel "the enormity of the slightest departure from the metaphysics they assume to be connected with the standard faith" (6.3). If science thrives on continuity, theology seems to thrive on discontinuity.

4. Development and growth are essential to science as a living

[4]In support of this view Peirce refers to the reception which greeted Tyndall's proposal to measure the efficacy of prayer by experimental statistics. "Instead of thanking Tyndall for the idea . . . the clergy to a man shrank back in terror, thus conclusively betraying to every eye their own utter disbelief in their own dogma. They pronounced it an impious proposition. But there was nothing more impious in it than in any other sort of inquiry into religion except this—that they feared it would bring all 'talkee-talkee' to an end." (1.660; cf. 6.515)

process. This development is towards greater perfection of knowledge, or closer approximation to the truth. But "the seminarists and religionists generally have at all times and places set their faces against the idea of continuous growth. That disposition of intellect is the most catholic element of religion. Religious truth having been once defined is never to be altered in the most minute particular." (1.40)   Consequently, the church as an institution has fought bitterly "by fire and sword all the great advances in the true sciences" (*ibid*). Its opposition has never proved to be effective, of course, since in the end the hated doctrines have had to be accepted (1.151). But religious conservatism has always sought to block the path of scientific progress.

Now the history of this conflict discloses that science becomes steadily stronger the older it grows, whereas theologically dominated religion just as steadily languishes. "Like a plucked flower, its destiny is to wilt and fade. The vital sentiment that gave it birth loses gradually its pristine purity and strength, till some new creed treads it down." (6.430)   The moral to be drawn is surely that the four attributes of science mentioned above are the source of its health, while the corresponding attributes of religion are the cause of its decline. If, therefore, religion is to be revitalized, it should discard the attributes which have vitiated it, and adopt those of its ancient enemy.

But is such a procedure possible? Peirce believes it is, provided the following things are done. First, religion must divorce itself from theology. This involves the recognition that religious beliefs are not statements professing to have truth-value, but are formulae upon which we will act. "Religion is a practical matter" (6.216). Accordingly, its beliefs are "practically infallible for the individual—which is the only clear sense the word 'infallibility' will bear" (1.633). Secondly, theology as the science of religious beliefs must (*a*) realize its irrelevance to religious practice, (*b*) surrender its pretensions to theoretical infallibility, and (*c*) develop an inquiring spirit which will enable it to grow. In other words, theology must reform its method by following the pattern of science. Thirdly, men must have greater faith in the unity of truth. "It is a damnable absurdity indeed to say that one thing is true in theology and another in science" (6.216). Provided the conclusions in each domain are put forward provisionally rather than dogmatically, the fact that they may *now* clash does not imply that they will *always* do so. Future inquiry will certainly bring about modifications on both sides, and these modifications may ultimately lead to general agreement.

The day has come . . . when the man whom religious experience most devoutly moves . . . while adhering to the essence of religion, and as far as possible to the church . . . will cast aside that religious timidity that is forever prompting the church to recoil from the paths into which the Governor of history is leading the minds of men, a cowardice that has stood through the ages as the landmark and limit of her little faith, and will gladly go forward, sure that truth is not split into two warring doctrines, and that any change that knowledge can work in his faith can only affect its expression, but not the deep mystery expressed. (6.432)

This change of attitude would finally obliterate the conflict between science and religion. For how could there be any opposition between theory and practice, if the two realms were to be completely separated? Moreover, no reason would remain why a theology which had reformed its method should clash with science. Each could go its own way untrammelled by the other, seeking only to discover truth. Under these circumstances, there would be no point in trying to reconcile the results of theology and science prematurely, as Paul Carus proposed to do in his journal *The Open Court*. Although Peirce contributed to that journal from time to time, he remained sceptical about its fundamental policy. Commenting on it in the *Nation* in 1890, he asks why religion and science should not "seek each a self-development in its own interest, and then, if as they approach completion, they are found to come more and more into accord, will not that be a more satisfactory result than forcibly bending them together now in a way that can only disfigure both? For the present, a religion which believes in itself should not mind what science says; and science is long past caring a fig for the thunder of the theologians."[5]

In order that permanent peace may prevail, it is not quite sufficient that religion should become "animated by the scientific spirit" (6.433). Science must also reflect something of the religious spirit. It must come to recognize that experimental inquiry is the learning of a great lesson which is being taught to men by their Creator. For "God's beneficence is in nothing more apparent than in how in the early days of science Man's attention was particularly drawn to phenomena easy to investigate and how Man has ever since been led on, as through a series of graduated exercises, to more and more difficult problems" (2.769). Hence, science is literally "knowledge of God's truth" (1.239). The vehicles of this knowledge are the manifold facts of nature. To a science fully conscious of its own purpose, therefore, nature must

[5]*Nation*, vol. L (1890), p. 119. Cf. 6.603.

appear as "something great, and beautiful, and sacred, and eternal, and real—the object of its worship and its aspiration" (5.589). Not only are qualities the symbols of a Divine plan being worked out in living realities (5.119), but the laws of nature themselves are "ideas or resolutions" in the Divine consciousness (5.107). The study of natural phenomena, then, ought to be undertaken in "the spirit of joy in learning ourselves and in making others acquainted with the glories of God" (1.127). Such a religiously motivated science can unite in a happy "marriage" with a scientifically motivated religion!

But it is now time to proceed to the details of Peirce's theology or "religious metaphysics." Here, three classical issues come up for examination, namely, God, Freedom, and Immortality. We shall review his opinions on these issues in order.

6. THE NATURE AND REALITY OF GOD

Peirce's doctrine of God represents the culminating point of his transcendentalism. Like the great theological metaphysicians of the past, he believed that man can obtain knowledge on such ultimate matters. This knowledge is derived from the twin sources of perception and thought. Yet it must of necessity be less certain than the results of inquiry in other fields, since "man has no such genius for discoveries about God . . . as he has for physical and psychical science" (6.491). Analogical reasoning must suffice to establish the broadest conclusions. And as for the details, "we only wildly gabble about such things" (6.509). We should obviously not expect minute accuracy on so transcendent a theme.

Let us first consider the meaning of the central idea. "If a pragmaticist is asked what he means by the word 'God,' he can only say that just as long acquaintance with a man of great character may deeply influence one's whole manner of conduct, so that a glance at his portrait may make a difference . . . so if contemplation and study of the physico-psychical universe can imbue a man with principles of conduct analogous to the influence of a great man's works or conversation, then that analogue of a mind—for it is impossible to say that *any* human attribute is *literally* applicable—is what he means by 'God'" (6.502). In other words, the fact that the investigation of nature teaches us to live in accordance with her ways, strongly suggests the presence of "some vast consciousness, who . . . is a Deity relatively to us" (5.107). Various theologians warn us not to attribute reason to the Deity or to make the mistake of believing that His Mind is at all like ours. But Peirce contends that our ability to predict the course of nature by means of scientific discoveries "is proof conclusive that, though we cannot think any thought of God's, we can catch a fragment of His Thought, as it were" (6.502).

We must, however, tread warily here. "Consciousness" and "mind" are hard enough to define in relation to the human, let alone the Superhuman. Certainly, if we mean by "consciousness" the general sensation of the brain or some part of it, or some visceral or bodily sensation, then "God probably has no consciousness" (6.489). It would be better to speak of Him as a "disembodied spirit." Similarly, all we know of "mind" is derived from the actions of animals with brains and ganglia like ourselves. "To apply such a word to *God* is precisely like the old pictures which show him like an aged man leaning over to look out from above a cloud. Considering the *vague intention* of it, as conceived by the *non-theological* artist, it cannot be called false, but rather ludicrously figurative." (6.199)

With more assurance we may follow tradition in defining God as *Ens Necessarium* and Creator of All (6.452; 6.489). The Creative Activity which is an inseparable attribute of Him has been manifesting itself not only throughout the infinite past, but is manifesting itself now, and will continue into the infinite future (6.506). "Vain as it is to attempt to bring to light any definite meaning from the idea, it is nevertheless true that *all reality* is due to the creative power of God" (6.505). Time as something real is therefore the result of creation (6.506), and He cannot Himself be subject to it (4.67). Neither is He subject to growth in the sense in which this applies to the universe as a whole. Yet it would be wrong to deny all growth to His nature (6.466). The case is the same with purpose. It is less false to speak of it as one of God's attributes than to think of Him as having no purpose. Finally, when we predicate omnipotence, omniscience, and perfection of Him, we are using the three words in the vaguest sense (6.508-509). We must not take the word "perfection" here to imply anything specifically moral (for God is surely above all self-restraint or law), but to imply "aesthetic spiritual perfection" (6.510).

Summing up, then, the nature of God for Peirce is represented in an essentially vague conception of an *Ens Necessarium:* the Supreme Creator of all that has been, is, or will be; a perfect, omniscient, omnipotent spiritual Being; a transcendent Person, whose relation to the world is that of infinite love. Although outside time, God is not without a kind of development whereby He comes to reveal Himself in the progressive evolution of the cosmos.

Since some philosophers will pronounce this conception to be a figment, Peirce's next task is to try and show that it signifies a reality. But how is this to be done? Certain methods have to be ruled out immediately. Pure deductive argument is useless; and scientific method, with its emphasis on prediction and experiment, is inapplicable. The belief in God's reality can therefore only be fixed by non-rational means. Peirce actually employs three such means: (1) the appeal to feeling or instinct, (2) the appeal to direct perception, and (3) the appeal to a mode of thought which he calls "musement." It is to be noted that he speaks of the *reality* rather than the *existence* of God, because "to exist" means for him "to react with other like things in the environment." In that sense, to say that God "exists" would be fetichism (6.495). What we wish to establish is His reality, or total independence of the thought of any human beings.

1. The most secure basis for a belief in God is immediate feeling or instinct. "An appeal to one's own instinct . . . is to argument what substance is to shadow, what bed-rock is to the built foundations of a cathedral" (6.503). When we first awake to reflective thought we find the idea of God already present in our minds. It is there as a strong, satisfying, instinctive belief. Everybody initially accepts it, as they do other common-sense notions. But if they begin to reason about it they will inevitably run into difficulties, for the simple reason that the moment you try to render precise the vague conceptions of common sense, you change them. This is the error into which the sceptical scientists have fallen. They think that because the belief in God cannot be given an exact formulation, it is therefore unfounded (6.496). What an absurd conceit! The plain man who trusts to his natural sentiments, and accepts the belief as it arises spontaneously in his heart, is on far more solid ground (6.486). Similarly, "we, one and all of us, have an instinct to pray; and this fact constitutes an invitation from God to pray" (6.516). It, like the idea of God, should be accepted, not merely because of its origin, but because it is a source of "great spiritual good and moral strength" (*ibid.*).

2. For those who have eyes to see, an immediate perception of God's reality is possible. When we gaze at the living spontaneity and manifoldness of the world, we are enjoying "a direct, though darkling, perception of God" (6.613). Likewise, when we open our heart, "which is also a perceptive organ," we see Him (6.493). This is what we

should expect, for from what other source could our idea of God come "if not from direct experience" (*ibid*)? How is it, then, that the reality of this Being can be doubted by anyone? "The only answer that I can at present make," Peirce declares, "is that facts that stand before our face and eyes and stare us in the face are far from being, in all cases, the ones most easily discerned" (6.162). At any rate, once a man *has* discerned them, he has "as good reason—putting aside metaphysical subtilties—to believe in the living personality of God as he has to believe in his own. Indeed, *belief* is a word inappropriate to such direct perception." (6.436)

3. In an article entitled "A Neglected Argument for the Reality of God," published in the *Hibbert Journal* for 1908, Peirce develops his doctrine of "musement." This is the name he gives to "a certain agreeable occupation of mind" which he thinks is not as commonly practiced as it deserves to be. In consists in casting aside all serious purpose and allowing one's thoughts to drift about freely. Such an attitude is not like reverie, a vacant or dreamy state. On the contrary, it is akin to "pure play . . . a lively exercise of one's powers" (6.458). As the muser lets his thoughts play over the subject of the breadth, depth, and unspeakable variety of the cosmos, with its myriad inter-connections and homogeneities, and then drifts to a contemplation of the vast panorama of evolution, "the idea of God's Reality will be sure sooner or later to be found an attractive fancy, which the Muser will develop in various ways. The more he ponders it, the more it will find response in every part of his mind, for its beauty, for its supplying an ideal of life, and for its thoroughly satisfactory explanation of his whole threefold environment" (6.465). The result will be the production of a truly religious belief in His reality and His nearness (6.486). But since any process of thought which tends to produce a definite belief is an argument (6.456), we have here a "humble argument" for God's reality, open to every honest man. On the whole, it has probably made more worshippers than any other (6.486).

Now the "neglected argument" to which Peirce alludes in the title of his essay consists in showing "that the humble argument is the natural fruit of free meditation, since every heart will be ravished by the beauty and adorability of the Idea, when it is so pursued" (6.487). Were theologians prepared to take this seriously, they could make a very strong case for the belief in God as "a fundamental ingredient" of the soul of man. Any such theological elaboration would, of course, lack the religious vitality of the "humble argument." We should have simply "a vindicatory description" of the manner in which that argument actually functions in the lives of human beings. But the result would be a theology having a far closer relevance to religion than is usually the case.

There is a further side to this matter which Peirce considers important. When viewed in relation to logical methodeutic, the "humble argument" appears as an instance of the initial stage of all scientific inquiry—"the stage of observing the facts, or variously rearranging them, and of pondering them until, by their reactions with the results of previous scientific experience, there is 'evolved' (as the chemists word it) an explanatory hypothesis" (6.488). That is to say, the belief in God is an example of abductive inference. Yet it differs from the general run of abductions in three respects. (i) The hypothesis has a vastly greater initial plausibility than other deliberately formed hypotheses. Indeed, "so hard is it to doubt God's Reality, when the Idea has sprung from Musements, that there is great danger that the investigation will stop at this stage, owing to the indifference of the Muser to any further proof of it" (*ibid.*). (ii) The hypothesis, unlike those formulated in science, has to remain so vague that no determinate, experiential consequences which can be put to the test are derivable from it. "How, for example, can we ever expect to be able to predict what the conduct would be, even of an omniscient being, governing no more than one poor solar system for only a million years or so? How much less if, being also omnipotent, he be thereby freed from all experience, all desire, all intention!" (6.489) (iii) Nevertheless, the hypothesis has a commanding and most beneficial effect upon the whole conduct of life of those who adopt it. This more than counteracts the deficiency noted under (ii), especially in the eyes of a pragmaticist (6.490).

Granting the similarity between musement and abductive inference, it is still not possible to establish in this way the truth of the belief in God's reality. For even in empirical science abduction is not a process which validates hypotheses; it simply presents them *for* validation, *via* induction. Consequently, the most we can say is that just as an enormous number of the hypotheses spontaneously suggested in abduction have subsequently been verified, so in the case of this one its very "naturalness" is an argument of no small weight in favor of its truth—despite the fact that the latter cannot be experientially confirmed. Yet at bottom Peirce set little store by such considerations. They represent but a momentary intrusion of his natural-

ism into a domain that is alien to it. "One cannot logically infer the
existence of God; one can only know Him by direct perception"
(6.613). His reality is so fully certified by the heart that the head can
add nothing vital to the belief. This is the final verdict of Peirce's transcendentalism.

It will be appropriate here to give a specific illustration of the
quasi-mystical vein in Peirce, to which I have already referred. The
illustration is taken from a passage in which he is describing his own
experience with the process of musement.

I have often occasion to walk at night, for about a mile, over an entirely
untravelled road, much of it between open fields without a house in sight.
The circumstances are not favorable to severe study, but are so to calm
meditation. If the sky is clear, I look at the stars in the silence, thinking
how each successive increase in the aperture of a telescope makes many
more of them visible than all that had been visible before. The fact that
the heavens do not show a sheet of light proves that there are vastly more
dark bodies, say planets, than there are suns. They must be inhabited, and
most likely millions of them with beings much more intelligent than we are.
For on the whole the solar system seems one of the simplest; and presumably under more complicated phenomena greater intellectual power will be
developed. What must be the social phenomena of such a world! . . . Let
a man drink in such thoughts as come to him in contemplating the physico-
psychical universe without any special purposes of his own; especially the
universe of mind which coincides with the universe of matter. The idea of
there being a God over it all of course will be often suggested; and the
more he considers it, the more he will be enwrapt with Love of this idea.
He will ask himself whether or not there really is a God. If he allows
instinct to speak, and searches his own heart, he will at length find that
he cannot help believing it. I cannot tell how every man will think. I know
the majority of men, especially educated men, are so full of pedantries . . .
that they cannot think straight about these things. But I can tell how a man
must think if he is a pragmatist. (6.501)

7. GOD AND THE WORLD

We have on several occasions caught a glimpse of Peirce's opinions
about the relation of God to the world. It is now time to attempt an
orderly presentation of these opinions, so far as the textual evidence
makes this possible.

In the strict sense of the term, God is the only Being who is fully
real (2.532). Created things have degrees of reality but fall short of
perfection. Prior to the creation of the universe God was in some
obscure way identical with the ideal world of boundless possibility
from which the actual world has grown; for "the starting-point of the

Universe, God the Creator, is the Absolute First" (1.362). Once qualities, along with space and time, become actual, the world exists as something other than God. He is not immanent in but is perpetually creating it (5.496). This process is the one metaphysics designates as "cosmic evolution." Hence, "a genuine evolutionary philosophy . . . is so far from being antagonistic to the idea of a personal creator that it is really inseparable from that idea" (6.157). And the far-off divine event towards which evolution moves is God completely revealed.

Among created things, human beings appear as the "children of God" (1.316). His relation to us is that of a Father who loves, and therefore undertakes to educate, His offspring. "In general, God is perpetually creating us, that is developing our real manhood, our spiritual reality. Like a good teacher, He is engaged in detaching us from a False dependence upon Him." (6.507) Naturally, it is impossible for us to understand the details of this process. "We do not know his inscrutable purposes, nor can we comprehend his plans" (1.143). All we know with certainty is that He loves us. Of that we are assured through our "direct perception of" and our "personal communication with" Him (6.162). Consequently, no matter what agitations or calamities may afflict the individual, he must remain firm in the faith that all is for the best. "Though his desperate struggles should issue in the horrors of his rout, and he should see the innocents who are dearest to his heart exposed to torments, frenzy and despair, destined to be smirched with filth, and stunted in their intelligence, still he may hope that it be best *for them,* and will tell himself that in any case the secret design of God will be perfected through their agency; and even while still hot from the battle, will submit with adoration to His Holy will" (6.479).

Yet man, like a wayward child, frequently refuses to obey the law of love which God has decreed for His creatures. Peirce sees this refusal concretely exemplified in the commercial civilization which surrounds him. It is characterized by "the worship of business, the life in which the fertilizing stream of genial sentiment dries up or shrinks to a rill of comic tit-bits" (1.673). Aided and abetted by the economists, the belief has developed that "greed is the great agent in the elevation of the human race and in the evolution of the universe" (6.290). Intelligence brought into the service of greed, it is urged, will guarantee the justest prices, the fairest contracts, and the most socially beneficial conduct. Those who denounce the "atrocious villanies" of this doctrine are dubbed "sentimentalists," among whom

Peirce proudly includes himself (6.292). For a sentimentalist is one who accepts the teaching of Christ, that "progress comes from every individual merging his individuality in sympathy with his neighbors," in contradistinction to those who believe "that progress takes place by virtue of every individual's striving for himself with all his might and trampling his neighbor under foot whenever he gets a chance to do so" (6.294). No society organized on the basis of the latter doctrine, Peirce contends, can escape eventual ruin. In a prophetic passage he declares that "the Gradgrind banner has been this century long flaunt-ing in the face of heaven, with an insolence to provoke the very skies to scowl and rumble. Soon a flash and quick peal will shake economists quite out of their complacency, too late. The twentieth century, in its latter half, shall surely see the deluge-tempest burst upon the social order—to clear upon a world as deep in ruin as that greed-philosophy has long plunged it into guilt." (6.292) Thus will mankind be chas-tised for its flagrant denial of the Divine law of love.

Another aspect of God's relation to the world may be seen in the life of reason. From this perspective, the universe "is a vast represen-tamen, a great symbol of God's purpose, working out its conclusions in living realities" (5.119). Now every symbol has attached to it cer-tain indices of reactions and icons of qualities. The part such qualities and reactions play in an inference made by a human being is identical with the part they play in nature as a whole. That is to say, the uni-verse is a gigantic argument of which man grasps but a few of the inferential steps. This vast logical process has an important esthetic side. For "the Universe as an argument is necessarily a great work of art, a great poem . . . just as every true poem is a sound argument" (*ibid.*). Perhaps it would be more apt to compare it with a painting. Every quality in a premiss is like an elementary colored particle in the painting. The sum of these particles produces "the intended Quality that belongs to the whole as whole. That total effect is beyond our ken; but we can appreciate in some measure the resultant Quality of parts of the whole." (*Ibid.*) The laws which prevail throughout the universe are best interpreted as ideas or resolutions in the Divine consciousness (5.107), so that of the three modes of being, actuality seems to be the only one alien to Him. Yet even it will ultimately become subject to His will, since "God completely revealed, is the Absolute Second" (1.362).

Are there any grounds for believing that He ever alters the course of events, or causes the laws of nature to be violated in individual

cases? Have miracles occurred, and do they still occur? In his brief
examination of this question Peirce expresses the following views.
(*a*) No decision on it can be reached by *a priori* arguments, as Hume
quite properly pointed out. The issue can only be settled by appealing
to evidence (6.514). (*b*) We have no conclusive evidence for the
happening of any miracle, past or present; and in the existing state
of scientific knowledge, such a thing seems "altogether improbable"
(2.750). Even the evidence for the miracles of Jesus is unconvincing
to a modern mind, "unless the general divinity of the Christian religion
be assumed" (6.538). (*c*) Yet science can no more categorically deny
miracles than it can assert them (1.90). Hume's argument against
them in his *Enquiry* failed to attain its objective, and was less adequate
philosophically than Bishop Butler's defense of them in his *Analogy*.
The definition Hume virtually *uses* (in contrast to the one he gives)
"is that a miracle is something the like of which has never been known
to happen" (6.537). In that sense can we be certain no miracles happen nowadays? "I do not feel so sure of it," Peirce declares (6.514).
What about the surprising developments with which the history of
science is studded, such as Becquerel's chance discovery of radio-
activity? What about the extraordinary manner in which men of genius
crop up quite unexpectedly in the course of civilization? These occurrences are just as unique and isolated as any miracle could be. No;
the only sound conclusion is that from the standpoint of science the
whole question is an open one. (*d*) But from the standpoint of religion the case is different. Here "it seems plain . . . that miracles are
intrinsic elements of a genuine religion" (6.446). What reason is unable to deny at the level of theory, faith may legitimately affirm in
the interests of practice.

8. FREEDOM AND IMMORTALITY

The two remaining subjects that come within the purview of religious metaphysics, Freedom and Immortality, may be dealt with
together. It is not difficult to forecast the kind of thing Peirce will say
about them, when we bear in mind his previous discussion of necessitarianism on the one hand, and of the nature of the self on the other.[6]

His early comments on freedom have a slightly different emphasis
from those which occur after 1880. Prior to that date he accepted the
doctrine of determinism as true of the realm of physical events
(cf. 5.539 n.), but did not accept it as true of psychical events. Hence,

[6]Cf. chap. vii, sec. 3; chap. ix, sec. 5.

his concern at this time was to show that there need be nothing paradoxical in admitting both "fate" and "freedom." After he rejected
physical determinism, he limited himself to insisting on the genuine-
ness of our experience of freedom in voluntary action, against the
wholly unwarranted dogma of the necessitarians.

In the course of his paper on "How to Make Our Ideas Clear,"
Peirce remarks that "the question of free-will and fate in its simplest
form, stripped of verbiage, is something like this: I have done something of which I am ashamed; could I, by an effort of the will, have
resisted the temptation, and done otherwise?" (5.403). The philosophical reply is that we have here not a question of fact, but a question of the formulation of certain propositions. The moralist says: "If
you had resisted the temptation, you could have done otherwise." The
determinist, on the contrary, declares: "Even if you had resisted the
temptation, you could not have done otherwise." Now it is usually
assumed that one of these propositions must be true and the other
false. But a little reflection will convince us that since both are conditional propositions, and since a conditional proposition can *only* be
false when its antecedent is true, the two propositions in question
must both be true. For in each case the antecedent is "a false supposition"; and there can be no objection to contradictory consequences
following from such a supposition (*ibid.*). The proposition asserted
by the determinist and the proposition asserted by the indeterminist
"are perfectly consistent, and only serve to reduce the supposition
that you did not try to an absurdity" (5.339). Peirce has no intention
of suggesting that both sides in this controversy are right. Indeed, he
thinks the determinists make statements which are quite unproven,
such as "that every act of will is determined by the strongest motive"
(5.339 n.). What he does intend to affirm is that the question whether
a man *could* have taken a line of conduct which in fact he did *not* take,
was "the origin of the whole doubt; that, had it not been for this question, the controversy would never have arisen; and that this question
is perfectly solved in the manner . . . indicated" (5.403).

As soon as he became convinced of the falsity of necessitarianism,
Peirce had no need to "reconcile" it with the belief in free will. For
the latter is only denied by those who are so blinded by a preconceived
theory that they cannot see obvious facts—the most obvious of all being
that everybody *in practice* is conscious of his freedom when he wills
to do a given act. We must not confuse willing with desiring, Peirce
insists. A desire is fully actual the instant it occurs; but willing does

not take place until something is done. Even a man who tries to move an object too heavy for him to stir achieves in large measure what he directly willed to do, namely, to contract certain muscles. Now desire no doubt implies "a tendency to volition, and though it is a natural hypothesis that a man cannot *will* to do that which he has no sort of desire to do, yet we all know conflicting desires but too well, and how treacherous they are apt to be; and a desire may perfectly well be discontented with volition, i.e., with what the man *will* do. The consciousness of that truth seems to me to be the root of our consciousness of free will." (1.331)

Such an admission ought not to cripple in any way the sciences which deal with the physical basis of personality, provided the distinction between the matter and the form of living things is carefully observed. Few people will care to deny that "the existence of an individual man is a totally different thing from the existence of the matter which at any given instant happens to compose him, and which is incessantly passing in and out" (1.220). The man's existence depends on how the material constituents in question are arranged or formed. Freedom may be an attribute of the man as an organized whole, without in the least being an attribute of the *parts* of the whole. Hence, for example, "every action of Napoleon was such as a treatise on physiology ought to describe. He walked, ate, slept, worked in his study, rode his horse, talked to his fellows, just as every other man does. But he combined those elements into shapes that have not been matched in modern times." (4.611) Because physiology can show a necessary cause for each action, it cannot be inferred that Napoleon was lacking in the freedom to choose the direction his career should take.

The highest, and perhaps in the end the sole type of freedom is self-determination or self-control. It seems to be "the capacity for rising to an extended view of a practical subject instead of seeing only temporary urgency. This is the only freedom of which man has any reason to be proud; and it is because love of what is good for all on the whole, which is the widest possible consideration, is the essence of Christianity, that it is said that the service of Christ is perfect freedom." (5.339 n.) In order to achieve such a comprehensive view, man must be guided by reason, not by impulse or desire. He therefore "*can*, or if you please is *compelled*, to make his life more reasonable*. What other distinct idea than that, I should be glad to know, can be attached to the word liberty?" (1.602)

The immortality of the soul was a question in which Peirce reported he had but "slight interest" (6.520). A philosopher who not merely rejects the conception of mind as a spiritual substance but also regards the empirical phenomenon of selfhood as wholly ephemeral, can scarcely be expected to excite himself over the problem of surviving bodily death. There is one sense, of course, in which immortality has to be admitted by everyone. "A man of character leaves an influence living after him. It is living: it is personal. In my opinion, it is quite proper to call that a future life. Jesus so spoke of it when he said he would always be with us. It is in some respects more fit to be made the subject of a promise than any other kind of future life." (6.519) But this is not the kind of immortality which concerns the plain man. What he wishes to know is whether "after death we shall retain or recover our individual consciousness, feeling, volition, memory, and, in short . . . all our mental powers unimpaired" (6.548).

Now we may approach this question from two very different standpoints. The first is a purely theoretical one in which we seek the verdict of science on the matter. Here we shall find, Peirce affirms, that the evidence is highly unfavorable to any form of personal survival. The unanimous verdict of the biological sciences is that there exists an intimate dependence "of healthy mind-action upon the state of the body. There are, also, those rare cases of double consciousness where personal identity is utterly destroyed or changed, even in this life. If a man or woman, who is one day one person, another day another, is to live hereafter, pray tell me which of the two persons that inhabit the one body is destined to survive?" (6.551) Even common sense is coming to reject the doctrine that the soul is able to endure apart from its animal body. Reflection on the most familiar occurrences of life, such as sleep, faintings, bodily illness, insanity, etc., inevitably points to that conclusion (6.577-578).

Has psychical research anything to contribute to the discussion? Peirce refers in this connection to the work by Gurney, Myers, and Podmore, *Phantasms of the Living*, which, among other things, purports to establish the fact of telepathic communication. The authors' most impressive arguments "are based upon the doctrine of probabilities," Peirce comments, "and these I have examined with care. I am fully satisfied that these arguments are worthless, partly because of the uncertainty and error of the numerical data, and partly because the authors have been astonishingly careless in the admission of cases ruled out by the conditions of the argumentation." (6.549) Furthermore, even if we were to accept the apparitions of spiritualism at their face value, what would they prove? Nothing particularly cheerful.

"These ghosts and spirits exhibit but a remnant of mind. Their stupidity is remarkable. They seem like the lower animals. If I believed in them, I should conclude that, while the soul was not always at once extinguished on the death of the body, yet it was reduced to a pitiable shade, a mere ghost, as we say, of its former self." (6.550)

Another thing that may lead us to doubt the reality of apparitions, Peirce remarks with sly humor, is their painful solemnity. They don't behave in the way we should expect disembodied spirits to behave.

I fancy that, were I suddenly to find myself liberated from all the trials and responsibilities of this life, my probation over, and my destiny put beyond marring or making, I should feel as I do when I find myself on an ocean steamer, and know that for ten days no business can turn up, and nothing can happen. I should regard the situation as a stupendous frolic, should be at the summit of gayety, and should only be too glad to leave the vale of tears behind. Instead of that, these starveling souls come mooning back to their former haunts, to cry over spilled milk. (*Ibid.*)

It seems plain, then, that the evidence collected by psychical research for any kind of personal survival is negligible. This is not to say that such research should be discountenanced. On the contrary, it "should receive every encouragement." For "scientific men, working in something like scientific ways, must ultimately reach scientific results" (6.587). But at present the doctrine of immortality can gain no support from that quarter. "In short," Peirce concludes, "the utter unlikeness of an immortal soul to anything we cannot doubt, and the slightness of all the old arguments [for] its existence, appear to me to have tremendous weight" (6.552).

Yet this whole matter must also be appraised from the standpoint of practice. Here, we may properly call attention to the inconclusiveness of the evidence purporting to *disprove* the doctrine of immortality. Take just a single point. "When a part of the brain is extirpated we find the result is that certain faculties are lost. But after a time they are recovered. How can this be? The answer given is that other parts of the brain learn to perform these functions. But after all, we do not know more than that if anything happens to the hemispheres, memory is deranged. It is a most wonderful thing if all we remember is really preserved in the cells of the cerebrum." (6.520) We are still so much in the dark about the physiological and psychological aspects of the human mind, that a man would be foolish to permit scientific considerations to affect his religious beliefs. He should say to himself: "If I am in another life it is sure to be most interesting; but I cannot imagine how it is going to be with *me*. . . . Beyond that, I simply am content to be in God's hands." (6.519)

This brings to a close our account of Peirce's transcendentalism. Its speculative breadth and originality, together with its vigorous affirmation of traditional doctrines, give it a distinctive place among the metaphysical constructions of occidental philosophy. Where it suffers by comparison with such works as Spinoza's *Ethics* and McTaggart's *The Nature of Existence* is in its lack of logical "connective tissue." In this respect it is a mere torso; or rather, it is like a vast mountain range seen afar off through the mists. At crucial points the details are wholly lacking. That is why one can sympathize with Morris Cohen's judgment, when he said of Peirce's speculative philosophy: "I am certain that he never could have completed this work, i.e. I cannot in my own imagination see how the various lines of his thought can be made to meet."[7] One can also understand how Chief Justice Holmes could write, after he had finished reading the essays reprinted in *Chance, Love and Logic* (1923): "I feel Peirce's originality and depth—but he does not move me greatly—I do not sympathize with his pontifical self-satisfaction. He believes that he can, or could if you gave him time, explain the universe. He sees cosmic principles when I should not dare to see more than the limit of our capacities, and his reasoning in the direction of religion &c., seems to me to reflect what he wants to believe—in spite of his devotion to logic."[8]

If the position I have taken in the present study is sound, the unfinished character of Peirce's transcendentalism is what one would expect to find. For the construction of a "system" of philosophy was not his primary intellectual concern. He makes this plain repeatedly in private correspondence with his brother "Jem," with Mrs. Ladd-Franklin, with William James, and with various other people. "The only thing I have ever striven to do in philosophy," he wrote to James in 1909, "has been to analyze sundry concepts with exactitude, . . . that being my only claim to consideration."[9] Yet side by side with this naturalistic motif was his transcendentalism which, although less powerful, attracted him to speculative metaphysics *malgré lui*. In the next and concluding chapter I shall discuss some of the possible sources of these conflicting tendencies, in the circumstances of his life and thought.

[7] *Journal of Philosophy, Psychology and Scientific Methods*, vol. XIII (1916), p. 727.

[8] Quoted from "The Holmes-Cohen Correspondence," edited with a foreword by F. M. Cohen, *Journal of the History of Ideas*, vol. IX (1948), p. 34.

[9] Quoted in R. B. Perry, *The Thought and Character of William James* (Boston, 1935), vol. II, p. 438.

XI

PEIRCE'S CAREER

1. PURPOSE OF THE PRESENT CHAPTER

THE considerations advanced in Parts One and Two are the evidence on which my interpretation of Peirce must rest. Since, however, the interpretation has been put forward as a hypothesis, some weight will be added to it if it can be shown to have an antecedent probability. This is what I shall endeavor to do in the remaining pages. Taking for granted the principle that a philosopher's temperament determines in large measure his basic assumptions, and that his temperament is in turn a result of inherited characteristics together with environmental influences, I shall raise the following question. Is it at all *likely* that Peirce's background, training, personal associations, and mental development could have been the source of opposite tendencies in his thought? The answer, I believe, will prove to be in the affirmative. The circumstances of his life were such as to encourage, if not to cause, both naturalistic and transcendental elements in his philosophy.

To support this contention it will be necessary to review those aspects of his environment and personal career which have a bearing on the tendencies in question. No attempt will be made, of course, to produce a history of American philosophy in the nineteenth century, or to write a biography of Peirce himself.[1] I shall merely single out the more important influences to which he was subject, and try to show their relevance to the interpretation which has been given.

[1] The former of these tasks has now been definitively accomplished in Herbert W. Schneider's *A History of American Philosophy* (New York, 1946), chaps. v-viii; the latter is something yet to be done. The best short account of Peirce's life is the article by Paul Weiss in the *Dictionary of American Biography*, vol. XIV. Mr. Feibleman also deals with this subject in *An Introduction to Peirce's Philosophy* (New York, 1946), chap. i. I am particularly indebted to Professor Weiss's excellent article for factual information.

2. BACKGROUND AND TRAINING

Peirce came of a family with a marked aptitude for mathematics and exact reasoning. His father was Professor of Mathematics at Harvard College for almost half a century, and had much to do with the development of the science in America during his lifetime. An older brother James, and a third cousin, Benjamin Osgood Peirce, also taught mathematics at Harvard for a number of years. Charles seems to have possessed the family aptitude in fullest measure. Appearing first in the form of a youthful interest in puzzles, card tricks, code languages, etc., it matured under the tutelage of his father, so that the latter expected his son to surpass him in mathematics. It is reported that J. J. Sylvester, the most distinguished mathematician in the country at the time, spoke of Charles as "a far greater mathematician than his father." But the son's gifts were destined to be employed, as we have seen, in the analysis of the basic conceptions of mathematics, logic, and philosophy.

Charles's analytical powers were strengthened by the training received from his father. "He educated me," Charles once wrote, "and if I do anything it will be his work." Benjamin Peirce was a man of strong intellect and character, deeply versed in the sciences, and a lover of poetry and the arts. The impression he left on his students was an indelible one. In the case of his son, however, he employed somewhat Spartan methods of education. Thus, while Charles was still of tender age, he was given a table of logarithms, with one example of how to use it to find the logarithm of a number, and another to illustrate the multiplication of numbers by logarithms. Beyond that the boy had to fend for himself in the matter. Desiring to teach his son the art of concentration, Peirce senior would from time to time play rapid games of double-dummy with him—beginning at 10 P.M. and lasting until sunrise! Every error made was subjected to sharp criticism as the games proceeded. This exercise may have helped Charles to develop the remarkable powers of endurance which he retained throughout life, and which enabled him to work at his desk for many hours every day.

When he began in his teens to read the works of the philosophers, his father would induce him to repeat some of their demonstrations, "and in a very few words would usually rip them up and show them empty. In that way the bad habits of thinking that would otherwise have been indelibly impressed upon me by these mighty powers, were,

I hope, in some measure, overcome." (3.405) He goes on to relate that at the time the *Critique of Pure Reason* was looming large in his studies, "my father . . . pointed out to me lacunae in Kant's reasoning which I should probably not otherwise have discovered" (1.560). Charles looked back on these lessons in critical thinking with a feeling of gratitude. They led him to conclude that "the best thing for a fledgling philosopher is close companionship with a stalwart practical reasoner" (3.405).

It seems appropriate to connect certain similarities of doctrine, especially in matters of religion, with the influence of the father on the son. At any rate, we find that Benjamin was as staunch a theist as Charles, and for much the same reason. According to report, the former believed in a special adaptation of the human mind to nature, which could only be accounted for by assuming that "the mind of man and that of Nature's God must work in the same channels."[2] He also held it to be unsound for man to reason in detail about religious questions. "In approaching the forbidden limits of human knowledge, it is becoming to tread with caution and circumspection . . . a wise philosophy will beware lest it strengthen the arms of atheism, by venturing too boldly into so remote and obscure a field of speculation as that of the mode of creation which was adopted by the Divine Geometer."[3] There can be little doubt that Charles must have heard such views expressed in the household; though, since the family was Unitarian, theology can scarcely have bulked large in its conversation.

Another side of the boy's personality that developed with his father's encouragement was his sensory and esthetic discrimination. Delicacy of palate was particularly stressed; so much so, that Charles once placed himself for two months "at monstrous expense" under the tutelage of a *sommelier,* and became a competent wine-taster. The affective dimension of his existence was of deep interest to him. In the Harvard lectures on pragmatism he speaks about the systematic course of training he has undergone in discriminating his feelings. "I have worked with intensity for many hours a day every day," he says, "to train myself to this; and it is a training which I would recommend to all of you" (5.112). The predominance of the category of feeling in his thought, as well as the subtleties of his phenomenological analysis,

[2] Cf. *Benjamin Peirce (1809-1880),* by Various Hands (Oberlin, Ohio, Mathematical Association of America, 1925), p. 6.
[3] *Astronomical Journal,* vol. II (1851), p. 19. Quoted in the *Dictionary of American Biography,* vol. XIV, article on "Benjamin Peirce."

are undoubtedly connected with his interest in the affective aspect of experience.

Such training was superimposed on a nature already ardent and even sentimental. For Charles not only inherited superlative intellectual powers, but also intense emotions. In later years he regretted that he had been brought up with so loose a rein that these emotions were never wholly mastered. The failure to acquire a sufficient degree of "moral self-control" in his youth caused him to "suffer unspeakably." The tragic implications of this for his personal life need not be touched on here. But we must note one consequence which has a bearing upon our main concern, namely, the conflict he experienced between the dictates of his intellect and those of his instincts or feelings. He makes the point clearly in an autobiographical passage written in 1902. "There are some questions about which I, and I suppose it is the same with every thinking man, find these two voices quite at odds, my reason temperately but decidedly asserting that I ought to act in one way, my instincts, whether hereditary or conventional I cannot tell, most emphatically and peremptorily, though with no pretence to rationality, giving reason the lie" (2.172). The form which this conflict takes in his philosophy has been sufficiently discussed in the preceding chapters.

At about the age of twelve, Charles's lifelong interest in experimental techniques began. On his own initiative he set up a chemical laboratory in which he undertook some fairly complex experiments in qualitative analysis. The experience thus gained served him well, for when, following an A.M. in Mathematics at Harvard, he took his Sc.B. in Chemistry, the latter degree was awarded *summa cum laude,* the first of its kind in the history of the college. He must have continued to research in this field intermittently, since as late as 1892 we hear of him "inventing" a method to prevent injury to goods being bleached by electricity. His knowledge of both inorganic and organic chemistry seems to have been unusually wide.

The other fields in which he familiarized himself with the details of scientific inquiry were astronomy, geodesy, and psychology. During his association with the Harvard Observatory, where he was an assistant for three years, he carried out the investigations published in *Photometric Researches* (1878)—the only book to appear from his pen while he was alive. According to expert judgment it contains material that is still valuable. As a member of the United States Coast Survey from 1861 until about 1891, he not only learned the technique of sur-

veying, but conducted a variety of experiments on the determination
of gravity with the aid of the pendulum.[4] In 1875 he was the first
American delegate to attend an International Geodetic Conference in
Europe, at which he reported his findings. The chief of these was that
pendulum experiments were subject to a hitherto undetected error.
This contention met with great opposition at first; but subsequent inquiry proved that he was right, and at a later conference he received
a vote of thanks and approval. Specialists declared themselves impressed by the originality and precision of his work. While lecturer in
Logic at Johns Hopkins University (1879-84), Peirce collaborated
with Joseph Jastrow in a series of psychological experiments. The results were presented to the National Academy of Sciences in a paper
entitled "On Small Differences in Sensation," published in the
Academy's *Proceedings* for 1884. In the light of his experience in these
fields, it is not surprising that Peirce should say: "I run up my colors
and declare myself scientific specialist" (6.560); or that he could
describe himself as having "inhabited a laboratory from the age of six
until long past maturity" (5.411).

3. PERSONAL ASSOCIATIONS

In addition to the association with his father, which belongs in a
special category, Peirce was influenced by intercourse with other personalities. While still a child, he saw distinguished visitors in his home,
and heard them converse with his parents. Scientists such as Agassiz,
Gibbs, Asa Gray, and Sylvester, as well as literary figures such as
Longfellow, Oliver Wendell Holmes, Margaret Fuller, and Emerson,
were frequent guests of the family. They formed an important part of
the environment in which the boy was reared.

Shortly after he ceased to be an undergraduate, Peirce became
intimate "in a philosophical rather than a personal way," with Chauncey Wright. The latter was known in Cambridge as a mathematician
with strong interests in the philosophy of science. Peirce describes him
as "one of the most acute followers of J. S. Mill" (1.4), having "gone
over" to Mill from the Kantian position of Hamilton (5.64). In fact,
Wright was a vigorous defender of thorough-going naturalism and
empiricism.[5] He and Peirce did battle "almost daily" for a period of

---

[4]See the list of publications in *Chance, Love and Logic*, edited by M. R.
Cohen (New York and London, 1923), pp. 312-13.

[5]Cf. Philip P. Wiener's interesting article, "Chauncey Wright's Defence of
Darwin and the Neutrality of Science," *Journal of the History of Ideas*, vol. VI
(1945), pp. 19-45.

about two years over the relative merits of Mill vs. Kant, and over the philosophical significance of Darwinism. These "mental fisticuffs without gloves" against a strong antagonist were of immense value to Peirce, though he could sometimes refer disparagingly to Wright's intellectual powers.[6] While Peirce's transcendentalism made him regard Wright as an opponent, the two men also had a great deal in common. It is significant, for example, that in indicating his relation to the members of "The Metaphysical Club," Peirce should place himself alongside Wright and James as "men of science, rather scrutinizing the doctrines of the metaphysicians on their scientific side than regarding them as very momentous spiritually" (5.12). After Wright's death in 1875, Peirce proposed to James that they should bring out a memorial volume as a tribute to what they had learned from their old "boxing-master." The association with Wright must, therefore, have helped to strengthen Peirce's naturalism.

Mention of that curiously obscure group, "The Metaphysical Club,"[7] suggests the names of other individuals to whose conversation and ideas Peirce was indebted. One of the "most interested fellows" was the lawyer Nicholas St. John Green, a disciple of Jeremy Bentham. "His extraordinary power of disrobing warm and breathing truth of the draperies of long worn formulas, was what attracted attention to him everywhere. In particular, he often urged the importance of applying Bain's definition of belief as 'that upon which a man is prepared to act.' From this definition, pragmatism is scarce more than a corollary; so that I am disposed to think of him[8] as the grandfather of pragmatism." (5.12)   A somewhat more aloof member of the "Club" was F. E. Abbot, for whose book *Scientific Theism* (1885) Peirce had profound admiration (cf. 1.20; 4.1; 5.423). Abbot's defense of "scholastic realism" as a necessary presupposition of scientific knowledge, and his teleological or vitalistic version of evolution, were doctrines congenial to Peirce's mind.

Among men of his father's generation whose influence Peirce felt were Louis Agassiz and Henry James senior. The former, with whom Peirce studied for a few months (1.205 n.), was a bitter enemy of

[6]Thus, in a letter to James in 1909, Peirce speaks of "that acute but shallow fellow, Chauncey Wright, whom I only availed myself of as a whetstone of wits." Quoted in R. B. Perry, *The Thought and Character of William James* (Boston, 1935), vol. II, p. 439.

[7]Cf. Philip P. Wiener, "Peirce's Metaphysical Club and the Genesis of Pragmatism," *Journal of the History of Ideas*, vol. VII (1946), pp. 1-16.

[8]Does the "him" refer to Bain or to Green?

Darwinism. He declared it far more likely that species had arisen through successive acts of creation on the part of the Supreme Being, than through a purely natural process of evolution. Indeed, he considered the diverse orders of species to be thoughts in the Creator's mind, owing their survival or extinction to His plan for the cosmos. These ideas were expressed in Agassiz's *Essay on Classification* which, as we have seen, Peirce regarded highly and used in his own classification of the sciences. On various occasions he held conversations with Henry James senior, the Swedenborgian (cf. 4.402 n.), and deeply pondered his books.[9] *Substance and Shadow*, Peirce thought, contained the "obvious" and "everlasting" solution of the problem of evil (6.287; 6.507). Other ideas which occur in Henry James and reoccur in Peirce are, the doctrine of the "sheer and abject phenomenality of selfhood in man," the conception of God as "infinite Love," the view of cosmic evolution as a process of Divine creation, and the belief in the reality of a "spiritual world."[10] Both Agassiz and Henry James, then, served to encourage Peirce's transcendentalism.

Of his younger contemporaries, William James was the only one with whom Peirce became unreservedly intimate. The personal relations between the two men, as well as the philosophical influence of Peirce on James, have been fully discussed in Professor Perry's study.[11] Our interest here is in the extent to which James may have influenced Peirce. So far as positive doctrine is concerned the latter appears to owe almost nothing to the former. But it is probable that the stimulation of James's conversation and writing led Peirce to sharpen the formulation of many of his own ideas. This is particularly true with regard to the pragmatic maxim (cf. 5.3; 5.414). James's predilection for nominalism, pluralism, and individualism may have had the effect of causing Peirce (by way of reaction) to accentuate his scholastic

---

[9] Henry James's *The Secret of Swedenborg: Being an Elucidation of His Doctrine of the Divine Natural Humanity* was reviewed sympathetically in the *North American Review* for April, 1870, pp. 463-68. Although unsigned, the article is attributed to "C. S. Peirce" by Austin Warren in his *The Elder Henry James* (New York, 1934), p. 264, and the internal evidence goes far to support this. Peirce speaks of the work as presenting "some very interesting and impressive religious views"; and adds, "to many a man who cannot fully understand it, it will afford, as it has us, much spiritual nutriment."

[10] Cf. William James, Introduction to *The Literary Remains of Henry James* (Boston, 1885), pp. 69, 36 n., 37; and Henry James, Sr., *The Social Significance of Our Institutions* (Boston, 1861), *passim*. Relevant quotations are also given in Schneider, *A History of American Philosophy*, pp. 306-7 and 332.

[11] *The Thought and Character of William James*, especially vol. I, chap. XXXII and vol. II, chaps. LXXV and LXXVI.

realism, his monism, and his social theory of reality. Intellectually, the friends were at opposite poles and had great difficulty in understanding one another. Emotionally, they were by no means unlike, as may be seen in the kinship of many of their views on religion. James, with his keen psychological insight, detected "the genuine vein of sentiment and softness" beneath Peirce's rather cold exterior.[12] Peirce, on the other hand, though he could be severely critical of James's lapses from sound logic, entertained a deep affection for him as an individual. "Who, for example, could be of a nature so different from his as I? He so concrete, so living; I a mere table of contents, so abstract, a very snarl of twine. Yet in all my life I have found scarce any soul that seemed to comprehend, naturally, not my concepts, but the mainspring of my life better than he did. He was even greater in the practice than in the theory of psychology." (6.184)

The man among his contemporaries who probably understood Peirce's concepts best was Josiah Royce. There was a far closer philosophical affinity between Royce and Peirce than between the latter and William James. When Royce's Gifford Lectures, *The World and the Individual,* were published, Peirce reviewed them very favorably in the pages of the *Nation.*[13] The first review is mainly taken up with showing the close similarity between Royce's metaphysical system and another position, which is a thinly disguised version of the one favored by Peirce himself. Both lead to a conception of an Absolute. About 1903, Peirce wrote a short introduction to his earlier papers, "The Fixation of Belief" and "How to Make Our Ideas Clear," in which he acknowledged "not indeed the Existence, but yet the Reality, of the Absolute, nearly as it has been set forth, for example, by Royce in his *The World and the Individual,* a work not free from faults of logic, yet valid in the main" (5.358 n.). Since this is the first occasion on which Peirce explicitly announces that his theory of inquiry presupposes an Absolute, it seems reasonable to attribute the new doctrine to the ideas of Royce. We know that Peirce was studying *The World and the Individual* at this time, and also that he and Royce held conversations on philosophical matters during Peirce's visits to Cambridge.[14]

---

[12]Cf. *ibid.,* vol. II, p. 117.

[13]The First Series was reviewed in the *Nation,* vol. LXX (1900), and the Second Series in vol. LXXV (1901).

[14]Cf. Perry, *The Thought and Character of William James,* vol. II, pp. 413, 425.

A good deal could be written about the likenesses between Peirce's speculative metaphysics and Royce's absolutism which would reinforce the belief in their mutual influence on one another. Two of the more important points may be mentioned in passing. (*a*) Both men agree that thought has an essential relation to action. But the action concerned is not individual bodily motion; it is a process already intellectualized or generalized in terms of an ultimate purpose ingredient in it. Hence, both make the same criticism of James on this issue. They charge him, in effect, with reducing theory to practice, i.e. with subordinating thought to the exigencies of action in particular, human situations. Such a doctrine Peirce characterized as "a stoical axiom" which appealed to him more at the age of thirty than at the age of sixty (5.3). (*b*) For both Peirce and Royce the ultimate end ingredient in all action is a *moral* end. Even the ostensibly detached investigations of science must be understood in this light. As Royce once put it, "all search for truth is a practical activity, with an ethical purpose."[15] The purpose in question, however, is not man's but God's. It is a transcendent purpose, a *summum bonum*, which expresses the character of the Divine plan being worked out in the cosmos. This kind of pragmatism, as Peirce observed to Mrs. Ladd-Franklin, "has the gratifying effect of encouraging the simplest ideas of religion and anthropomorphic ideas of the Absolute."[16]

4. PHILOSOPHICAL STUDIES

It is rather remarkable that the first two books on philosophy which Peirce studied should symbolize the opposite tendencies in his thought. One of the books was Whateley's *Logic*, the discovery of which proved to be an exciting and decisive experience. Strange though it may seem, the work turned him into a permanent lover of the subject, opened up the domain of logical analysis, and pointed his mind in the direction of semiotic. A few years later, he launched upon "a most painstaking study" of Schiller's *Briefe über die ästhetische Erziehung des Menschen* with his friend Horatio Paine. This turgid product of German roman-

---

[15] *The Philosophy of Loyalty* (New York, 1908), p. 326.

[16] Cf. *Journal of Philosophy, Psychology and Scientific Methods*, vol. XIII (1916), p. 720. Yet Peirce once wrote to James regarding Royce's *The World and the Individual:* "I don't think it very good taste to stuff it so full of the name of God. The Absolute is, strictly speaking, only God in a Pickwickian sense, that is, in a sense that has no effect. Forgive the garrulity that comes of my eremitical life and God bless you!" Quoted in Perry, *The Thought and Character of William James*, vol. II, p. 425.

ticism made an indelible impression upon him. Schiller's stress on the primacy of feeling and sentiment in the life of man undoubtedly influenced Peirce's transcendentalism.

From Schiller came his initial interest in the philosophy of Kant. Before reaching maturity, Peirce tells us, he "devoted two hours a day to the study of Kant's *Critic of the Pure Reason* for more than three years, until I almost knew the whole book by heart, and had critically examined every section of it" (1.4). With the detailed effects of this study on Peirce's thought we cannot be concerned here. But one general effect was to give powerful reinforcement to his naturalism. Kant's rejection of the classical conception of metaphysics as a "speculative science," and his insistence that there can be no genuine knowledge which transcends experience, are reflected in the ideas which we have surveyed in Part One. Peirce saw clearly that "Kant . . . is nothing but a somewhat confused pragmatist" (5.525). For "the Kantist has only to abjure from the bottom of his heart the proposition that a thing-in-itself can, however indirectly, be conceived; and then correct the details of Kant's doctrine accordingly, and he will find himself to have become a Critical Common-sensist" (5.452).

Now the application of the pragmatic maxim to "ontological metaphysics" exposes nearly all its propositions as either "meaningless gibberish" or "downright absurd." "So that all such rubbish being swept away, what will remain of philosophy will be a series of problems capable of investigation by the observational methods of the true sciences" (5.423). Much of Kant's work is precisely along these lines, and for it Peirce has the profoundest admiration. He reminds us that the philosopher of Königsberg "always remained a physicist who had taken up philosophy"—which is the way Peirce thinks of himself (1.7)—and that his "great strength in logical analysis" was akin to the power that can be observed "in all strong scientific intellects."[17] Kant's position as "the King of modern thought" (1.369) is due to the fact that he possessed "in a high degree all seven of the mental qualifications of a philosopher:

1. The ability to discern what is before one's consciousness.
2. Inventive originality.
3. Generalizing power.
4. Subtlety.
5. Critical severity and sense of fact.

[17]*Nation*, vol. LXXV (1902), pp. 209-11.

6. Systematic procedure.
7. Energy, diligence, persistency, and exclusive devotion to philosophy." (1.522)

In short, Kant was a genuine "laboratory philosopher," not a "seminary philosopher" like Fichte, Schelling, or Hegel.

But there were other sides of Kant's work which also influenced Peirce. For instance, he was impressed by the architectonic which underlies the *Critique of Pure Reason*, and he refers with approval to Kant's "universally and justly lauded parallel" between philosophy and a piece of architecture (1.176). Like a great public building whose structure expresses "the depths of the architect's soul," a philosophical doctrine is "meant for the whole people." It is not a private affair intended for the edification of the few, but something public and general, containing "the message with which an age is charged and which it delivers to posterity" (*ibid.*). Moreover, just as a building is drawn in blueprint before its construction is undertaken, so a philosophy needs to be deliberately planned from the beginning (1.177). It is absurd for a thinker to attack his problems piecemeal as they arise in his experience. They can only be properly dealt with if they are considered in the light of a comprehensive system whose features have been determined *a priori*. From Kant, therefore, Peirce's predilection for philosophizing in the grand manner received substantial support. Indeed, the "edifice" he proposed to erect (1.1), owed more than a little to those German metaphysicians whose arguments he judged to have "little weight" (1.5), but whose ways of thinking were deeply ingrained in his nature (1.4).

Peirce's classification of the sciences provides a significant illustration of the effect of architectonic on his thought. We have had occasion to mention this at several previous points in the discussion, but the matter is important enough to be referred to again. It is one thing to conduct an empirical survey of the sciences with a view to tracing their interrelationships. It is quite another thing to set up a hierarchical scheme in which the "superior" sciences hand down principles to the "inferior." The former procedure will yield a provisional map of human inquiry in diverse fields. The latter procedure enables deductive considerations to take precedence over observation, and thus paves the way for non-naturalistic conclusions. Thus, when Peirce describes mathematics as the science which seeks to discover the necessary consequences of abstractly formulated hypotheses, he is giving a factual account of the matter. But when he further characterizes it as the "highest" science, whose principles determine in advance the results of subordinate sciences (e.g., that phenomenology can only find three ultimate categories), he is permitting his architectonic to dictate *a priori* what must be the case. The implications of this for the whole of his transcendentalism have been explored sufficiently above. Those who hold that Peirce's "system" is the heart of his philosophy quite naturally stress the role of his architectonic. Yet we have to remember that he could also write: "An *a priori* philosophy ought not to pronounce in advance upon the truth of anything which is capable of verification or refutation by subsequent experience. But beyond the realm of verification, truth and falsity lose their meanings. Hence the moment a philosopher, upon *a priori* or epistemological grounds, enunciates any proposition whatever as true, we are warned to be upon our guard against some jugglery. Where we have no scientifically observed facts to go upon, the prudent thing is to confess our downright ignorance."[18]

The final aspect of Kant which probably had an influence on Peirce is the doctrine that the moral is superior to the logical faculty in man, or that practical reason has pre-eminence over theoretical reason. For Kant, theoretical reason is limited to the realm of phenomena, whereas practical reason can transcend that realm and put man into touch with the noumenal world. In Peirce, this doctrine takes the form of the dependence of logic upon ethics. Logical or scientific inquiry is not simply action directed towards the resolution of specific problems, by using hypotheses, predictions, and empirical verifications. It is action directed towards the realization of an ultimate end or *summum bonum*. Furthermore, on this approach, a man can only reason logically by identifying himself with the interests of an unlimited community (Kant's "Kingdom of Ends") and abjuring selfish concerns. Hence a moral imperative lies at the basis of sound reasoning.

While we are on this subject, it will be well to summarize sharply the antithesis between Peirce's naturalism and his transcendentalism in regard to it. According to his naturalism, scientific inquiry is a method of fixing beliefs by bringing them into accord with the character of the actual world. This is its purpose and aim. Abstract conceptions such as "truth" and "reality" are defined in terms of the method. The result is the production of certain regulative ideas, such as the notion of the "concordance of an abstract statement with the ideal limit towards

[18]*Ibid.*, vol. LVII (1893), p. 394.

which endless investigation would tend to bring scientific belief"
(Truth), or of "the object represented in the opinion destined to be
ultimately agreed to by all who investigate" (Reality). For his transcendentalism, however, the purpose and aim of scientific inquiry is
the promotion of the *summum bonum*. But our belief in the metaphysical reality of this "ultimate end of all action" cannot be scientifically attested, since inquiry presupposes it. Hence, recourse must be
had to the deliverances of feeling or to *a priori* arguments.

Returning to Peirce's philosophical studies, we learn that he proceeded from Kant "to an admiring study of Locke, Berkeley, and
Hume" (1.560). The lucidity of British thought strongly appealed to
him, for "clearness is the first merit of a philosopher" (6.614). By the
time discussions were being held at "The Metaphysical Club," Peirce's
ideas had acquired "the English accent" (5.12). Of the three thinkers,
Hume influenced him least. When Paul Carus suggested that the doctrines of Peirce and Hume were "closely allied," Peirce was roused to
a vigorous protest. "Never, during the thirty years in which I have
been writing on philosophical questions, have I failed in my allegiance
to realistic opinions . . . while all that Hume has to say is said at the
instance and in the interest of the extremest nominalism" (6.605).
Locke is frequently mentioned with words of praise. Peirce thinks
"the celebrated *Essay Concerning Humane Understanding*" contains
"the first steps in profound analyses" of a great many problems, such,
for example, as the analysis of probability (2.649; 2.696). He declares
that Locke's definition of experience[19] "should be accepted as definite,
and as a landmark that it would be a crime to displace or disturb"
(5.611). The procedure used by Locke to arrive at "those clean definitions that strew the pages of the *Essay*" is an excellent illustration of
the pragmatic principle. This principle is even more apparent in the
work of Berkeley, who "on the whole has more right to be considered
the introducer of pragmatism into philosophy than any other one
man."[20] Both Locke and Berkeley advanced Peirce's interest in semiotic, through their treatment of the relation of thought to signs.

In later years, Peirce developed considerable admiration for the
Scottish thinkers, Reid and Hamilton. He subscribed to their view that
we have a direct perception of the external world (5.539), and considered Reid, in particular, to have a "subtle" and "well-balanced"

---

[19]*Essay concerning Human Understanding*, Bk. II, chap. ɪ, sec. 2.
[20]Perry, *The Thought and Character of William James*, vol. II, p. 425.
Cf. 6.482.

mind (5.444). It was to Reid's common-sense position in philosophy that he declared his adhesion, "under certain inevitable modifications" (*ibid.*). Against the people who dismissed Hamilton as "antiquated," Peirce was wont to argue that his writings are at least as good as those of J. S. Mill, and in the case of the notes on Reid, "are especially worthy of attention" (6.590). Kantianism tinged with common sense was more congenial to Peirce than extreme empiricism.

After studying the British philosophers, he turned next "to Aristotle's *Organon, Metaphysics,* and psychological treatises, and somewhat later derived the greatest advantage from a deeply pondering perusal of some of the works of mediaeval thinkers . . . most especially from John of Duns, the Scot . . . and William of Ockham" (1.650). Although he occasionally calls himself an Aristotelian (1.618; 5.77 n.), Peirce's thought was never significantly affected by the philosophy of the Stagirite. The one doctrine which appears to have taken root in his mind was Aristotle's insistence on the divorce of theoretical science from the concerns of practice. We have observed the place of this doctrine in Peirce's transcendentalism, where it is linked with ideas far more Platonic than Aristotelian. How far the influence of Plato came to him directly from a study of the *Dialogues,*[21] and how far it came indirectly through the doctrines of Duns Scotus, one finds it difficult to say. The laudatory references to Scotus in the *Collected Papers* (e.g. 2.166; 4.28; etc.) are not accompanied by extensive indications of doctrinal indebtedness. We may recall, however, such important points of similarity in the views of the two philosophers as their conception of universals, their treatment of individuation, and their separation of philosophy from religion. Ockham, "beyond question the greatest nominalist that ever lived" (1.29), not only represented for Peirce the powerful challenge of that position, but bequeathed to posterity the "razor" which Peirce judged to be an indispensable weapon for philosophy.

In general, what Peirce admired in the ancients and the scholastics was the thoroughness of their logical analysis. It never occurred to him to advocate a return to their doctrines. Hence, even in the case of Duns Scotus, he says: "If his logic and metaphysics, not slavishly worshipped, but torn away from its mediaevalism, be adapted to modern culture, under continual wholesome reminders of nominalistic criticisms, I am convinced that it will go far toward supplying the

[21]Cf. Editors' note to 1.584.

philosophy which is best to harmonize with physical science. But other conceptions have to be drawn from the history of science and from mathematics." (1.6)   The value which the work of these thinkers has for a modern is due to the fact that they were animated by the true scientific spirit (1.33). They practiced, albeit in a crude and inchoate way, "that Analytic Method to which modern physics owes all its triumphs" (1.64). "They were minute and thorough in their knowledge of such authorities as they had, and they were equally minute and thorough in their treatment of every question which came up" (1.31). That is why a laboratory-philosopher can learn much from the study of their writings. These writings will be vastly more illuminating to him than the efforts of "the whole Hegelian army," who think the analytic method ought to be supplanted "by the 'Historic Method,' which studies complex problems in all their complexity, but which cannot boast any distinguished successes" (1.64).

This brings us to the question of Peirce's relation to Hegel. Here we find an interesting case of attraction and repulsion, arising from the fact that Peirce's transcendentalism drew him towards, while his naturalism drove him away from Hegelianism. He tells us that at the time of his early studies all he knew of Hegel came from one secondary source—Augusto Vera's *Introduction à la philosophie de Hégel* (1855)— which was sufficient to repel him (4.2). By 1868 he had apparently begun to examine the subject at first hand, since a letter by him in the *Journal of Speculative Philosophy* for that year makes specific reference to Hegel's *Werke* (6.626). This was one of two communications on the subject of "being" and "nothing," which the Hegelian editor, Harris, characterized as an impressive statement of the "anti-speculative" position. Peirce was undoubtedly sensitive to the challenge of St. Louis Hegelianism, which was being promulgated by Harris and others in the pages of the *Journal.* Yet he insists that "there was no influence upon me from Hegel, unless it was of so occult a kind as to entirely escape my ken" (5.38).

From the standpoint of naturalism, Hegel's dialectic seems to Peirce simply "the method of inclinations" (5.382 n.). Hence he declares: "My whole method will be found to be in profound contrast to that of Hegel; I reject his philosophy *in toto*" (1.368). The dialectical method "has the defect of not working at all if you think with too great exactitude" (1.544). Such a defect creates havoc, especially in the field of logic. Peirce is therefore able to demonstrate with ease that Hegel's arguments against syllogism depend on an elementary confusion (5.332). He also points out the error involved in Hegel's assumption that from given premises only one conclusion can be drawn. This is simply not the case in the logic of relatives (6.313; 3.396 ff.). Hegel, of course, cannot be blamed for his failure to realize this. But he can be blamed for ignoring the study of mathematics, particularly since he "has for his chief topic the importance of continuity, which was the very idea the mathematicians and physicists had been chiefly engaged in following out for three centuries" (1.41). Consequently, "most of what is true in Hegel is a darkling glimmer of a conception which the mathematicians had long before made pretty clear, and which recent researches have still further illustrated" (6.31). As for the more sweeping conclusions presented in the *Wissenschaft der Logik,* they are wholly nugatory. "I have never met with an attempt to state a transcendental argument with precision which began to convince me. At any rate, when I examine the logics of more or less Hegelian tendency which have appeared in the last quarter of a century, I must decline to allow any weight to such flummery." (2.35)

Yet Peirce confesses that "vague applications" of Hegel's method "recommend themselves to my faith" (*ibid.*). If he does not strictly belong among Hegelians, he is nevertheless "strongly drawn to them" (4.50). There can be no doubt that Hegel is "in some respects the greatest philosopher that ever lived" (1.524). His "plan of evolving everything out of the abstractest conception by a dialectical procedure [is] far from being so absurd as the experientialists think" (1.368). Had he only accorded proper recognition to immediate feeling and brute reaction as ingredients of reality, "pragmaticists might have looked up to him as the great vindicator of their truth" (5.436). Even as matters stand, however, "pragmaticism is closely allied to the Hegelian absolute idealism" (*ibid.*). Thus, Peirce holds that his categories "agree substantially with Hegel's three moments" (2.87). Similarly, the latter's objective logic is the model Peirce has in mind when he elaborates a speculative cosmology (6.214 ff.), and when he argues that signs have a "life" of their own, "so that—the requisite vehicle being present—they will go through a certain order of development" (2.111). No wonder, then, that his transcendentalism can lead him to say: "My philosophy resuscitates Hegel, though in a strange costume" (1.42).

Sometimes Peirce was prepared to identify this costume as the one worn by another post-Kantian, namely, Schelling. "My views were probably influenced by Schelling," he writes to James in 1894, "by all stages of Schelling, but especially by the *Philosophie der Natur.* I consider Schelling enormous; and one thing I admire about him is the freedom from the trammels of system, and his holding himself uncommitted to any previous utterance. In that he is like a scientific man. If you were to call my philosophy Schellingism transformed in the light of modern physics, I should not take it hard."[22] A few of the more familiar ideas of the German thinker which recur in Peirce's transcendentalism are the notion that the laws of Nature are materialized "laws of reason," that Nature is living not mechanical, that matter is "extinct mind," that it is characterized by opposition or polarity, and that the universe is to be understood in terms of an "evolution" towards an ultimate goal. Even the poetic language in which Schelling clothes these ideas is not wholly absent from the *Collected Papers.*

Another facet of this influence which must be mentioned is Peirce's relation to New England Transcendentalism. He was himself aware of the possibility that he had been affected by it.

I may mention, for the benefit of those who are curious in studying mental biographies, that I was born and reared in the neighborhood of Concord— I mean in Cambridge—at the time when Emerson, Hedge, and their friends were disseminating the ideas they had caught from Schelling, and Schelling from Plotinus, from Boehm, or from God knows what minds stricken with the monstrous mysticism of the East. But the atmosphere of Cambridge held many an antiseptic against Concord transcendentalism; and I am not conscious of having contracted any of that virus. Nevertheless, it is probable that some cultured bacilli, some benignant form of the disease, was implanted in my soul, unawares, and that now, after long incubation, it comes to the surface, modified by mathematical conceptions and by training in physical investigations. (6.102)

Without entering upon a detailed discussion, we may note the resemblance between Peirce's transcendentalism and that of the New Englanders in regard to the following points. (*a*) Feeling or sentiment is a sounder guide in practical life than logic. The pronouncements of the heart are to be preferred here to those of the head. (*b*) Yet ideas, being Platonic essences, are more important than actions, since the general has a higher value than the particular. (*c*) The outer world of physical events, no less than the inner world of man's consciousness, is a manifestation of God's presence in the cosmos, the "language" in which His plan is unfolding itself. (*d*) Reality is one not many;

[22]Perry, *The Thought and Character of William James,* vol. II, pp. 415-16. Cf. 6.605.

monism rather than pluralism expresses the ultimate truth about things. (*e*) Evil is not an irreducible component of reality, for all that happens is in conformity with the Divine Nature, and must therefore be good when viewed *sub specie aeternitatis*. In these respects, at least, Peirce was in complete agreement with such a transcendentalist as Emerson.[23]

The final aspect of Peirce's studies which must be touched on has to do with logic. In this field, both his historical and his systematic knowledge were profound. He used Prantl's *Geschichte der Logik im Abendlande* as a guide-book in historical matters. Although his general feeling towards the work was one of gratitude (4.26), he did not hesitate to criticize it harshly (2.218) and even violently (2.323 n.). The more measured criticisms clearly spring from an exact knowledge of the particular texts concerned. The revolutionary developments in logic that were beginning in his own day became known to him through his study of De Morgan's memoir about 1866 (1.562). The following year he read a paper to the American Academy of Arts and Sciences based on the ideas of Boole—then practically unknown to Americans—and made valuable improvements in the Boolean system (cf. 3.1 ff.). His technical contributions to the subject during the next two decades placed him in the front rank of logicians. The excellence of his researches was recognized by Schröder in his compendious *Vorlesungen über die Algebra der Logik*, which more or less summed up the century's developments in the field. Peirce's close examination of this work is revealed in his long paper, "The Logic of Relatives," published in the *Monist* in 1897 (cf. 3.456-552). Well could he say about that time: "I am a logical analyst by long training, you know" (1.160). No man in America, and few men in the world, had a better right to the title.

5. SUMMARY AND CONCLUSION

We may now draw together the diverse considerations reviewed in this chapter, and suggest their relevance to Peirce's philosophical outlook.

The main influences which helped to form his naturalism were: his native capacity for exact thinking and analysis; the intensive training in this activity which he received from his father; his detailed acquaintance with the experimental procedures employed in chemistry,

[23]Cf. Frederick I. Carpenter, "Charles Sanders Peirce: A Pragmatic Transcendentalist," *New England Quarterly*, vol. XIV (1941), pp. 34-48.

astronomy, geodesy, and psychology; his association with scientists working in those fields; discussions with Chauncey Wright and Nicholas St. John Green at the Metaphysical Club; his minute examination of Kant's *Critique of Pure Reason;* his study of the British Empiricists, the Scottish Realists, Aristotle's *Organon,* and the late medieval logicians; his wide knowledge of contemporary works in formal logic, such as those of De Morgan, Boole, Jevons, Schröder, etc., and also in inductive logic, such as those of Whewell, Mill, Venn, etc.

Among the influences which determined his transcendentalism were: a strongly emotional, sensuous nature; a vein of deep religious feeling, akin to mysticism, in his temperament; the religious convictions of his father; personal association with such anti-naturalistic thinkers as Henry James senior, Louis Agassiz, F. E. Abbot, William James, and Josiah Royce; the study of the German romantics, particularly Schiller, Schelling, and Hegel; Kant's architectonic and, to a lesser degree, his moral philosophy; the "climate of opinion" produced by New England Transcendentalism.

In no sense does the above purport to be an exhaustive account of Peirce's mental biography. Still less does it pretend to "explain" his unique and distinctive personality, the living figure who combined these various influences in his written and spoken discourse. There is a striking vignette of the living Peirce contained in one of John Jay Chapman's letters, which is well worth quoting in this connection.

Went to the Century, where I happened to sit down next to Charles Peirce, and stayed talking to him ever since, or rather he talking. He is a most genial man—got down books and read aloud. He began by saying Lincoln had the Rabelais quality. It appears he worships Rabelais. He read passages from Carlyle in a voice that made the building reverberate. He also read from an Elizabethan Thomas Nash—a great genius whom he said Carlyle got his style from, but he is wrong. Nash is better . . . and Peirce read with oriflamme appreciation. He then talked about—plasms—force, heat, light— Boston, Emerson, Margaret Fuller, God, Mammon, America, Goethe, Homer, Silver, but principally science and philosophy—a wonderful evening. It was ask and have, and, and, but that he talked himself positively to sleep with exertion, he would be talking yet, and I have many more things I want to ask him, chiefly Helmholtz. He is a physical mathematician mechanician, that sort of a man of a failed life so far as professional recognition goes, but of acknowledged extraordinary ability, and is positively the most agreeable person in the city. He is a son of old Professor Peirce, is about 55 and is like Socrates in his willingness to discuss anything and his delight in posing things and expressing things. In fact I got to answering him in the style of Plato's dialogues. . . . He has a theory that the laws of mind and matter are the same and he don't believe in the conservation of energy. He explained this at length—and he frightened two or three gentlemen who came near while he was doing it so that they won't come to the Club for a month. They looked at him in wonder, crossed themselves, and went away.[24]

Nothing remotely comparable to this vivid picture is aimed at in the present chapter. All it seeks to do is to establish the antecedent probability of the hypothesis that there are opposite tendencies in Peirce's thought. It is my contention that an independent survey of the broad circumstances of his career suggests the hypothesis as worthy of being put to the test. The positive evidence for it has been assembled in the central part of the book.

If my interpretation is sound, how may we best envisage Peirce's place in the history of American philosophy? It would be presumptuous to offer a dogmatic answer to this question in a paragraph. But I shall hazard the following opinion for what it may be worth. Peirce's subtle, original, and wide-ranging intellect was struggling to break loose from the patterns of thought typical of his own century, and to point the way to the leading conceptions of the next. His naturalism I take to be the measure of his success in this struggle. It is directly "in the general line of growth" of the ideas which dominate the philosophical arena today. That is why it is a major influence in the development which is going on—a development which, as Professor Schneider has conjectured,[25] will doubtless issue in a new tradition whose details are as yet unformulated. But no thinker can emancipate himself completely from the influences of the past or present. Hence, in Peirce's transcendentalism we see the effect of the ideas characteristic of the post-Kantian period in America. I strongly doubt, therefore, whether Peirce is properly regarded as the "founder" of any existing philosophical movement, or whether his significance lies in a comprehensive "system" to which we should return. On the contrary, it is as an enormously rich and stimulating *point de départ* for contemporary thought that I believe he ought to be studied.

This comment would be superfluous were it not that the present enthusiasm for Peirce may end by making him the object of a cult. Nothing could be more out of harmony with the spirit of his philo-

---

[24]*John Jay Chapman and His Letters*, edited by M. A. DeWolfe Howe (Boston, 1937), pp. 94-96.

[25]Cf. *A History of American Philosophy*, p. vii.

sophy, or more repugnant to him personally. As he put it in the draft of a preface to a projected work:

My book will have no instruction to impart to anybody. Like a mathematical treatise, it will suggest certain ideas and certain reasons for holding them true; but then, if you accept them, it must be because you like my reasons, and the responsibility lies with you. Man is essentially a social animal; but to be social is one thing, to be gregarious is another: I decline to serve as bellwether. My book is meant for people who *want to find out;* and people who want philosophy ladled out to them can go elsewhere. There are philosophical soup-shops at every corner, thank God! (1.11)

To approach such a man as though he were an oracle is to show him scant respect. All he asks of his readers is "a high faith in the reality of knowledge, and an intense desire to find things out" (1.14). By studying him in this spirit we not only honor his memory, but we learn to appreciate him as the pioneer that he was. And in so doing, we understand the truth of William James's remark that Peirce "is a gold-mine of ideas for thinkers of the coming generation."

APPENDIX

Peirce's Entry in the Harvard Class Book of 1859

AN amusing sidelight is cast on the youthful Peirce by his entry in the Harvard Class Book of 1859 at the time of his graduation. Permission to reproduce the entry here has been kindly granted by the Custodian of the Harvard University Archives, Dr. C. K. Shipton.

Peirce.

1839

September 10. Tuesday. Born

1840.

Christened

1841

Made a visit to Salem which I distinctly remember

1842

July 31. Went to church for the first time

1843.

Attended a marriage

1844.

Fell violently in love with Miss W and commenced my education

1845

Moved into new house on Quincey St.

1846.

Stopped going to Ma'am Sessions and began to go to Miss Wares —
a very pleasant school where I learnt much and fell violently
in love with another Miss W whom for distinctions Sake
I will designate as Miss W!

1847.

Began to be most seriously and hopelessly in love. Sought to
drown my care by taking up the subject of Chemistry — an
antidote which long experience enables me to recommend as
Sovereign.

1848.

Went to dwell in town with my uncle C. H. Mills and went
to School to the Rev. T. H. Sullivan, where I received my

first lessons in elocution.

1849.

In consequence of playing truant and bathing in the frog-pond, was taken ill. On my recovery, I was recalled to Cambridge and admitted a member of the Cambridge High School.

1850.

Wrote a "History of Chemistry."

1851.

Established a printing-press.

1852.

Joined a debating Society.

1853.

Set up for a fast man and became a bad school-boy.

1854.

Left the High School with honor after having been turned out several times. Worked at Mathematics for about six months and then joined Mr. Dixwell's school in town.

1855.

Graduated at Dixwell's and entered College.
Read Schiller's Æsthetic Letters & began the study of Kant.

1856.

Sophomore. Gave up the idea of being a fast man and undertook the pursuit of pleasure.

1857.

Junior. Gave up the pursuit of pleasure and undertook to enjoy life.

1858.

Senior. Gave up enjoying life and exclaimed "Vanity of vanities!

INDEX OF PROPER NAMES

INDEX OF SUBJECTS

Ah! Peirce was right. His "minuter logic"
Could only avail towards what he sought
As the scrawl on an infant's slate
To a cartoon of Raphael.

Hugh MacDiarmid, *The Divided Bird.*

A CATALOGUE OF SELECTED DOVER BOOKS
IN ALL FIELDS OF INTEREST

A CATALOGUE OF SELECTED DOVER BOOKS
IN ALL FIELDS OF INTEREST

WHAT IS SCIENCE?, *N. Campbell*
The role of experiment and measurement, the function of mathematics, the nature of scientific laws, the difference between laws and theories, the limitations of science, and many similarly provocative topics are treated clearly and without technicalities by an eminent scientist. "Still an excellent introduction to scientific philosophy," H. Margenau in *Physics Today*. "A first-rate primer . . . deserves a wide audience," *Scientific American*. 192pp. 5⅜ x 8.
60043-2 Paperbound $1.25

THE NATURE OF LIGHT AND COLOUR IN THE OPEN AIR, *M. Minnaert*
Why are shadows sometimes blue, sometimes green, or other colors depending on the light and surroundings? What causes mirages? Why do multiple suns and moons appear in the sky? Professor Minnaert explains these unusual phenomena and hundreds of others in simple, easy-to-understand terms based on optical laws and the properties of light and color. No mathematics is required but artists, scientists, students, and everyone fascinated by these "tricks" of nature will find thousands of useful and amazing pieces of information. Hundreds of observational experiments are suggested which require no special equipment. 200 illustrations; 42 photos. xvi + 362pp. 5⅜ x 8.
20196-1 Paperbound $2.00

THE STRANGE STORY OF THE QUANTUM, AN ACCOUNT FOR THE GENERAL READER OF THE GROWTH OF IDEAS UNDERLYING OUR PRESENT ATOMIC KNOWLEDGE, *B. Hoffmann*
Presents lucidly and expertly, with barest amount of mathematics, the problems and theories which led to modern quantum physics. Dr. Hoffmann begins with the closing years of the 19th century, when certain trifling discrepancies were noticed, and with illuminating analogies and examples takes you through the brilliant concepts of Planck, Einstein, Pauli, Broglie, Bohr, Schroedinger, Heisenberg, Dirac, Sommerfeld, Feynman, etc. This edition includes a new, long postscript carrying the story through 1958. "Of the books attempting an account of the history and contents of our modern atomic physics which have come to my attention, this is the best," H. Margenau, Yale University, in *American Journal of Physics*. 32 tables and line illustrations. Index. 275pp. 5⅜ x 8.
20518-5 Paperbound $2.00

GREAT IDEAS OF MODERN MATHEMATICS: THEIR NATURE AND USE, *Jagjit Singh*
Reader with only high school math will understand main mathematical ideas of modern physics, astronomy, genetics, psychology, evolution, etc. better than many who use them as tools, but comprehend little of their basic structure. Author uses his wide knowledge of non-mathematical fields in brilliant exposition of differential equations, matrices, group theory, logic, statistics, problems of mathematical foundations, imaginary numbers, vectors, etc. Original publication. 2 appendixes. 2 indexes. 65 ills. 322pp. 5⅜ x 8.
20587-8 Paperbound $2.25

THE MUSIC OF THE SPHERES: THE MATERIAL UNIVERSE — FROM ATOM TO QUASAR, SIMPLY EXPLAINED, *Guy Murchie*
Vast compendium of fact, modern concept and theory, observed and calculated data, historical background guides intelligent layman through the material universe. Brilliant exposition of earth's construction, explanations for moon's craters, atmospheric components of Venus and Mars (with data from recent fly-by's), sun spots, sequences of star birth and death, neighboring galaxies, contributions of Galileo, Tycho Brahe, Kepler, etc.; and (Vol. 2) construction of the atom (describing newly discovered sigma and xi subatomic particles), theories of sound, color and light, space and time, including relativity theory, quantum theory, wave theory, probability theory, work of Newton, Maxwell, Faraday, Einstein, de Broglie, etc. "Best presentation yet offered to the intelligent general reader," *Saturday Review*. Revised (1967). Index. 319 illustrations by the author. Total of xx + 644pp. 5⅜ x 8½.
21809-0, 21810-4 Two volume set, paperbound $5.00

FOUR LECTURES ON RELATIVITY AND SPACE, *Charles Proteus Steinmetz*
Lecture series, given by great mathematician and electrical engineer, generally considered one of the best popular-level expositions of special and general relativity theories and related questions. Steinmetz translates complex mathematical reasoning into language accessible to laymen through analogy, example and comparison. Among topics covered are relativity of motion, location, time; of mass; acceleration; 4-dimensional time-space; geometry of the gravitational field; curvature and bending of space; non-Euclidean geometry. Index. 40 illustrations. x + 142pp. 5⅜ x 8½.
61771-8 Paperbound $1.35

HOW TO KNOW THE WILD FLOWERS, *Mrs. William Starr Dana*
Classic nature book that has introduced thousands to wonders of American wild flowers. Color-season principle of organization is easy to use, even by those with no botanical training, and the genial, refreshing discussions of history, folklore, uses of over 1,000 native and escape flowers, foliage plants are informative as well as fun to read. Over 170 full-page plates, collected from several editions, may be colored in to make permanent records of finds. Revised to conform with 1950 edition of Gray's Manual of Botany. xlii + 438pp. 5⅜ x 8½.
20332-8 Paperbound $2.50

MANUAL OF THE TREES OF NORTH AMERICA, *Charles Sprague Sargent*
Still unsurpassed as most comprehensive, reliable study of North American tree characteristics, precise locations and distribution. By dean of American dendrologists. Every tree native to U.S., Canada, Alaska; 185 genera, 717 species, described in detail—leaves, flowers, fruit, winterbuds, bark, wood, growth habits, etc. plus discussion of varieties and local variants, immaturity variations. Over 100 keys, including unusual 11-page analytical key to genera, aid in identification. 783 clear illustrations of flowers, fruit, leaves. An unmatched permanent reference work for all nature lovers. Second enlarged (1926) edition. Synopsis of families. Analytical key to genera. Glossary of technical terms. Index. 783 illustrations, 1 map. Total of 982pp. 5⅜ x 8.
20277-1, 20278-X Two volume set, paperbound $6.00

IT'S FUN TO MAKE THINGS FROM SCRAP MATERIALS,
Evelyn Glantz Hershoff
What use are empty spools, tin cans, bottle tops? What can be made from
rubber bands, clothes pins, paper clips, and buttons? This book provides
simply worded instructions and large diagrams showing you how to make
cookie cutters, toy trucks, paper turkeys, Halloween masks, telephone sets,
aprons, linoleum block- and spatter prints — in all 399 projects! Many are easy
enough for young children to figure out for themselves; some challenging
enough to entertain adults; all are remarkably ingenious ways to make things
from materials that cost pennies or less! Formerly "Scrap Fun for Everyone."
Index. 214 illustrations. 373pp. 5⅜ x 8½.   21251-3 Paperbound $1.75

SYMBOLIC LOGIC and THE GAME OF LOGIC, *Lewis Carroll*
"Symbolic Logic" is not concerned with modern symbolic logic, but is instead
a collection of over 380 problems posed with charm and imagination, using
the syllogism and a fascinating diagrammatic method of drawing conclusions.
In "The Game of Logic" Carroll's whimsical imagination devises a logical game
played with 2 diagrams and counters (included) to manipulate hundreds of
tricky syllogisms. The final section, "Hit or Miss" is a lagniappe of 101 additional puzzles in the delightful Carroll manner. Until this reprint edition,
both of these books were rarities costing up to $15 each. Symbolic Logic:
Index. xxxi + 199pp. The Game of Logic: 96pp. 2 vols. bound as one. 5⅜ x 8.
                                                      20492-8 Paperbound $2.50

MATHEMATICAL PUZZLES OF SAM LOYD, PART I
selected and edited by M. Gardner
Choice puzzles by the greatest American puzzle creator and innovator. Selected
from his famous collection, "Cyclopedia of Puzzles," they retain the unique
style and historical flavor of the originals. There are posers based on arithmetic,
algebra, probability, game theory, route tracing, topology, counter and sliding
block, operations research, geometrical dissection. Includes the famous "14-15"
puzzle which was a national craze, and his "Horse of a Different Color" which
sold millions of copies. 117 of his most ingenious puzzles in all. 120 line
drawings and diagrams. Solutions. Selected references. xx + 167pp. 5⅜ x 8.
                                                      20498-7 Paperbound $1.35

STRING FIGURES AND HOW TO MAKE THEM, *Caroline Furness Jayne*
107 string figures plus variations selected from the best primitive and modern
examples developed by Navajo, Apache, pygmies of Africa, Eskimo, in Europe,
Australia, China, etc. The most readily understandable, easy-to-follow book in
English on perennially popular recreation. Crystal-clear exposition; step-by-
step diagrams. Everyone from kindergarten children to adults looking for
unusual diversion will be endlessly amused. Index. Bibliography. Introduction
by A. C. Haddon. 17 full-page plates, 960 illustrations. xxiii + 401pp. 5⅜ x 8½.
                                                      20152-X Paperbound $2.25

PAPER FOLDING FOR BEGINNERS, *W. D. Murray and F. J. Rigney*
A delightful introduction to the varied and entertaining Japanese art of
origami (paper folding), with a full, crystal-clear text that anticipates every
difficulty; over 275 clearly labeled diagrams of all important stages in creation.
You get results at each stage, since complex figures are logically developed
from simpler ones. 43 different pieces are explained: sailboats, frogs, roosters,
etc. 6 photographic plates. 279 diagrams. 95pp. 5⅜ x 8⅜.
                                                      20713-7 Paperbound $1.00

PRINCIPLES OF ART HISTORY,
H. Wölfflin
Analyzing such terms as "baroque," "classic," "neoclassic," "primitive," "picturesque," and 164 different works by artists like Botticelli, van Cleve, Dürer, Hobbema, Holbein, Hals, Rembrandt, Titian, Brueghel, Vermeer, and many others, the author establishes the classifications of art history and style on a firm, concrete basis. This classic of art criticism shows what really occurred between the 14th-century primitives and the sophistication of the 18th century in terms of basic attitudes and philosophies. "A remarkable lesson in the art of seeing," *Sat. Rev. of Literature.* Translated from the 7th German edition. 150 illustrations. 254pp. 6⅛ x 9¼. 20276-3 Paperbound $2.25

PRIMITIVE ART,
Franz Boas
This authoritative and exhaustive work by a great American anthropologist covers the entire gamut of primitive art. Pottery, leatherwork, metal work, stone work, wood, basketry, are treated in detail. Theories of primitive art, historical depth in art history, technical virtuosity, unconscious levels of patterning, symbolism, styles, literature, music, dance, etc. A must book for the interested layman, the anthropologist, artist, handicrafter (hundreds of unusual motifs), and the historian. Over 900 illustrations (50 ceramic vessels, 12 totem poles, etc.). 376pp. 5⅜ x 8. 20025-6 Paperbound $2.50

THE GENTLEMAN AND CABINET MAKER'S DIRECTOR,
Thomas Chippendale
A reprint of the 1762 catalogue of furniture designs that went on to influence generations of English and Colonial and Early Republic American furniture makers. The 200 plates, most of them full-page sized, show Chippendale's designs for French (Louis XV), Gothic, and Chinese-manner chairs, sofas, canopy and dome beds, cornices, chamber organs, cabinets, shaving tables, commodes, picture frames, frets, candle stands, chimney pieces, decorations, etc. The drawings are all elegant and highly detailed; many include construction diagrams and elevations. A supplement of 24 photographs shows surviving pieces of original and Chippendale-style pieces of furniture. Brief biography of Chippendale by N. I. Bienenstock, editor of *Furniture World.* Reproduced from the 1762 edition. 200 plates, plus 19 photographic plates. vi + 249pp. 9⅛ x 12¼. 21601-2 Paperbound $3.50

AMERICAN ANTIQUE FURNITURE: A BOOK FOR AMATEURS,
Edgar G. Miller, Jr.
Standard introduction and practical guide to identification of valuable American antique furniture. 2115 illustrations, mostly photographs taken by the author in 148 private homes, are arranged in chronological order in extensive chapters on chairs, sofas, chests, desks, bedsteads, mirrors, tables, clocks, and other articles. Focus is on furniture accessible to the collector, including simpler pieces and a larger than usual coverage of Empire style. Introductory chapters identify structural elements, characteristics of various styles, how to avoid fakes, etc. "We are frequently asked to name some book on American furniture that will meet the requirements of the novice collector, the beginning dealer, and . . . the general public. . . . We believe Mr. Miller's two volumes more completely satisfy this specification than any other work," *Antiques.* Appendix. Index. Total of vi + 1106pp. 7⅞ x 10¾.
21599-7, 21600-4 Two volume set, paperbound $7.50

CATALOGUE OF DOVER BOOKS

THE BAD CHILD'S BOOK OF BEASTS, MORE BEASTS FOR WORSE CHILDREN, and A MORAL ALPHABET, *H. Belloc*
Hardly an anthology of humorous verse has appeared in the last 50 years without at least a couple of these famous nonsense verses. But one must see the entire volumes — with all the delightful original illustrations by Sir Basil Blackwood — to appreciate fully Belloc's charming and witty verses that play so subacidly on the platitudes of life and morals that beset his day — and ours. A great humor classic. Three books in one. Total of 157pp. 5⅜ x 8.
20749-8 Paperbound $1.00

THE DEVIL'S DICTIONARY, *Ambrose Bierce*
Sardonic and irreverent barbs puncturing the pomposities and absurdities of American politics, business, religion, literature, and arts, by the country's greatest satirist in the classic tradition. Epigrammatic as Shaw, piercing as Swift, American as Mark Twain, Will Rogers, and Fred Allen, Bierce will always remain the favorite of a small coterie of enthusiasts, and of writers and speakers whom he supplies with "some of the most gorgeous witticisms of the English language" (H. L. Mencken). Over 1000 entries in alphabetical order. 144pp. 5⅜ x 8.
20487-1 Paperbound $1.00

THE COMPLETE NONSENSE OF EDWARD LEAR.
This is the only complete edition of this master of gentle madness available at a popular price. *A Book of Nonsense, Nonsense Songs, More Nonsense Songs and Stories* in their entirety with all the old favorites that have delighted children and adults for years. The Dong With A Luminous Nose, The Jumblies, The Owl and the Pussycat, and hundreds of other bits of wonderful nonsense. 214 limericks, 3 sets of Nonsense Botany, 5 Nonsense Alphabets, 546 drawings by Lear himself, and much more. 320pp. 5⅜ x 8. 20167-8 Paperbound $1.75

THE WIT AND HUMOR OF OSCAR WILDE, *ed. by Alvin Redman*
Wilde at his most brilliant, in 1000 epigrams exposing weaknesses and hypocrisies of "civilized" society. Divided into 49 categories—sin, wealth, women, America, etc.—to aid writers, speakers. Includes excerpts from his trials, books, plays, criticism. Formerly "The Epigrams of Oscar Wilde." Introduction by Vyvyan Holland, Wilde's only living son. Introductory essay by editor. 260pp. 5⅜ x 8.
20602-5 Paperbound $1.50

A CHILD'S PRIMER OF NATURAL HISTORY, *Oliver Herford*
Scarcely an anthology of whimsy and humor has appeared in the last 50 years without a contribution from Oliver Herford. Yet the works from which these examples are drawn have been almost impossible to obtain! Here at last are Herford's improbable definitions of a menagerie of familiar and weird animals, each verse illustrated by the author's own drawings. 24 drawings in 2 colors; 24 additional drawings. vii + 95pp. 6½ x 6. 21647-0 Paperbound $1.00

THE BROWNIES: THEIR BOOK, *Palmer Cox*
The book that made the Brownies a household word. Generations of readers have enjoyed the antics, predicaments and adventures of these jovial sprites, who emerge from the forest at night to play or to come to the aid of a deserving human. Delightful illustrations by the author decorate nearly every page. 24 short verse tales with 266 illustrations. 155pp. 6⅝ x 9¼.
21265-3 Paperbound $1.50

THE PRINCIPLES OF PSYCHOLOGY,
William James
The full long-course, unabridged, of one of the great classics of Western literature and science. Wonderfully lucid descriptions of human mental activity, the stream of thought, consciousness, time perception, memory, imagination, emotions, reason, abnormal phenomena, and similar topics. Original contributions are integrated with the work of such men as Berkeley, Binet, Mills, Darwin, Hume, Kant, Royce, Schopenhauer, Spinoza, Locke, Descartes, Galton, Wundt, Lotze, Herbart, Fechner, and scores of others. All contrasting interpretations of mental phenomena are examined in detail—introspective analysis, philosophical interpretation, and experimental research. "A classic," *Journal of Consulting Psychology.* "The main lines are as valid as ever," *Psychoanalytical Quarterly.* "Standard reading ... a classic of interpretation," *Psychiatric Quarterly.* 94 illustrations. 1408pp. 5⅜ x 8.
20381-6, 20382-4 Two volume set, paperbound $6.00

VISUAL ILLUSIONS: THEIR CAUSES, CHARACTERISTICS AND APPLICATIONS,
M. Luckiesh
"Seeing is deceiving," asserts the author of this introduction to virtually every type of optical illusion known. The text both describes and explains the principles involved in color illusions, figure-ground, distance illusions, etc. 100 photographs, drawings and diagrams prove how easy it is to fool the sense: circles that aren't round, parallel lines that seem to bend, stationary figures that seem to move as you stare at them — illustration after illustration strains our credulity at what we see. Fascinating book from many points of view, from applications for artists, in camouflage, etc. to the psychology of vision. New introduction by William Ittleson, Dept. of Psychology, Queens College. Index. Bibliography. xxi + 252pp. 5⅜ x 8½.
21530-X Paperbound $1.50

FADS AND FALLACIES IN THE NAME OF SCIENCE,
Martin Gardner
This is the standard account of various cults, quack systems, and delusions which have masqueraded as science: hollow earth fanatics. Reich and orgone sex energy, dianetics, Atlantis, multiple moons, Forteanism, flying saucers, medical fallacies like iridiagnosis, zone therapy, etc. A new chapter has been added on Bridey Murphy, psionics, and other recent manifestations in this field. This is a fair, reasoned appraisal of eccentric theory which provides excellent inoculation against cleverly masked nonsense. "Should be read by everyone, scientist and non-scientist alike," R. T. Birge, Prof. Emeritus of Physics, Univ. of California; Former President, American Physical Society. Index. x + 365pp. 5⅜ x 8.
20394-8 Paperbound $2.00

ILLUSIONS AND DELUSIONS OF THE SUPERNATURAL AND THE OCCULT,
D. H. Rawcliffe
Holds up to rational examination hundreds of persistent delusions including crystal gazing, automatic writing, table turning, mediumistic trances, mental healing, stigmata, lycanthropy, live burial, the Indian Rope Trick, spiritualism, dowsing, telepathy, clairvoyance, ghosts, ESP, etc. The author explains and exposes the mental and physical deceptions involved, making this not only an exposé of supernatural phenomena, but a valuable exposition of characteristic types of abnormal psychology. Originally titled "The Psychology of the Occult." 14 illustrations. Index. 551pp. 5⅜ x 8. 20503-7 Paperbound $3.50

FAIRY TALE COLLECTIONS, *edited by Andrew Lang*
Andrew Lang's fairy tale collections make up the richest shelf-full of traditional children's stories anywhere available. Lang supervised the translation of stories from all over the world—familiar European tales collected by Grimm, animal stories from Negro Africa, myths of primitive Australia, stories from Russia, Hungary, Iceland, Japan, and many other countries. Lang's selection of translations are unusually high; many authorities consider that the most familiar tales find their best versions in these volumes. All collections are richly decorated and illustrated by H. J. Ford and other artists.

THE BLUE FAIRY BOOK. 37 stories. 138 illustrations. ix + 390pp. 5⅜ x 8½.
21437-0 Paperbound $1.95

THE GREEN FAIRY BOOK. 42 stories. 100 illustrations. xiii + 366pp. 5⅜ x 8½.
21439-7 Paperbound $1.75

THE BROWN FAIRY BOOK. 32 stories. 50 illustrations, 8 in color. xii + 350pp. 5⅜ x 8½.
21438-9 Paperbound $1.95

THE BEST TALES OF HOFFMANN, *edited by E. F. Bleiler*
10 stories by E. T. A. Hoffmann, one of the greatest of all writers of fantasy. The tales include "The Golden Flower Pot," "Automata," "A New Year's Eve Adventure," "Nutcracker and the King of Mice," "Sand-Man," and others. Vigorous characterizations of highly eccentric personalities, remarkably imaginative situations, and intensely fast pacing has made these tales popular all over the world for 150 years. Editor's introduction. 7 drawings by Hoffmann. xxxiii + 419pp. 5⅜ x 8½.
21793-0 Paperbound $2.25

GHOST AND HORROR STORIES OF AMBROSE BIERCE,
edited by E. F. Bleiler
Morbid, eerie, horrifying tales of possessed poets, shabby aristocrats, revived corpses, and haunted malefactors. Widely acknowledged as the best of their kind between Poe and the moderns, reflecting their author's inner torment and bitter view of life. Includes "Damned Thing," "The Middle Toe of the Right Foot," "The Eyes of the Panther," "Visions of the Night," "Moxon's Master," and over a dozen others. Editor's introduction. xxii + 199pp. 5⅜ x 8½.
20767-6 Paperbound $1.50

THREE GOTHIC NOVELS, *edited by E. F. Bleiler*
Originators of the still popular Gothic novel form, influential in ushering in early 19th-century Romanticism. Horace Walpole's *Castle of Otranto*, William Beckford's *Vathek*, John Polidori's *The Vampyre*, and a *Fragment* by Lord Byron are enjoyable as exciting reading or as documents in the history of English literature. Editor's introduction. xi + 291pp. 5⅜ x 8½.
21232-7 Paperbound $2.00

BEST GHOST STORIES OF LEFANU, *edited by E. F. Bleiler*
Though admired by such critics as V. S. Pritchett, Charles Dickens and Henry James, ghost stories by the Irish novelist Joseph Sheridan LeFanu have never become as widely known as his detective fiction. About half of the 16 stories in this collection have never before been available in America. Collection includes "Carmilla" (perhaps the best vampire story ever written), "The Haunted Baronet," "The Fortunes of Sir Robert Ardagh," and the classic "Green Tea." Editor's introduction. 7 contemporary illustrations. Portrait of LeFanu. xii + 467pp. 5⅜ x 8.
20415-4 Paperbound $2.50

EASY-TO-DO ENTERTAINMENTS AND DIVERSIONS WITH COINS, CARDS, STRING, PAPER AND MATCHES, *R. M. Abraham*

Over 300 tricks, games and puzzles will provide young readers with absorbing fun. Sections on card games; paper-folding; tricks with coins, matches and pieces of string; games for the agile; toy-making from common household objects; mathematical recreations; and 50 miscellaneous pastimes. Anyone in charge of groups of youngsters, including hard-pressed parents, and in need of suggestions on how to keep children sensibly amused and quietly content will find this book indispensable. Clear, simple text, copious number of delightful line drawings and illustrative diagrams. Originally titled "Winter Nights' Entertainments." Introduction by Lord Baden Powell. 329 illustrations. v + 186pp. 5⅜ x 8½. 20921-0 Paperbound $1.00

AN INTRODUCTION TO CHESS MOVES AND TACTICS SIMPLY EXPLAINED, *Leonard Barden*

Beginner's introduction to the royal game. Names, possible moves of the pieces, definitions of essential terms, how games are won, etc. explained in 30-odd pages. With this background you'll be able to sit right down and play. Balance of book teaches strategy — openings, middle game, typical endgame play, and suggestions for improving your game. A sample game is fully analyzed. True middle-level introduction, teaching you all the essentials without oversimplifying or losing you in a maze of detail. 58 figures. 102pp. 5⅜ x 8½. 21210-6 Paperbound $1.25

LASKER'S MANUAL OF CHESS, *Dr. Emanuel Lasker*

Probably the greatest chess player of modern times, Dr. Emanuel Lasker held the world championship 28 years, independent of passing schools or fashions. This unmatched study of the game, chiefly for intermediate to skilled players, analyzes basic methods, combinations, position play, the aesthetics of chess, dozens of different openings, etc., with constant reference to great modern games. Contains a brilliant exposition of Steinitz's important theories. Introduction by Fred Reinfeld. Tables of Lasker's tournament record. 3 indices. 308 diagrams. 1 photograph. xxx + 349pp. 5⅜ x 8.20640-8Paperbound $2.50

COMBINATIONS: THE HEART OF CHESS, *Irving Chernev*

Step-by-step from simple combinations to complex, this book, by a well-known chess writer, shows you the intricacies of pins, counter-pins, knight forks, and smothered mates. Other chapters show alternate lines of play to those taken in actual championship games; boomerang combinations; classic examples of brilliant combination play by Nimzovich, Rubinstein, Tarrasch, Botvinnik, Alekhine and Capablanca. Index. 356 diagrams. ix + 245pp. 5⅜ x 8½. 21744-2 Paperbound $2.00

HOW TO SOLVE CHESS PROBLEMS, *K. S. Howard*

Full of practical suggestions for the fan or the beginner — who knows only the moves of the chessmen. Contains preliminary section and 58 two-move, 46 three-move, and 8 four-move problems composed by 27 outstanding American problem creators in the last 30 years. Explanation of all terms and exhaustive index. "Just what is wanted for the student," Brian Harley. 112 problems, solutions. vi + 171pp. 5⅜ x 8. 20748-X Paperbound $1.50

CATALOGUE OF DOVER BOOKS

Social Thought from Lore to Science,
H. E. Barnes and H. Becker
An immense survey of sociological thought and ways of viewing, studying, planning, and reforming society from earliest times to the present. Includes thought on society of preliterate peoples, ancient non-Western cultures, and every great movement in Europe, America, and modern Japan. Analyzes hundreds of great thinkers: Plato, Augustine, Bodin, Vico, Montesquieu, Herder, Comte, Marx, etc. Weighs the contributions of utopians, sophists, fascists and communists; economists, jurists, philosophers, ecclesiastics, and every 19th and 20th century school of scientific sociology, anthropology, and social psychology throughout the world. Combines topical, chronological, and regional approaches, treating the evolution of social thought as a process rather than as a series of mere topics. "Impressive accuracy, competence, and discrimination . . . easily the best single survey," *Nation*. Thoroughly revised, with new material up to 1960. 2 indexes. Over 2200 bibliographical notes. Three volume set. Total of 1586pp. 5⅜ x 8.
20901-6, 20902-4, 20903-2 Three volume set, paperbound $9.00

A History of Historical Writing, *Harry Elmer Barnes*
Virtually the only adequate survey of the whole course of historical writing in a single volume. Surveys developments from the beginnings of historiography in the ancient Near East and the Classical World, up through the Cold War. Covers major historians in detail, shows interrelationship with cultural background, makes clear individual contributions, evaluates and estimates importance; also enormously rich upon minor authors and thinkers who are usually passed over. Packed with scholarship and learning, clear, easily written. Indispensable to every student of history. Revised and enlarged up to 1961. Index and bibliography. xv + 442pp. 5⅜ x 8½.
20104-X Paperbound $2.75

Johann Sebastian Bach, *Philipp Spitta*
The complete and unabridged text of the definitive study of Bach. Written some 70 years ago, it is still unsurpassed for its coverage of nearly all aspects of Bach's life and work. There could hardly be a finer non-technical introduction to Bach's music than the detailed, lucid analyses which Spitta provides for hundreds of individual pieces. 26 solid pages are devoted to the B minor mass, for example, and 30 pages to the glorious St. Matthew Passion. This monumental set also includes a major analysis of the music of the 18th century: Buxtehude, Pachelbel, etc. "Unchallenged as the last word on one of the supreme geniuses of music," John Barkham, *Saturday Review Syndicate*. Total of 1819pp. Heavy cloth binding. 5⅜ x 8.
22278-0, 22279-9 Two volume set, clothbound $15.00

Beethoven and His Nine Symphonies, *George Grove*
In this modern middle-level classic of musicology Grove not only analyzes all nine of Beethoven's symphonies very thoroughly in terms of their musical structure, but also discusses the circumstances under which they were written, Beethoven's stylistic development, and much other background material. This is an extremely rich book, yet very easily followed; it is highly recommended to anyone seriously interested in music. Over 250 musical passages. Index. viii + 407pp. 5⅜ x 8.
20334-4 Paperbound $2.25

THREE SCIENCE FICTION NOVELS,
John Taine
Acknowledged by many as the best SF writer of the 1920's, Taine (under the name Eric Temple Bell) was also a Professor of Mathematics of considerable renown. Reprinted here are *The Time Stream*, generally considered Taine's best, *The Greatest Game*, a biological-fiction novel, and *The Purple Sapphire*, involving a supercivilization of the past. Taine's stories tie fantastic narratives to frameworks of original and logical scientific concepts. Speculation is often profound on such questions as the nature of time, concept of entropy, cyclical universes, etc. 4 contemporary illustrations. v + 532pp. 5⅜ x 8⅜.
21180-0 Paperbound $2.50

SEVEN SCIENCE FICTION NOVELS,
H. G. Wells
Full unabridged texts of 7 science-fiction novels of the master. Ranging from biology, physics, chemistry, astronomy, to sociology and other studies, Mr. Wells extrapolates whole worlds of strange and intriguing character. "One will have to go far to match this for entertainment, excitement, and sheer pleasure . . ."*New York Times*. Contents: The Time Machine, The Island of Dr. Moreau, The First Men in the Moon, The Invisible Man, The War of the Worlds, The Food of the Gods, In The Days of the Comet. 1015pp. 5⅜ x 8.
20264-X Clothbound $5.00

28 SCIENCE FICTION STORIES OF H. G. WELLS.
Two full, unabridged novels, *Men Like Gods* and *Star Begotten*, plus 26 short stories by the master science-fiction writer of all time! Stories of space, time, invention, exploration, futuristic adventure. Partial contents: *The Country of the Blind, In the Abyss, The Crystal Egg, The Man Who Could Work Miracles, A Story of Days to Come, The Empire of the Ants, The Magic Shop, The Valley of the Spiders, A Story of the Stone Age, Under the Knife, Sea Raiders*, etc. An indispensable collection for the library of anyone interested in science fiction adventure. 928pp. 5⅜ x 8.
20265-8 Clothbound $5.00

THREE MARTIAN NOVELS,
Edgar Rice Burroughs
Complete, unabridged reprinting, in one volume, of Thuvia, Maid of Mars; Chessmen of Mars; The Master Mind of Mars. Hours of science-fiction adventure by a modern master storyteller. Reset in large clear type for easy reading. 16 illustrations by J. Allen St. John. vi + 490pp. 5⅜ x 8½.
20039-6 Paperbound $2.50

AN INTELLECTUAL AND CULTURAL HISTORY OF THE WESTERN WORLD,
Harry Elmer Barnes
Monumental 3-volume survey of intellectual development of Europe from primitive cultures to the present day. Every significant product of human intellect traced through history: art, literature, mathematics, physical sciences, medicine, music, technology, social sciences, religions, jurisprudence, education, etc. Presentation is lucid and specific, analyzing in detail specific discoveries, theories, literary works, and so on. Revised (1965) by recognized scholars in specialized fields under the direction of Prof. Barnes. Revised bibliography. Indexes. 24 illustrations. Total of xxix + 1318pp.
21275-0, 21276-9, 21277-7 Three volume set, paperbound $8.25

HEAR ME TALKIN' TO YA, *edited by Nat Shapiro and Nat Hentoff*
In their own words, Louis Armstrong, King Oliver, Fletcher Henderson, Bunk Johnson, Bix Beiderbecke, Billy Holiday, Fats Waller, Jelly Roll Morton, Duke Ellington, and many others comment on the origins of jazz in New Orleans and its growth in Chicago's South Side, Kansas City's jam sessions, Depression Harlem, and the modernism of the West Coast schools. Taken from taped conversations, letters, magazine articles, other first-hand sources. Editors' introduction. xvi + 429pp. 5⅜ x 8½.   21726-4 Paperbound $2.00

THE JOURNAL OF HENRY D. THOREAU
A 25-year record by the great American observer and critic, as complete a record of a great man's inner life as is anywhere available. Thoreau's Journals served him as raw material for his formal pieces, as a place where he could develop his ideas, as an outlet for his interests in wild life and plants, in writing as an art, in classics of literature, Walt Whitman and other contemporaries, in politics, slavery, individual's relation to the State, etc. The Journals present a portrait of a remarkable man, and are an observant social history. Unabridged republication of 1906 edition, Bradford Torrey and Francis H. Allen, editors. Illustrations. Total of 1888pp. 8⅜ x 12¼.
                    20312-3, 20313-1 Two volume set, clothbound $30.00

A SHAKESPEARIAN GRAMMAR, *E. A. Abbott*
Basic reference to Shakespeare and his contemporaries, explaining through thousands of quotations from Shakespeare, Jonson, Beaumont and Fletcher, North's *Plutarch* and other sources the grammatical usage differing from the modern. First published in 1870 and written by a scholar who spent much of his life isolating principles of Elizabethan language, the book is unlikely ever to be superseded. Indexes. xxiv + 511pp. 5⅜ x 8½. 21582-2 Paperbound $3.00

FOLK-LORE OF SHAKESPEARE, *T. F. Thistelton Dyer*
Classic study, drawing from Shakespeare a large body of references to supernatural beliefs, terminology of falconry and hunting, games and sports, good luck charms, marriage customs, folk medicines, superstitions about plants, animals, birds, argot of the underworld, sexual slang of London, proverbs, drinking customs, weather lore, and much else. From full compilation comes a mirror of the 17th-century popular mind. Index. ix + 526pp. 5⅜ x 8½.
                    21614-4 Paperbound $2.75

THE NEW VARIORUM SHAKESPEARE, *edited by H. H. Furness*
By far the richest editions of the plays ever produced in any country or language. Each volume contains complete text (usually First Folio) of the play, all variants in Quarto and other Folio texts, editorial changes by every major editor to Furness's own time (1900), footnotes to obscure references or language, extensive quotes from literature of Shakespearian criticism, essays on plot sources (often reprinting sources in full), and much more.

HAMLET, *edited by H. H. Furness*
Total of xxvi + 905pp. 5⅜ x 8½.
                    21004-9, 21005-7 Two volume set, paperbound $5.25
TWELFTH NIGHT, *edited by H. H. Furness*
Index. xxii + 434pp. 5⅜ x 8½.   21189-4 Paperbound $2.75

La Boheme by Giacomo Puccini,
translated and introduced by Ellen H. Bleiler
Complete handbook for the operagoer, with everything needed for full enjoyment except the musical score itself. Complete Italian libretto, with new,
modern English line-by-line translation—the only libretto printing all repeats;
biography of Puccini; the librettists; background to the opera, Murger's La
Boheme, etc.; circumstances of composition and performances; plot summary;
and pictorial section of 73 illustrations showing Puccini, famous singers and
performances, etc. Large clear type for easy reading. 124pp. 5⅜ x 8½.
20404-9 Paperbound $1.25

Antonio Stradivari: His Life and Work (1644-1737),
W. Henry Hill, Arthur F. Hill, and Alfred E. Hill
Still the only book that really delves into life and art of the incomparable
Italian craftsman, maker of the finest musical instruments in the world today.
The authors, expert violin-makers themselves, discuss Stradivari's ancestry, his
construction and finishing techniques, distinguished characteristics of many
of his instruments and their locations. Included, too, is story of introduction
of his instruments into France, England, first revelation of their supreme
merit, and information on his labels, number of instruments made, prices,
mystery of ingredients of his varnish, tone of pre-1684 Stradivari violin and
changes between 1684 and 1690. An extremely interesting, informative account
for all music lovers, from craftsman to concert-goer. Republication of original
(1902) edition. New introduction by Sydney Beck, Head of Rare Book and
Manuscript Collections, Music Division, New York Public Library. Analytical
index by Rembert Wurlitzer. Appendixes. 68 illustrations. 30 full-page plates.
4 in color. xxvi + 315pp. 5⅜ x 8½.   20425-1 Paperbound $2.25

Musical Autographs from Monteverdi to Hindemith,
Emanuel Winternitz
For beauty, for intrinsic interest, for perspective on the composer's personality,
for subtleties of phrasing, shading, emphasis indicated in the autograph but
suppressed in the printed score, the mss. of musical composition are fascinating
documents which repay close study in many different ways. This 2-volume
work reprints facsimiles of mss. by virtually every major composer, and many
minor figures—196 examples in all. A full text points out what can be learned
from mss., analyzes each sample. Index. Bibliography. 18 figures. 196 plates.
Total of 170pp. of text. 7⅞ x 10¾.
21312-9, 21313-7 Two volume set, paperbound $5.00

J. S. Bach,
Albert Schweitzer
One of the few great full-length studies of Bach's life and work, and the
study upon which Schweitzer's renown as a musicologist rests. On first appearance (1911), revolutionized Bach performance. The only writer on Bach to
be musicologist, performing musician, and student of history, theology and
philosophy, Schweitzer contributes particularly full sections on history of German Protestant church music, theories on motivic pictorial representations
in vocal music, and practical suggestions for performance. Translated by
Ernest Newman. Indexes. 5 illustrations. 650 musical examples. Total of xix
+ 928pp. 5⅜ x 8½.   21631-4, 21632-2 Two volume set, paperbound $4.50

THE METHODS OF ETHICS, *Henry Sidgwick*
Propounding no organized system of its own, study subjects every major methodological approach to ethics to rigorous, objective analysis. Study discusses and relates ethical thought of Plato, Aristotle, Bentham, Clarke, Butler, Hobbes, Hume, Mill, Spencer, Kant, and dozens of others. Sidgwick retains conclusions from each system which follow from ethical premises, rejecting the faulty. Considered by many in the field to be among the most important treatises on ethical philosophy. Appendix. Index. xlvii + 528pp. 5⅜ x 8½.
21608-X Paperbound $2.50

TEUTONIC MYTHOLOGY, *Jakob Grimm*
A milestone in Western culture; the work which established on a modern basis the study of history of religions and comparative religions. 4-volume work assembles and interprets everything available on religious and folkloristic beliefs of Germanic people (including Scandinavians, Anglo-Saxons, etc.). Assembling material from such sources as Tacitus, surviving Old Norse and Icelandic texts, archeological remains, folktales, surviving superstitions, comparative traditions, linguistic analysis, etc. Grimm explores pagan deities, heroes, folklore of nature, religious practices, and every other area of pagan German belief. To this day, the unrivaled, definitive, exhaustive study. Translated by J. S. Stallybrass from 4th (1883) German edition. Indexes. Total of lxxvii + 1887pp. 5⅜ x 8½.
21602-0, 21603-9, 21604-7, 21605-5 Four volume set, paperbound $11.00

THE I CHING, *translated by James Legge*
Called "The Book of Changes" in English, this is one of the Five Classics edited by Confucius, basic and central to Chinese thought. Explains perhaps the most complex system of divination known, founded on the theory that all things happening at any one time have characteristic features which can be isolated and related. Significant in Oriental studies, in history of religions and philosophy, and also to Jungian psychoanalysis and other areas of modern European thought. Index. Appendixes. 6 plates. xxi + 448pp. 5⅜ x 8½.
21062-6 Paperbound $2.75

HISTORY OF ANCIENT PHILOSOPHY, *W. Windelband*
One of the clearest, most accurate comprehensive surveys of Greek and Roman philosophy. Discusses ancient philosophy in general, intellectual life in Greece in the 7th and 6th centuries B.C., Thales, Anaximander, Anaximenes, Heraclitus, the Eleatics, Empedocles, Anaxagoras, Leucippus, the Pythagoreans, the Sophists, Socrates, Democritus (20 pages), Plato (50 pages), Aristotle (70 pages), the Peripatetics, Stoics, Epicureans, Sceptics, Neo-platonists, Christian Apologists, etc. 2nd German edition translated by H. E. Cushman. xv + 393pp. 5⅜ x 8.
20357-3 Paperbound $2.25

THE PALACE OF PLEASURE, *William Painter*
Elizabethan versions of Italian and French novels from *The Decameron,* Cinthio, Straparola, Queen Margaret of Navarre, and other continental sources — the very work that provided Shakespeare and dozens of his contemporaries with many of their plots and sub-plots and, therefore, justly considered one of the most influential books in all English literature. It is also a book that any reader will still enjoy. Total of cviii + 1,224pp.
21691-8, 21692-6, 21693-4 Three volume set, paperbound $6.75

THE WONDERFUL WIZARD OF OZ, *L. F. Baum*
All the original W. W. Denslow illustrations in full color—as much a part of
"The Wizard" as Tenniel's drawings are of "Alice in Wonderland." "The
Wizard" is still America's best-loved fairy tale, in which, as the author expresses
it, "The wonderment and joy are retained and the heartaches and nightmares
left out." Now today's young readers can enjoy every word and wonderful picture of the original book. New introduction by Martin Gardner. A Baum
bibliography. 23 full-page color plates. viii + 268pp. 5⅜ x 8.
20691-2 Paperbound $1.95

THE MARVELOUS LAND OF OZ, *L. F. Baum*
This is the equally enchanting sequel to the "Wizard," continuing the adventures of the Scarecrow and the Tin Woodman. The hero this time is a little
boy named Tip, and all the delightful Oz magic is still present. This is the
Oz book with the Animated Saw-Horse, the Woggle-Bug, and Jack Pumpkin-
head. All the original John R. Neill illustrations, 10 in full color. 287pp.
5⅜ x 8.
20692-0 Paperbound $1.75

ALICE'S ADVENTURES UNDER GROUND, *Lewis Carroll*
The original *Alice in Wonderland*, hand-lettered and illustrated by Carroll
himself, and originally presented as a Christmas gift to a child-friend. Adults
as well as children will enjoy this charming volume, reproduced faithfully
in this Dover edition. While the story is essentially the same, there are slight
changes, and Carroll's spritely drawings present an intriguing alternative to
the famous Tenniel illustrations. One of the most popular books in Dover's
catalogue. Introduction by Martin Gardner. 38 illustrations. 128pp. 5⅜ x 8½.
21482-6 Paperbound $1.00

THE NURSERY "ALICE," *Lewis Carroll*
While most of us consider *Alice in Wonderland* a story for children of all
ages, Carroll himself felt it was beyond younger children. He therefore provided this simplified version, illustrated with the famous Tenniel drawings
enlarged and colored in delicate tints, for children aged "from Nought to
Five." Dover's edition of this now rare classic is a faithful copy of the 1889
printing, including 20 illustrations by Tenniel, and front and back covers
reproduced in full color. Introduction by Martin Gardner. xxiii + 67pp.
6⅛ x 9¼.
21610-1 Paperbound $1.75

THE STORY OF KING ARTHUR AND HIS KNIGHTS, *Howard Pyle*
A fast-paced, exciting retelling of the best known Arthurian legends for young
readers by one of America's best story tellers and illustrators. The sword
Excalibur, wooing of Guinevere, Merlin and his downfall, adventures of Sir
Pellias and Gawaine, and others. The pen and ink illustrations are vividly
imagined and wonderfully drawn. 41 illustrations. xviii + 313pp. 6⅛ x 9¼.
21445-1 Paperbound $2.00

Prices subject to change without notice.

Available at your book dealer or write for free catalogue to Dept. Adsci,
Dover Publications, Inc., 180 Varick St., N.Y., N.Y. 10014. Dover publishes more
than 150 books each year on science, elementary and advanced mathematics,
biology, music, art, literary history, social sciences and other areas.